REVISITING THE ELEGY IN THE BLACK LIVES MATTER ERA

Revisiting the Elegy in the Black Lives Matter Era is an edited collection of critical essays and poetry that investigates contemporary elegy within the black diaspora. Scores of contemporary writers have turned to elegiac poetry and prose in order to militate against the white supremacist logic that has led to the recent deaths of unarmed black men, women, and children. This volume combines scholarly and creative understandings of the elegy in order to discern how mourning feeds our political awareness in this dystopian time as writers attempt to see, hear, and say something in relation to the bodies of the dead as well as to living readers. Moreover, this book provides a model for how to productively interweave theoretical and deeply personal accounts to encourage discussions about art and activism that transgress disciplinary boundaries, as well as lines of race, gender, class, and nation.

Tiffany Austin, PhD, was born on April 26, 1975, in Murfreesboro, Arkansas, to the union of Anthony (Tony) Eric Austin and Ruth Ann May, who later moved to Kansas City, Missouri, in 1977. Tiffany joined the ancestors on Saturday, June 23, 2018. During her career, Tiffany taught at Florida Memorial University, Mississippi Valley State University, and most recently at the University of The Bahamas. She was also a widely published poet, with her chapbook *Étude* appearing in 2013. Of this volume, her mentor Sterling Plumpp noted, "Austin's genius is her unusual gift for metaphor and allusion." Others recognized Tiffany's genius too, with her poems appearing in such prestigious outlets as *Callaloo*, *Obsidian III*, *African American Review*, *Coloring Book: An Anthology of Poetry and Fiction by Multicultural Writers*, *Warpland*, *pluck!*, *The Journal of Affrilachian Arts and Culture*, *Valley Voices*, *Auburn Avenue*, *TriQuarterly*, *Sycorax's Daughters*, and *Moko: Caribbean Arts and Letters*. Tiffany was a teacher, writer, poet, activist, and feminist. Never one for titles, she was moved instead by both action and passion. She was incomparable, generous, artistic, and authentic—a beautiful soul who will live on in the many artistic and personal seeds she planted and nurtured.

Sequoia Maner is a poet-scholar and Mellon Teaching Fellow of Feminist Studies at Southwestern University. She earned her B.A. in English from Duke University and her M.A. and Ph.D. degrees in English from the University of Texas at Austin. She is coeditor of *Revisiting the Elegy in the Black Lives Matter Era*. Her dissertation and book project, *Liberation Aesthetics in the #BlackLivesMatter Era*, examines how experimental poetics and performance bolster black social movements. Her essay on the performance of "quiet interiority" as collective praxis in Beyoncé's *Lemonade* is published in the journal *Meridians: feminism, race, transnationalism* and her poem "upon reading the autopsy of Sandra Bland," finalist for the 2017 Gwendolyn Brooks Poetry Prize, is published in *Obsidian: Literature & Arts of the African Diaspora*.

Emily Ruth Rutter is Assistant Professor of English at Ball State University, where she teaches courses in Multi-Ethnic American and African American Literature. She is the author of two monographs: *Invisible Ball of Dreams: Literary Representations of Baseball behind the Color Line* (University Press of Mississippi, 2018) and *The Blues Muse: Race, Gender, and Musical Celebrity in American Poetry* (University of Alabama Press, 2018). Her research has been published in the journals *African American Review*, *South Atlantic Review*, *Studies in American Culture*, *Aethlon*, and *MELUS*. Her book chapter on African American women poets appears in *A Cambridge History of Twentieth-Century American Women's Poetry*, and a book chapter on Amiri Baraka and sports is forthcoming in *Some Other Blues: New Perspectives on Amiri Baraka* (Ohio State UP, 2021).

darlene anita scott is Associate Professor of English at Virginia Union University. She is a poet and visual artist whose research explores corporeal performances of trauma and the violence of silence. Her poetry has appeared in journals including *J Journal*, *Quiddity*, and *The Baltimore Review*, among others. Her art has been featured in *The Journal*, an arts and literature magazine of Ohio State University, and at The Girl Museum, a virtual museum celebrating girls and girlhood. Recipient of support from the Virginia Commission for the Arts, Delaware Division of the Arts, Tennessee Commission for the Arts, and College English Association, scott's most recent project is a multimedia exploration, *Breathing Lessons*, which explores the role of the good girl as it is applied to girls of color.

Routledge Research in American Literature and Culture

REVISITING THE ELEGY IN THE BLACK LIVES MATTER ERA

Edited by
Tiffany Austin, Sequoia Maner,
Emily Ruth Rutter, and
darlene anita scott

Routledge
Taylor & Francis Group

NEW YORK AND LONDON

First published 2020
by Routledge
52 Vanderbilt Avenue, New York, NY 10017

and by Routledge
2 Park Square, Milton Park, Abingdon, Oxon, OX14 4RN

Routledge is an imprint of the Taylor & Francis Group, an informa business

© 2020 Taylor & Francis

The right of Tiffany Austin, Sequoia Maner, Emily Ruth Rutter, and
darlene anita scott to be identified as the authors of the editorial material,
and of the authors for their individual chapters, has been asserted in
accordance with sections 77 and 78 of the Copyright, Designs and Patents
Act 1988.

Library of Congress Cataloging-in-Publication Data
A catalog record for this book has been requested

ISBN: 978-0-367-27638-6 (hbk)
ISBN: 978-0-367-32158-1 (pbk)
ISBN: 978-0-367-85354-9 (ebk)

Typeset in Bembo
by Apex CoVantage, LLC

This book is dedicated in loving memory to Dr. Tiffany Austin
(1975–2018)

CONTENTS

PART III
Elegists as Activists 177

FIGURES

ACKNOWLEDGMENTS

We thank Christina Sharpe, Opal Tometi, Alicia Garza, Patrisse Khan-Cullors, Mahogany L. Browne, and Amanda Johnston for the inspiration you provide. We are grateful for Howard Rambsy II's and Tony Medina's willingness to help develop this work, and for Howard's website, culturalfront.org, which is an invaluable resource for scholars and students of black poetry. We thank Kelly Lessard for her photograph of the National Memorial for Peace and Justice that adorns this book cover. Thanks also to Toni Austin and Ruth Austin for their support of this project.

darlene is indebted to her coeditors for offering balance as her world tilted; for holding her always in light; to Tiffany Austin for entrusting her with friendship, wisdom, and the best belly laughs. She thanks the usual suspects: Niel and Solomon for holding and giving her space; her wombmate and best twin, Dr. Doreen Scott-Baker; the rest of the squad: Denise, Dianne, Debra; the shoulders on which she stands: Ernest Scott and Gloria Scott; and to the Vermont Studio Center, The Watering Hole, and Rahikya Wilson for giving her a where and a way to settle into the elegy of her body and make it something that can hopefully be of use.

Sequoia thanks the artists, poets, and writers in her life who encourage her to dream big and work smart: to keep moving, keep building. She gives particular thanks to Amanda Johnston for her wisdom, courage, space-making, and fierce sense of sisterhood. She thanks the Andrew Mellon Foundation for generous grants that have provided the stability to complete and promote this project. She thanks poets Evie Shockley and Patricia Smith for reading and recognizing early versions of the work. She also thanks *The Feminist Wire* and the Furious Flower Poetry Center for publishing her #BlackLivesMatter elegies. Sequoia thanks the NEH Institute for hosting "Black Poetry after the Black Art," a workshop that took place in the summer of 2015 where many of the contributors to this book met and forged alliances. She thanks the mentors in her life including Helena

Woodard, Tony Bolden, Chad Bennett, Deborah Paredez, Jennifer Wilks, Lisa Moore, Kevin Quashie, and Eric Pritchard for reading early drafts of this work; illuminating avenues and pathways; and encouraging her to live in creative and critical spaces always and at once. She thanks loved ones including her mother, Dr. Denise Valerie Maner, her husband, Keith Woodard, and her homegirls: Beth Consetta Rubel, Yvette DeChavez, and drea brown.

Emily wants to thank Tiffany Austin, without whom this volume would have never been conceived, as well as darlene and Sequoia for making this the most meaningful project of her, career. She is also grateful to her African American Studies students, especially Adriana Arthur, Kaylah Bell, Dachele Dycus, Aric Fulton, Natalia Langham, Jalynn Madison, Dillon O'Nail, Lauren Reynolds, KeAyra Williams, and Morgan Williams, for engaging in an incredibly generative dialogue with her about elegy, Black Lives Matter, and everything in between. She also wants to thank her friends, colleagues, and family who have supported this project, especially Mike Begnal, Kiesha Warren-Gordon, Sharon Lynette Jones, Kendra Lowery, Debbie Mix, Angela Jackson-Brown, Simon Balto, Max Felker-Kantor, Rachel Fredericks, Pat Collier, Vanessa Rapatz, Molly Ferguson, Katy Didden, Sreyoshi Sarkar, Ben Bascom, Mary Parish, Maureen Gallagher, Lyn Jones, Kristin Cipollone, Lindsay Griffin, Rachel Bachenheimer, Lora Klein, Lauren Erickson, Diane Rodelli, Ginger Carter, the Rutter clan, and Jasmine and Jathan Taylor. Thanks also to Cole Brayfield for his assistance on the index and the volume's companion website: https://revisitingtheelegy.org/.

Every effort has been made to clear rights on poetry excerpts. The authors would like to thank the following for providing permission to quote their works in this volume:

LAUREN K. ALLEYNE: "Elegy for Tamir" and "Poetry Workshop after the Verdict" have been reprinted with the permission of the author.

TIFFANY AUSTIN: "Dark Milk: After Basquiat" and "Peaches" have been reprinted with the permission of the author.

PAULA BOHINCE: "The Flint River" first appeared on *The Rumpus* and has been reprinted with the permission of the author.

LUCILLE CLIFTON: Grateful acknowledgment to Boa Press for permission to excerpt lines from "jasper texas 1998," "the photograph: a lynching," and "alabama 9/15/63" from *The Collected Poems of Lucille Clifton*.

DANIELLE LEGROS GEORGES: "Poem of History and "As Falling Star" originally appeared in *The Dear Remote Nearness of You* (Barrow Street Press, 2016). They have been reprinted with the permission of the author.

ANGELA JACKSON-BROWN: "I Must Not Breathe" originally appeared in *House Repairs* (Negative Capability Press, 2018). It has been reprinted with the permission of the author.

BETTINA JUDD: Grateful acknowledgment to Black Lawrence Press for allowing us to reprint material from *Patient*.

SEQUOIA MANER: Thank you to *The Feminist Wire* in which "Black Boy Contrapuntal" was originally published, and to *Obsidian: Literature and Arts in the African Diaspora* in which "upon reading the autopsy of Sandra Bland" was originally published in (vol. 43, no. 22 [2017]: 116).

SHANE MCCRAE: Grateful acknowledgment to Wesleyan University Press for permission to excerpt lines from *In the Language of My Captor*.

TONY MEDINA: "Senryu for Trayvon Martin" and "From the Crushed Voice Box of Freddie Gray" have been reprinted with the permission of the author.

CLAUDIA RANKINE: Thank you to Graywolf Press for permission to excerpt lines from *Citizen: An American Lyric*. Thanks also to Penguin UK for permission to quote passages from *Citizen: An American Lyric*.

EVIE SHOCKLEY: Grateful acknowledgment to Wesleyan University Press for allowing us to reprint "dependencies" from *the new black* and "buried truths" from *semiautomatic*.

TRACY K. SMITH: Grateful acknowledgment to Graywolf Press for permission to excerpt lines from *Wade in the Water*.

JERRY WEMPLE: "Nickle Rides" has been reprinted with permission of the author.

PREFACE

"WHERE WILL ALL THAT BEAUTY GO?"

A Tribute to Poet-Scholar Tiffany Austin

Emily Ruth Rutter

I write this dedication to my friend and coeditor of this volume, Dr. Tiffany Austin. She passed away from complications from a minor foot surgery on June 23, 2018. These are circumstances that affirm the wisdom of the adage "truth is stranger than fiction," for I never would have predicted that a book about mourning would also pay elegiac tribute to one of its editors. Tiffany and I collaborated for many months on *Revisiting the Elegy in the Black Lives Matter Era*, and in the wake of her death I decided to forge ahead with the project with the assistance of darlene anita scott and Sequoia Maner. We are collectively resolved to make this the beginning, not the end of Tiffany's legacy.

I first met Tiffany at the 2015 Issues in Critical Investigation Symposium on the African Diaspora at Vanderbilt University, where she gave an engaging and provocative poetry reading with her friend Destiny Birdsong. Tiffany and I discovered a mutual love of the blues, and we struck up a friendship that grew over the last few years. I invited her to give a reading at my home institution, Ball State University, and to discuss her poetry with my students. Unfortunately, the visit was scheduled for November 9, 2016, the day after the worst election in living memory. Tiffany arrived late on November 8, and because we were catching up on the long drive from the Indianapolis airport to Muncie, Indiana, we were not listening or paying attention to the election results. We only discovered that the unthinkable had transpired late that night, and then we spent a mournful morning discussing how we would negotiate this turn of events. It is no exaggeration to say that Tiffany saved me, my students, and my colleagues from utter despondency that day. We went to my classes, read her poems, discussed music and the lyric and how to read oblique references with curiosity rather than frustration. She gave a beautiful reading that night from "A South in Sound: A Photo Essay," a work that I will turn to shortly. My students would not stop talking to her after the reading, as they felt a kind of gravitational pull catalyzed by the meditative beauty of her elegiac verse. When we discussed the date for her visit, we were not thinking about Trump, Russia, white nationalism, and all the rest. We were thinking about a propitious time for her poetry, and on that score we were right.

Later, Tiffany wrote a poem about her visit, entitled "After an Election," which conveys her own wide-ranging emotions, but which also speaks to the alternating feelings of despair and defiance coursing through the arteries of much of the American body politic that fateful night and the long day that followed:

> Before entering the hotel room, I walk to a Chinese restaurant—it's near midnight, but they let me in, not telling me about results. Once in the bed, I finally call my mother to hear the news. She keeps saying, I love you. I think about when I visit and I lie next to her. When you're that close, I've always felt you must reveal. She once told me, I think people are punished by the children they bear. I am her child and I wonder what she is being punished for. Having her palms read? I say this to her because I'm angry. I say this because I almost believe her. She can't believe the election results. I'm half asleep, so I can. The next day, I'm before students near tears, not there, near anger, and I talk about Melvin Tolson, and labor, and my grandmother. In the middle of it all, a young man eagerly says we need to talk afterwards. He's the one that his professor tells me asks if she painted the work before he says something of Basquiat in an art gallery. I smile at him.[1]

As Tiffany writes, she talked that day about "labor," a word that performs double duty here in its reference to both birth (of children, of poetry, of innovative ideas) and the arduous work of resilience and resistance ("near tears, not there, near anger") in a white-supremacist patriarchal society.

To me, "After an Election," is also a form of elegy—a lament for the hope that perhaps we should have never quite believed in but was so tantalizingly in its sway. A few lines later, for example, Tiffany considers the precarious lives of her family, especially her nephews, who she is reminded of by my eager student:

> still I want my nephew to be as perfect as the bursting skin of the sausage on the grill swallowing sweat. No. I don't get to speak to the young man afterwards. I hug young women instead. They are braver than I am and give me something of myself. But I'm on the plane back to an island. And I'm trying to hold on to what Toni Morrison says—to think about work. I keep going back to her. She brings up *Absalom! Absalom!* in a journal article— better to commit incest than have a drop of black blood. I remember saying something similar to my father and asking him about it because he knew the bible. He couldn't talk about it. He had finished using his voice. He was tired. I'm tired. We're still afraid of the dark continents. Women. Africa. I admit I don't have hope or I have hope in the names of my students who

talk about not being a woman, being a gachapon, never about race, and a professor asking them to write about a lovesome thing. My sister is named Toni and she has three sons. The last email I sent her said, "You know Zora was controversial. Her life—she cut and was cut." "And, Nina, that freedom costs." They stop my heart, these students, again, before me. I have hope—in names like Jarrod, Ide, and Tisunne.[2]

This paratactic lyricism is one of the hallmarks of Tiffany's verse, swerving among wide-ranging associations but never losing the intimate rhythm she establishes with the reader. Engaging with Tiffany's "After an Election" and much of her oeuvre is like being coaxed into taking an unfamiliar journey in which she asks you to relinquish your expectation of following the map but still to trust that she will get you home, weary perhaps from the foreboding roads you have traveled but nevertheless reassured by the enlightenment and solidarity she has offered. This poem also makes a gesture toward consolation that I think is key to honoring Tiffany in particular and to engaging with the poetry put forward in *Revisiting the Elegy in the Black Lives Matter Era* more generally. "I have hope," she concludes, but not in the institutions that are "still afraid of the dark continents. Women. Africa." Instead, Tiffany found "hope—in names like Jarrod, Ide, and Tisunne." Even as we spill grief-stricken ink over the innumerable names like theirs in the pages that follow, we join Tiffany in our unwavering investment in the "lovesome" young men and women who we, too, want to protect.

In his 1963 memoir *The Fire Next Time*, James Baldwin similarly ruminates on the fate of the boys he grew up with in Harlem who were abandoning hope of rising beyond their subjugated status. "What," Baldwin asks, "will happen to all that beauty? *What will happen to all that beauty?*"[3] Through his rather urgent interrogative, Baldwin, who is remembering his peers even as he is writing in the present tense and considering the future, denies his readers the solace of emotional distance. Much like the contemporary elegists that are the subject of this book, Baldwin refuses to remain silent as the dominant society not only denies black boys and men their beauty but also their humanity. In both the lyric poem "Where will all that beauty go?" and "A South in Sound: A Photo Essay," Tiffany riffs on Baldwin's line, and a version of this question has been haunting me since her death: *What will we do without all that beauty?*

Because I am both a writer and poetry devotee, my answer has been to put fingers to keyboard, and try to honor the rich textures of Tiffany's verse, as well as to realize our shared vision for *Revisiting the Elegy in the Black Lives Matter Era*, one of her final projects. In this volume, Tiffany and I set out to consider the recent outpouring of elegiac poetry and prose responding to the state-sanctioned deaths of unarmed black men, women, and children. We had been discussing a concerted resistance to consolation in black-authored elegies, and we had also ourselves wondered what to do in the face of so much death and grief. For example, Tiffany's "A South in Sound: A Photo Essay" speaks to the ways in which the Delta landscape archives a traumatic diasporic past and present, braiding together her current observations and reflections with the traumatic history that refuses to be silent. This seemingly placid South, Tiffany seems to say, is a din of ghostly voices:

> In Itta Bena, Mississippi, right outside of Greenwood, or Greenwood right outside of it, older black men sit in trucks or on benches in a downtown with a clinic, an auto shop and an on-again-off-again barbecue spot. Then there is Greenwood, and I think about SNCC and Bob Moses. The town still carries the quiet and the smothered fury of that past time, of Moses, in its smell. You drive a bit and come to Money Road—there, Robert Johnson's reputed gravesite beside a small church, and farther down, the purposefully dilapidated store where Emmett Till allegedly whistled at a white woman. So many blues sites, so many sites central to a violent racial history, and it's no wonder that this—the blues and civil rights—is what the state seems to be selling lately. I had to pass the "Welcome to Mississippi: Birthplace of America's Music" sign upon entering. Yet, the commemoration of the Emmett Till plaque on the Sumner courthouse front yard was not well attended by "whites" in the area. There are places I'm told not to visit in Greenwood; it is speculated that a black man was recently hanged behind the local Walmart, and a local doctor was accused in a murder-for-hire scheme, allegedly hiring two black youngsters to kill a local attorney. Beside markers, the architecture of neighborhoods like Glendora that resembles South American shantytowns. What is happening in Mississippi? Visiting up North again, I tell a stranger, I've moved to Mississippi, and her face changes. But is this place any different from any other in this country? I'm an outsider here, but I sense that there is still a dangerous gyration in the South. I'm an insider here, and I sense that there is still a dangerous gyration in these United States. While journeying to the local book store, I watch the three older white men daily standing at the courthouse front in Greenwood endorsing the continued flying of the Confederate flag. I stare and let the car drive itself. I hear about frat parties at the refurbished shacks sold as a tourist attraction. There are so many stories in this place, not only about Robert Johnson being poisoned by jealousy. In the "here" of the Delta, amid the rich soil, from a local poet, I listen to, "It's true if you hear it."[4]

The boundaries between inside and outside, here and there are not simply arbitrary. There are differences between the strangeness and alterity of North and South, and there are places where outsiders struggle to discern what is and is not real in the "story" the place tells itself. Yet one of the keen insights of Tiffany's photographic prose-poem is that we need to "hear" the truth of "smothered fury" not only in Itta Bena, Mississippi, but everywhere.

Although it is probably best described as sui generis, "A South in Sound" could also be added to the long list of Emmett Till poems. Both his infamous killing and the promise of his young life extinguished so painfully pervades Tiffany's vision of the Delta terrain. Juxtaposing haiku-like poetry, lyrical prose, and a photograph of a dilapidated iron bridge above the muddy waters of the Tallahatchie River, Tiffany stages a kind of reckoning. She reflects not only on the dangers of the past but also the oppressive forces still conspiring against the "young ones" from Money, Mississippi, these many decades later:

Death eats.
But they tell me we can live a full life.
What about a sweet smiling boy?

We pass young ones like him; they wave, especially the one in a wheel-chair. I don't know their stories. But I know the story. Out of the car now, we walk to the bridge that leads from a clean church, down a woody path, to crowded trees on the other side. The water is batter below—brown and browner. I look for the brown underneath. On the drive back, I stop to ask the young boys, "Who attends the church nearby, Where were its members during a killing?" But they have lighter fluid. We're now driving to the barn house near the cotton gin that's become a museum. I remember a beauty salon in a shotgun house, a building with no name on it, but fronted by a community of men, women, children. They wave listlessly.[5]

Tiffany's imagery educes a feeling of tension and unease here that nearly defies language. These figures, whose heartrending traumas and joys have so long been ignored, "wave listlessly," perhaps saying goodbye, or saying hello, or even call-ing out an SOS, but not expecting an adequate response from any of these expressions.

This passage in particular and "A South in Sound" more generally is also a deep blues, a music and ethos that Tiffany treasured. Ralph Ellison's description in "Richard Wright's Blues" seems apt:

The blues is an impulse to keep the painful details and episodes of a brutal experience alive in one's aching consciousness, to finger its jagged grain, and to transcend it, not by the consolation of philosophy but by squeezing from it a near-comic, near-tragic lyricism.[6]

"A South in Sound" masterfully steadies itself on the "jagged grain," as Tiffany provides a kind of consolation but not in the conventional elegiac turn; rather, through its panoply of Delta characters, she affirms the value of yearning (another blues trope).

As this photographic prose-poem concludes, Tiffany features an image of a gaggle of young black men gathered around several shotgun houses juxtaposed with her "near-comic, near-tragic lyricism":

> In Louise, boys boast with their naked chests beside an empty snow cone truck.
> I imagine the taste mora.
> Where will all that beauty go?
>
> What if this was theirs—the boys who nod, who always show some naked-ness, making the jewelry they wear more pronounced? One of them who could be an owner of his own land in Belzonia drives me in his old pick-up truck from church to the piece he hopes to buy one day and do something with. Corn? Catfish? Homes? I ask him what he does for fun. He drives me to the sound of water. He fishes. He hunts with his father, and his father, and sometimes his aunt. He fishes.[7]

While there are no prototypical blues trains to ride out of town or broken hearts to mourn and mend, here Tiffany captures a desire for transcendence beyond the abject poverty and grim statistical odds stacked against these "naked"-chested young men, vulnerable to an unforgiving world. The boy in the "old pickup truck" "fishes" and "hunts," searching for possibility and agency in a region that has persistently punished black people who dared to transgress their curtailed existence.

When I presented a version of this tribute to Tiffany at the 2018 Issues in Critical Investigation Symposium at Vanderbilt, where we first met three years earlier, the scholar Kinitra Brooks offered another portrait of the Delta, one filled with her personal memories of cultural and communal nourishment. She recalled hip hop and blues music, love and laughter, and, ultimately, a kinship not defined by the bonds of oppression. Dialoguing with Kinitra brought me back to the flexibility of Tiffany's title: "*A* South in Sound," not "*The* South." As with the multimodality of her photographic prose-poem, Tiffany recognized the textured sounds, images, and language she captured so vividly were only one version of an unfolding, multifarious story. There are many Souths to listen for, her title affirms. Thus, while Tiffany was drawn to the Delta region and rendered it with an unrivaled poignancy, she did not choose to set down roots there, moving to the Bahamas instead, and always keeping her mind open to the possibility of still other horizons. Wherever she went, as the saying goes, she took herself, a self that listened well and set those voices and images down in the eloquent verse she leaves behind.

The last time I saw Tiffany was in Las Vegas at the MELUS (Multi-Ethnic Literature of the U.S.) Conference. After a few days of panels, we decided to see *Purple Rain: The Prince Tribute Show*, which Tiffany thought might help to resolve the grief she felt after Prince's recent passing. It was a very Vegas-style show, and we danced and laughed, and even each splurged for a photograph with the cast afterward. On the ride over to the show, Tiffany said how glad she was that she met me, emphasizing the hopefulness in forging a sincere bond. I shied away from expressing how much I valued our friendship, dodging the intimacy of the compliment with "right back at you" or some such nonsense. We exchanged dozens of emails between then and her death, but that moment looms large because it encapsulates so well the difference between us. Namely, Tiffany was willing to take the emotional risk occasioned by the moment, willing to give her whole vulnerable self over to the cause of human connection—a quality that made her not only a cherished friend but also a moving writer.

Indeed, she was always urging others to move beyond the first response to the deeper, braver one that lay in waiting. The book you hold in your hands may not have even come to pass had it not been for her dissuading me from letting the specter of my white body (and the inherent privileges I enjoy as a result) provide an escape hatch from addressing both the chronic nature of black death in this country and the artistic responses to the grief that these immeasurable losses cause. Specifically, the idea for the book grew out of a series of panels we cochaired at the 2018 Midwest Modern Language Association Conference, and two of our panelists, darlene anita scott and J. Peter Moore, are now essential voices in this volume. I remember being asked after giving my paper on elegiac strands in the work of Danez Smith and Aracelis Girmay about what I planned to do next with this research. Would this become an article, part of a book, or some other scholarly endeavor? I expressed my uncertainty, suggesting that perhaps I, a white woman, was not the one to write extensively about black grief. My essay had posed precisely these questions: What are the ethics of grieving? What kind of artistic response is most appropriate? Who, ultimately, are these elegies for?

I remember Tiffany saying something to me and (the room at large) like, "I want you to push past those anxieties because we all have to bear witness; we all have to take part." I wish I could remember her precise words because I felt, once again, as if she had paved a way forward for me and all of us to confront America's original sin and its various (and often pernicious) manifestations today. In other words, Tiffany was urging me to continue to engage in antiracist writing and activism, rather than to simply say, "I'm white, so it's not my responsibility." At one of our later panels, another scholar expressed her exacerbation with her white students for their blindness to black pain in a film she showed them, and Tiffany urged her, too, to move beyond that frustration in order to find a way to talk, to make herself and them more vulnerable. Tiffany urged all of us to chip away at the barriers and boundaries that so often foreclose the possibility of understanding. This was Tiffany in her element, able to face the cruelest of human realities but also to take the next step toward radical forms of love and transformation. In fact, in my last lengthy email from her, she told me about breaking her foot in Cuba and the strangers who ensured her care. "When I fell and was in so much pain," she wrote, "I was immediately surrounded by many who were truly concerned about me and made sure I made it to the hospital. How do you repay that?"

Rather than wallow about being immobile and needing surgery, Tiffany's attention was on crafting an appropriate response to human kindness.

Now as I reflect on Tiffany's work, I am reminded of the poignant truth of Audre Lorde's claim in "Poetry Is Not a Luxury": "Poetry is the way we help give name to the nameless so that it can be thought."[8] What Tiffany offers is just that, a new way of seeing and knowing. As she herself noted in an interview before her visit to Ball State,

> I'm trying to work out something in my poetry, and I like for audiences to take that journey with me. I truly believe if we use new language, our perspectives and how we engage with problems change as well. I do not have a target audience; I only hope for one that is willing to listen.[9]

How fitting that Tiffany's last major project was one that showcases artists-activists working in community to find ways to remedy the endemic anti-black racism that has plagued our nation since its infancy.

Even as your journey in this world has come to an end, we are here listening to the legacy you have left behind, Tiffany. We hear you in the prophetic "Peaches," one of two of your poems in this volume, when you offer: "I'm tender there. / I'll go because tender can lay upon tender." We hear you further in the volume in "Dark Milk: After Basquiat's Painting," in which you expose the pain and alienation teeming in so many of our elegiac renderings: "Who says beauty is here somewhere / when where do you come from means / you don't belong here." We are listening in the pages that follow, as we pursue affirmative answers to your pressing question: "Where will all that beauty go?"

Notes

1. Tiffany Austin, "After an Election," *Auburn Avenue* (Autumn/Winter 2017), https://www.theauburnavenue.com/after-an-election.
2. Ibid.
3. James Baldwin, *The Fire Next Time*, in *The Price of the Ticket: Collected Nonfiction, 1948-1985* (New York: St. Martin's Press, 1985), 379.
4. Tiffany Austin, "A South in Sound: A Photo Essay," *Triquarterly* 151 (Winter/Spring, 2017), www.triquarterly.org/issues/issue-151/south-sound-photo-essay (accessed July 5, 2018).
5. Ibid.
6. Ralph Ellison, "Richard Wright's Blues," in *Shadow and Act* (New York: Random House, 1964; New York: Vintage, 1995), 78.
7. Austin, "A South in Sound."
8. Audre Lorde, "Poetry Is Not a Luxury," in *Sister Outsider: Essays and Speeches* (Freedom, CA: Crossing Press, 1984; Freedom, CA: Crossing Press, 2007), 37.
9. Tiffany Austin, "An Interview with Tiffany Austin," by *#bsuenglish*, Ball State University English Department, November 2, 2016, http://bsuenglish.com/blog/2016/11/02/tiffany-interview/ (accessed July 5, 2018).

INTRODUCTION TO *REVISITING THE ELEGY IN THE BLACK LIVES MATTER ERA*

Emily Ruth Rutter, Sequoia Maner, Tiffany Austin, and darlene anita scott

> "The wrongheaded question that is asked is, What kind of savages are we? Rather than, What kind of country do we live in?"
> —*Claudia Rankine, "The Condition of Black Life Is One of Mourning"*[1]

The murder of Trayvon Martin on February 26, 2012, and his killer's exoneration in June of the following year set the stage for the contemporary liberation movement known as Black Lives Matter and the newly invigorated conversations about systemic racism currently underway—conversations in which creative writers have taken active and visible roles. Their writings attempt to answer poet Claudia Rankine's apposite question—"What kind of country do we live in?"—with a clear-eyed poignancy that acts as a bulwark against apathy and complacency. In this volume, we, too, ruminate on the nation's inequitable state of affairs as we turn our attention to the genre most associated with mourning: the elegy. What kinds of elegiac responses are most appropriate to police killings, the surveillance of black communities, and the slow violence of socioeconomic disparities, among other structural forms of racism?[2] How have and how must contemporary elegists innovate within and against the tradition of elegy to account for bodies deemed disposable by the state? In what ways does the elegiac mode facilitate healing, helping us to cope with, meditate on, and work to build healthy, sustainable futures informed by this systemic pattern of loss? How do we productively interweave theoretical and personal accounts to encourage discussions about art and activism that transgress disciplinary boundaries? Ultimately, what role does elegiac writing play in both the political movements for and personal commitments to black lives? These are the questions that *Revisiting the Elegy in the Black Lives Matter Era* centralizes.

While this is the first and only edited collection to address contemporary elegy within the black diaspora, we enrich ongoing creative and scholarly exchanges regarding the poetics and politics of mourning. In recent years, several monographs, essay collections, and creative anthologies have addressed the state-sanctioned deaths of unarmed black men, women, and children. Scholarly works such as *Pursuing Trayvon Martin: Historical Contexts and Contemporary Manifestations of Racial Dynamics* (2014), *Trayvon Martin, Race, and American Justice: Writing Wrong* (2014), and *Deadly Injustice: Trayvon Martin, Race, and the Criminal Justice System* (2015), among others, usefully contextualize the structural injustices that led to the deaths of young black men from Emmett Till to Amadou Diallo and Trayvon Martin, as well as the exonerations of their killers. In *Pursuing Trayvon Martin*, George Yancy and Janine Jones aver that "Trayvon Martin's death was a 'postmortem event,'" for "black bodies have become 'marked for death' within a white racist semiotic field."[3] The critical essays in *Revisiting the Elegy* enhance this scholarly discussion by attending to the cultural work performed by creative writers on behalf of victims of institutionalized racism. Several recent collections, including *A Gathering of Words: Poetry and Commentary for Trayvon Martin* (2012), *Stand Our Ground: Poems for Trayvon Martin & Marissa Alexander* (2013), *Killing Trayvons: An Anthology of American Violence* (2014), *Resisting Arrest: Poems to Stretch to the Sky* (2016), and *Of Poetry and Protest: From Emmett Till to Trayvon Martin* (2016), have also gathered innovative responses to the chronic devaluing of black life. In his introduction to *Of Poetry and Protest*, Michael Warr succinctly sums up the objectives of his and other like-minded anthologies: "We hope to expose and project poetic consciousness on the issue of police killing more broadly in the Public Square."[4] Interlacing creative and scholarly approaches to systemic violence that is both immediate and gradual, *Revisiting the Elegy* moves this dialogue in new and provocative directions by calling particular attention to poetic renderings of black grief.

With our focus on the elegy, this volume also builds on the work of Karla F. C. Holloway's *Passed On: African American Mourning Stories* (2002), which blends deeply personal ruminations with scholarly examinations of a variety of twentieth-century texts. Holloway argues that "African Americans' particular vulnerability to an untimely death in the United States intimately affects how black culture both represents itself and is represented."[5] While she does not examine the elegy genre, Holloway makes the case that "the dead and the ways of our dying have been as much a part of black identity as have been the ways of our living."[6] This perpetual state of mourning that began when the first enslaved Africans arrived on American shores makes the task of African American elegists distinct. Loss is not singular, in other words, but it is a constituent part of the *lived* experience of black Americans. As Christina Sharpe queries in her recent *In the Wake: On Blackness and Being* (2016):

What does it mean to defend the dead? To tend to the Black dead and dying: to tend to the Black person, to Black people, always living in the push toward our death? It means work. It is work: hard emotional, physical, and intellectual work that demands vigilant attendance to the needs of the dying, to ease their way, and also to the needs of the living.[7]

Both caretaking and grieving are the underappreciated, unremunerated labors of blackness that are invisible to most white Americans for whom the loss of a loved one does not require mounting a defense of the beloved's character, or remaining ever-vigilant about the care that the dying receive in a medical system that, as Sharpe notes, assumes that "blacks feel less pain."[8] Focusing specifically on the elegy, the poems and essays collected here make legible this uneven national response to the suffering of the living and the mourning of the dead, both performing the kind of "wake work" that Sharpe describes and encouraging readers to become part of the vigil.

The Princeton Handbook of Poetic Terms defines the elegy as

> a lyric, usually formal in tone and diction, suggested either by the death of an actual person or by the poet's contemplation of the tragic aspects of life. In either case, the emotion, originally expressed as a lament, finds consolation in the contemplation of some permanent principle.[9]

Black writers have long been drawn to this form, but they have also adapted it to the sociohistorical and cultural circumstances that distinguish the experiences of African Americans in a white-supremacist nation. For example, in his landmark study of elegy, *Poetry of Mourning: The Modern Elegy from Hardy to Heaney* (1994), Jahan Ramazani observes that "Langston Hughes and other African American poets have altered the elegy to address issues traditionally excluded from its repertoire, such as racial strife, lynching, and urban poverty."[10] In *American Elegy: The Poetry of Mourning from the Puritans to Whitman* (2007), Max Cavitch similarly examines several elegies composed by enslaved black Americans for whom "to mourn publicly at all was to consecrate ties of feeling and of blood that often lay under the heaviest interdictions."[11] In an essay examining Paul Laurence Dunbar's elegies, Marcellus Blount also highlights the political stakes of black-authored elegies: "In African American elegies, race often stands for community, and that sense of community is often structured through a figurative glimpse of the past."[12] Citing the elegiac work of Lucille Clifton and Elizabeth Alexander, Emily J. Lordi concurs that "representations of grief construct an ever-expanding black community, one that comprises 'murdered sons' as well as imagined future members."[13] Elegists of African descent, we might say, invest in this ancient form less because of its utility for expunging individual grief and more for its capacity to affirm black solidarity in the face of a hostile, often violent white majority.

Phillis Wheatley's *Poetry on Various Subjects, Religious and Moral* (1773), the first poetry collection published by an African American, includes a number of elegies,[14] though we might date the explicit use of the form as a lyrical tool of both black resistance and empowerment to the post-Reconstruction period in general and the 1895 death of Frederick Douglass in particular. For example, Paul Laurence Dunbar, perhaps that era's most famous black poet, penned an eponymous Douglass elegy which mourns "the passing of her noblest born," while also, as Blount notes, working to persuade "readers that the black generations from which Douglass's leadership issues will continue even without him."[15] A similar movement from lamentation to an affirmation of communal resolve characterizes Henrietta Cordelia Ray's "In Memoriam (Frederick Douglass)," a poem first published in the elegiac collection *In Memoriam: Frederick Douglass* (1897). Ray begins solemnly, noting "ours is a grief that will outlast / The civic splendor," but by the poem's final stanza, she exhorts her readers to honor Douglass's legacy through their own activism.[16] "But courage! no great influence can die," she exclaims, and then assures her readers that their work must be both steadfast and collective: "We are a people now, no more forlorn."[17] Elegies for Douglass continued well into the twentieth century, with poets such as Robert Hayden and Maya Angelou, among others, invoking his legacy, as Ray did over a century ago, as a reminder of the *ongoing* struggle to realize the nation's democratic creed.

Indeed, at least since Douglass's death, distinct waves of black-authored elegies have signified not only the collective mourning of an individual but also an era's structure of sociopolitical feeling. To this end, Harlem Renaissance poets made use of the elegiac mode during the 1920s and 30s as they responded to the pervasive lynching of black men and women. While grief certainly forms the backbone of many of these poems, they function less in the service of consolation and more as a vehicle for exposing the violent white scapegoating of black citizens in the wake of World War I, as the nation underwent rapid technological, demographic, and economic transformations. First published in the avant-garde periodical *Fire!!*, Helene Johnson's "A Southern Road" (1926) aptly represents the common themes and tropes that characterize lynching poems of the Harlem Renaissance period. Johnson mourns not a named figure but one representative of the thousands tortured and burned with impunity by white communities, concluding the poem by rendering the victim Christ-like against the backdrop of a merciless Southern landscape: "*A solemn tortured shadow in the air.*"[18]

While lynching poems marked an era of activism against the brutality of Jim Crow-era "white rage,"[19] elegies mourning the gruesome murder of 14-year-old Emmett Till signified the formal commencement of the Civil Rights movement. Till's story bears revisiting: On August 28, 1955 in Money, Mississippi, two white men, Roy Bryant and J.W. Milam, terrorized and brutalized Till, a Chicago native visiting family in Money, after the teenager allegedly whistled at Bryant's wife, Carolyn. Bryant and Milam pistol-whipped and shot Till, and then tied his neck to a cotton gin and drowned his body in the Tallahatchie River. As the Appendix to this volume makes clear with its long list of Till elegies, his murder galvanized poet-activists to take up the Civil Rights agenda, while Till has also remained an intergenerational touchstone invoked to underscore the nation's refusal to engage in meaningful truth and reconciliation about its devastating investment in anti-black racism. Spanning decade and style, Langston Hughes, Gwendolyn Brooks, Al Young, James A. Emanuel, Wanda Coleman, Audre Lorde, Elizabeth Alexander, Cornelius Eady, Douglas Kearney, Jericho Brown, and Marilyn Nelson are only a few of the poets who have utilized the elegiac mode to express their grief, anger, and defiance of the white-supremacist forces that led to Till's death, as well as the exoneration of his killers.[20] For example, Lorde's "Afterimages" (1982) ruminates on the image of Till's bloated, mutilated body at his open casket funeral, affirming that, even decades after Till's murder, an elegiac pivot toward consolation is not possible. Especially in Lorde's description of Till's spectral presence—"the ghost of a black boy / whistling"[21]—we can appreciate the role that elegies play in archiving the racial traumas about which white America often suffers amnesia. Further, in continuously *saying Till's name*, generations of poets have reminded readers that the white-supremacist ideologies that structured American life during the 1950s have neither been fully redressed nor eradicated.

If Till's death and the elegies mourning him are linked to the Civil Rights movement and its unfinished business, the "Coltrane poem," another key subgenre of African American elegy, is one of the hallmarks of the Black Arts Movement of the 1960s and 70s.[22] These poems do not grieve anti-black racism as much as they attend to the potential loss of artistic innovation signified by avant-garde saxophonist John Coltrane's death from liver cancer in 1967. To this end, Jayne Cortez's "How Long Has Trane Been Gone" (1969) registers concern that Coltrane's memory will fade from social consciousness, as with so many path-breaking black artists before him. The poem concludes, therefore, with a live, pressing question: "How long / Have black people been gone."[23] Lamenting and fomenting in one stroke, Cortez uses this elegy to call attention to the sociopolitical stakes that exceed Coltrane's death. As Kimberly Benston avers of "Coltrane poems," the poet "engages loss by revaluing the meaning of Coltrane, the meaning of death, the meaning of blackness, and the meaning of meaning," and through this elegiac process, the poet, "re-members and sings on."[24] In other words, Cortez and the scores of other Coltrane elegists harness the power of the word to reconcile the saxophonist's absence (and even absence itself), while vowing to extend the tradition of radical innovation that his oeuvre exemplifies.

Although distinct in the sociohistorical flashpoints to which they respond, elegies for Frederick Douglass, lynching victims, and Emmett Till, as well as Black Arts–era "Malcolm X" and "Coltrane poem[s]," are characterized by their shared utilization of elegiac tropes to counter white hegemonic narratives on the one hand and to honor black life on the other. Performing literary labor in the service of Black Power, Black Arts Movement poets in particular shored up the relationship between art and activism that continues to hold sway as current writers work in concert with Black Lives Matter and the network of organizations that comprise the Movement for Black Lives. Extending a politically potent elegy tradition nurtured by their literary precursors, contemporary writers[25] are also shifting its contours in response to an evolving technological landscape that includes the real-time footage of violence against black bodies by law enforcement, as well as the viral sharing of artistic responses to these episodes. High-profile lamentations by singer Beyoncé Knowles-Carter and rapper Kendrick Lamar (among others) have garnered attention and praise,[26] but poetry, perhaps especially the elegy, has been one of the most utilized and poignant genres for expressing both grief and outrage at the chronic devaluation of black life. For example, the group Black Poets Speak Out (#BPSO) has created, among other initiatives, an online platform for writers to lodge their poetic protests against state-sanctioned killings; each video begins with the declaration, "I am a black poet who will not remain silent while this nation murders black people. I have a right to be angry."[27] Amanda Johnston, cofounder of Black Poets Speak Out, shares the group's vision in an interview with Sequoia Maner, a coeditor of this book, saying, "This is in the legacy of black poetics which has always been political and never shied away from that work, but done it in different ways. This is our phase, our now."

This felicitous phrase, "Our now," refers to both the black arts renaissance and black liberation movements currently (and inseparably) underway. Tellingly, "a recent survey by the National Endowment for the Arts revealed that poetry readership doubled among 18-to-34-year-olds over the past five years."[28] This exponential rise was arguably catalyzed not only by the web and social media outlets that have made poetry more accessible, but also by the proliferation of politically conscious verse that has engaged readers in the structural inequities that threaten black lives and blunt collective black empowerment. In her aptly titled essay in the *New York Times*, "Political Poetry Is Hot Again," poet Tracy K. Smith drew a related conclusion about the political utility of the lyric: "Lately [the lyric "I"] seems concerned with seeking revelation not in privacy, but in community. Not in the meditative mind but in bustling bodies in shared space, in the transactions our physical selves are marked and marred by."[29] Enacting change within the context of community is a hallmark of the contemporary elegies gathered and explicated here, as well as the titles listed in this book's Appendix. Indeed, the elegy has proven to be a vital vehicle for countering white media representations that either ignore black pain or individualize it, eclipsing systemic forms of oppression in the process. Within these works, the "I" often manifests as an elegiac "we," and readers are encouraged to become more than passive bystanders. Instead, they are enjoined to participate in the liberation struggle, refusing the enervating forces of state violence, social apathy, and sociocultural amnesia about America's racially unjust past and present.

Contemporary elegies carve out a *public* space for black grief, while decidedly resisting the turn toward consolation that often characterizes the poetic form. To this end, Mark Strand and Eavan Boland describe the prototypical trajectory of the elegy: "It sets out the circumstances and character of a loss. It mourns for a dead person, lists his or her virtues, and seeks consolation beyond the momentary event."[30] By contrast, the aptly titled poem "not an elegy" from Danez Smith's collection *Don't Call Us Dead* (2017) invokes the genre of elegy even while casting aside its utility for addressing the routine extinguishing of black life.[31] In her collection *The Black Maria* (2016), Aracelis Girmay puts similar pressure on elegiac conventions by yoking together the recent deaths of thousands of refugees traveling from North Africa to Europe with the spate of police killings of unarmed African Americans. To accommodate this range of tragedies, Girmay develops the concept of "elelegy": "*elelegy* means to place itself in both the English elegiac tradition and the ululatory traditions of grieving and joy in cultures of North and East Africa."[32] Fusing these two traditions—one focused on conjuring and communing and the other on consolation and redemption—Girmay maps a new elegiac path, attentive to the language and forms used for mourning and what they reveal about the perils of black life past and present, within American borders and well beyond them.

Alternatively, in her tour-de-force *Citizen: An American Lyric* (2014), Claudia Rankine lists in fading black ink recent victims of police brutality, including Jordan Russell Davis, Eric Garner, John Crawford, Michael Brown, Akai Gurley, Tamir Rice, Walter Scott, Freddie Gray, Sharonda Coleman-Singleton, Cynthia Hurd, Susie Jackson, Ethel Lee Lance, DePayne Middleton Doctor, Clementa Pinckney, Tywanza Sanders, Daniel L. Simmons, Sr., Myra Thompson, Sandra Bland, and Jamar Clark, not to mention the African American men, women, and children that Rankine both mourns and anticipates in the repeated phrase "In Memory of" inscribed on the white glossy page that bears these names.[33] In what surely is an unprecedented move, Rankine has continued to augment this list, with *Citizen* on its eighteenth printing as of June 2018 with no clear end in sight to the systemic anti-black violence the poet tracks.[34] As this volume's essays, poems, and Appendix demonstrate, Rankine, Smith, and Girmay are only a few of the pathbreaking writers who have renovated the elegy to speak to current sociopolitical exigencies, especially aligning themselves with the aims of the Black Lives Matter movement.

Our title invokes Black Lives Matter specifically because it is the most influential and disruptive racial justice movement of the era, a movement that speaks to the wide range of political commitments held by elegists and critics gathered here. Begun in 2013 by Alicia Garza, Patrisse Khan-Cullors, and Opal Tometi in response to the acquittal of George Zimmerman, 17-year-old Trayvon Martin's killer, #BlackLivesMatter "is now a member-led global network of more than 40 chapters."[35] As Garza explains, "Our members organize and build local power to intervene in violence inflicted on Black communities by the state and vigilantes."[36] Barbara Ransby recently noted,

Tens of thousands of people participated in Black Lives Matter protests in some form between 2013 and 2017. At the height of the protests a Pew poll indicated that over 40 percent of Americans were sympathetic to the Black Lives Matter movement, as they understood it. In the same period, the term

Black Lives Matter was tweeted over a hundred thousand times per day.[37] (emphasis in original)

What may have begun as a hashtag is now an international black liberation movement with hundreds of thousands of leaders and followers of all generations and racial hues.

Also key is that the architects of this movement are black women who have made intersectional and genderqueer frameworks central to the Black Lives Matter platform. Such a focus means that, while Trayvon Martin, Michael Brown, Tamir Rice, Eric Garner, Freddie Gray, John Crawford, Walter Scott, and other black men and boys are remembered, both on the streets and on the page, women such as Sandra Bland, Charleena Lyles, Aiyana Stanley-Jones, Korryn Gaines, Rekia Boyd, and others are also not forgotten. This intersectional focus likewise means that activists and writers are keenly attentive to the ramifications of racism that may not explode our Twitter feeds but are no less destructive to black communities. As Garza avers, "Black poverty and genocide is state violence"; moreover,

> Black women continue to bear the burden of a relentless assault on our children and our families and that assault is an act of state violence. Black queer and trans folks bearing a unique burden in a hetero-patriarchal society that disposes of us like garbage and simultaneously fetishizes us and profits off of us is state violence.[38]

In this book, we also take an expansive view of "state violence," attending to elegiac responses to police shootings of unarmed black men, women, and children, alongside slower but no less pernicious forms of violence such as environmental racism and systemic neglect by the medical industry. Put another way, we consider politically conscious elegies in capacious terms, recognizing the myriad ways in which writers, readers, and activists may mobilize against white, hetero-patriarchal dominance and the havoc it wreaks.

Several relevant histories have also enriched our understanding of the origins of Black Lives Matter, as well as the through-lines between this current movement and activist movements of decades past. Notably, Patrisse Khan-Cullors, cofounder of Black Lives Matter, published the first memoir of the movement, *when they call you a terrorist* (2018), which opens with a foreword by activist Angela Davis. Khan-Cullors recounts the lived experiences that forged her freedom fighting, noting "Like many of the people who embody our movement, I have lived my life between the twin terrors of poverty and the police. . . . I carry the memory of living under that terror."[39] Her powerful memoir captures the quotidian nature of state violence in the lives of poor people and sets the stakes for immediate and robust racial justice. Scholar Keeanga-Yamahtta Taylor's *From #BlackLivesMatter to Black Liberation* (2016) considers why black liberation catalyzed by abusive policing became exigent during the presidency of Barack Obama, the first black man elected to the nation's highest office. How, in other words, did this culminating moment in the long struggle for black inclusivity in American power structures yield no tangible gains for black liberation, and why has American inequality increased despite perceived gains like the Civil Rights Act of 1964? If Taylor questions the efficacy of black liberation by asking, "Can we get free in America?," she ultimately affirms the transformative potential of antiracist work: "It is the struggle itself that can compel people to push for more."[40] Moreover, Barbara Ransby's *Making All Black Lives Matter: Reimagining Freedom in the Twenty-First Century* (2018) outlines the genesis and organizational structure of Black Lives Matter, as well as its potential for reimagining the social distribution of power. Rather than focus on police killings, Ransby showcases "visionary young Black activists who, inspired by Black feminist teachings and practice, are embracing new modes of leadership as they attempt to build a movement that creates transformative possibilities."[41] We take our cues from Khan-Cullors, Taylor, and Ransby who see within Black Lives Matter a struggle for a society not predicated on gross social inequalities and which is, therefore, not reliant on state surveillance and police violence to discipline marginalized communities; thus, *Revisiting the Elegy in the Black Lives Matter Era* invests in the possibilities engendered by activists and artists engaged in the struggle for liberatory transformation.

Divided into three parts—"Elegiac Reconfigurations," "Hauntings and Reckonings," and "Elegists as Activists"—the volume is structured to give readers a *multifaceted* understanding of the contemporary poetics and politics of mourning. Our first section, "Elegiac Reconfigurations," focuses on recent innovations of the elegiac form to speak to the chronic, institutionalized assault against people of African descent. The section commences with Tony Medina's poems, which redact through sharp-tongued renditions of the killings of Trayvon Martin and Freddie Gray. In "Senryu for Trayvon Martin," he riddles out chaos in the Japanese form meant for satire: "Gunpowder blinds / The eye of justice reckless / As a dumb vigilante." Medina continues with this ironic tone in "From the Crushed Voice Box of Freddie Gray," in which the voice of Gray punctures our sensibilities about mourning:

> I am the Magic Negro
> The Black Houdini
> Who done it
> Done it to him self
>
> I brokes my own spine
> After hogtying myself
> Into a pretzel even
> Houdini who done it
> Would envy

Medina suggests the ways in which the victims of police brutality are often transformed in the wake of their deaths into criminals who somehow deserved their fate, thereby deflecting culpability from the justice system and its officers. Similarly, through the anaphoric "I must," Angela Jackson-Brown's poem "I Must Not Breathe" enumerates all of the self-abnegating expectations placed on people of African descent as they prepare to encounter police officers. For example, "I must not breathe too loudly or too quietly," and "I must grin and show all my teeth." Jackson-Brown solemnly concludes with the declaration: "I must not get stopped but if I run, I must be prepared to die. I must be prepared to die." "Elegiac Reconfigurations" also includes innovative elegies by poets Lisa Norris, Anne Lovering Rounds, Paula Bohince, Jerry Wemple, Emily Jo Scalzo, Sequoia Maner, and Steffan Triplett.

Our first chapter in this section is Laura Vrana's "Denormativizing Elegy: Historical and Transnational Journeying in the Black Lives Matter Poetics of Patricia Smith, Aja Monet, and Shane McCrae," which reads Smith's *Incendiary Art* (2017), Monet's *My Mother Was a Freedom Fighter* (2017), and McCrae's *In the Language of My Captor* (2016) as examples of contemporary collections that "reveal how Western linear time and national borders support ideologies reliant on devaluing black lives." As Vrana notes in her chapter, these texts are aesthetically diverse:

> Smith's work heavily utilizes inherited forms, rhyme, and metrical patterns; Monet's draws on spoken word styles descended from Black Arts Movement aesthetics, incorporating fast-paced wordplay and informal devices like eschewing capitalization; and McCrae's deploys excess white space and unexpected lineation and mid-word enjambment, visually evoking innovations currently affiliated predominantly with academic poetry.

Yet what draws these poets together is their insistence that elegy neither be bound up in a hegemonic American identity, nor emblematic of a teleological reading of history. Instead, Vrana argues, Smith, Monet, and McCrae mobilize elegiac tropes to destabilize nationalistic conceptions of belonging, as well as "facile comparisons between past and present injustices," thereby envisaging "a future in which these elegiac interventions prove less necessary."

Next, we turn to Maureen Gallagher's "The Didactic and Elegiac Modes of Claudia Rankine's *Citizen: An American Lyric*," which considers Rankine's award-winning collection through the lens of the elegiac, the didactic, and Tina Chen's pedagogical commitment to "an ethics of knowledge." Emphasizing the saliency of Rankine's collection for poetry specialists, undergraduate students, and the general public, Gallagher outlines (à la Chen) the ways in which Rankine facilitates *process*-oriented reading that actively refuses closure. Specifically, "*Citizen*'s concurrent deployment of the elegiac and didactic modes ultimately promotes an epistemological orientation that allows for white readers' development of an ethical sensibility in the BLM era." Gallagher concludes that, rather than the strident prescriptions often associated with the didactic mode, *Citizen* enjoins white readers in particular to engage in an ongoing learning process, whereby they are taught "twenty-first century lessons in how blacks live, how blacks die, how to mourn, and how to resist."

Anne Rashid's "Lucille Clifton's and Claudia Rankine's Elegiac Poetics of Nature" then offers another view on formal renovations of the elegy by examining the ways in which public occasional poems from Rankine's *Citizen* and from Lucille Clifton's *Blessing the Boats: New and Selected Poems, 1988–2000* not only challenge elegiac turns toward consolation but also pastoral imperatives in nature poetry. Rather than the didactic and pedagogical modes proposed by Gallagher's reading of *Citizen*, Rashid's essay suggests that Rankine and Clifton

> cross the divide between the human and nonhuman, establishing a collective responsibility for their readers to reckon with past and present racism, while both drawing on and subverting the traditional conventions of the pastoral and the elegy.

In so doing, these poets unsettle a naturalized distance that (white) readers may feel toward both state-sanctioned violence and the scars that the natural landscape bears from such atrocities. In their distinct ways, Rankine and Clifton thus encourage "readers to confront anti-black hate crimes, to contend with the guilt and culpability that white people may feel, and, ultimately, to take action against persistent racist violence."

J. Peter Moore's "'in terrible fruitfulness': Arthur Jafa's *Love Is the Message, the Message Is Death* and the Not-Lost Southern Accent" also surveys a contemporary elegiac landscape but pushes the artistic frameworks beyond the written word. Moore's chapter examines cinematographer Arthur Jafa's *Love Is the Message, the Message is Death* (*LMMD*) alongside poet and theorist Fred Moten, placing Moten's previously unpublished poem "southern pear trees" in "affective proximity" with Jafa's short film. Moore contends that "*LMMD* reads as elegy to the extent that it reads Black Lives Matter as an injunction to rethink the conventions of elegy." Further, "*LMMD* demonstrates the profound ways in which loss is constitutive of black culture and artists such as Jafa reimagine that loss through affective and dialogic modes of expression." As the chapter concludes, Moore also notes with characteristic eloquence that "*LMMD* arises out of sustained decay, reclaims the bloomspace of neglect, and registers the South as no bounded place on the map, but rather a symphony of open questions." Indeed, Moore's pairing of Jafa and Moten facilitates needed rumination on the residue of creative and sociopolitical friction—what the chapter terms "rubbing"—that tends to "loss and its refusal."

In our second section, "Hauntings and Reckonings," we engage critical and creative responses to the specter of white privilege, environmental racism, neo-colonialism, and a health-care system that has long ignored and abused the black body. To this end, Danielle Legros Georges's "Poem of History" reflects on the ways in which the very structures that assure protection are bound up in anti-black violence:

> The University sprawls like a beast. How beautiful
>
> Its lawns, its evening lights. Patrolled by dark
> Guards drawn from the dark city's periphery,
>
> An irony not lost on them, posted in inky
> Corners, shielding the people of the University
>
> From others like them. Inside and out. The confines
> Of safety. The black jungle. The grey jungle.
>
> The towers, the lush avenues, the colossal
> Structures. The sources of knowledge.
>
> A dark flower. A guarding of history.

As Georges suggests, institutions charged with public safety, including universities, are often the same ones that perpetuate the stereotypes of "The black jungle." Moreover, within these sanctified settings, dark-skinned men and women are tasked with safeguarding the privileged from "others like them"; these are the "dark flower[s]," Georges rues, that become entangled in their own marginalization.

Also confronting the specter of white dominance, Lauren K. Alleyne's "Elegy: For Tamir" begins by informing us, "This was going to be a curse poem—/ me hexing the man who ghosted you." Yet the speaker reveals later, "This, I understand, is the grief talking. / This is the unchained melody of rage." While this poem conveys grief and righteous rage, it also moves beyond melancholy, beyond consolation, beyond exaltation. Alleyne, in her poem, again:

> But to write his haunting is to name you
> hell and you have been misnamed enough,
> sweet boy. I make of these words an altar,
> instead. I breathe this poem into a prayer,
> each syllable a taper burning in memory
> of you. Sweet boy, let me build you here
> a new body, radiantly black, limber, poised
> to become its most beautiful becoming.

Becoming most aptly renames the work that Alleyne and her contemporaries perform, as they struggle with ways to encounter and engage these deaths that require ongoing vigils. Alongside Alleyne and Georges, darlene anita scott's elegiac crown of sonnets, as well as poems by Sean Murphy, Sarah Giragosian, Tiffany Austin, and Charlie Braxton, reckon with the grief and wreckage wrought by white supremacy.

Our first chapter in "Hauntings and Reckonings" is Almas Khan's "Black Lives Matter and Legal Reconstructions of Elegiac Forms," which examines elegiac interventions in a legal discourse that continues to justify the killings of unarmed black citizens in particular and the nation's racially stratified privileges in general. As Khan shows, there is a long tradition of African-descended poet-lawyers whose work is infused with a new urgency in the age of both Black Lives Matter and the presidency of Donald J. Trump, whose support for white-supremacist ideologies is well documented. Drawing on critical race theory to explicate recent elegiac writings by poets Evie Shockley and Reginald Dwayne Betts and federal court judge Damon J. Keith, Khan's chapter particularly demonstrates the ways in which mourning and rage can be reframed "to expand the elegy's power to directly impact the development of equal rights for people of color." Although Judge Keith, Shockley, and Betts approach public mourning with distinct aims in mind, Khan observes notable parallels in their fusing of "legal critiques into elegiac forms," as well as their investment in historical reckoning, advocating a poetics of action in an era with increasingly high racial stakes.

Sequoia Maner's "Anatomizing the Body, Diagnosing the Country: Reading the Elegies of Patricia Smith," which, like Vrana's essay, examines Smith's 2017 collection *Incendiary Art*, also returns to her 1993 collection *Close to Death (C2D)*, Smith's first extended wrestling with elegy in the midst of state-inflicted violence toward black people. In these collections, Maner argues, Smith, "explodes the elegiac mode into dazzling possibilities by returning to familiar scenes and lingering concerns, discovering new pathways to grapple with racism and sexism's graphic reproduction." As sites for analysis, the chapter explores Smith's reworking of the Emmett Till poem alongside a lyrical engagement with both a mourning mother figure and the autopsy report, through which Maner argues that Smith "redirects readers from the gruesome condition of the anatomized body to the violent nature of the murderous State." As the chapter concludes, Maner invokes Fred Moten's conception of fugitivity in order to consider the entropic nature of Smith's elegies, whereby "the murdered/martyred body suspires a catching catalysis among the living."

Deborah M. Mix's "'A Diagnosis Is an Ending': Spectacle and Vision in Bettina Judd's *Patient.*" also explores the spectral presence of black women's bodies. As Mix explains, Judd's 2014 collection *Patient.*:

> seeks to understand and undermine contemporary attitudes toward black pain and dis-ease in part by taking us back to the foundational period in which assumptions about black women's bodies and experiences were established in the structures of medicine in the United States.

Objectified and ignored, the ghosts of black women, including Esmin Green, Joice Heth, Anarcha Westcott, Betsey Harris, and Lucy Zimmerman, require more than the recognition of individualized loss; instead, Judd's poetry calls for an honest accounting of the intersecting, interlocking forms of racism and sexism that have led to repeated violations of the tenets encoded in the Hippocratic Oath. For Mix, Judd's elegies are only the beginning of the reckoning that *Patient.* demands, for the collection decidedly "refuses elegiac resolution in favor of a rationale for resistance and change." As Mix's chapter emphasizes, we need not only attend to the present racialized and gendered disparities in the medical system, we need also to reckon with the haunting roots of these inequities.

In our third and final section, "Elegists as Activists," we showcase the relationship between art and activism that has been invigorated in recent years, while also highlighting a long tradition of black elegiac resistance. In "Uniform; or things I would paint if I were a painter," for example, Cameron Barnett refuses the gallery of snapshots of white power flooding our screens, picturing instead: "Malcolm X with a sheriff's cap on, chin strap tightened," "Eric Garner / wearing a six-pointed badge" and "'Black Lives Matter' chiseled at the feet of the Lincoln Memorial." Further, Kimmika Williams-Witherspoon's "No Indictment (On the Death of Sandra Bland)" renders her elegy for Bland as a hortatory chant:

> No indictment
> Or warrant in hand—
> Forgive us Sandra.
> *Justice*
> Not served!

In the language of protest, Williams-Witherspoon's clipped staccato lines not only voice outrage, they also call us to action.

In addition to Barnett and Williams-Witherspoon, "Elegists as Activists" includes poems of resistance by Chris Campanioni, Tiffany Austin, Jacqueline Johnson, Nicholas Rianard Goodly, and Jason Harris. Our first chapter in this section is Licia Morrow Hendriks's "'A Cause Divinely Spun': The Poet in an Age of Social Unrest," which traces a genealogy of elegist-activists beginning with Countee Cullen's "Scottsboro, Too, Is Worth Its Song" (1934), a poem that marks a crucial moment, whereby the elegist chides American poets for their own silence regarding what Hendriks describes as the nation's "willful blindness to its own moral bankruptcy." Glancing back in order to address the poetic-political exigencies of the present, Hendriks's chapter examines Tracy K. Smith's rendering of the transformative power of love in the elegies included in *Wade in the Water* (2018). Pairing Cullen with Smith, the chapter traces

> the evolution of the philosophical outlook and artistic vision of African American poets who achieve a place in the national canon while using

that platform to crusade for the eradication of race-based prejudice and discrimination in American institutions and public life, as well as in the residual personal sentiments of the purportedly culturally enlightened.

The "contemporary protest elegy," Hendriks concludes, is currently performing "the transformative cultural work of raising consciousness and defining a generational agenda."

In "Edwidge Danticat's Elegiac Project: A Transnational Historiography of U.S. Imperialist State Violence," Maia L. Butler and Megan Feifer draw attention to another high-profile elegist-activist: the award-winning author Edwidge Danticat. Examining the elegiac inflections of several of Danticat's recent *New Yorker* pieces, Butler and Feifer underscore the connection between "her role as a public intellectual, which hinges on the performance of 'faithful witnessing' in the space of the opinion editorial" and her acclaimed fiction and nonfiction. Moreover, Butler and Feifer argue that Danticat renovates Black Lives Matter discourse, "showing how transnational dimensions of imperial violence are integral to the ongoing project of determining, enforcing, and policing citizenship in the U.S., the Dominican Republic, and Haiti." Reading Danticat's oeuvre through the lens of Achille Mbembe's concept of necropolitics and Jennifer L. Shoaff's attention to "civil death, social apartheid, and administrative genocide," Butler and Feifer also suggest that Danticat's elegiac project exceeds lamentation. Instead, Danticat calls for a reckoning with the "continued abuses of imperial power against black subjects at home and on the move."

In his lyric essay "Loving You Is Complicated: Empire of Language #4," Brother Yao (Hoke S. Glover III) continues in this elegist-as-activist vein while combining creative and critical modes. Moving between the lyric, narrative, and aphoristic, Brother Yao considers the role of both poetry and hip hop—specifically, Kendrick Lamar's groundbreaking album *To Pimp a Butterfly* (2015)—in the Movement for Black Lives. Drawing attention to the frustrations and difficulties accompanying the cultural work of the black poet, Brother Yao ruminates on the institutionalized biases within the arts industry, as well as in every other facet of black American life. He concludes the chapter with a poignant look at the 2015 Baltimore Riots (ignited by the death of Freddie Gray while in police custody) and the failure of language, and more particularly poetry, to adequately account for the range of emotions that manifests on the streets: "What awards shall be given to the riots? What poems can be written in the face of death? To what do we owe the fist? To what do we owe the young unpoetic standing in front of riot gear in a sector of the empire, whose officials run the camp like the wild, wild, wild west?" These are the live questions that Brother Yao poses to us as readers, artists, activists, teachers, mentors, and, above all, citizens.

Following Brother Yao's chapter, we turn to coeditor Sequoia Maner's aforementioned interview with Black Poets Speak Out's Amanda Johnston. Their conversation emphasizes the sociocultural impact of this group in particular and the current marriage of multimodal art and activism in general. Following the interview are links to Black Poets Speak Out's teaching tools. In the back of the volume, you will also find prompts for discussion to accompany the chapters and poetry, as well as an Appendix that includes black-authored historical and contemporary elegies, pertinent criticism, and other suggestions for continued study. We have designed these resources to be useful for readers and educators, both in and outside of academe.

Taken together, this collection's interview, essays, poems, and additional resources elucidate how mourning feeds our political awareness in this dystopian time, as black writers attempt to see, hear, and say something to the bodies of the dead as well as to living readers. Not unlike protest chants of "no justice, no peace" and "say her name," these writers emphasize that solace is not the desired outcome when the dead are victims of institutionalized oppression. Indeed, if elegy holds the promise of communion with the deceased and of puncturing the boundary, however briefly, between *what was* and *what is*, then the critics and creative writers included here identify in contemporary elegy further boundary-breaking potential, whereby the possibilities of a more equitable *what could be* take shape. Moreover, while we focus on a specific literary form, our volume provides a model for how to engage in productive dialogue through both theoretical and deeply personal accounts, transgressing disciplinary boundaries in the process. We hope that rich conversations ensue, as we all consider the roles we play in the recognition of black loss and the care for black lives.

Notes

1. Claudia Rankine, "The Condition of Black Life is One of Mourning." *The Fire This Time: A New Generation Speaks About Race*, ed. Jesmyn Ward (New York: Scribner, 2016), 147.
2. We adapt the term "slow violence" from Rob Nixon, who describes "a violence that occurs gradually and out of sight, a violence of delayed destruction that is dispersed across time and space, an attritional violence that is typically not viewed as violence at all" (Rob Nixon, *Slow Violence and the Environmentalism of the Poor* [Cambridge, MA: Harvard University Press, 2011], 2).
3. George Yancy and Janine Jones, "Introduction," in *Pursuing Trayvon Martin: Historical Contexts and Contemporary Manifestations of Racial Dynamics*, eds. Yancy and Jones (Lanham, MD: Lexington Books, 2013), 20.
4. Michael Warr, "Introduction," in *Of Poetry and Protest: From Emmett Till to Trayvon Martin*, eds. Warr and Philip Cushway (New York: W. W. Norton, 2016), 13.
5. Karla F. C. Holloway, *Passed On: African American Mourning Stories* (Durham, NC: Duke University Press, 2002), 2.
6. Ibid., 8.
7. Christina Sharpe, *In the Wake: On Blackness and Being* (Durham, NC: Duke University Press, 2016), 10.
8. Ibid.
9. Alex Preminger, ed., "Elegy," in *The Princeton Handbook of Poetic Terms* (Princeton, NJ: Princeton University Press, 1986), 62.
10. Jahan Ramazani, *Poetry of Mourning: The Modern Elegy from Hardy to Heaney* (Chicago: University of Chicago Press, 1994), 135.

11. Max Cavitch, *American Elegy: The Poetry of Mourning from the Puritans to Whitman* (Minneapolis: University of Minnesota Press, 2007), 18.

12. Marcellus Blount, "Paul Laurence Dunbar and the African American Elegy," *African American Review* 41, no. 2 (2007): 241.

13. Emily J. Lordi, "[B]lack and Going On Women: Lucille Clifton, Elizabeth Alexander, and the Poetry of Grief," *Palimpsest: A Journal on Women, Gender, and the Black International* 6, no. 1 (2017): 45.

14. Antonio T. Bly notes that of the 39 poems that comprise *Poems on Various Subjects, Religious and Moral*, nearly half of them are elegies, and furthermore, "one-quarter of the poems she wrote after the publication of her book are also elegies" ("'On Death's Domain Intent I Fix My Eyes': Text, Context, and Subtext in the Elegies of Phillis Wheatley," *Early American Literature* 53, no. 2 [2018]: 320). See also Gregory Rigsby's "Form and Content in Phillis Wheatley's Elegies," *CLA Journal* 19, no. 2 (1975): 248–57.

15. Blount, "Paul Laurence Dunbar," 239.

16. Henrietta Cordelia Ray, "In Memoriam (Frederick Douglass)," in *The Portable Nineteenth-Century African American Women's Writers*, eds. Hollis Robbins and Henry Louis Gates, Jr. (New York: Penguin, 2017), 353, 356.

17. Ibid., 356.

18. Helene Johnson, "Southern Road," in *Shadow Dreams: Women's Poetry of the Harlem Renaissance*, ed. Maureen Honey (New Brunswick, NJ: Rutgers University Press, 2006), 190. A similar description of the lynched black body as a martyr appears in Langston Hughes's 1931 poem "Christ in Alabama" (*The Collected Poems of Langston Hughes*, ed. Arnold Rampersad [New York: Vintage, 1994]: 143).

19. Carol Anderson, *White Rage: The Unspoken Truth of Our Racial Divide* (New York: Bloomsbury, 2016), 4. According to Anderson, "The trigger for white rage, inevitably, is black advancement. It is not the mere presence of black people that is the problem; rather, it is blackness with ambition, with drive, with purpose, with aspirations, and with demands for full and equal citizenship" (Anderson, *White Rage*, 4).

20. See Howard Rambsy II's *Cultural Front* blog entry, "A Checklist of Emmett Till Poems," for a more comprehensive list: www.culturalfront.org/2017/01/a-checklist-of-emmett-till-poems.html (accessed August 20, 2018). Also, see this volume's tribute to the late Tiffany Austin, who wrote movingly about Till and his legacy in her lyrical photo essay "A South in Sound." Finally, see the Appendix to *Revisiting the Elegy in the Black Lives Matter Era*.

21. Audre Lorde, "Afterimages," in *The Collected Poems of Audre Lorde* (New York: W. W. Norton, 1997), 339.

22. The Malcolm X poems of Black Arts–era writers Sonia Sanchez, Haki Madhubuti, Carolyn Rodgers, Etheridge Knight, Gwendolyn Brooks, and Margaret Walker, among others, constitute another dimension of black elegy.

23. Jayne Cortez, *Celebrations and Solitudes: The Poetry of Jayne Cortez* (New York: Strata-East, 1974).

24. Kimberly Benston, *Performing Blackness: Enactments of African-American Modernism* (New York: Routledge, 2000), 148.

25. Alongside poetry, novelists like Jesmyn Ward and journalists like Ta-Nehisi Coates wrestle with matters of documenting, contextualizing, and mourning the dead. See *Men We Reaped* (2013) and *Sing, Unburied, Sing* (2017) by Ward and *Between the World and Me* (2015) and *We Were Eight Years in Power* (2017) by Coates. For a more comprehensive catalog of art produced in tandem with the Movement for Black Lives, see the Appendix to *Revisiting the Elegy in the Black Lives Matter Era*.

26. Among other messages of support for Black Lives Matter, Beyoncé's visual album, *Lemonade* (2016), features Sybrina Fulton, Trayvon's Martin's mother, Lesley McSpadden, Michael Brown's mother, and Gwen Carr, Eric Garner's mother, holding photographs of their slain sons. See Beyoncé, *Lemonade*, Tidal, 1:05, April 23, 2016,

http://listen.tidal.com/ (accessed August 20, 2018). Kendrick Lamar's albums *To Pimp a Butterfly* (2015) and *DAMN* (2017) both incorporate Black Lives Matter themes, such as mourning the slain black victims of police violence. Notably, both Beyoncé and Lamar incorporate poetry into their experimental soundscapes as *Lemonade* features the poetry of Warshan Shire and *To Pimp a Butterfly* integrates the stylings of spoken word and revolves around an unfolding poem to Tupac Shakur. The track "Alright" on Lamar's album *To Pimp a Butterfly* has become a consistent rallying cry among Black Lives Matter supporters. During his 2016 Grammy performance, Lamar lodged a more explicit protest of systemic racism when he referenced February 26, 2012, the day Martin was shot and lamented, "This is modern-day slavery." See James West, "Watch Kendrick Lamar's Incredible Grammy Performance," *Mother Jones* video, 5:50, February 15, 2016, accessed May 1, www.motherjones.com/mixed-media/2016/02/kendrick-lamar-grammy-performance (accessed August 20, 2018).

27. "About Us," #BlackPoetsSpeakOut, http://blackpoetsspeakout.tumblr.com/About (accessed August 20, 2018).

28. Jesse Lichtenstein, "How Poetry Came to Matter Again: A Young Generation of Artists is Winning Prizes, Acclaim, and Legions of Readers While Exploring Identity in New Ways," *TheAtlantic.com*, September 2018, www.theatlantic.com/magazine/archive/2018/09/chen-chen-aziza-barnes-layli-long-soldier/565781/ (accessed August 20, 2018).

29. Tracy K. Smith, "Political Poetry Is Hot Again. The Poet Laureate Explores Why, and How," *The New York Times Book Review*, December 16, 2018, www.nytimes.com/2018/12/10/books/review/political-poetry.html (accessed December 16, 2018).

30. Mark Strand and Eavan Boland, *The Making of a Poem: A Norton Anthology of Poetic Forms* (New York: W. W. Norton, 2000), 168.

31. Danez Smith, "Not an Elegy," in *Don't Call Us Dead* (Minneapolis: Graywolf Press, 2017), 67–68.

32. Aracelis Girmay, "Elelegy," in *The Black Maria* (Rochester, NY: BOA Editions, 2016), 108.

33. Claudia Rankine, *Citizen: An American Lyric* (Minneapolis: Graywolf Press, 2017), 134.

34. "Citizen in the Classroom," Graywolf Press, www.graywolfpress.org/citizen-classroom (accessed January 20, 2019).

35. Alicia Garza, "A Herstory of the #BlackLivesMatter Movement," *The Feminist Wire*, October 7, 2014, www.thefeministwire.com/2014/10/blacklivesmatter-2/ (accessed August 20, 2018).

36. Ibid.

37. Barbara Ransby, *Making All Black Lives Matter: Reimagining Freedom in the Twenty-First Century* (Berkeley: University of California Press, 2018), 1.

38. Garza, "A Herstory of the #BlackLivesMatter Movement."

39. Patrisse Khan-Cullors and Asha Bandele, *When They Call You a Terrorist: A Black Lives Matter Memoir* (New York: St. Martin's Press), 2018.

40. Keeanga-Yamahtta Taylor, *From #BlackLivesMatter to Black Liberation* (Chicago: Haymarket Books, 2016), 217–18.

41. Ransby, *Making All Black Lives Matter*, 9.

PART I

Elegiac Reconfigurations

Tony Medina

Senryu for Trayvon Martin

Skittles bag
Pockmarked holey
Bleeds in rain puddle

Hoodie hides
No blood, tears, or
Eyes shut by wet grass

Screams pierce night sky
A father's stomach pits
My boy! My boy!

Shot through sky
Skittles like Roman candle bursts
Blood from open chest

Stars squint and stare
Raindrops glare in moonlight
Witnessing bloodletting

Mourning grass
Like wet face of boy
Screaming *bloody murder*

Gunpowder blinds / The eye of justice reckless / As a dumb vigilante

Silence of blood clouds
Night drizzle where wind
Whistles through hole in can

Empty bag of Skittles
Crushed can of iced tea
Last game with father

Rain chews night air
Gnaws at brown boy flesh
Grinning teeth of bullets

Rain stains brown boy's
Back as blood pours from chest
Turning the green grass red

How blues is born
Rain falls steady on dead end
Street strewn with black body

Mama's cries hang
On rain hooks ornamenting
Night wind's grin

Blood petals pock
Grim face of grass like lotus
On rain slick back of black boy

Not enough lifetimes
To take back powder burn cries
To piece my boy back

Tony Medina

From the Crushed Voice Box of Freddie Gray

I am the Magic Negro
The Black Houdini
Who done it
Done it to him self

I handcuffed my own
Damn self
I threw myself
In the back of the patrol car

My hands shackled
Behind my back
Slaveship cargo
Ago

I am the Magic Negro
The Black Houdini
Who done it
Dooze it to him
Self him black self

See, Ma? No hands!

I snatched the pistol
From the white man's
Mind
From the back of the
Patrol car—

Suck on dis, Houdini!
I grabs the gun
And shoot my
Self in the chest
Neo-colonial style

The autopsy report says
Damn—
Would've been easier
To walk on water

I bet you a quarter
He done shot himself

I am the Magic Negro—
Spineless—

I brokes my own spine
After hogtying myself
Into a pretzel even
Houdini who done it
Would envy

Only to turn myself
Into a human pinball
Rattling around
The steel gullet
Of a Negro pickup truck

Once reserved for newly-
Arrived Potato Famine
New York Irish drunks
Down on their luck—

Me—*moi*—
It is I who was
Othello—
Oh hell no—

Yes—me
The Magic Negro
The Black Houdini
Who done it—
Dooze it all the time

To him self
His own
Damned self

Angela Jackson-Brown

I Must Not Breathe

If I am stopped by the cops I must be quiet. I must not breathe.
I must not ask questions. I must not breathe.
I must not move.
I must not breathe. I must not talk back.
I must be compliant. I must not breathe.
I must not film the cop.
I must not call family or friends. I must not breathe.
I must not put my hands up or down. I must not breathe.
I must cooperate. I must be docile.
I must stay in the car or get out, depending on the mood of the cop.

I must not breathe too loudly or too quietly.
I must only do what I am told even if what I am told to do goes against my
basic civil rights.
I must not breathe.
I must hope that the cop is having a good day.
I must hope that the cop is a "good cop." I must hold my breath and not
breathe. I must not be suicidal.
I must not be angry. I must be civil.
I must be obedient.
I must grin and show all of my teeth.
I must shuffle and dance, but only on cue.
I must not get stopped but if I run,
I must be prepared to die.
I must be prepared to die.

Anne Lovering Rounds

American Diptych

Passing ████████████████████████
Passing█████████████████████████████
Passing ████████████████████████████████

██
███████████████████████████████████████
██████████████████████████████████████
█████ I leave██ lilac ██████
█leave ████████████████████████████████ spring

I cease from my song ████████████████████

██

Yet ████████████████████████████████
█████████████ chant ████████████████
███
███
██
█████████ all my days and lands-█████████████████
████████████████ chant ██████████████
████████████████████████████████████

Passing
Passing
Passing

                I leave   lilac
     leave   spring

I cease from my song

Yet
                        chant

                        all my days and lands-
                              chant

Jerry Wemple

Nickel Rides
For Freddie Gray

I.
Back in the days when your grandfather's father,
maybe his father, was a young man down at the shore
amusement piers or the scruffy city lots over near

the wrong side of town, they used to call them nickel rides.
Steel boxes jacking up and down, bucking around,
make your back feel like it was worked over with crowbar,

your hips like they was smacked with a plank.
Back in my day, word was out about those nickel rides
on the Philly streets. I was in from the country, hard

down by the river and the woods, but even
I knew what was what. Saw clear enough that one day
while stretching my legs near the 30th Street station

waiting in between long-run trains, when the paddy wagon
pulled up and four cops jumped out, jumped a man I hardly
noticed, whacking him good with long sticks. I figured soon

enough that I needed to take a left, cross the street,
head up another, act like never saw nothing, especially
a side-vision glance of him being cuffed and dumped

in the back of the wagon for a nickel ride. That unit
screech-lurching down the street like the driver wanted
to bust the brakes and run out all the gas all at once.

II.
First off, the war on drugs is a concept. There ain't a war on drugs;
there's a war on people. All wars have casualties, atrocities.
All wars have losers. Only some wars have winners. Tonight

I see Charm City up in flames. Orange tongues of fire taunt
us from brick buildings. The old people say it's just as it was
back in the King riot, nearly fifty years ago. They say

the neighborhood ain't changed much since those days.
We had one good store. Now it's burnt. Kids too young to remember
Tupac let alone Reverend King dodge in and out of focus,

like they were spun off their own nickel rides, dazed from the experience.
Philly, Baltimore, D.C.—I'm not much for cities. But a twist of fate,
a change of luck, and I could've been. Missed being born in Baltimore,

city of my conception, by a few weeks or a month. I got a parcel of kin
buried in the German saint's cemetery in the Manayunk section of Philly.
Generation or two before them it isn't hard to fathom *other* blood kin,

all those years removed, being sold in an auction lot in swampy D.C.
Of course, there's a war on despair, too, though not official
and having no spokesperson. It's often erratic, explosive even,

but is long-going like the rest. Likewise, despair too is a concept,
and so needs a people enemy. And sometimes it's them, but in the end it's us.
Me, I avoid the nickel rides. I watch on my TV what's happening

one hundred fifty miles downriver in slacked-jawed sorrow.

1

DENORMATIVIZING ELEGY

Historical and Transnational Journeying in
the Black Lives Matter Poetics of Patricia
Smith, Aja Monet, and Shane McCrae

Laura Vrana

The genre of elegy is intrinsically fraught with irresolvable contradictions: between the desire for consolation, and the need to deny that any compensation for the one lost is possible; between individuating the elegized through personalized details, and acknowledging death's universality; and between those recurring tropes that have long shaped elegy, and the innovation required to grapple with any loss that feels singular. Such contradictions abide in elegies focused solely on commemorating private losses, without consciously considering societal ramifications. But, because of slavery's unnatural violence, black elegists have historically experienced these pressures in distinctive ways, since elegy could arguably only be effective in serving abolitionist goals by depicting individual losses as representative of the institution.

Responding to contemporary iterations of this problem, black Americans murdered in publicized instances of state violence must often be elegized in ways that innovate within and around expectations of the genre. Embracing contradictions[1] drives this formally and ideologically innovative work of reinventing elegy now in vogue among African American poets grappling with the psychological and social tensions produced by such deaths. For instance, the traditional elegiac desire to portray the deceased as singular can feel incompatible with advocating institutional reform, which demands demonstrating how a loss participates in systemic injustice. Further, contemporary black poets tend not to distance or objectify the dead[2] but rather to identify with those lost, since what Christina Sharpe—in the indispensable study mentioned in the introduction—terms "wake work" mandates confronting the possibility of the speaker becoming the next one slain.

This chapter argues that elegiac poems in Patricia Smith's *Incendiary Art* (2017), Aja Monet's *My Mother Was a Freedom Fighter* (2017), and Shane McCrae's *In the Language of My Captor* (2017) respond to these contradictions by expanding the genre across the boundaries often constructed in American elegy between nations and temporal periods. Their poems reveal that these national and temporal boundaries tend to silence institutional critique, serving to buttress claims that it is always "too soon" to shift attention from individual deaths toward reform. In refusing those boundaries, Smith, Monet, and McCrae draw attention to the transnational continuities and historical duration of struggles against racism, shifting notions of readers' ethical obligations. These poets demonstrate that "black mourning troubles the temporal logic"—and implicit national logic—"of Freud's framing of melancholia and mourning,"[3] revealing how Western linear time and national borders support ideologies reliant on devaluing black lives. Thus, poetically troubling the transparency of those systems of representation helps to weaken these hierarchies and disrupt the constant "weather"[4] of anti-black violence they prop up.

These three writers' poetics are quite distinctive: Smith's work heavily utilizes inherited forms, rhyme, and metrical patterns; Monet's draws on spoken word styles descended from Black Arts Movement aesthetics, incorporating fast-paced wordplay and informal devices like eschewing capitalization; and McCrae's deploys excess white space and unexpected lineation and mid-word enjambment, visually evoking innovations currently affiliated predominantly with academic poetry. These stylistic differences reinforce the texts' thematically unique focal points. Smith links past murders like that of Emmett Till to the present, while raising in new ways traditionally elegiac questions about distance from or intimacy with those more recently lost. Monet's tone channels the confrontational approach of Black Lives Matter activism in connecting Middle Eastern and American struggles. Finally, McCrae produces imaginative, meditative thought experiments colliding the distant past and the twenty-first century. But ultimately, all three differentiate their turns to history from those encouraged by the widespread view that "the slave past provides a ready prism for apprehending the black political present."[5] They illustrate instead that probing the unruly temporal and spatial parameters of black mourning produces fresh ethical relations to the past in an age of disappointment over black leaders' failure to "connect the sins of the past to the crimes of the present"[6] and in ways that might meaningfully alter current discourse around time, nation, and the loss of black lives.

Beyond standard elegiac efforts to represent the ambiguity around temporality often induced by the rupture of loss,[7] elegy by black poets demonstrates that normative views of temporality and their impact on relationships with the dead help maintain the repressive institutions killing those mourned. Hence, crafting elegies that exceed the timeframe of the deceased's lived experiences works to counteract that repression through rejecting Western linear temporality. For instance, by weaving intimate details about long-lost ancestors into elegies for those recently lost, Smith, Monet, and McCrae undermine fixed ideas about chronology and claims that time progresses teleologically, accompanied by inexorable progress. Writing elegy that strains against Western boundaries of time also engenders more ethically complex relations to the past. As R. Clifton Spargo highlights, under normal societal views, "[t]o mourn ethically would be to mourn in such a way that the memory of the dead might serve the living."[8] Yet any professed commitment to learning from the past is rendered superficial by the century-long trend in Western nations[9] toward attenuating rituals of mourning, which discourages substantial engagement with what the past might teach. Sharpe demonstrates well why redefining the norms of mourning and temporal relationships to the dead, outside current state-sanctioned parameters, is hence especially essential for those of African descent. She seeks "a method of encountering a past that is not past."[10] that is more suitable to the conditions wherein death becomes an "interminable event."[11] These conditions yield poets like Smith, Monet, and McCrae, who violate conventional temporal representational practices in order to "transform spaces for and practices of an ethics of care (as in repair, maintenance, attention)."[12]

Beyond the general reaction in all elegy "against the American pathology of compulsory cheerfulness,"[13] African American poets also confront the specifically racialized repression of non-normative views of death. Such repression is traceable to the denial of burial rituals during enslavement, a method of exerting control over the slaveholder's property beyond the temporal and geographical bounds of an individual life by attempting to quash spiritual practices among those left behind, often through measures as extreme as withholding a body from interment. Against continuing iterations of such forces, "[t]he power of the Black Lives Matter movement . . . is that it preserves this act of mourning"[14] and, in the words of Claudia Rankine—from whose ruminations on the 2015 Charleston massacre the epigraph for this volume is drawn—"keep[s] mourning an open dynamic."[15]

Simultaneously, Smith, Monet, and McCrae violate the sense of nationhood that elegy has historically aided in constructing by refusing to allow the loss addressed to reinforce hegemonic constructions of the meanings of life and appropriate deployments of death, and by refusing to respect borders in determining which losses deserve to be mourned. Cavitch shows that elegy has contributed to shaping and articulating national identity, particularly through widely read poems for heroes like Washington and Lincoln.[16] These famous American elegies have helped craft national boundaries delineated by whiteness. Contemporary black elegy helps remake that nationhood, pushing against normative Western views of national identity and socially sanctioned temporalities and politics of mourning to innovate a space for black American belonging and citizenship.

Hence non-conventional notions of temporality and spatiality in Black Lives Matter elegies reconstruct the tradition of American elegy in a mode resistant to nationalistic agendas interested in elegizing only certain losses. Elegizing individuals whose murders elicit less public outcry inserts them into historical narratives that comprise definitions of the nation. The traditional view may be that "[e]mbedded in mourning is a requirement to interrogate our cultural expressions of grief," a requirement that always involves "a humbling recognition that there is nothing more one could have done or might still do for the other."[17]

But such a tepid notion is inadequate when facing the state-sanctioned murders of black Americans. To genuinely fulfill that requirement to interrogate expressions of grief, Smith, Monet, and McCrae in often "obliquely elegiac poems"[18] thwart facile comparisons between past and present injustices.[19] They contribute to Sharpe's "wake work" by exploding temporal and geographic boundaries, envisioning solidarity that defies the nation-state and clichéd ideas that the past can be tidily mapped onto the present. To render porous through elegiac innovation the boundaries of temporality and nation by which responses to black deaths are normativized is to disrupt the power of the white-supremacist state, hopefully contributing to a future in which these elegiac interventions prove less necessary.

Patricia Smith's *Incendiary Art*

Smith's text may adhere most recognizably both to conventions of American elegy and to views of the past as a cipher for interpreting the present, for *Incendiary Art* links prior victims of lynching's violence—most prominently Emmett Till—with twenty-first-century losses. Yet these poems' obvious engagement with the genre makes it easy to overlook how the text shatters temporal ideologies traditionally espoused in elegy via three strategies: Smith (1) disavows chronological progression, jumping between periods to insist that the moral arc of our nation does not inexorably bend toward progress, and that relationships between mothers and lost children defy temporal parameters of mourning; (2) simultaneously draws close and distances the dead, to complicate claims that we can learn readily from those gone; and (3) asserts the inadequacy of mourning practices that do not address systemic circumstances producing that death, contradicting expectations that elegies focus on individuating the deceased. Her linking of past and present not only elucidates the historic roots of violence, but also illustrates that doing so without acting upon that knowledge yields "no moral."[20]

The work's eponymous central sequence, a series of poems scattered throughout the text titled "Incendiary Art" followed by subtitles ranging from "MOVE, Philadelphia, 1985" through "The Body," proceeds in no (chrono)logical order, moving from 1985, to 1968, to 1963, to 1992, to 1921, to 2014, to an undated last piece, destabilizing the fantasy of teleological progress. This repetition with differences demonstrates the cyclical recurrence of similar, and yet importantly distinctive, instances of systemic violence: These poems juxtapose the deaths of, for example, Sandra Bland and victims of the 1921 Tulsa race riots. Smith performs a balancing act, respecting individual loss through intricate detail but also acknowledging that past eras can never be fully imagined. This parallel unknowability regarding both past incidents, and more recent violence enacted against those Smith did not know personally, is further evoked by repeating titles in the evocative "Emmett Till: Choose Your Own Adventure" sonnet sequence. She also repeats poetic phrases, such as "up to their necks in fuel"[21] and "up to your neck in fuel,"[22] affectively recreating the pervasiveness of the white supremacy that ravages black life—and that leaves no language for the temporal ongoingness of black motherhood after a child is killed.

For the text reinforces the disjunction of "still" remaining a mother once one inhabits a category for which our culture has no term that would serve as the inverse of orphan. In this mode, Smith writes of Mamie Till Mobley: "*She / a mama, still.*"[23] This lack of terminology is encapsulated in Smith's representation of mothers sharing the narratives of children slain by police, who are caught between temporalities of what was and what should have been, forced to raise their children's children. Despite the frequency with which such reversals occur for black mothers, parents mourning children remains unnamable within Western conventions, an experience that thus will not "ever sound familiar"[24] linguistically but is all too familiar within the black community. Overall then, such temporal jumps and reversals deny the moralizing that old-fashioned elegiac approaches fumble toward, especially through Smith's ethically complex choices like including a section elegizing black girls slain by their own (black) fathers.

In parallel, Smith erects distance between herself as a poet and those slain with whom she had no relationship, emphasizing that simplistic moral lessons can rarely be derived simply from connecting the past to present circumstances. While the text is awash in reactions to losses of black life, just one piece openly evokes the genre: "Elegy," the longest poem of the book, is for Smith's father, whose life she elucidates in detailed anecdotes up through his death by gun violence. This particularity is birthed by a relationship that cannot exist between Smith and those elegized whom she never knew, an intimacy rendered possible by the accumulation of the more distant black dead paid tribute to in the less sprawling preceding pieces. For, contrasting with the free verse of "Elegy," many poems in *Incendiary Art* inhabit forms like sestinas and pantoums.[25] Exhibiting such formal control when mourning those one did not know counteracts the tendency to imply that past black lives lost can speak directly to those who are attuned in the present, maintaining affective distance even as "Elegy" then brings the speaker into closer intimacy with loss.

The work's essential opening poem, "That Chile Emmett in That Casket," also performs this balancing between drawing Till close and holding him at bay as someone whose death looms so large that he himself is always already unknowable. The *Jet* photograph—intended by Mamie "to make *whites* see just how destructive their racism was"[26]—is evoked to emphasize how "both the photo and its deployment are universal aspects of black childhood."[27] But Smith highlights that this threatening deployment of the photo is not effecting change and merely makes the child protagonist aware of her failings. Even the poem's unusual second-person narration reinforces emotional distance between poet and the scenario depicted: "But there were / no pictures of you anywhere. You sparked no moral. You were alive."[28] This ambivalence sets up the ambiguity that permeates the text, refusing to paint blameless victims and clear morals. The repetition implied by the black elder who warns the child, "*Lord, they kilt that chile more than one time,"*[29] positions Till's murder as one in a long line, but also suggests the inuring that can occur in listeners, like this child speaker, who hear the tale too often. Simply repeating Till's story without finding innovative ways to represent its temporal disjunctions, as Smith does throughout the broader structure of the collection, is depicted as ineffectual both politically and aesthetically.

For likely the two most memorable portions of *Incendiary Art* are its revisions of the Till story that query what could have been, and the nine sequential pages each starkly containing only the phrase "The gun said: *I just had an accident.*"[30] These Till poems imagine the life this boy deserved—and yet explore the other threats he would certainly have encountered in a white-supremacist culture even had he survived Mississippi. Similarly, that eerie phrase anthropomorphically spoken by the gun evokes childlike innocence, but these pages are implicated in the immediately surrounding narratives of black Americans killed in police custody. Hence, the repetition of these sequences asserts the necessity of viewing each loss as unique, yet situating it within systems that produce it.

The text's ending, then, by juxtaposing personal reflections on her father with a final Till "Choose Your Own Adventure" and the last "Incendiary Art" poem bars readers from arriving at tidy conclusions about progression from distant mourning to intimate loss. While mothers visiting their incarcerated sons in one poem "[f]eel like we are in another country,"[31] Smith insists that these poems and the losses that they address are deeply American. The desire of black citizens to stake "teary claim to *Oh say can we see*, slapdashing through lyric and mutilating that meandering key, we still want a verse that just happens not to be there"[32] exposes the lie of that national anthem, in a poem that alludes to the blithe white ability to believe that gun violence should not impact their non-black lives. Thus Smith's temporally jarring moves demonstrate that the moral arc of the universe may not always bend toward justice, unless we conceive of temporal boundaries anew or shatter them altogether. Refusing to find direct language for such experiences of loss (in favor of euphemisms that seek to control black mourning) produces only repetition, whereas Smith seeks innovative futures.

Aja Monet's *My Mother Was a Freedom Fighter*

Also imagining innovative futures, Monet's collection inserts murders of African American women into a transnational framework that explicitly asserts solidarity with oppressed groups in Middle Eastern countries, just as Black Lives Matter activists did during the Ferguson rebellions.[33] This destabilizing of national borders, coupled with glances back in time that assert a lineage of powerful female freedom fighters as influential in the present moment despite their having physically passed, together strains standard definitions of elegy. Further, Monet's humanizing of those like Palestinians who are excluded from the purview of American national policy subverts the supposed autonomy of national borders, an approach amplified by a style reliant on internal rhyme and rhythms that mirror hip-hop rather than Smith's tight forms. These two poets, despite divergent aesthetics, parallel one another in their insistence that responding to the ongoingness of black death requires collapsing temporal eras and defying the nation-state's parameters, by expanding ideas about which victims prove worthy of attention and asserting joy as integral to mourning.

The omnipresence of the threat of death to inhabitants of the black diaspora is elucidated early in Monet's collection, when the speaker describes what it is like to "feel like you are always near death"[34] in the hospitals of "inner healing." There, the speaker depicts "the spirits that be / in every room i entered, watching over us / all knowing and being" and how she eventually ceased visiting those in the process of dying because "everywhere i went people were sick / dying in public." This poem captures the constricting, inept nature of rituals surrounding and views of death in its final lines:

> we prescribe the suffering
> people we love die alone
> people afraid to love die alone
> we watch people die alone, in secret
> as if it weren't happening.[35]

Another speaker proclaims that "everywhere we go / i am a single mother mourning / in public,"[36] again showing the universality of the achronological experience of being a childless mother in the black community. Monet's repeated gestures toward the pain that results from such mourning occurring "in public" indicates that conventional ideas of mourning as private are available only to the privileged, whether because anti-black racism forces loss into political visibility or because everyday losses mourned by black women are denied the significance of time to mourn privately in a white-supremacist society.

Reversing the circumstances of that previous speaker as "a single mother," Monet is positioned in uncomfortable proximity to death by references to the possibility of the speaker having never been born because her mother considered abortion. Composing such verses in the first person especially situates the poet—and readers—closer to the experience, forcing intimacy with a topic that provokes hesitancy about whether to revel in or reject those circumstances that ultimately prompted the mother to keep what seems to have been an unwanted child. In this way, Monet implicitly evokes Gwendolyn Brooks's famed, and famously ambiguous, "the mother" as a precursor, fittingly so given Brooks's role as a pioneering modern black elegist with her complex poems for Till and others. This moral morass dominates the end of the first section of *Freedom Fighter*, where Monet writes:

> i owe my life
> to the woman
> who stopped my mother

on the b56
on her way
to the abortion clinic
and told her

you have a poet coming.[37]

Later, the speaker in what could be the same (or a similar) scenario becomes the mother rather than the child-poet, forcing readers to inhabit the discomfiting shoes that would prompt pondering such a choice. This poem, "the emerging woman after aborting a girl," portrays with great empathy the paradoxical conditions that produce such non-choices and thus demystifies death, bringing it into closer communion with the everyday than Western mourning allows. But such closeness need not yield (only) desperation or sorrow in Monet's poetry; instead, she depicts grappling with such losses through love, joy, and active resistance that can help diasporic people "be not dismayed / be defiant and deliberate / always, be"[38] against forces of normativization that strive to erase them.

One of those defiant resistant strategies as enacted in her poetics inheres in an innovative temporality that involves bringing maternal ancestors to life, through interweaving seemingly autobiographical anecdotes and vital ancestral diasporic spiritual concepts. These nonlinear temporal gestures reveal the need to, as one reviewer puts it, "ground yourself in the heroic past to lift yourselves to a heroic future,"[39] such that the poems feel prophetic even though this same review acknowledges that prophets tend to be "bestow[ed] their proper title" only "once they're safely in the grave."[40] Monet asks that we perform that bestowing, but also that we refuse to see these ancestors as "safely" in the grave. A brief poem "on asking my grandmother about santeria" links Santeria spiritual practices with one of the most recognizable Black Lives Matter slogans, demonstrating the relevancy of rituals often relegated to the past or derided as foolish by white power structures. Further, such poems inhabit a different relationship to the past than is allowed by the prevalent framing that views the degradation of enslavement as a context key to comprehending present oppression. In place of primarily communicating intergenerational trauma, these poems proffer the intergenerational transmission of joy, love, survival, and triumph.

Transnationally, this new relationship to mourning through joy and triumph proves especially essential when these poems emphasize that violent struggle is a worldwide project resulting from the global reach of colonialism and imperialism—and that joyous resistance to that violence is equally widespread. In a diasporic world stretching from "children in dakar" to slain female protestors like Iranian Neda Agha-Soltan and Palestinian freedom fighters, Monet illustrates the need for solidarity between those women of "#sayhername" and those she addresses in "a voice from azadi square" and "the giving tree." The latter poem juxtaposes in its last lines an italicized refrain that evokes the omnipresence of violence in contested Palestinian territory with an acknowledgment of the speakers' guilt: "*They came in violently*, she says. / we came in violently. displaced, black, and american. still, still. / she fed us."[41] The parallel phrases juxtaposed with only the subjects "*They*" and "we" altered demonstrates American complicity in this Middle Eastern conflict. Yet despite the unlikelihood of this bond in the face of American disregard toward these victims, the "[d]isplaced, black" American citizens are nevertheless granted sustenance in an act of generosity that creates "still[ness]" against the frenzied movement of warfare's destruction, always "still" ongoing.

Monet's poems thus formally and thematically embody radical solidarity and demand that readers act, revealing their power to do so. Every speaker and character in this text is equally granted the possibility of political significance: "a transwoman dancing with herself in a crowded room for the first time / is too, a protest / a mother in Hebron dresses her daughter in dreams, existence / is too, resistance."[42] The interweaving of losses more readily viewed as political (due to their participation in international conflicts) and personal in *My Mother Was a Freedom Fighter* creates a diasporic feminist ethos of solidarity around mourning—and corresponding celebration. Against the question "what purpose do i have in Palestine / lest we forget june jordan or alice walker,"[43] Monet defiantly demonstrates the import of crafting innovative elegiac practices, across boundaries of nation and time and in defiance of state-approved notions of appropriate mourning for black lives. Her text asserts the multiple valences of mourning, its tones of celebration as well as valediction, powerfully contradicting societal normativizing of responses to lost black lives.

Shane McCrae's *In the Language of My Captor*

McCrae's National Book Award-nominated work pushes this innovation farthest of all, elegizing the present while disavowing speaking about it directly. His view that turning to the past proves his most effective approach for addressing the present renders McCrae's poetics a vital intervention in the innovative contemporary black elegiac project.[44] Emphasizing the ubiquity of death in the black experience, McCrae intertwines childhood memories, Civil War histories, commentary on white-dominated exploitation across eras, and oblique references to Black Lives Matter. Through this anti-chronological interweaving, he stretches and strains societally sanctioned definitions of the appropriate temporalities of mourning and of the supposedly shared values of our nation-state, countering reductive conceptions of the conventional labor of relating to the past.

The living death of white supremacy—and the need for the means of responding to that atmosphere without oversimplifying the so-called lessons of the past—dominates McCrae's collection. From the opening sequence spoken by a haunting "captive" in a human zoo, to persona poems voiced by the historic figure of "Jim Limber the adopted mulatto son of Jefferson Davis," to pieces fictionalizing an early black film star named Banjo Yes, each of McCrae's persona poems demonstrates how exploiting oppressed peoples for entertainment has been fundamental to American history and the reinscription of living death. Illustrating that the wide-ranging voices across disparate eras brought together in his collection all share in common such experiences of repression, McCrae refuses popular narratives that paint those in positions of power who have died as absolved of sin or above criticism by virtue of historical distance. Such absolution seems to be applied only to (white) figures like Jefferson Davis and never to those they exploit and/or kill, and so McCrae's juxtaposing of real people and fictional personae highlights that normativized ideas of time and nationhood rely on overly simplistic moralizing that must be thwarted for all our sakes.

While *In the Language of My Captor* does not explicitly connect American violence to international struggles as Monet's work does, its opening section consists of ethically meditative poems in the voice of a "captive" in a human zoo, evoking the historical imprisonment of figures like Saartjie Baartman (the so-called Hottentot Venus) throughout the international realms implicated in colonialist enterprise. These pieces unsettlingly situate that captivity in no particular era, reminding us that imperial conquest has always included capitalist exploitation of black bodies, merely taking different forms over the centuries. This "captive" speaker perspicaciously analyzes his voyeurs and captors, transitioning from laughter at their inane worldview to sorrow ("I used to laugh at him but now I grieve"[45]), and exposing the shallowness of such Western concepts as that of monotheism and "privacy," the latter of which relies on a distinction between intimate private space and public exposure that Monet also shows to be untenable in the black experience. Indeed, McCrae's captive comprehends the universality of the human condition more deeply than the spectators:

> when I met new people
> The first thing I assumed was
> they were just like me
>
> ...And so at first I thought the white men
>
> ...had been
> whitened by the sun ...
> I thought they didn't
>
> Know they were dead.[46]

The desire to "[h]elp" and the assumption that everyone is "like me" is quashed by captivity, but this speaker in return gains deep insights into the breadth of white exploitation. That insight emerges in the final words of the first section, where he rails against describing his homeland "[i]n the language of my captor,"[47] yet expresses sympathy for those captors and an awareness of the expansive ways of being "dead."

Similarly depicting historically repugnant circumstances as rife with complexity, one of McCrae's personae, Jim Limber, reflects on the fact that the president of the Confederacy, Jefferson Davis, adopted a mixed-race child during the Civil War. In particular, McCrae shows Jim ruminating on a white man's facile postbellum words:

> the dead don't see

> No important differences between the Ne-
> gro and the White the dead don't see no bad
> In folks if what bad they done they ain't free-
> ly chose to do the dead don't see no good

> In folks if what good they done they ain't hoped
> To do.[48]

The fact that these claims feel familiar today yet are believably spoken by a nineteenth-century character illustrates the pervasiveness of myths about death's equalizing power and the pervasiveness of white-supremacist violence repeatedly disproving such an idyllic notion. Thus, McCrae suggests that his ability to envision a complex, not wholly negative, relationship between Jim and his adoptive parents is enabled by the historical gulf between the poet and the situation. That choice not only shows that similarly ethically ambiguous circumstances are still obtained in relationships between black and white Americans across the supposedly equalizing boundary between death and life, but it also demonstrates the telescopic view that temporal distance allows beyond simple moralizing.

It is because of the power in this distance that McCrae just once in this text crafts an overt Black Lives Matter elegy: It is no coincidence that he elegizes one of the youngest widely known figures, Tamir Rice, murdered for child's play that anti-black stereotypes render dangerous in white police officers' eyes. "Banjo Yes Plucks an Apple from a Tree in a Park" is dedicated to Rice, though its fictional early black film star speaker lived a century before Rice's 2014 murder, requiring a temporal perspective that would be deemed impossible by linear conceptions of time. Banjo Yes has to this point been a lighthearted character who humorously, albeit with forethought that reveals his intellect, takes advantage of stereotypes to position himself advantageously, such that he might become a wealthy performer able to marry white women and transgress certain boundaries. Here, however, pondering an apple leads him to somber queries:

> a real

> Apple don't taste no sweeter than a movie
> Apple it ain't crisper but it's some better
> A nigger eats an apple in a movie
> It ain't no apple it's a big fat water-

> melon man it's fried chicken it's all that

> bullshit a nigger eats but he ain't eating.[49]

Spectators' ability to transmogrify fact into whatever confirms their racialized assumptions makes the apple bitter, a symbol of Banjo Yes's constant self-awareness of who is watching and why.

The final lines, "I waste my mind / Trying to read white folks' minds I'll tell you what / An apple is it's death it's my child dead,"[50] devastatingly link McCrae's imagined early twentieth-century character to Tamir's murder. Positioning the minstrel-like figure of Banjo Yes as forced to consume the Edenic apple—and as consumed, in turn, by the desire to keep such knowledge of good and evil from future black children—rings powerfully, evoking how frequently such Biblical imagery has been used perniciously to prop up white-supremacist ideologies. This poem draws a direct line from the exploitation of imperialistic exploration, to that of the film industry, to the loss of childhood innocence embodied in a toy gun being read as something else entirely due to stereotypes propagated by those preceding forces. Elegizing Tamir in McCrae's innovative mode involves indirection, temporal distance, and interrogating exploitation long enacted by American entertainment.

Ultimately, the "language of my captor" of the collection's title effectively creates distance between the poet and his subject, and between readers and that which we often want clearly spelled out, complicating standard assumptions about the ethics of the past and present. The memoir-like poems of the text's middle section describe a grandfather who "wouldn't have been ashamed to admit that he believed white people were superior"[51] but would have vehemently eschewed being labeled a white supremacist. Such distinctions between how people openly describe their beliefs, and their frequent unashamed admission of such beliefs if only an unpleasant label can be avoided, embodies how McCrae grapples best with ugliness in the present by sidestepping its specific circumstances. Such indirection, rather than mere attempts to provide facile terms meant to improve society without further substantial action, can reveal ways forward. And these poems' depiction of the complexities of love and freedom—of how Jim Limber could feel a kind of warped love even for the Confederate leader, and of how a white captor's anxieties about his own freedom that shape his mistreatment of a captive might be *almost* comprehensible—shatter the boundaries frequently erected around black mourning. McCrae depicts all of these histories as equally and foundationally American, underpinned by shameful impulses that connect us all and thereby require us to engage in collective reckoning.

Conclusion

The "death" of the poet as a culturally relevant figure has been proclaimed for generations; yet writing *about* death in the innovative modes that the poets discussed here are doing seems to be revivifying the art. Much as all elegy "develops by feeding off a multitude of new deaths, including the body of its own traditions,"[52] black elegy has been given new life by the outpouring of work produced in relation to the Black Lives Matter movement. Even more important is the fact that readers are attending to this verse more responsively than ever before. As Austin, Maner, Rutter, and scott highlight in the introduction, it seems unlikely to be a coincidence that poetry readership in the U.S. is increasing for the first time in years[53] just as the devastation wrought by murders of people of color is generating poetic reactions that spread more widely than ever. New technologies expand the borders of time and space that once constrained reading, creating instantaneity and simultaneity that reveal the constructed nature of Western concepts of time and space.

The combined force of this new poetics and new means of dissemination makes this moment ripe for considering elegy anew. Poets like Patricia Smith, Aja Monet, and Shane McCrae encourage such a shift in thinking, insisting that elegizing black lives demands expanding the temporal conventions of the genre and its relationship to views of American nationhood. The "refuge and consolation"[54] offered by grappling with the past rather than the present for McCrae might feel to some like an evasion of the necessity of using art to counteract present horrors. But it is also vital to counter the obligation often imposed on black poets that they serve as spokespeople for certain issues. As such, temporal and geographical expansiveness enables new avenues for these poets to execute the project expected of them. Some truer justice may emerge from understanding that normativized forms of relating to the dead inhabit too narrow a framework of temporality, geography, and American identity; Smith, Monet, and McCrae help us reconceptualize those frames.

Notes

1. Ramazani refers to this: "At first glance, the phrase 'African-American elegy' might seem to be either a contradiction in terms or a redundancy. A contradiction in terms because 'elegy' has been defined as a European form. . . . And yet a redundancy because African-American poems have often been characterized as what W. E. B. Du Bois called 'Sorrow Songs,' inevitably elegizing a long history of racial oppression and

murder. But 'African-American elegy' is neither oxymoronic nor pleonastic." See Jahan Ramazani, *Poetry of Mourning: The Modern Elegy from Hardy to Heaney* (Chicago: University of Chicago Press, 1994), 135.

2. Ramazani notes that "[a]s a genre, it [premodern elegy] had typically shaped and ordered grief, had abstracted and objectified the dead"; see Ramazani, *Poetry of Mourning*, 18. Hammond refers to "[t]he objectification of the dead" that "reinforced the simultaneously harsh and consolatory thrust of" American puritan elegy; see Jeffrey A. Hammond, *The American Puritan Elegy: A Literary and Cultural Study* (Cambridge: Cambridge University Press, 2000), 164. Connolly argues that "Lowell objectifies" the poets he elegizes; see Sally Connolly, *Grief and Meter: Elegies for Poets After Auden* (Charlottesville: University of Virginia Press, 2016), 193.

3. Margo Natalie Crawford, "The Post-Neo-Slave-Narrative," *The Psychic Hold of Slavery: Legacies in American Expressive Culture* (New Brunswick: Rutgers University Press, 2016), 70.

4. See Christina Sharpe, *In the Wake: On Blackness and Being* (Durham: Duke University Press, 2016), 102–34.

5. Stephen Best, "On Failing to Make the Past Present," *Modern Language Quarterly,* 73, no. 3 (September 2012): 453.

6. Keeanga-Yamahtta Taylor, *From #BlackLivesMatter to Black Liberation* (Chicago: Haymarket Books, 2016), 138.

7. See R. Clifton Spargo, "The Contemporary Anti-Elegy," *The Oxford Handbook of the Elegy,* ed. Karen Weisman (New York: Oxford University Press, 2010), 417.

8. See R. Clifton Spargo, *The Ethics of Mourning: Grief and Responsibility in Elegiac Literature* (Baltimore: Johns Hopkins University Press, 2004), 19.

9. Ramazani, *Poetry of Mourning*, 10–23.

10. Sharpe, *In the Wake,* 13.

11. Ibid., 19. Ruha Benjamin similarly elaborates on the importance of black "afterlives," highlighting the "repertoire of invoking the slain to vivify collective action. Scholar of modern slavery Zhaleh Boyd connects this form of invocation to the idea of 'ancestral co-presence.' She refers to hashtag signifiers, like #SayHerName, as gathering points that make present the slain and call upon recent ancestors—Tamir Rice, Sandra Bland, Michael Brown, Ayana Jones, and so many others—as spiritual kin who can animate social movements. . . . Co-presence, in short, troubles the line between the biological living and dead." See Ruha Benjamin, "Black AfterLives Matter: Cultivating Kinfulness as Reproductive Justice," *Boston Review,* July 16, 2018 (accessed January 1, 2019), n.p., http://bostonreview.net/race/ruha-benjamin-black-afterlives-matter.

12. Sharpe, *In the Wake,* 131.

13. Ramazani, *Poetry of Mourning,* 17. He highlights: "Moreover, ethnic, racial, religious, and sexual minorities in England and America, including some Jews, Muslims, African Americans, Irish Americans, and gays, have preserved or reinvented rituals long abandoned by most white middle-class mourners in these countries; sometimes they have even harnessed mourning and its rituals as oppositional practices. Nevertheless, elegists as diverse as the Anglo-Irish Yeats and the Ulster-Catholic Heaney, the African American Hughes and the gay-Jewish Ginsberg and Rich, have all witnessed and responded to changes in mourning customs wrought by modernization." See Ramazani, *Poetry of Mourning,* 22. What he does not discuss at length is that one of the foundational conditions of modernization has been the violent repression of minority groups.

14. Mary Unger, "Literary Justice in the Post-Ferguson Classroom," *MELUS,* 42, no. 4 (Winter 2017): 99.

15. Claudia Rankine, "The Condition of Black Life Is One of Mourning," in *The Fire This Time: A New Generation Speaks About Race,* ed. Jesmyn Ward (New York: Scribner, 2016), 150.

16. See Max Cavitch, *American Elegy: The Poetry of Mourning from the Puritans to Whitman* (Minneapolis: University of Minnesota Press, 2007), 80–107. Cavitch also illustrates that elegy has helped "variously to configure, legitimate, and disrupt national identifications by both crossing and articulating divisions of class, race, gender, religion, sexuality, and politics"; see Cavitch, *American Elegy,* 15.

17. Spargo, *Ethics,* 37.

18. Cavitch, *American Elegy,* 110.

19. None of these works incorporates paratext, which is noteworthy given the frequent appearance of such documentation in recent poetry collections that depict history. This absence suggests that these projects are less invested in drawing connections between past and present than in reshaping the notion that the past can yield tidy lessons.

20. Patricia Smith, *Incendiary Art* (Evanston: Northwestern University Press, 2017), 6.

21. Ibid., 10.

22. Ibid., 31.

23. Ibid., 33.

24. Ibid., 73.

25. Mark Strand and Eavan Boland call the pantoum "a perfect form for the evocation of a past time," since "the reader takes four steps forward, then two back." See *The Making of a Poem: A Norton Anthology of Poetic Forms,* eds. Mark Strand and Eavan Boland (New York: W. W. Norton, 2001), 44.

26. Jonathan Farmer, "'Up To Their Necks In Fuel': On Patricia Smith's *Incendiary Art,*" *Kenyon Review,* Web (accessed January 1, 2019), n.p., https://www.kenyonreview.org/reviews/incendiary-art-by-patricia-smith-738439/.

27. Ibid.

28. Smith, "That Chile Emmett in That Casket," 6.

29. Ibid., 5.

30. Ibid., 93–101.

31. Ibid., 29.

32. Ibid., 15.

33. See Taylor, *From #BlackLivesMatter,* 162.

34. Aja Monet, *My Mother Was a Freedom Fighter* (Chicago: Haymarket Books, 2017), 34.

35. Ibid.

36. Ibid., 119.

37. Ibid., 39.

38. Ibid., 146.

39. Josh Roark, "Book Review: My Mother Was a Freedom Fighter by Aja Monet," *Frontier Poetry,* May 24, 2017, web (accessed October 30, 2018), n.p., https://www.frontierpoetry.com/2017/05/24/book-review-mother-freedom-fighter-aja-monet/.

40. See Ibid.

41. Monet, *My Mother,* 82.

42. Ibid., 145.

43. Ibid., 87.

44. Shane McCrae, "Episode 11: Shane McCrae," interview with Rachel Zucker, *Commonplace: Conversations with Poets (and Other People),* November 1, 2016, web (accessed January 1, 2019), 21:20–27:00, https://www.commonpodcast.com/home/2016/10/29/episode-11-shane-mccrae.

45. Shane McCrae, *In the Language of My Captor* (Middletown, CT: Wesleyan University Press, 2016), 4.

46. Ibid., 13–14.

47. Ibid., 13.

48. Ibid., 77.

49. Ibid., 61.

50. Ibid., 62.
51. Ibid., 32.
52. Ramazani, *Poetry of Mourning,* 8.
53. Iyengar details that the greatest gains have occurred among young adults, women, adults with only some college education, and ethnic minorities; the latter now read poetry at a greater rate than white Americans. This suggests that poetry's appeal to groups traditionally believed to be disinterested in the genre is increasing—a fact that Iyengar attributes primarily to offerings like Poetry Out Loud, but also acknowledges may be produced by social media. See Sunil Iyengar, "Taking Note: Poetry Reading Is Up—Federal Survey Results," *Art Works Blog,* National Endowment for the Arts, June 7, 2018, web (accessed January 1, 2019), n.p., https://www.arts.gov/art-works/2018/taking-note-poetry-reading-%E2%80%94federal-survey-results.
54. McCrae, "Episode 11," 33:10.

2

THE DIDACTIC AND ELEGIAC MODES OF CLAUDIA RANKINE'S *CITIZEN: AN AMERICAN LYRIC*

Maureen Gallagher

Claudia Rankine's *Citizen: An American Lyric* has been the rare book of innovative poetry with expansive reach and relatively widespread name recognition within the academy[1] and beyond. It has become a *New York Times* bestseller, winner of several awards, and upon release was widely—and glowingly—reviewed in the popular press, thus garnering the attention of a broader audience who rarely reads poetry. Images of the book, with its recognizable cover art—a photograph of *In the Hood*, David Hammons's 1993 art piece depicting the detached hood of a dark sweatshirt—has pervaded the public sphere: During the 2016 presidential primary campaign season, a photograph went viral of a woman reading the book while seated in the audience of a Trump Rally;[2] a copy of the book is gifted to a character in Spike Lee's 2017 Netflix reboot of *She's Gotta Have It*.[3] Within academia, it has quickly become a "must-read," and, for many professors and college-level instructors, also a "must-teach."[4]

In this chapter, I suggest that the remarkable reception of *Citizen* hinges on its instructional role for readers—not only, but certainly significantly, white readers—during the Black Lives Matter (BLM) era. Many have noted that the text is framed by scenes of learning, as it opens with a childhood memory that is set in a classroom, while the final section concludes with the declarative statement: "It was a lesson."[5] The overarching "lesson" aligns with the tenets of the BLM movement and can be summarized as follows: the continued pervasiveness of white-supremacist ideologies results in black individuals suffering from relentless emotional, physiological, and violent—even fatal—injuries. Moreover, the text "teaches" readers to see the connections between high-profile killings and everyday experiences of anti-black racism, or what Rankine has referred to the white mindset of "internalized dominance."[6]

With its unambiguous messages, *Citizen* disrupts the assumptions of many poets and poetry critics—especially those who align with "avant-garde" or "experimental" practices—who have long eschewed "didactic" poetry. One poet-critic who has disagreed with these detractors, Jonathan Holden, argued in 1991 that poetry would once again be relevant for a broader public if it *is* didactic: "A great many people in America *want* moral instruction. They want poetry with a 'message.' . . . the didactic is a line of development which, if persuaded artfully, might further enlarge the estate of our poetry."[7] *Citizen* is a book that exemplifies Holden's prediction: It has been so well-received not *despite* but *because* of its commitment to "moral instruction." My argument thus contrasts with critics and reviewers who deemphasize[8] or disavow *Citizen* as didactic.[9] Indeed, while *Citizen* plays a role in renewing American poetry's relevance to a wider public, its strategies can also transform poetry specialists' considerations of the didactic mode.

I argue further that, as the object lessons of *Citizen* hinge on the crucial need to publicly mourn black lives cut short by violence, *Citizen* also operates within the black American elegiac tradition.[10] In particular, *Citizen* explores the black subject as one engaged in the elegiac process of "melancholic mourning," as conceptualized by Jahan Ramazani. According to Ramazani, in the modern elegy, subjects engage in "ambivalent and protracted grief," which departs from both the healing consolations of traditional elegy and "the psychoanalytic ideal of therapeutic art."[11] The unresolved process of melancholic mourning emerges from the "impossibility of preserving a pristine space apart, of grieving for the dead amid the speed and pressure of modern life."[12] Ramazani makes a special case of black elegies, which often speak to the collective experiences of "racial strife, lynching, and urban poverty."[13] The articulation of "[p]rotracted and unresolved mourning" in modern black elegies are like blues songs, where personal feelings, including "anger, despair, grim laughter, and self-punishment," linger melancholically, while "the social and racial contexts of such feelings" are always present.[14] I apply Ramazani's argument in order to situate *Citizen* within the lineage of modern black elegy in the twenty-first century. Indeed, in the digital age, the "impossibility of preserving a pristine space apart" for mourning the loss of black lives is heightened through media saturation, including the circulation of smart phone videos, excruciating social media–driven interrogation of the minutiae of black victims' lives, and cable channel pundits pandering to their audiences through the *de facto* criminalization of black men, women, and children. *Citizen* contributes a twenty-first-century model for mourning for those who have died as a result of state-sanctioned violence. The melancholic mourning in *Citizen* is paradoxical: Both a central preoccupation and impervious to resolution; both circumscribed by the white gaze within media-driven narratives and also a form of resistance to white supremacy; both cataclysmic and woven into the fabric of everyday black life.

In what follows, I first consider these paradoxes with the context of pedagogical scholarship that foregrounds ethical considerations for white readers of multicultural literary texts. I apply these pedagogical insights to explore how *Citizen* positions white readers as learners. Next, I demonstrate the utility of considering the didactic alongside the elegiac mode in an examination of *Citizen*. I then turn to the ways that *Citizen* instructs its readers in the complexities and unresolved tensions of mourning in the Black Lives Matter era. Through its commitments to both instruction and mourning, *Citizen* illustrates the capaciousness and relevance of the elegiac and the didactic modes in contemporary innovative poetry.

Reconfiguring the Didactic Mode Through an "Ethics of Knowledge"

The *Princeton Encyclopedia of Poetry and Poetics* describes the didactic as a "mode" of poetry in the Western tradition that "intends 'useful teaching,'" which, from antiquity, encompasses both metaphysical/theological inquiry and practical, "how-to" advice (such as farming techniques). The editors assert that, while it has assumed radically different genres and approaches over the centuries, the "didactic mode is very much alive" in twentieth- and twenty-first-century literature.[15] Since the advent of "High" Modernism, however, many American poets and critics use the term "didactic" to delegitimize a certain poem, poet, or poetic movement.[16] Nevertheless, there have been many politically committed projects in American poetry over the last century in which at least part of the objective can be described as instructive: for example, documentary poetic projects of the 1930s, and, in the 1960s and 1970s, poetry affiliated with the Black Arts Movement, anti-Vietnam war protests, and second-wave and black feminisms. Thus, in one sense, poetry's potential or intentions to teach readers certain lessons is a tie that binds American verse and poetry scholarship throughout the twentieth and into the twenty-first century. At the same time, there has been scant attention paid to didactic poetry as a specific mode,[17] since "[c]ritical theory ... has tended either to skirt the issues or to convert the didactic mode into related categories."[18]

I argue that much can be gained by directly considering *Citizen* in the didactic mode. I propose a reconception of the didactic mode with an emphasis on "ethics of knowledge," based on Tina Chen's and Ann-Marie Dunbar's pedagogical arguments.[19] Chen's literary pedagogy focuses on teaching American novels written by authors of color to predominantly white college students. Chen argues that it is essential to reconfigure, or even oppose

> many of the traditional goals we set in order to evaluate pedagogical "success," (goals that include "mastering" the material, cultivating points of identification in order to effect intellectual inquiry, and producing in our students the pleasures that motivate academic enterprise).[20]

Instead, teachers, critics, and readers should approach "multiethnic literature" with an ethical orientation "in the production of knowledge about those who are culturally different from themselves."[21] Chen emphasizes the need to avoid objectifying, and thereby dehumanizing, the subject(s) represented in a literary text. Her argument emphasizes that the pleasure of learning about "racial and cultural others" should not originate from the (white) reader's conceptual domination or degradation of nonwhite characters and people: "teaching contemporary literary texts . . . affords us opportunities to strategize with our students the corruption of desire, the re-education of pleasure, and the refusal of mastery."[22] Rather than an epistemology conceptualized as "mastery" or "intellectual accomplishment," Chen emphasizes an epistemology grounded in "sensitivity to the ethical responsibilities such study demands."[23] Compellingly, Chen turns to "the literature itself" for models of ethical orientation "towards the study of alterity."[24] While her study focuses on novels, I apply her concept of "ethics of knowledge" by examining the "cues" in the text of *Citizen*, an innovative, hybrid text of lyric, images, and nonfiction prose.

My argument also draws on the insights of Ann-Marie Dunbar, who builds on Chen's "ethics of knowledge" in her examination of ethics and pedagogy in the "multicultural American literature classroom."[25] Dunbar delineates the "twin pitfalls" of white students who read "multicultural texts"—"universalizing and othering."[26] Dunbar sympathetically describes "universalizing" as white students' well-intentioned attempts at identification with literary subjects; she notes that this approach is often encouraged by teachers. Here Dunbar follows Chen, who pinpoints the origins of "universalizing" as rooted in the "humanistic impulse."[27] While readers identifying with subjects of literary texts can arguably be a productive experience, Dunbar observes that white identification with nonwhite subjects can lead to a flattening of crucial historical and racial differences. On the other hand, the opposite pitfall is that white students may end up "reifying alterity" by essentially concluding, "'these people are totally different from me.'"[28] Dunbar extends Chen's pedagogical approach, emphasizing that instructors foreground "the construction of whiteness itself, which can help students develop a clearer sense of their own positionality in relation to texts."[29] Such a pedagogical approach begins "multicultural" literature study with a focus on whiteness in order to decenter the white subject as a universal norm.

I draw on the language from Chen's and Dunbar's pedagogical insights to articulate how *Citizen* inhabits the didactic mode. Rankine constructs a text which highlights and decenters whiteness so fundamentally that white readers are never able to rest complacently within a stance of either universalizing or othering the black subject. I read *Citizen* as a text that encompasses both poles of didactic poetry's preoccupations as articulated in antiquity: its "lessons" are at once metaphysical and grounded in considerations of "how to" (or, often, "how *not* to") engage in interracial interactions in everyday life. I argue, further, that *Citizen*'s concurrent deployment of the elegiac and didactic modes ultimately promotes an epistemological orientation that allows for white readers' development of an ethical sensibility in the BLM era.[30] If traditional understandings of the didactic poem and the elegy are presumed to have a predetermined *telos*—mastery of a particular learning objective in the didactic mode, and a healing consolation arrived at by way of the elegiac—*Citizen* involves a learning process that necessarily *resists* a narrative of grief with any neat closure. Neither offering (nonblack) readers complete knowledge of "black life," nor delivering the consolations of resolved mourning, *Citizen* blends the didactic and elegiac modes in order to situate both learning about and grieving of black lives as an intertwined, relentless, and open-ended process.

Citizen: Blending the Elegiac and Didactic Modes

Many popular reviews and interviews with Rankine emphasize the book's extensive chronicling of quotidian "microaggressions."[31] *Citizen* memorably opens with black subject(s) experiencing an overwhelming aggregation of slights and humiliations inflicted upon them by white friends, colleagues, neighbors, and passerby. While the earliest sections explore episodes from daily life, they are fundamentally interwoven with later sections of the text that focus on both historical and contemporaneous deaths of black men, women, and children. *Citizen* links everyday anti-black racism—across the range of white callousness, hypervigilance, and fear—to the very same conditions that enable the fatal neglect of thousands during Hurricane Katrina, the over-policing of black subjects, and the high-profile killings of black men and boys. By juxtaposing the everyday and the catastrophic, *Citizen* teaches (nonblack) readers about the threat of violence and death that casts an ever-present shadow on black inhabitants of the U.S. and within the global black diaspora.

Or, as declared in the title of the op-ed that Rankine penned for *The New York Times*, "The Condition of Black Life Is One of Mourning." Rankine's essay appeared in June 2015 on the occasion of the white-supremacist Dylann Roof's massacre of nine parishioners in the historical Emanuel African Methodist Episcopal Church in Charleston, South Carolina. Directly aligning her values with the BLM movement, Rankine articulates how black lives are continually constrained by the threat of white-supremacist violence. Rankine's op-ed clarifies the didactic lessons of *Citizen* as necessarily intertwined with the elegiac, namely that the threat of state-sanctioned, violent death shapes daily life for black individuals.

In terms of the instruction of white readers of *Citizen* in particular, it is necessary to consider Rankine's use of the second person, which is a key pedagogical strategy for decentering whiteness. Many reviewers and literary critics have discussed the startling and innovative choice of the second person for the speaking subject, which has been read as deeply involving, even implicating the reader.[32] The "you" also has been read as demonstrating our intrinsic interrelatedness—the second person depends on the first person, and vice versa.[33] Moreover, in interviews Rankine states that the "you" draws on the idea that, historically, blacks are in the position of the "second person," never the "first person";[34] therefore, the "you" can be read to emphasize that there is a second America that is often invisible and subordinate to dominant, white America.[35]

In addition to previous critical considerations of the second person, I suggest that the "you" can also be read as positioning the reader as learner. With its broad scope, the second person carries with it an awareness that there are multiple audiences who will receive these texts differently. At the same time, I suggest that *Citizen* comments upon how "you" in conversational language can mean "anyone in general," but ironically undercuts that tendency: In most episodes, the "you" must be a black subject, a discovery that allows white readers to be alert to the presumed whiteness of the subject in so many literary and cultural texts. Therefore, white reader-learners are dislodged from the comfort zone of the universal white subject.

The content of passages examining black-white encounters also serves to decenter whiteness. A passage early in Section I describes racial tensions that disrupt the "fragile, tenuous" dynamics of black-white friendship: "sometimes your historical selves, her white self and your black self, or your white self and her black self, arrive with the full force of your American positioning."[36] When the text instructs white readers to be conscious of their white positionality by highlighting the "battle between the 'historical self' and the 'self self,'"[37] Rankine identifies the tension between the reality of subjectivity constructed through sociohistorical contexts and the ideology of universal humanism. As Richard Dyer notes, whites have long been able to avoid considerations of whiteness as a historical construction.[38] Standing in stark contrast is the black subject, ever conscious of the "historical self," which *Citizen* emphasizes as one marked by profound grief and loss: The loss of history prior to the Euro-American slave trade; the loss of full rights of citizenship; the violent loss of so many black lives.

Moreover, this passage comments on the precarious "attachment" between black and white friends as always endangered, even in the most mundane of daily encounters. The text starts with an interracial friendship marked by the simpatico energy of "compatible personalities," but then shifts to a moment of racial tension that "wipe[s] the affable smiles right from your mouths."[39] Both figures risk the loss of a friendship. However, within the predominantly white, middle-class networks of professional connections and intimacies invoked in the opening section of *Citizen*, the "black self" is simply more vulnerable. *Citizen* thus begins with moves that resist white readers' attempts to universalize or identify easily with black experience. As a result, the opening of *Citizen* fulfills the pedagogical practices that Dunbar advances: By decentering whiteness, readers are compelled to consider their "own positionality in relation to texts."

Citizen's flat tone works in tandem with the second-person to resist the individualizing of emotional responses to anti-black racism. For example, when the recognition of racial difference in an interracial friendship "wipe[s] the affable smiles right from your mouths," the text observes a change of facial expressions, rather than the subjects emoting directly and dramatically. The flatness is also constructed on commentary that swings between micro and macro views of a given conflict. The text alternately focuses on a specific moment of conflict (the disappearing smiles) and situates that moment in broader historical and social contexts (the arrival of "the full force of your American positioning"). In his consideration of *Citizen*, Charles Legere makes a case for the flatness of tone within affective terms, encompassing both despondency and anger, thus reflecting the political powerlessness of the subject in the twenty-first century.[40] Conversely, Heather Love's microsociological approach to reading *Citizen* situates the text within the traditions of documentary poetry and the "online genre of microaggressions."[41] While Love recognizes many possible readings of the second person subject, she ultimately argues that the text's flatness primarily shows "Rankine's alignment of her lyric voice with technologies of surveillance and with the Hawk-Eye camera. . . . By identifying herself with the camera rather than with a traditional expressive lyric 'I,' Rankine turns a cold eye on racialized trauma, including her own."[42]

While placing Rankine's text within the tradition of documentary poetics is certainly valid, particularly episodes involving interracial *encounters*, Love's reading elides much of Rankine's extensive exploration of interiority, which is the realm of conventional lyric: feelings, reflections, descriptions of bodily sensations. Like Legere, I read the tonal flatness of the text as speaking to a range of negative feelings. I add to this insight the consideration that numerous less explored passages of *Citizen*, both prose-like and lyrical, encompass subjective interiority and explore invisible effects and embodied affects that are unable to be captured on any kind of surveillance camera. It is imperative to consider the many instances of subjective reflection that recur throughout *Citizen*, wherein the flatness of tone is sustained through dispassionate descriptions, but the focus shifts towards the subject's feelings and embodied responses.

Rather than the lyric subject as camera, *Citizen* advances a subject that is more accurately described as engaged in the elegiac process of melancholic mourning. The black subject, enervated by constant vigilance and the ongoing accumulation of insults, is recurrently described through many sections of *Citizen* as afflicted: vulnerable, exhausted, aching, sighing, nauseous. The experiences of embodied affect are recognizable to any reader, but the occasions of those bodily responses are particular to black experience: The particularities of the daily assault of racist microaggressions, the phenomenon of John Henryism,[43] and embodied grief in response to the black community's experiences of police brutality and hate crimes. For white readers, recalibrating the perception of black emotion is crucial, as mainstream American culture relentlessly constrains and proscribes the possibilities for blacks' expression of feelings. Thus, the text's model of twenty-first-century melancholic mourning instructs readers in pervasive grief as the "Condition of Black Life."

Many less-examined prose and lyrical sections of *Citizen* illustrate melancholic mourning through descriptions of the black subject's embodied experiences. For example, nausea is invoked early in Section I: "An unsettled feeling keeps the body front and center. The wrong words enter your day like a bad egg in your mouth and puke runs down your mouth, a dampness drawing your stomach in toward your rib cage."[44] This passage demonstrates the subject's interiority as constituted through exteriority. "The wrong words enter your day like a bad egg in your mouth" can refer to the experience of any number of the book's episodes of microaggressions where whites compel the black subject to absorb contempt or insensitivity. The text's unpleasant descriptions—"puke" that "runs down your mouth," "a dampness" on the torso, a revolting stench that inspires self-loathing from "Your own disgust at what you smell"[45]—demonstrates how the effects of internalized racism take a toll on the body through nausea, disgust, and enervation. *Citizen* legitimizes black anguish through a recurring focus on involuntary bodily reactions, with numerous descriptions of sighs, vomit, aches, and fatigue.

The text repeatedly returns to the individual's embodied and interior effects of racism, ultimately enacting the anguish that follows the "battle between the 'historical self' and the 'self self.'"[46] The experiences of the "'self self'" are undeniable in their constancy, immediacy, and bodily discomfort: "To your mind, feelings are what create a person, something unwilling, something wild vandalizing whatever the skull holds. Those sensations form a someone. The headaches begin then."[47] But then, the text asks, how to square these pressing and real experiences of feelings and bodily aches with the ways the "world" shapes "you"? Rankine turns to metaphors of burial and storage: "The world is wrong. You can't put the past behind you. It's buried in you; it's turned your flesh into its own cupboard."[48] The textual description of internalized, embodied grief both invites empathetic understanding from white readers and an emphasis on racial difference. Rankine's treatment of black interiority is crucial, for it sustains the humanity of the subject: All readers can relate to "wild" feelings, bodily aches, forces beyond our control. Yet on another level, because of this passage's placement in *Citizen* after the accumulation of so many experiences of anti-black racism, the (attentive) white reader cannot slip into an understanding of a black subject's grief as an articulation of any "universal" human condition. By providing cues that curtail white readers' ability to universalize or other black subjects, *Citizen* offers instructions in how to develop an "ethics of knowledge" about racial difference.

"In Memory of Trayvon Martin": Lynching Elegy

Section VI marks a shift in content in *Citizen*, for it participates in the black elegiac tradition of the lynching poem, most prominently through the prose-poem "In Memory of Trayvon Martin." The verbal text is followed by the photograph of the 1930 lynching of J. Thomas Shipp and Abraham Smith in Marion, Indiana, with the hanged black bodies under erasure. The text starts with the stereotype of black men and boys as criminal, "My brothers are notorious," only to counter this stereotype immediately: "They have not been to prison." The text then situates this "notorious" behavior within the conditions of daily life within white dominance: "They have been imprisoned. The prison is not a place you enter. It is no place."[49] In other words, the white surveillance gaze always already criminalizes and constrains black men and boys, making prison "no place" because it can be any place. The text continues to resist the stereotype of criminal black masculinity: "My brothers are notorious. They do regular things, like wait. On my birthday they say my name. They will never forget that we are named."[50] In contrast to lawless behavior, the text emphasizes activities—waiting, celebrating, remembering—that suggest caution and emphasize familial and community ties. The initial lines suggest what Ramazani and Marcellus Blount conceptualize as the black elegiac tradition of responding to collective concerns.[51] The shared experience of "my brothers" is tense: They are continually policed, waiting, on edge. Also, the text's insistence of the importance of "my birthday" and names— "They will never forget that we are named"—counters the mainstream culture's erasure of black victims of the criminal justice system through recognition of each individual as a member of a community.[52]

Further, "In Memory of Trayvon Martin" identifies Martin's 2012 death as a lynching by situating it within the historical and social contexts of black men and boys constrained by state control and threat of violence: "the years of passage, plantation, migration, of Jim Crow segregation, of poverty, inner cities, profiling, of one in three, two jobs, boy, hey boy, each a felony, accumulate into the hours inside our lives where we are all caught hanging, the rope inside us, the tree inside us, its roots our limbs, a throat sliced through."[53] This inventory of social injustices insists on the elegiac as an element of everyday life in black America, past and present. The image of the lynching tree describes the collective black experience of the internalized threat of racial violence: Both the "tree" where "we are all caught hanging" and the weaponized "rope" exist "inside us." At once elegiac and didactic, this passage is invested in teaching (nonblack) readers that, contrary to the mythos of American individualism, black men and boys "have been imprisoned" by the legacy of slavery and segregation that continues today through social inequalities that have been actively perpetuated by police practices, the prison industrial complex, and endemic poverty.

At the same time, it is significant that the verbal text of this lynching elegy puts the black corpse under erasure, just as the accompanying photo does. The grief articulated in a lynching poem is vulnerable to the reification of alterity by white readers; the murdered black subject is in danger of becoming ossified into the familiar figure of a victim—reduced to a mutilated body, lacking agency, an object of spectacle. Instead, "In Memory of Trayvon Martin" describes the black collective as *both* experiencing a heightened vulnerability while *also* generating startling beauty out of melancholic mourning. After the reference to the "tree inside us," the poem abruptly shifts from violence to regenerative beauty: "a throat sliced through and when we open our mouths to speak, blossoms, o blossoms, no place coming out, brother, dear brother, that kind of blue."[54] Rankine uses the classical lyric trope of apostrophe in the repetition, "o blossoms," which self-consciously highlights the artifice of the image of budding flowers emerging from a corpse. Rather than blood and gore, Rankine disrupts reader's expectations with "blossoms," an image of beauty and new life that stands in for black creativity. The wording "kind of blue" references the 1959 Miles Davis' jazz album masterpiece by the same name, thus pointing towards excellence in black artistry as borne from the melancholic mourning that, as Ramazani argues, permeates the blues, blues poetry, and jazz.[55] Tellingly, the music that emerges "when we open our mouths to speak" is nonverbal, echoing James Baldwin's insight that the black American has only been able to "tell his story" through "his music."[56] Thus, the text characterizes the wounded black subject as the creator of miraculous beauty, demonstrating an agency and resilience that resists white readers' reduction of blacks to victimhood.

Significantly, "In Memory of Trayvon Martin" alternates between the black collective and the black speaking subject's individual loss of a beloved intimate. I suggest that this alternation further resists the white reader's potential reification of the black subject as "other." In the aftermath of a high-profile, violent death of black person, the white response of pity is both well-rehearsed and fleeting, as Rankine discusses in the aforementioned op-ed, "The Condition of Black Life Is One of Mourning." "In Memory of Trayvon Martin" starts and returns to the bereaved subject in order to individualize, and therefore humanize, black individuals' shock, loss, and grief. After the imagery of the "tree inside" and "blossoms," the prose-poem continues in the first person by describing a disrupted phone call with her brother, an implicit reference to the Trayvon Martin case: Martin was on his cell phone with a girlfriend when neighborhood watch volunteer George Zimmerman spotted and confronted him. The speaker worries about losing communication with her brother: "I say good-bye before anyone can hang up. Don't hang up. My brother hangs up though he is there. I keep talking. The talk keeps him there." The use of the first-person speaker is all the more noticeable in a book notable for deployment of the second person. Fragments of their (one-sided?) telephone conversation turn to the weather and surroundings: "The sky is blue, kind of blue. The day is hot. Is it cold? Are you cold? It does get cool. Is it cool? Are you cool?"[57] The speaker articulates dread, worry, desperation, bewilderment. She knows she needs to say good bye, but that early farewell itself occurs all too soon, indicative of a life cut off prematurely, suddenly, violently.

The prose-poem also includes pointed wordplay. For example, the metaphorical "hanging up" references the historical phenomenon of lynching by hanging. The question "Are you cool?" shifts away from anodyne comments about the weather to the speaker seeking reassurance that the brother is fine. The repetition of the term "cool" alludes to another landmark album by Miles Davis, *The Birth of Cool*, released in 1957. The repetition underscores the imperative for black men and boys to remain "cool" and restrained as a survival tactic within white supremacy. In the context of this prose-poem, the sought-after reassurance of the brother as "cool" (arguably the ultimate American slang expression that originated from African American Vernacular English) is rendered with dramatic irony, even absurdity, in the context of Trayvon's imminent death. Readers know that this phone conversation is to be a final one; communication with Trayvon would be irrevocably ended. "You" are not cool.

Rankine's text shows no move towards closure or consolation in what Ramazani articulates as "violent and irresolvable grief."[58] Instead, it ends with a desperate plea: "don't hang up. Wait with me. Wait with me though the waiting might be the call of good-byes."[59] In this decrescendo, the tone of "In Memory of Trayvon Martin" shifts from outraged to plaintive, a strategy that allows for white readers to shift from an appreciation of racial difference to an invitation to empathize with the figure of the individual survivor, grieving the loss of a loved one. Consequently, "In Memory" resists the "twin pitfalls" of both universalism and the objectification of racial difference. Melancholic mourning is both situated within the historical and social particularities of black life and evinces individual grief as resistance towards loss.

The "Self Self" vs. the "Historical Self"

After Section VI's exploration of social injustices and highly publicized killings, Section VII returns to the internal battle waged between the "self self" and the "historical self," culminating in a lyric exploration of a black individual's existential crisis as occasioned by destabilizing loss. The poem begins the subject as "immanent you" who experiences far more certainty of their bodily existence than their selfhood: "you" have come of age "understanding" that you "are not anyone, worthless."[60] This untenable social positionality emerges from the black body as rendered paradoxically invisible and hypervisible by the white gaze. The text's repetition of the phrase, "Hey you—," indicates how the white world interpellates the black subject through constant surveillance while denying personhood: "You nothing. / You nobody."[61] As a result, since "[t]he outside comes in—" the black subject has the continual experience of "[s]lipping down burying the you buried within."[62] This phrase echoes earlier burial metaphors in order to underscore the black subject as compelled to internalize the "world['s]" "furious erasure."[63] While the black subject is condemned to be continually "fighting off / the weight of nonexistence," what is stable is "your certain ache"—bodily pain that "coexists" with "your own weight."[64]

Here we have the opposite of the Cartesian *cogito*: the black subject, continually denied full citizenship in the commonweal, doubts the existence of a "self self." Whereas Descartes's famous thought experiment distrusted bodily sensations for their ephemerality, *Citizen* underscores the persistence and permanence of the embodied experience of black grief: "You are not sick, you are injured— / you ache for the rest of life."[65] The result is an existential crisis occasioned by the grief of the loss of self: "The worst injury is feeling you don't belong so much / to you—."[66] The black subject of *Citizen* is wounded, carrying grief in his/her "flesh," while the sense of stable selfhood remains elusive. Rankine's text teaches readers how racism leads to grief and loss that is integral—or perhaps, threatening—to black subject formation. Following Section VI's exploration of the collective contexts of social injustices, Section VII's focuses on how individual grief manifests in embodied suffering and existential crisis. Thus, Rankine demonstrates that the embodied experiences of ongoing, unresolved mourning is fundamental to black life.

Conclusion

When critics frame texts as "didactic" vs. "open," they tend to conflate all teaching strategies with lecture. Alternatively, via *Citizen*, I have adumbrated an updated model of didactic poetry that is attentive to Rankine's elegiac commitments while also informed by contemporary student-centered pedagogy scholarship. It is revealing that the very strategy—the use of "you"—that Rankine describes as part of "keep[ing] the text open" directly emerges from her own teaching experiences, as she describes in an interview with Meara Sharma:

> I didn't want to race the individuals. Obviously [the reader] will assume— "She's black, he must be white," etc.—but I wanted those assumptions to be made. Because amid this post-racial thing, sometimes I'll have a student who says, "I don't really think about race. I don't *see* race." And then I'll ask, "Well, how do you read this?" And they say, "Oh, that's a black person, that's a white person." So clearly, you're race-ing these people in order to understand this dynamic. I wanted that positioning to happen for readers.[67]

In the terms of pedagogical theory, Rankine's classroom exchange is easily recognized as an example of student-centered, active learning. I suggest that *Citizen* offers a model of didactic poetry that is open enough to facilitate the student construction of knowledge through the process of discovery and self-reflection.

In other words, *Citizen* illustrates that the didactic can be a much more flexible mode than critics usually presume; indeed, the didactic can conceptualize knowledge in terms other than "mastery." In the end, doesn't learning happen most effectively when learners are both *guided* and *invited* to discover how to construct knowledge—and ideally, an "ethics of knowledge"—for themselves? *Citizen* provides a unique opportunity for literary critics to consider how the didactic mode can provide a model of how to reject mastery, particularly when the text focuses on racial difference. In Rankine's book, the didactic blends with the elegiac in order to offer twenty-first-century lessons in how blacks live, how blacks die, how to mourn, and how to resist. For white readers in particular, learning involves the ongoing lessons of how to reject "internalized dominance" and reshape the white imagination.

Notes

1. *Citizen* has already garnered an impressive range of critical interpretations, including Angela Hume's compelling placement of Rankine's text as engaged in a project of "antiracist ecopoetics" ("Toward an Antiracist Ecopoetics: Waste and Wasting in the Poetry of Claudia Rankine," *Contemporary Literature* 57, no. 1 [2016]: 79–110); Bella Adams's focus on critical race theory and legal scholarship ("Black Lives/White Backgrounds: Claudia Rankine's *Citizen: An American Lyric* and Critical Race Theory," *Comparative American Studies* 15, nos. 1–2 [2017]: 54–71); Leigh Gilmore's exploration of artistic revisitations of Hurricane Katrina ("Refugee | Citizen: Mediating Testimony through Image and Word in the Wake of Hurricane Katrina," *a/b: Auto/Biography Studies* 32, no. 3 [2017]: 673–81, doi:10.1080/08989575.2017.1339447)]; Linda Voris's critical consideration of role of memory in experimental writing ("'The Curious Props': Placing Memory in Recent Experimental Writing: Claudia Rankine's *Citizen: An American Lyric* (2014) and Bhanu Kapil's, *Incubation: A Space for Monsters* [2006]," *West Branch* 82 [2016]: 72–78).

2. And controversy has been good for sales. *New Republic* reported on a spike in the book's sales after the photo of the woman reading *Citizen* went viral. See Alex Shephard, "Minutes," *The New Republic*, 2015, https://newrepublic.com/minutes/124386/poetry-one-winner-trump-presidency.

3. Chris Cabin, "'She's Gotta Have It' Review," *Collider*, November 23, 2017, collider.com/shes-gotta-have-it-review-netflix/.

4. Two examples of web-based sources geared towards teaching *Citizen* include discussion questions posted on the Graywolf Press website (www.graywolfpress.org/books/citizen) and an "Online Teaching Symposium" featured on the *Southern Humanities Review* website: www.southernhumanitiesreview.com/teaching-citizen-an-shr-online-symposium.html.

5. Claudia Rankine, *Citizen: An American Lyric* (Minneapolis: Graywolf Press, 2014), 159.

6. Rankine credits Robin DiAngelo for the phrase "internalized dominance." See Claudia Rankine, "In Our Way: Racism in Creative Writing," *Association of Writers & Writing Programs*, October/November 2016, www.awpwriter.org/magazine_media/writers_chronicle_view/4120/in_our_way_racism_in_creative_writing.

7. Jonathan Holden, *The Fate of American Poetry* (Athens: University of Georgia Press, 1991), 80.

8. See Heather Love, "Small Change: Realism, Immanence, and the Politics of the Micro," *Modern Language Quarterly* 77, no. 3 (2016), https://doi.org/10.1215/00267929-3570678. Love mentions the possible "pedagogical" approach of *Citizen* in a footnote, observing that the text exhibits "[t]ones and stances that might be read as pedagogical—interrogative, corrective, patient, exasperated" (437 n14). Love's tentative concession that the text's stance "might be read as pedagogical" illustrates a scholarly desire to avoid the taboo of the didactic. Also see Parul Sehgal, "Sister Outsider: Claudia Rankine's Poetic Reflections on 'Invisible Racism,'" *Book Forum*, 21, no. 4 (December-January 2015–2016), www.bookforum.com/inprint/021_04/13924.

9. For example, my argument differs from the interpretation made by Marjorie Perloff who, in her blurb on the back cover of *Citizen*, states, "Rankine is never didactic: she merely *presents* . . . allowing you to draw your own conclusions," *Citizen: An American Lyric* (Minneapolis: Graywolf Press, 2014).

10. My emphasis on *Citizen* as operating within the tradition of black elegy thus departs from Michael LeMahieu's thought-provoking reading of Rankine's book within the lineage of the Civil War elegy as refracted through the significant influence of Robert Lowell's 1964 "For the Union Dead." See Le Mahieu, "Robert Lowell, Perpetual War, and the Legacy of Civil War Elegy," *College Literature*, 43, no. 1 (Winter 2016): 91–120.

11. Jahan Ramazani, *Poetry of Mourning—The Modern Elegy from Hardy to Heany* (Chicago: University of Chicago Press, 1994), 28–29.

12. Ibid., 14.
13. Ibid., 135.
14. Ibid., 140.
15. T. V. F. Brogan and S. J. Kahn, "Didactic Poetry," *The Princeton Encyclopedia of Poetry and Poetics*, 4th ed., eds. Roland Green, Stephen Cushman, and Clare Cavanagh (Princeton, NJ: Princeton University Press, 2012), http://proxy.library.cmu.edu/login?url=https://search.credoreference.com/content/entry/prpoetry/didactic_poetry/0?institutionId=1200.
16. It would be inaccurate to say that modernist poets were the first to critique "didactic" poetry in English; many prominent nineteenth-century poets also derided the didactic in poetry.
17. Two monographs that treated the "didactic" mode directly in the twentieth-century Anglo-American scene were authored by Willard Spiegelman, *The Didactic Muse: Scenes of Instruction in Contemporary American Poetry* (Princeton, NJ: Princeton University Press, 1989) and Joanna Durczak, *Treading Softly, Speaking Low: Contemporary American Poetry in the Didactic Mode* (Lublin: Wydawnictwo UMCS, 1994). Since neither book examines any black poetry, nor are either much interested in direct lessons that convey a particular political message, deeper consideration of their arguments is not relevant for the present purposes.
18. Brogan and Kahn, "Didactic Poetry."
19. Tina Chen, "Towards an Ethics of Knowledge," *MELUS* 30, no. 2 (2005): 158, www.jstor.org/stable/30029853.
20. Ibid., 158–59.
21. Ibid., 158.
22. Ibid., 159.
23. Ibid., 163.
24. Ibid., 158.
25. Ann-Marie Dunbar, "Between Universalizing and Othering: Developing an Ethics of Reading in the Multicultural American Literature Classroom," *College English* 42, no. 1 (2013): 26.
26. Dunbar, "Between Universalizing and Othering," 29, 26.
27. Chen, "Towards an Ethics of Knowledge," 158.
28. Dunbar, "Between Universalizing and Othering," 29.
29. Ibid., 30.
30. One limitation of my reading is that it focuses on *Citizen* as a text as "taught" to white American readers, when of course the text's actual readership is racially, culturally, and nationally diverse. Part of this limitation is my own identity position; as a white American reader, I enter the text through the limited knowledge of my own white experience, and I do not want to presume by making assumptions about the experiences of nonwhite readers. My discussion also emphasizes the text's white readership because the framework draws upon the scholarship of Chen and Ann-Marie Dunbar, whose pedagogy is based on teaching literature written by authors of color to predominantly white student-readers. Despite the emphasis on white readership in what follows, its function as a "wake-up call" for white readers is not the only way in which *Citizen* functions within the didactic mode. The text may resonate as instructional in entirely differently ways for black readers, as well as for readers from racial backgrounds beyond the black-white binary.
31. See, for example, Dan Chiasson, "Color Codes." *The New Yorker*, October 27, 2014; and Meara Sharma, "Claudia Rankine on Blackness as the Second Person," *Guernica*, November 17, 2014. Erica Hunt's thoughtful review does observe the grief at the heart of *Citizen*, although considerably more space is devoted to the topic of microaggressions. Erica Hunt, "All About You," *Los Angeles Times Book Review*, December 8, 2014, https://www.newyorker.com/magazine/2014/10/27/color-codes.
32. See Hunt, "All About You," and Ron Charles, "Claudia Rankine's Editor on the Genius of 'Citizen,'" *The Washington Post*, January 21, 2015. https://www.washingtonpost.com/news/arts-and-entertainment/wp/2015/01/21/claudia-rankines-editor-on-the-genius-of-citizen/.

33. Sandra Lim, "Interview with Claudia Rankine, 2014 National Book Award Finalist, Poetry," *National Book Foundation*, 2014, www.nationalbook.org/nba2014_p_rank ine_interv.html#.WGqf9CMrJ-U.
34. Meara Sharma, "Claudia Rankine on Blackness as the Second Person," *Guernica*, November 17 2014, www.guernicamag.com/blackness-as-the-second-person/.
35. Alexandra Schwartz, "On Being Seen: An Interview with Claudia Rankine From Ferguson," *The New Yorker*, August 22, 2014, www.newyorker.com/books/page-turner/seen-interview-claudia-rankine-ferguson.
36. Rankine, *Citizen*, 14.
37. Ibid., 14.
38. See Richard Dyer, *White: Essays on Race and Culture* (London: Routledge, 1997).
39. Rankine, *Citizen*, 14.
40. Charles Legere, "21st-Century American Poetry in the Anglosphere," *Anglistik: International Journal of English Studies* 26, no. 2 (2015): 105–12, https://angl.winter-verlag.de/article/angl/2015/2/9.
41. Love, "Small Change," 419.
42. Ibid., 441.
43. Rankine, *Citizen*, 11.
44. Ibid., 8.
45. Ibid.
46. Ibid., 14.
47. Ibid., 61.
48. Ibid., 63.
49. Ibid., 89.
50. Ibid.
51. Ramazani, *Poetry of Mourning*, 174 and Marcellus Blount, "Paul Laurence Dunbar and the African American Elegy," *African American Review* 41, no. 2 (2007): 239–46.
52. The importance of remembering names underscores Rankine's commitment to memorializing those killed in government-sanctioned violence, as is evident in the continually updated "In Memory" page, discussed on page 15 of the Introduction to this volume.
53. Rankine, *Citizen*, 89–90.
54. Ibid., 90.
55. Ramazani, *Poetry of Mourning*, 138.
56. James Baldwin, "Many Thousands Gone," *Notes of a Native Son* (Boston: Beacon Press, 1955), 24. The complete quote, which I have truncated, is directly relevant to the project of *Citizen*, for it celebrates the miracle of black American music while also critiquing the willed ignorance of white America: "It is only in his music, which Americans are able to admire because a protective sentimentality limits their understanding of it, that the Negro in America has been able to tell his story."
57. Rankine, *Citizen*, 90.
58. Ramazani, *Poetry of Mourning*, 135.
59. Rankine, *Citizen*, 90.
60. Ibid., 139.
61. Ibid., 142.
62. Ibid., 141.
63. Ibid., 142.
64. Ibid., 139.
65. Ibid., 143.
66. Ibid., 146.
67. Sharma, "Claudia Rankine on Blackness as the Second Person."

3

LUCILLE CLIFTON'S AND CLAUDIA RANKINE'S ELEGIAC POETICS OF NATURE

Anne M. Rashid

Continuing the work of the Civil Rights and Black Power movements, Black Lives Matter activists have documented and resisted centuries of anti-black violence and degradation. As part of that resistance, many African American poets have turned the trauma of witnessing this violence into elegies that implicate structures of power that are reinforced by white supremacy, police violence, and white privilege. Two of these poets, Lucille Clifton and Claudia Rankine, set many of their elegiac poems in nature, bringing race, trauma, and injustice into a powerful and troubling juxtaposition with the natural world. In this chapter, I will focus on elegiac poetics in Clifton's *Blessing the Boats: New and Selected Poems 1988–2000* and Rankine's *Citizen: An American Lyric* (2014). In distinct ways, Clifton and Rankine reimagine people, histories, and places that have been erased, forgotten, and silenced. In the process, they cross the divide between the human and nonhuman, establishing a collective responsibility for their readers to reckon with past and present racism, while both drawing on and subverting the traditional conventions of the pastoral and the elegy.

Clifton's and Rankine's elegiac poems belong to the genre of literature of environmental justice, integrating nature imagery in order to draw readers' attention to continued racial injustices, both on the micro and macro levels. As Evie Shockley observes,

> The insistence upon protecting poetry's aesthetic purity from the (racialized) taint of political issues and socio-historical contexts can be seen as a futile—if ideologically powerful—attempt to construct a binary opposition between inextricably related categories. The dichotomization of 'political poetry' and 'nature poetry' should be understood as a particular instantiation of the larger divide that has been articulated between politics and aesthetics.[1]

Angela Hume goes on to posit that "[t]his dichotomy poses challenges to African American poets in particular, whose experiences of nature have always been suffused with the political, given America's history of racism. . . . what I would call a poetics of environmental justice."[2] Viewed through the lens of environmental justice poetry, several of the poems in Rankine's *Citizen: An American Lyric* (2014) and Clifton's *Blessing the Boats: New and Selected Poems 1988–2000* resist this dichotomy between the natural and sociopolitical realms as they shed light on twentieth- and twenty-first-century atrocities committed against black people.

These poets also situate their work within a long tradition of black elegy that can be traced back to the origins of African American letters, as noted in this volume's Introduction. According to Marcellus Blount, "In African American elegies, race often stands for community, and that sense of community is often structured through a figurative glimpse of the past."[3] Blount notes that "the elegy works as part of slavery's masculinist figurative legacy" and that it has tended to be a way for male poets to "enact a rite of passage between men."[4] He alludes to "When Lilacs Last in the Dooryard Bloom'd," Whitman's elegy to Abraham Lincoln, and Dunbar's elegy to Frederick Douglass, and notes the inherent aspirations both Whitman and Dunbar shared in becoming great poets by writing these tributes to fallen masculine heroes, and thus, writing themselves into the tradition in the process.[5] Clifton and Rankine, as black women poets, seem to be doing something quite distinct in their elegies. They are certainly concentrated on community, but they resist the practice of writing themselves into an Anglo-American tradition, opting instead to subvert pastoral and elegiac conventions by using them in new ways. In writing tributes to the dead who have been wrongfully killed, they are not looking for acclaim. By centering their writing on acknowledging the wrongs done to their communities, they remedy the future by inciting their readers to do something to prevent future crimes.

In this chapter, I will analyze Clifton's more public occasional poems in *Blessing the Boats*, focusing on the historical violence done to African Americans. Rankine, in *Citizen*, also incorporates public occasional poems, responding to specific acts and sites of violence in the recent past. However, many of this collection's poems are compiled from multiple experiences of micro- and macroaggressions she gleaned from personal conversations and interviews with African American colleagues and friends. Like Clifton, she takes on personas to force the reader to grapple with racism and violence in different settings. Moreover, Rankine and Clifton rewrite the elegy by integrating nature imagery into their poetry about violence and trauma from past and recent hate crimes. Typically, the elegy is employed to comfort the reader, provide solace, and celebrate the deceased. Their use of elegy, however, like their use of the anti-pastoral, unsettles readers in order to provoke them into action. According to Jahan Ramazani,

> Over the course of the twentieth century, poets have drawn upon and transformed an age-old language of mourning, alloying the profound insights

of the past with the exigencies of the present. Out of this fusion they have forged a resonant yet credible vocabulary for grief in our time—elegies that erupt with all the violence and irresolution, all the guilt and ambivalence of modern mourning.[6]

Both Clifton and Rankine incorporate "a resonant yet credible vocabulary for grief in our time," bearing witness to the deep injustices that continue to affect black communities, often through nature imagery, which figures as complicit in the violence done toward black bodies. Taken together, Clifton's and Rankine's elegies enjoin readers to confront anti-black hate crimes, to contend with the guilt and culpability that white people may feel, and, ultimately, to take action against persistent racist violence.

As she explores the volatile territory of the past and present in *Blessing the Boats*, Clifton creates a space for rupture and unsettling nature imagery. Clifton doesn't use nature as the pastoral tradition's locus of escape; instead, she shows how even the natural setting unrelentingly evokes the violence of the past. Her poems about racial violence are purposefully antipastoral; nature offers no relief since many crimes were committed in "pastoral" settings. Camille Dungy notes that in poems by people of African descent, natural landscapes are often "tainted by a legacy of racially motivated brutality," but at the same time offer "the promise of a future unfettered by fear [which] is realized through the natural forces of change."[7] She further explains, "Given the active history of betrayal and danger in the outdoors, it is no wonder that many African Americans link their fears directly to the land that witnessed or abetted centuries of subjugation."[8] These natural sites—trees, rivers, and pastures—hold memories of lynching, drowning, and torture, and Clifton asserts a collective responsibility to remember past injustices and resists making nature beautiful in elegiac tributes to victims of hate crimes. In an interview with Hilary Holladay, Clifton says she models herself after the old preacher who said, "I come to comfort the afflicted and to afflict the comfortable."[9] She memorializes those who have been the victims of racist hate crimes throughout history and expresses no tolerance for further violence.

Clifton's elegy for James Byrd, "jasper texas 1998," specifically drew resistance from some readers because, choosing to speak from Byrd's decapitated head left on a back road after he was dragged to death by a group of white men in a pickup truck, the poem made them uncomfortable. The rural setting connects this murder to lynchings of earlier history. In the pastoral tradition, these places would typically be settings for healing. Instead, they are sites for violence. According to Mary Jane Lupton, "The poem 'jasper texas 1998' offers no solace through art; there is no softening, no epiphany, no drawing back. The poet urges neither pacifism nor racial harmony in her elegy."[10] There is instead a feeling of exasperation with humanity that would commit such a heinous act. In an interview with Michael Glaser, Clifton reflects upon her writing of this poem and the accusation that she "played the race card" in it. She explained that she was pleased that it drew this sort of reaction, since too often people equate her acceptance "in the world" with acceptance of the status quo: "It's like, because I can speak about race, and because I have friends who are not African American, it must be that I think everything is OK, that I don't feel racism because, after all, I'm OK. But I've got a cousin who's not OK, you know what I mean? And I have friends who are of my race who are not OK, and I am not always OK."[11] Clifton expresses a deep, ethical commitment to represent the racism she and many in the black community have experienced in her writing. In this same interview, she goes on to explain,

> My poetry is not about "how does it look." It's about "how does it feel." You know?. . . . It's not about the surface of things. I hope it's more than that. I hope it is about humans who are deeper than that. And it's certainly not about forgetting—it's about remembering, because memory is what we have.[12]

Clifton grounds her poems in how it *feels*—to be a victim of a racist hate crime, to be an onlooker, to be one who is left behind to remember. Not feeling "OK" and forcing her readers to remember the violence of the past and the present is a hallmark of Clifton's writing. In persona poems, she tells the stories of those who are not here to tell them due to violence, imagining what they might say now if they had voices. She implicates everyone, including her readers, by using nature to connect black and white experience in such a way that insists it is a privilege to forget—and, furthermore, to perpetuate silence about violent deaths perpetuates the trauma.

In the second stanza of "jasper texas 1998," the speaker wonders why he should consider a white man a brother and then goes on to ask who exactly is the human: "the thing that is dragged or the dragger?"[13] The questions call attention to the pressing hopelessness that Byrd himself probably felt, but also speaks to what other African Americans feel in light of hate crimes like these that continue to plague American society. His death serves as a jarring reminder that racism and violence are still very much linked, and so are the plights of living and dead African Americans. The sun offers no relief: It "is a blister overhead."[14] This metaphor connotes violence and pressure, and the speaker thinks, "if i were alive i could not bear it."[15] In the end, "hope bleeds slowly from [his] mouth / into the dirt that covers us all."[16] This image demands that we all have a collective responsibility to right past wrongs and make the present violence end—since we occupy this space, here and now, and we will all be united under the dirt when we die. Although, she ends the poem with the speaker lamenting, "i am done with this dust. i am done,"[17] which suggests that he is fed up with living in this racist world—a world where such a crime could happen. Lupton notes that when this poem was first published and received a Pushcart Prize,

> some readers expressed hostility toward the prize-winning poem because Clifton seemed to be blaming whites for Byrd's treatment while withholding

her usual forgiveness. She said, "I don't want to be accessible to everyone. I'm really very private. As long as I tell the truth I don't see why my mission is to assure people that they are comfortable. I always wanted to be more outspoken. I guess I'm in a place all by myself."[18]

Clifton demonstrates that truth telling is more important than being amenable to her readers' feelings and making them comfortable. She notes that even though this outspokenness is unpopular, she must inhabit this role and space as a poet— even if that isolates her and makes her less accessible to readers. In these public elegies, Clifton, like many other contemporary black poets, performs risks in the name of justice.

Clifton also incorporates poignant and painful images of trees into her elegiac poems, suggesting their complex significance for a history of anti-black terrorism. To this end, in "the photograph: a lynching," Clifton refers to the lynching photographs taken by white spectators of African Americans' brutalized bodies hanging from trees. According to Daniel J. Martin, "The participants did not disguise themselves, and in fact lynchings were attended like social events with people drinking, being photographed next to the corpse, and taking away the victim's body parts as souvenirs."[19] Clifton highlights the spectacle of this event and the inanity and inhumanity of the audience in this seemingly pastoral setting. This poem is crafted as a series of questions that compel her readers to enter this horrific scene. By the last stanza, Clifton implicates readers, asking whether it is "all of us / captured by history into an / accurate album?"[20] Clifton draws her readers together under a "gathering sky" into this album of history, placing the onus on white readers to take collective responsibility for past wrongs (much like Rankine does in "February 26, 2012 / In Memory of Trayvon Martin" which will be discussed later). The nature imagery here calls upon white readers to both engage in truth and reckoning and to consider their complicity in the continued silence surrounding this horrific history. Clifton explains in an interview with Jacqueline Jones LaMon,

> I was asked once to write about landscape and the beauty of the trees. But I cannot—I will not—close part of my vision. I know what my history has been and it is a human history. Every time I see a tree I know somebody used to hang on that. . . . I'm not going to make others comfortable and not mention that. That's just the way I am. . . . I don't believe that as a poet I am here to make others feel good, feel happy. I'm supposed to chronicle what is so. And it would be nice to forget history, but we do it at our peril, as we have seen lately.[21]

Clifton's collective responsibility to remember past wrongs and injustices is a reminder that these events took place in the same environment we live in today. The nature surrounding us acts as a reminder, like the trees which appear complicit in these lynchings. As Dungy notes, African Americans can "look at trees and see history, many sources of horror," but they can also "look at trees and see grandeur, sources of sustenance, beauty, and shade."[22] In resisting the making of nature beautiful in these horrific moments in history, Clifton intentionally departs from the traditional elegiac and pastoral device of offering consolation.

Clifton also weaves natural imagery into an urban space of violence in her poem "alabama 9/15/63," an elegy to Cynthia, Carole, Denise, and Addie Mae, who lost their lives in the 1963 16th Street Baptist Church bombing in Birmingham, Alabama. This incident occurred in a city, so it's not located in a typical "pastoral" scene, but Clifton uses nature imagery to create an awareness of what happened to these little girls. She includes an interrogative structure, using the refrain "Have you heard the one about . . ." to introduce each question which adds a morbidly humorous tone to another grim, violent moment in history.[23] Clifton catches her readers off guard by pulling us into the poem to remember another deeply disturbing racist act. The four little girls, while practicing for the church choir, are "shattered into skylarks in the white" Birmingham light.[24] Both this sudden explosion and subsequent transfiguration of the children into black birds "known for their music" after the bombing create a moment of beauty in this otherwise horrific scene.[25] The light itself after the bombing is white, and could allude to the white light from the blast which has left its mark on the psyche of the people in Birmingham and beyond. It could also refer to the white perpetrators who planted the bomb and the ideology of white supremacy from which they acted. At the end of the poem, Clifton leaves us with a sense that "the blast / is still too bright to hear them play"—we cannot hear their heavenly music because of this despicable act of white-supremacist violence.[26] These girls become emblems of a heavenly pastoral landscape which we in this world cannot access. Their choir practice was interrupted by a bomb—and we will never know what the sound of their blended voices would be in song or who they could have become had they lived. Clifton suggests that only the dead have access to that beauty now.

The transformation of the girls into skylarks, known for their singing, implies that the girls' song continues on in heaven. In an interview with Grace Cavalieri, Clifton explains, "I feel that nothing is lost, that history is still here, now. And the only way to deal with history really, is to recognize that it is still part of us, which in our country we tend to not have done, as much as we might have."[27] This assertion haunts the last stanza of "alabama 9/15/63"—since there is a commentary on how people do forget, or neglect to hear the strains of the songs of the past.[28] All too often, we respond to violence with silence and move away from these moments into cultural amnesia. This silence impedes healing the wounds of racial violence and, Martin notes, "telling the story is essential . . . something important happens when people bring trauma out of the unconscious in order to . . . enfold and unfold it in narrative."[29] Clifton propels us back into the past with her elegies of African American trauma, and she utilizes an anti-pastoral poetics to remind us that this history of violence is still living in the here and the now, in both national and human-made environments.

Claudia Rankine takes up Lucille Clifton's call to innovate the elegy to compel her readers to keep horrific racial violence in mind, while enjoining them to confront and contend with present racism. In the 14-year interval between the publication of Clifton's *Blessing the Boats: New and Selected Poems 1988–2000* and the publication of Rankine's *Citizen: An American Lyric* (2014), there was an increased awareness of the systemic violence perpetrated against African American citizens. Rankine's volume was published in the midst of the beginnings of the Black Lives Matter movement and spoke to the feelings of many black people who were being bombarded on an almost daily basis with images and stories of more victims of police brutality. It catapulted Rankine into the national consciousness because *Citizen* spoke to the exigent need to confront racism and racist acts in this specific cultural moment. In an interview with Kate Kellaway, Rankine notes,

> Racism is complicated. White people feel personally responsible for racism when they should understand the problem as systemic. It is interfering as much with their lives as with the lives of people of colour. And racism can lodge in them. It isn't them yet it can become them if they are not taking notice.[30]

Rankine, like Clifton, makes her white readers uncomfortable to challenge their conceptions about race and racism. As Rankine puts it,

> White privilege is masterful at keeping invisible what remains sadly hyper-visible in certain communities. For black people, institutionally condoned murders are present every day. If you have a son, given the stats, you're going to be thinking: "What happens when he's out on his own? What happens if he accidentally puts his hands in his pockets at a moment that is wrong according to the white gaze?"[31]

Rankine forces her white readers to really examine their own privilege when it comes to their relative safety compared to members of the African American community, especially African American males. Rankine's book approaches the elegy with a juxtaposition of image and text, personal experience, and public violence.

In many of her elegiac poems, Rankine presents nature as a witness to hate crimes. Sometimes her speaker needs relief from the daily reminders of racism and actually begins to transform into nature to disconnect from the disturbing and often violent actions of humanity. Hume notes, "Between the most daily discriminatory microaggressions and the entrenched forms of structural racism that facilitate them in the first place, Rankine suggests, black bodies are rendered increasingly deindividuated and expendable."[32] At moments in *Citizen*, nature can provide temporary relief from the horrors of hate crimes and allow her speaker escape. In Part IV, Rankine includes instances where the speaker uses a simile to liken herself to an animal or something inanimate after encountering racism. At one point, the speaker reveals, "To live through the days sometimes you moan like a deer. / Sometimes you sigh. The world says stop that."[33] The world objects to her animal reactions to racist behavior, yet it is the only way she can make it from day to day. It is also significant that she chooses a deer, an animal long hunted and ritualistically killed in its natural environment year after year. It isn't dangerous, threatening, or harmful, yet still it is a target and a victim of violence.

In Part I, Rankine includes a photo of Kate Clark's artwork entitled "Little Girl," which superimposes a child's face on a deer form (caribou hide was used to create the piece).[34] This visual reinforces the elegies contained within *Citizen* by combining the image of a human with an often hunted animal. Later, the speaker admits that her sighing is not a sickness, yet "it is not the iteration of a free being."[35] The ruminant animal is not a free being, and neither is the human—the "worrying exhale of ache" holds her captive. The speaker is unable to express herself in ways that the rest of the world would understand. Through the animal, she can convey what is happening to her psyche. Later, she writes, "The world is wrong. You can't put the past behind you. It's / buried in you; it's turned your flesh into its own cupboard."[36] The speaker challenges "the world's" erasure of the history of racism, and Rankine suggests that the African American psyche stores the residual feelings impressed by the accumulated racist acts of past and present. The ruminant sigh or deer moan is a coping mechanism for this speaker who, in this section, represents African American women's experiences with racialized microaggressions and the precarity of living in a white supremacist, patriarchal, and militarized society.

By bringing the elegy together with nature, Rankine also takes on the role of truth teller in her writing about hate crimes. She pays homage in one elegy to Trayvon Martin, the black teenager in Florida who was killed by George Zimmerman, a white neighbor, while walking home one night in early 2012. In "February 26, 2016 / In Memory of Trayvon Martin," however, the speaker addresses the collective "brothers," instead of Trayvon specifically. She simultaneously implicates the larger system of institutionalized, targeted death and addresses the criminal justice system that has disproportionately punished African American young men. She focuses on the victims, alluding to the past violence done to the collective "brother," and "the rope inside us, the tree inside us, its roots our limbs,"[37] which prevents the collective speaker from having a voice. She invokes the accumulation of both micro- and macroaggressions which haunt the speaker, making a direct correlation between the psychological and physical violence done to so many African American men, women, and children, as well as the collective reader. Her use of "we" and "us" connotes this collective responsibility, much like Clifton's use of "we" in the last stanza of "the photograph: a lynching."[38] We are implicated, too: "we are all caught hanging, the rope inside us, the tree inside us, its roots our limbs," and even become the rope, the tree, the perpetrator of the violence.[39]

Rankine, like Clifton, draws the reader into the scene, creating an "accurate album"[40] of history. When we open our mouths to speak, all that comes out are flower blossoms and the blues, other elegiac expressions of mourning and remembrance. The speaker could be trying to speak out against the perpetual violence, but nothing comes out—nothing changes. There is a feeling of complicity and surrender, because not much has changed in all these years for all of our brothers (and sisters and children). According to Hume, Rankine's use of apostrophe contributes to the elegiac feeling in the poem. She concludes that "the loss is so overwhelming to the speaker that she becomes incapable of uttering, or claiming, a place and home for herself. To risk reckoning with one's black history and life conditions is always to risk becoming destabilized and *dis*placed—imprisoned by the 'no place' of one's own historical experience."[41] Hume goes on to note, "By gesturing toward the sky, Rankine suggests that African Americans cannot see nature without seeing a history of incarceration and violence."[42] She notes that Rankine's use of the infamous 1930 photo of a public lynching in Marion, Indiana, that omits the bodies of the three black men forces the viewer to look directly into the eyes of the white perpetrators of violence instead of focusing on the black bodies.

In another elegiac poem, Rankine specifically addresses the perpetrators of violence, indicting them directly and depicting the hate crime, using pathetic fallacy to show how nature responds to the horrific event. In "June 26, 2011 / In Memory of James Craig Anderson," Rankine writes of the murder of James Craig Anderson who was robbed, beaten, and run over by a pickup truck in a hate crime. She writes from multiple perspectives, with nature as witness in the motel parking lot in Jackson, Mississippi. Much like Clifton's approach in "jasper texas 1998," Rankine recreates the scene of the hate crime and alternates perspectives. She begins by personifying the pickup truck as the perpetrator of this hate crime. The pickup truck acts almost of its own volition, objectifying the nameless black subject. Inhabiting the voice of the pickup, Rankine similarly implicates all of us as witnesses, for as the sun rises to reveal this graphic scene, the sky turns red and mirrors the color of the blood on the asphalt. In this case, nature does not give comfort or allow escape from the murder—it reacts to the crime by streaking the sky red, reacting with horror to the scene. Rankine draws a sharp contrast between the natural landscape and the pickup. It isn't beautiful like this sunrise at dawn and, Rankine suggests, it is a witness to murder. She later questions the perpetrator of the crime, Deryl Dedmon, directly:

> James Craig Anderson is dead. What ails you, Dedmon?
> What up? What's up is James Craig Anderson is dead. So
> sorry. So angry, an imploding anger. It
> must let you go. It let you go.[43]

The repetition of "James Craig Anderson is dead" adds gravity to the crime's horror, by giving the victim a name and shifting blame away from the pickup, which is now "a figure of speech" to Dedmon and his anger. The speaker directly questions Dedmon throughout the poem, and by the end, his "imploding anger" let him go. This can be read in multiple ways—it lets him off the hook, or it is his undoing.

In "December 4, 2006 / Jena Six," Rankine again refuses to allow her readers to forget by addressing the perpetrators of recent racial violence. Incorporating tropes of the elegy and the pastoral, Rankine lyrically ruminates on the hate crime committed by a group of white teens in Jena, Louisiana, which motivated six African American high school students to retaliate by beating up Justin Barker, a white high school student. However, this poem omits racial signifiers in order to destabilize readers' racial positionings; the Jena boys and the landscape also merge, as do images of light and darkness. In the first stanza, the African American victim lays claim to nature, finding shelter from the rain under "the overhanging branches of the 'white tree.'"[44] In that moment, in the center of the school yard, he surprises himself by relating to past Civil Rights actions of sitting in white places—for example, at the "white" lunch counter and in the "white" section of the bus. The speaker asks, "did the hardness of the ground / cross the hardness of the seats in buses as he waited to be / noticed listening to the lift and fall of the leaves above him?"[45] The white boys become "a darkening wave as / dusk folded into night walking toward a dawn sun"[46] Already, there is a hostile tone—the boys "punching through the blackness as they noosed the rope looped around the overhanging branches of their tree."[47] They, too, lay claim to nature, noosing "their" tree with rope. They, too, surprise themselves, "at the center of the school yard thinking this / is how they will learn the ropes."[48] They, too, relate to their ancestors—but in this case, it is the perpetrators of lynchings.[49] Rankine's last line mirrors the last line of the first stanza, but in this case, she wonders if the boys give that look of hardness to the tree itself—and was that same hardness in the eyes of the racists who had come before these boys, a look passed down from generation to generation? Kimberly Ruffin notes, "When it came to this natural location, African American students were not welcome; they were not understood as full members of the school community; they were environmental others."[50] She goes on to explain,

> As evoked in the racialization of the schoolyard tree in Jena, a long history exists of making nonhuman nature reflect racist exploitation and violence. Long-standing environmental micro- and macroaggressions that reinforce oppression have left African Americans simultaneously separated from prime nonhuman natural resources and characterized as animalistic sub-humans.[51]

In Rankine's poem, the tree itself mirrors the racism of the white boys and the violent tradition they are continuing. At the same time, the poem reflects through its elegiac connection with the past the oppression which generations of black men and boys have suffered at the hands of white perpetrators.

Rankine's last stanza merges black and white together, but again, racial codes are not mentioned. It begins with the phrase, "Boys will be boys," revealing their common reaction "in the violence of / aggravated adolescence." However, their "ex- / periencing [of] the position of positioning" has different repercussions for the white and black teens. This is "a position / for only one kind of boy."[52] The speaker interjects "face it know it" to add import to this inequality, since the African American teens have already been *positioned*, marked to be the criminals and the weapons which explode the landscape. She adds, "then the / litigious hitting back is life imprisoned" at the end, a statement about how many African American men and boys are locked away for life for minor crimes, a fate that loomed heavy over the Jena Six when they were initially charged with attempted murder of Justin Barker.[53] According to Ruffin,

> Although the white student sustained relatively minor injuries, five of the Jena Six were charged with attempted murder. Across the United States, people saw the treatment of the Jena Six as representative of a national scourge: a criminal justice system that routinely minimizes or dismisses crimes perpetrated by whites and either falsely accuses blacks or inflates and unduly punishes black wrongdoing. A national outcry against the racial injustices brought into relief by the Jena Six culminated in a protest march that drew thousands to Jena on September 20, 2007, with solidarity protests around the country.[54]

Rankine, like many other Black Lives Matter–era poets, demonstrates an interest in connecting individual acts of brutality to the prison industrial complex. In this poem, there is a reckoning with the disproportionate punishment given to the African American teenagers because of their actions compared to the white teenagers. Even though this poem is not an elegy in the traditional sense, it harks back to hate crimes of the past where many African Americans lost their lives to lynching. Rankine's incorporation of nature imagery—the noosed tree, in this case—also reflects a link to the anti-pastoral, the tree as representation of the violence that countless trees were implicated in.

Indeed, this concept of "face it know it" is conveyed in Rankine's essay "The Condition of Black Life Is One of Mourning," where she considers how Mamie Till Mobley's insistence upon an open casket for her son Emmett drew attention to the horrific consequences of white supremacy:

> [Mamie Till] Mobley's refusal to keep grief private allowed a body that meant nothing to the criminal-justice system to stand as evidence. By placing both herself and her son's corpse in positions of refusal relative to the etiquette of grief, she "disidentified" with the tradition of the lynched

figure left out in public view as a warning to the black community, thereby using the lynching tradition against itself. The spectacle of the black body, in her hands, publicized the injustice mapped onto her son's corpse. "Let the people see what I see," she said, adding "I believe that the whole United States is mourning with me."[55]

Rankine argues that Mobley's act of showing the brutality her son's body endured is a powerful gesture toward the community. His body acts as evidence, and this mapping gives a sense of the black body as a territory, too, one his mother claims and carries back for the world to see. In some ways, Mamie Till Mobley herself reinforces the rejection of the pastoral ideal, by reclaiming him and exposing the injustice done to his body in a pastoral setting, implicating the ugliness of the river he was drowned in, while indicting the humans responsible for her son's murder.

Similarly in *Citizen*, Rankine uses the elegy to provoke her readers to remember past hate crimes, and to do something about present ones. In particular, Rankine challenges white readers to act against systemic racism and oppression by her use of the elegiac lyric, putting the white reader in a black person's shoes to experience the feeling of micro- and macroaggressions. Nature in her poetry could provide temporary respite, but often it is as intricately implicated as her readers are, as witnesses to racist acts. Her use of the pastoral is another device to pull the reader into the landscape where racist crimes were and are committed. When asked why it is so hard to call out racism in the aforementioned interview with Kellaway, Rankine explained, "Because making other people uncomfortable is thought worse than racism. It has taken me a while to train myself to speak out."[56] In ethical commitments and poetic strategy, Rankine, like Clifton, is a central figure of the black elegiac tradition who "face it know it," making her white readers uncomfortable in order to challenge their conceptions about race and racism. They cannot easily slip away into an inanimate form, distancing themselves from the horrors of racism. Hume notes,

> While the book is not ostensibly a work of ecological poetry or environmental criticism, one of *Citizen*'s most pointed critiques— . . . concerns the difficulty of relating to or identifying with one's environment when one has been othered by the dominant white society and, consequently, forced to live with greater amounts of environmental risk.[57]

She considers *Citizen* to have made "an important contribution to conversations among scholars of ecopoetics and environmental justice."[58] Indeed, through her elegiac, anti-pastoral poetics, Rankine emphasizes the continual challenges of being "othered."

Clifton's elegiac poetry, too, is involved in what Holladay describes as "sounding a clarion call, . . . serving as a moral witness at the turn of the millennium," and "her longtime readers who have read her work through the years are in a unique position to take heed."[59] In an interview with Naomi Thiers, Clifton responded,

> One of the strengths of poets is to notice what happens and to tell about it. A man in the audience at one of my readings said, "This is very interesting, but I can't really get into it because I'm a historian." And I said, "Me, too." What the poet does, ideally, is to talk about the history of the inside of people so that history is more than just the appearance of things.[60]

When asked about her assertion that if the Los Angeles Police Department read poetry they never would have beaten Rodney King, Clifton observed, "I am certain. They couldn't have done it so easily because poetry allows you to see beyond yourself, to try to reach toward the sameness in the other."[61] Clifton offers poetry as an antidote to the prevalence of police brutality, allowing for a space for empathy. This, combined with her concerted interest in speaking the truth about "the history of the inside of people" gives insight into her project of breaking down these barriers between people of different races.[62]

In striking ways, Clifton and Rankine integrate the anti-pastoral in their elegiac poetry about racial violence in order to compel their readers to remember our dark history and to pay attention to our present moment. These poems ask us to bear witness, but also encourage us to be active in the resistance to more violence done toward the African American community. Like the nature in these poems, we are implicated as these events unfold; we must take action to stop any further violence. Their poetry can push all of us to see beyond ourselves, "to try to reach toward the sameness in the other."[63]

Notes

1. Evie Shockley, "On the Nature of Ed Roberson's Poetics," *Callaloo* 33, no. 3 (2010): 729.
2. Angela Hume, "Toward an Antiracist Ecopoetics: Waste and Wasting in the Poetry of Claudia Rankine," *Contemporary Literature* 57, no. 1 (2016): 81.
3. Marcellus Blount, "Paul Laurence Dunbar and the African American Elegy," *African American Review* 41, no. 2 (2007): 241.
4. Ibid., 242.
5. Ibid.
6. Jahan Ramazani, *Poetry of Mourning: The Modern Elegy from Hardy to Heaney* (Chicago: University of Chicago, 1994), ix.
7. Camille Dungy, "Introduction: The Nature of African American Poetry," in *Black Nature: Four Centuries of African American Nature Poetry*, ed. Camille Dungy (Athens: University of Georgia Press, 2009), xxxiv.
8. Ibid., xxvi.
9. Hilary Holladay, *Wild Blessings: The Poetry of Lucille Clifton* (Baton Rouge: LSU Press, 2004), 142.
10. Mary Jane Lupton, *Lucille Clifton: Her Life and Letters* (Westport: Praeger, 2006), 78.

11. Michael Glaser, "I'd Like Not to Be a Stranger in the World: A Conversation/Interview with Lucille Clifton," *The Antioch Review,* 58, no. 3 (Summer 2000): 313.
12. Ibid.
13. Lucille Clifton, *Blessing the Boats: New and Selected Poems 1988–2000.* (Rochester: BOA Editions, 2000), 20.
14. Ibid.
15. Ibid.
16. Ibid.
17. Ibid.
18. Lupton, *Lucille Clifton,* 79.
19. Daniel J. Martin, "Lynching Sites: Where Trauma and Pastoral Collide," in *Coming into Contact: Explorations in Ecocritical Theory and Practice,* eds. Annie Merrill Ingram, Ian Marshall, Daniel Philippon, and Adam W. Sweeting. (Athens: University of Georgia Press, 2007), 96.
20. Clifton, *Blessing the Boats,* 19.
21. Jacqueline Jones LaMon, "The Healing World of Lucille Clifton," *Mosaic 17.* (January 2007), https://mosaicmagazine.org/lucille-clifton-interview/#.XJfpw7hWySp.
22. Dungy, "Introduction: The Nature of African American Poetry," *Black Nature,* xxxiv.
23. Clifton, *Blessing the Boats,* 21.
24. Ibid.
25. Ibid.
26. Ibid.
27. Grace Cavalieri, "The Poet and the Poem: An Interview with Lucille Clifton," *National Public Radio,* 2003, www.gracecavalieri.com/significantPoets/lucilleClifton1.html.
28. According to Hilary Holladay, Clifton's use of titles using specific locations and dates, "underscores the message that the poems make in no uncertain terms: racial oppression is an ongoing part of American life, and we would do well to face the problem head-on rather than pretend it belongs to some era long before our own." Hillary Holladay, "Black Names in White Spaces," *Southern Literary Journal* (2002): 131.
29. Martin, "Lynching Sites," 104.
30. Kate Kellaway, "Claudia Rankine: 'Blackness in the White Imagination has Nothing to Do with Black People,'" *The Guardian,* December 27, 2015, www.theguardian.com/books/2015/dec/27/claudia-rankine-poet-citizen-american-lyric-feature.
31. Claire Schwartz, "An Interview with Claudia Rankine," *TriQuarterly,* July 15, 2016, www.triquarterly.org/issues/issue-150/interview-claudia-rankine.
32. Hume, "Toward an Antiracist Ecopoetics," 80.
33. Claudia Rankine, *Citizen: An American Lyric* (Minneapolis: Graywolf, 2014), 59.
34. Kate Clark, *Little Girl,* 2008 in *Citizen,* 19.
35. Rankine, *Citizen,* 60.
36. Ibid., 63.
37. Ibid., 89, 90.
38. Clifton, *Blessing the Boats,* 19.
39. Hume writes of the tree imagery in one of Rankine's earlier poems, "American Light":

> Rankine throws into relief the complexity of environmental relations for African Americans. . . . The tree, a pastoral archetype, becomes a figure for danger and violence, bringing to mind the relationship between trees and lynching. In this way, Rankine explicitly realigns her pastoral inheritance from the Romantic tradition to that of what we might call a black pastoral tradition—one according to which nature is always implicated in histories of racialized violence. Hume, "Toward an Antiracist Ecopoetics: Waste and Wasting in the Poetry of Claudia Rankine," 96.

40. Clifton, *Blessing the Boats,* 19.

41. Hume, "Toward an Antiracist Ecopoetics," 99.
42. Ibid.
43. Rankine, *Citizen*, 95.
44. Ibid., 99.
45. Ibid.
46. Ibid.
47. Ibid.
48. Ibid.
49. Kimberly Ruffin notes,

> The white students' actions advanced the daily microaggression of unequal access to the school's outdoor resources to a macroaggressive, life-threatening gesture worthy of the designation "hate crime." The ease with which microaggressions around this tree escalated into macroaggressions reflects the union of environmental alienation and racism in the United States. All white students had to do was fashion rope into nooses and attach them to a tree to evoke centuries of brutal, racialized place- and power-keeping (Kimberly Ruffin, *Black on Earth: African American Ecoliterary Traditions* [Athens: University of Georgia Press, 2010], 4).

50. Ruffin, *Black on Earth*, 3.
51. Ibid., 4.
52. Rankine, *Citizen*, 101.
53. Ibid.
54. Ruffin, *Black on Earth*, 1–2.
55. Claudia Rankine, "The Condition of Black Life is One of Mourning," in *Charleston Syllabus: Readings on Race, Racism, and Racial Violence,* eds. Chad Williams, Kidada E. Williams, and Keisha N. Blain (Athens: University of Georgia Press, 2016), 72.
56. Kellaway, "Claudia Rankine."
57. Hume, Toward an Antiracist Ecopoetics," 79–80.
58. Ibid.
59. Holladay, *Wild Blessings*, 62.
60. Naomi Thiers, "Lucille Clifton," in *Truthtellers of the Times: Interviews with Contemporary Women Poets,* ed. Janet Mullaney Palmer (Ann Arbor: University of Michigan Press, 1998), 21.
61. Ibid.
62. Ibid.
63. Ibid.

4

"IN TERRIBLE FRUITFULNESS"

Arthur Jafa's *Love Is the Message, The Message Is Death* and the Not-Lost Southern Accent

J. Peter Moore

It is difficult to think about Arthur Jafa's *Love Is The Message, The Message Is Death* (2016) in the context of elegy and not be distracted by the absent presence that accompanies any effort to locate the now-famous video online. With its rhapsodic stitching of original and freely circulating footage, the seven-minute digital video, set to Kanye West's "Ultralight Beam," has garnered rapt responses from commentators, lending credence to the title of Nate Freeman's piece in *Art News:* "The Messenger: How a video by Arthur Jafa Became a Worldwide Sensation—and described America to Itself."[1] But the frenzy surrounding *LMMD* has done little to compromise the barriers preventing the editioned work from being absorbed back into the video-sharing websites from which it so conspicuously emerged. What does make its way into the open-access digital domain is an ever-expanding archive of videos produced in conjunction with official institutional programing, featuring Jafa in conversation with colleagues and curators. While they are no substitute for the film itself, these symposia register the complex voice responsible for the absented assemblage. A messenger, no doubt, Jafa, with his flair for thinking aloud—practiced in theoretical debates, sports radio hot takes, art history outtakes, and the story behind the story of black popular music—gives the viewer reason to stop searching for bootleg versions of the famous film and instead tarry there for a while in the presentation of its absence.

In one of these performances, Jafa speaks with film critic Amy Taubin at the School of Visual Arts in New York.[2] In the post-discussion Q&A, a participant begins his question with an aside: "Being from Mississippi as well, it's just really comforting to hear your accent and see you haven't lost it." Born in Tupelo and raised in Clarksdale, Jafa is not simply *from* the South, but *of* it, to the extent that, when he hears the comment from the audience, he cannot let it pass without letting out an exuberant "aahaa." At a similar event hosted by the Hammer Museum,

Jafa's good friend Greg Tate introduces him not as the cinematographer of Spike Lee's *Crooklyn*, Julie Dash's *Daughters of the Dust*, or Stanley Kubrik's *Eyes Wide Shut*, nor as the director of multiple music videos, nor as the visual artist featured in several international exhibits of renown.[3] Instead he chooses a title reflective of Jafa's contribution to all of these fields, lighting upon the label of "Southern oral storyteller." Jafa then proceeds to earn the title, regaling the Los Angeles audience with the legend of the Greasy Man: A successful attorney in Clarksdale who moonlit as a public menace, breaking into homes late at night, smearing his naked body with petroleum jelly and leaving his greasy mark on the furniture the victim had reserved for company. Despite being an offhand observation, the participant's original aside and Jafa's reply pose an entry point into what I want to argue are the two animating concerns of Jafa's work: Loss and location.

Keeping his phrasing in mind, the following writing concerns itself with something other than Jafa's Southern accent. Instead my concern lies in what we might call his not-lost accent. A space often associated with the elegiac, the South by way of the comment becomes that which the artist has managed to not lose. As worded, the comment presents loss as the framework for understanding what remains. In contrast to accent, a marked mode of pronunciation indexing regional distinction, a not-lost accent refers to those same features of cultural particularity, but goes further to think about the conditions that make possible their appearance. Anyone who has been on a road trip with a stubborn driver knows there is a significant conceptual distinction between being lost, being not-lost, and knowing where you are going. In a similar way, the not-lost accent is a way of thinking about cultural particularity beyond the binary of possession and dispossession. It addresses the many ways that loss, in the form of systemic neglect and disenfranchisement, affects cultural expressivity, while at the same time refuses to accept the conventional notion of loss as that which animates a conservative cycle of mourning and consolation. Instead, a not-lost accent imagines loss as a generative break, the rupture that makes possible, the radical relinquishing of wholeness in favor of fragmentation.

One final heuristic follows from the New York observation. The audience member states that it is comforting to hear Jafa's accent, but then switches from the auditory to the visual, stating that it's good to "see" that he had not lost it. While the synesthetic slip is characteristic of colloquial speech, the slip actually carries a great deal of precision. The phrase invites us to think about what it might mean to film with an accent, to edit with an accent, to speak in images with an accent. In what follows I argue that *LMMD* serves as evidence of Jafa's not-lost accent, pointing to the ways that his understanding of loss bears on the history of poetic elegy, its translatability to the filmic medium, its implications for black aesthetics, and its relationship to the discourse of Southern regionalism.

While no commentator to date has explicitly linked *LMMD* to the elegy, the surrounding discourse has succeeded in identifying a host of characteristics that support an analysis of the film as such. In nearly every account, respondents emphasize the overwhelming affective force of the film, referencing its "tremendous emotional power."[4] While reviewers are careful to emphasize the emotional range of the piece—from joy to anguish—they consistently return to the judgement that loss and the ecstatic structures of mourning set the tone. When loss is not explicitly engaged, images of triumph—political, athletic, and artistic—serve to expand the iconography of loss rather than simply offset it. A case in point comes in the opening shot. Instead of beginning with footage of police brutality, Jafa begins by reposting the viral clip of Charles Ramsay explaining to local news that he knew something was wrong when Amanda Berry, a "little pretty white girl," "ran into a black man's arms." Like the lyrical content of the blues, the comedic line takes the terror of racism and turns it into an expressive art of calculated coolness. It is the laugh born of loss, the loss of one's self-image to the prejudice of a dominant culture. By confronting a sense of loss that is more subtle and pervasive, Ramsay makes explicit the ubiquitous racism that posits blackness as a threat and thereby sustains the excessive police violence captured by citizen journalists and repurposed by Jafa. As much a product of the moment as it is a product of the unacknowledged past, *LMMD* reads as elegy to the extent that it reads Black Lives Matter as an injunction to rethink the conventions of elegy. In particular, *LMMD* demonstrates the profound ways in which loss is constitutive of black culture and artists such as Jafa reimagine that loss through affective and dialogic modes of expression.

Part of this rethinking involves selecting the aesthetic features of elegiac tradition that attract alteration. Though intensely modern in its media, the film is guided by several determinants that can be traced to the ancient context out of which elegy first emerged. As Peter Sacks attests, the earliest distinguishing feature of the elegiac verses of ancient Greece was not the subject matter but rather the metrical order and musicality. Recited over the "mournful pipe players called *aulos*," elegy emerges in close tandem with instrumental sound.[5] Jafa's film extends upon this tradition, modernizing the plaintive pipe with Kanye's ethereal synth C minor soundtrack. While conspicuously electronic in its sound, the song points back to older modes of electronic instrumentation that merge advanced circuitry with acoustical vibration. The sound resonates with the atmospheric oscillating hum of the Hammond B3 organ, held by many, including Ashon Crawley, as the constitutive sound of black Pentecostalism.[6] The rotating Leslie speaker, the amplification component of the B3, uses a Doppler spinning horn to create an organic tremolo that achieves the "mournful character" of ancient elegiac wind instruments.

The dominant referent of "Ultralight Beam" is the black church, a ritual context that carries its own connections to the history of elegy. As Sacks notes, the elegy can be traced to ritual offerings sacrificed to vegetation gods, and these ceremonial circumstances required a formalness, elevating elegy above daily affairs, conveying "the effect not only of an event but of a performance."[7] While the opening sample of four-year old Natalie Green praying represents a democratic populist embrace of the low-fidelity margins, the child's passionate speech carries the marks of ritual circumstance as she gets carried away with the rhetorical flourish of praise. With the voices of The Dream, Kelly Price, and Chance the Rapper latticing one another, "Ultralight Beam" foregrounds formalness. The ceremonial significance of the piece applies equally to Jafa's technique as a filmmaker. In those sequences of original footage, one finds a highly sophisticated sense of dynamic lighting and framing, which extends the distressed aesthetics of found footage, creating a high-style approximate to the preacherly vernacular of black oral tradition.

But Jafa's film also points to the ways in which the ceremonial effects of elegy have escaped the ritual context, seeping into the corners of file-sharing virtual space. As Maria Damon points out, despite the residual vestiges of the ceremonial ancient form, it remains one of the more publicly available modes of poetry.[8] Elegy is the form of poetry most non-poets find themselves writing when moved to compose verse. Jafa builds his film out of the everyday, but avoids documenting the conventional scenes of everyday elegy. Nowhere is Lebron warming up in his "I Can't Breathe" shirt, nowhere is footage of funeral wreaths or public defacement of confederate memorials. And only scant images point to the outpouring of support in cities like Ferguson. Yet Jafa's film in its attention to everyday life makes a case for seeing the elegiac in the most unlikely of spaces. If, as Frederick Douglass points out in his 1845 *Narrative of the Life*, that violence is the blood-stained gate of black becoming, *LMMD* seeks to understand the many physical and metaphysical valences of violence and death.[9] Instead of images of public mourning, Jafa establishes a context in which the hallmarks of commodified black culture become legible as instances of monstrous elegy. As Ernest Hardy states, Jafa offers a nuanced conception of monstrousness. "To be monstrous," claims Jafa, "is to be a thing or person that doesn't respect boundaries. . . . It's that [the figure deemed monstrous] changes itself and eludes definition as a survival technique."[10] From this perspective, monstrous mourning amounts to scenes of virtuosic enactment that emerge out of sorrow and anguish. The clearest example comes by way of the distressed footage he includes of public dance performances where performers defy gravity with a particular move known as the death drop. In falling back on one thigh, almost parallel with the floor, the dancer then uses the bent leg to thrust herself back to a standing position. These pirouetting flashes of embodied elegance resonate with familiar images of Civil Rights protestors thrown back by the force of water hoses and clubs, but with its titular reference to mortal loss, the death drop also testifies to the myriad ways in which the everyday reimagines the posture of mourning.

Though descriptive of the various tensions at play in the piece, the concept of the elegy stands at some remove from the medium of the moving image. Since the elegy in a contemporary context refers to such a broad range of techniques, its failure to represent a coherent genre makes it seem well-suited for cross-media traffic. But as Paul Coates points out, the rift between film and elegy is on display whenever filmmakers feel that in order to invoke the literary mode they must make an explicit reference to elegy in the title, as evident in Jafa's work. According to Coates, film's resistance to elegy belongs to its "refusal to set aside time for memorization and reflection."[11] If elegy is the remembrance of things past, then film with its "prosthetic memory" denies the passing, cradling the lost object into the continual present, removing the possibility of lingering in its absence. In its most popular iteration, narrative cinema, film follows a causal grammar incompatible with elegy, long associated with the irregular timetable of lyric, opposes. The result is a medium that does not easily allow for the two foundations of elegy: The distancing and the looking back across great distance.

According to Coates, films that stand the greatest chance of manifesting close ties to the elegiac are those that disrupt the temporal episteme of film. These include fictional undertakings that reconsider linear temporal succession, "breaking the [forward-moving] rules of narrative," and documentary films, which according to Coates, are well positioned "to trace, in near aleatory fashion, the contours of a situation and can [therefore] maintain a single note of lament far more easily than standard narrative fiction."[12] In analyzing the elegiac quality of both alinear narrative form and the documentary, Coates lists techniques which communicate the temporal rupture elegy necessitates. Through voiceover, a filmmaker narrates from the position of looking back, emphasizing filmic distance. Applying a musical soundtrack, the filmmaker introduces means of marking repetition, cultivating an awareness in the viewer that one scene might be sonically looking back on another. And finally the freeze frame, with its arresting sense of stasis, dislodges a moment from the procession of moving frames. Each of these features figure prominently in Jafa's film. Exhibiting the formal logic of a docu-poem, *LMMD* reaches for music in order to establish a liturgical order, manifesting a pattern indifferent to conventional logics of temporality. Jafa's voiceovers are not narrative in nature. Instead they bring diegetic sound to bear on certain images, such as President Obama singing "Amazing Grace" or a young man pleading with his mother to help him as the police place him in custody. While these instances do interrupt the temporal order of the piece, they challenge the desire for a stable position, removed from the past, where narration can take place outside of time. Without ever fully committing to the freeze frame, the film features overt rate manipulation. Numerous clips progress in a signature distinct from the mimetic standard of 24 frames per second. A boy jumps from stairs in slow motion, Bert Williams abruptly faints in an erratic manner indicative of hand-cranked projectors, Bobby Seale and Miles Davis, seen close up, move in minute increments, undermining the performativity of portraiture, and countless dancers shudder into an irregular ebb and flow of delay and advance.

In addition to these techniques, Jafa advances his own methods for invoking distance and retrospect, methods which serve less to reinforce his connection to elegy than to trouble its conventions. Picked up secondhand like so many things in Jafa's work, the concept of affective proximity sits at the heart of his self-declared obsession with recombining pictorial fragments. Attributing the concept to his friend and fellow filmmaker John Akomfrah, Jafa recalls, "He said something that struck me because I feel it's at the core of almost everything that I do. He said that essentially what he tries to do is take things and put them in some sort of affective proximity to one another."[13] Affective proximity names the gestalt dynamic inherent in collage and montage, wherein discrete clippings and found materials, once assembled, convey a signal that exceeds their constitutive sum. In much of Akomfrah's work, the strategy serves to trouble the cinematic grammar of causality, as he uses multichannel cinematic installations to screen two or three moving images simultaneously. The concurrent splay of images reorient the discourse around such issues as migration by showing interpenetrating images that emphasize both ecological and economic imperatives. Jafa's interest in affective proximity occurs primarily in its capacity as a framework for understanding the power of pattern to trouble contextual boundaries:

> Affective proximity is a thing that happens when two things come together. Certain things seek to be next to other things. When I would flip through these books, I would see an image, which was demanding to be emancipated from the context in which it found itself and placed next to where it was supposed to go. It was like the levee broke and I just started cutting everything up. It's a kind of ordering of things emerging and demanding to be themselves. It's as if there's a latent potentiality in things.[14]

Read in the light of Coates's treatment of cinematic elegy, affective proximity imagines distance as at once a temporal and spatial gap. In decontextualizing and recontextualizing the appropriated image, Jafa traverses a sense of historical distance, as his assemblages often shrink time by positing a relation between the contemporary and the past, and a sense of spatial distance by reducing the gaps that mark certain spaces as diametrically opposed. Footage of the paramilitary response to Ferguson comes into affective proximity with Civil Rights–era riot control. Footage of police violence comes into affective proximity with a late-night grinding dancefloor, which comes into affective proximity with a high-flying sports highlight, which comes into affective proximity with children at play. In bringing those images together, the film presents the great spatial and temporal distances that cultural forms travel. Heeding the animist volition of images, Jafa presents distance as the condition of possibility for connection.

Affective proximity, however, is not simply another means by which *LMMD* approaches the conventions of elegy; it also represents the clearest instance of Jafa reworking those conventions to take into consideration the ways in which loss shapes black culture and the ways in which black culture reshapes loss. As Jafa's comments suggest, proximity ostensibly applies to the contact zone that emerges when materials from different contexts come into relation. The foundational experience of affective proximity that concerns Jafa has overt pictorial implications but is not pictorial in nature. In his essay "My Black Death," the film-maker discusses "instances in which black aesthetics radically redirected Western art practice in the twentieth century," particularly the "advent of African 'art' in Europe," when "Europeans were confronted with artifacts that were essentially alien, i.e., they were the products of radically different assumptions about how one apprehends and responds to the world."[15] According to Jafa, of all the artists who drew inspiration from the objects, it was Marcel Duchamp who managed to offer the "smart[est]" intervention. "Duchamp peeped that these artifacts were, in fact, not art but instruments whose functionality had been arrested, and that much of their power was derived from their radically alienated, and de facto transgressive, relationship to the context in which they found themselves."[16] At its base, affec-tive proximity refers to this experience of aberrant being, the radical alienation Jafa attributes to the black body in a Western context. No idea stands as more central to the film, and Jafa's work in total, than the ontological becoming associ-ated with the moment in which African slaves ceased to imagine themselves as African and initiated an unending process towards the constitution of blackness as a mode of deterritorialized cultural affiliation. Turning away from the prospect of reconstituting an inviolable blood line to a nation-state of uninterrupted political and cultural belonging, the subjects of Jafa's film deny the bounded logic of self-possession and enlightenment subjectivity and a disavowal of the specter of natal belonging, consecrated around a notion of inviolable inalienable home place and origin. They make available contingent spaces of black dwelling within the scant structures provided: The sanctuary, the gym, the stage, the club, and the street. This ever-renewing project appears in each scene of Jafa's film, which in collecting the images of black people refusing that which was refused, presents a model of elegy constituted not by loss, but rather by the refusal of loss, or not-loss. The elegiac in his work functions not as an acknowledgment of momentary loss, which animates the search for a substitute, consolation, and the reassertion of proprietary rights, but as generative rupture, inciting a sociality at odds with the classic aim of elegy, the reconstitution of the autonomous subject.

This negation of negation and what it means for black variations on elegy finds sustained theorization in the work of Fred Moten:

> Elegy is related to tragedy to the extent that it mourns for that which is the condition of possibility of the tragic: (a desire for) home. But what is the relation between tragedy, elegy, and improvisation? Perhaps this: that what animates the tragic-elegiac is something more than home(lessness) and (the absence of) singularity and totality: perhaps also there is a certain constellation that exceed them, that exceed the structure of their oscillation between happiness and despair, resurrection and morning. What I'm talking about is ensemble and the improvisation that allows us to experience and describe it. It is our access to the "sexual cut" that "insistent perviousness evading each and every natal occasion," and "it allows us to move beyond

either the simple evasion of the abyss or the spatio-temporal discontinuity that impedes our direction (home) or the narcotic belief in some spectral reemergence from its depths: rather we might look at that temporal-spatial discontinuity as a generative break, one wherein action becomes possible, one in which it is our duty to linger in the name of ensemble and its performance.[17]

This break, which Moten refers to as a "temporal-spatial discontinuity," exceeds the articulation of what is lost, what is absent, that abiding sense of homelessness. It also exceeds the desire to be whole, which Moten phrases in Kantian terms of singularity, the self-fashioning individual subject, and totality, the vision of an all-encompassing social fabric, which absorbs without dissolving the singular. To exceed then is to refuse what has been refused. Rather than mourn for the loss and redress the absence, Moten imagines elegy as pointing to an abyss that cannot be sustained by the familiar stations of the liberal subject, shuttling between happiness and despair in pursuit of closure and a return to regularly scheduled efficiency. Instead for Moten elegy names something distinctly significant for the emergence of blackness as a concept of uprooted becoming. It reports the loss of origins, the experience of the break, the lingering in the gap that allows for unpredictable, transgressive, and emphatic action to take place in collective space. At base, then, Moten presses for a new understanding of elegy that acknowledges its relevance for the question of black diasporic culture by positing home or place of origins as the lost object animating a tradition of radicalism.

Elegy is black aberrant dwelling on spectacular display. Elegy is the articulation of the alienated who refuse the terms of their alienation and practice that refusal by remaining open to the contingency of improvisational commitment. As a compositional strategy, the phrase concerns an affective discharge that follows from the recontextualization of two assumable disconnected items. Underpinning this compositional notion of affective proximity sits the sense of lost home, lost origins, and generative rupture.

In *LMMD*, Jafa literalizes black radical alienation by juxtaposing images of black people with Hollywood depictions of extraterrestrial life. Amidst the footage of (un)common black folk and celebrities, all weaving between the poles of joy and despair, Jafa integrates clips of the xenomorph, the H.R. Giger creature from Aliens, and the colossal creature from Cloverfield. He clarifies their inclusion by calling attention to Martine Syms's "Mundane Afro-Futurist Manifesto," where she states, "The Mundane Afro-futurists recognize that we are not aliens."[18] In an effort to rethink stereotypical representations of black people as cosmological other, Syms thrust onto the "bonfires of the stupidities" such escapist conceits as "references to Sun Ra," "Jive-talking Aliens," and "References to Parliament Funkadelic and/or George Clinton." Though capacious enough to include its antithesis, the film makes apparent its commitment to taking seriously those representations of blackness that Syms antagonizes. He follows Syms's declaration with a shot of Odell Beckham, Jr. making a superhuman catch, before cutting to a close up of Okwui Okpokwasili, an American dancer from Nigeria whose work speaks to the experience of being construed as otherworldly in the West. Then in direct response to Syms's statement, Jafa cuts to a clip of a young black boy slapping his mother in public, screaming, "Mommy, wake up." The slap and pronouncements serve as chanticleer for the coming sequences in which Jafa splices together newsreel footage of black urban uprisings with filmic representations of extraterrestrials destroying cityscapes. "As is often the case with great science-fiction film," states Jafa, "*Aliens* is bound up with these ideas of the other. And the other, as far as it exists in the Western imagination, is bound up with who black people are imagined to be."[19]

As the notion of a not-lost suggests, radical alienation is not something to be mourned, nor is it simply the charge for ceaseless transgression. Jafa maintains a commitment to seeing, hearing, and feeling the forms of poetic dwelling that emerge when one accepts spatial/temporal dislocation as an opportunity to improvise. His work belongs to that tradition of radical black aesthetics that Moten situates "in the break," as Jafa circulates images of impossible sociality that cohere in the ostensibly incoherent. Home is what was lost, and this loss sets in motion a process of displacement, of systemic deprivation and political denial. But home, as the film points out, is also what was relinquished, as blackness in *LMMD* manifests as a series of social gatherings in which marginalized peoples are refusing that which had been stripped of them. Seen from this vantage, each scene in the film represents a monadic flashpoint, conveying within its unitary form a general truth about aberrant being. His subjects mobilize the strategies of detournment to make space habitable within a larger scene of precarity and trepidation. Charles Ramsey's comic delivery skews the white gaze of evening news. The swag surfin' that erupts in the basketball gym coordinates a sense of contingent belonging. Lateria Wooten reworking the gospel tradition makes the sanctuary a space of convivial sway. In *LMMD*, dance culminates in the synchronized ripple of ecstatic observers, working in tandem with the performer to consecrate the space. In this way, Jafa both marks loss as constitutive of black being and suggests the ways in which African-descended people reshape elegiac expression.

To return to the comments that opened this writing, the not-lost accent of the South is readily discernible in Jafa's awareness of aberrant black being and its fugitive potential for place-based improvisation. In reflecting on his upbringing in the South, the filmmaker consistently describes the experience as one informed by radical *alien*ation. In his essay on "Black Visual Intonation," Jafa begins by recounting a dream in which he and the xenomorph are "just chilling" in his childhood bedroom. His father and mother treat the alien as just another guest in the home.[20] The two sit in the room that has been marked as black by the "psychological music" coming from the record player: "You know, jazz, rock, reggae, anything that was strange." Just as the alien is raced black, the black domestic unit is classed as alien, and the South is read as that space where the two figures meet.

In "My Black Death," Jafa uses an anecdote of first seeing Stanley Kubrick's *2001: A Space Odyssey* to elaborate on the not-lost understanding of the South as a space forged out of radical alienation. As he tells it, the film, which he credits as the formative experience in his development as an artist, had made its way through its long distribution chain, finally reaching the small theater in Jafa's hometown. Flummoxed by the film, Jafa nevertheless reports feeling that his early life in Mississippi had prepared him to see some strange marvelous beauty in Kubrick's denuded tableau. "The film's slow, glacial pageantry impressed the altar boy in me," writes Jafa, "exposing me to what I'd identify now as a minimalist sensibility, a sensibility to which, I believe, I was predisposed by the flatness and austerity of the Delta."[21] As he states, the region not only primed him to see the lush variances of an otherwise austere scene, it also gave him perspective into the aberrant condition of the black monolith, standing out starkly against the context of the tawny prehistorical landscape.

> My family's move from the moderately progressive Tupelo to the essentially segregated Clarksdale, situated at the Delta's epicenter, had a cathartic impact, as did a continual and enmeshing confrontation with the extreme deprivations of the region and its abject pleasures. An exposure to the transfixing, and for me unprecedented, blackness of its inhabitants, their arresting beauty and dense corporeal being, the inescapable duality of absence and presence.[22]

The notion of blackness that shapes Jafa's understanding of elegy is one informed by a practice that he associates with the South, that of repurposing neglect into a range of radical social practices. *LMMD* attests to his awareness that the South is not the only place where such experiences can be found, but it also remains significant to the extent that it figures in his mind as a place of first exposure to "the dark matter of black being."[23]

Coda

On Saturday, March 24, 2018, I attended a panel conversation at the Whitney Museum in New York, on Zoe Leonard's "Strange Fruit" (1992–1997), which was on display in one of the institution's smaller galleries. Conceived as a personal meditation on the AIDS crisis, the piece consists of various fruits—bananas, avocados, lemons, oranges, grapefruits—emptied of their fleshy core and sewn back together, some with crude zippers and buttons, all in a late stage of decay, scattered on the floor. For his response, panelist Fred Moten read a poem written for the occasion, entitled "southern pear tree," which extends upon Leonard's titular gesture to Billie Holliday by drawing out a connection to Janie Crawford from Zora Neale Hurston's *Their Eyes Were Watching God* (1937), who gazes up in wonder at the matrimonial union of bee and bud beneath the eponymous pear tree. A week earlier, while traveling with students in Berlin, I arranged for a tour of the Julia Stoschek gallery, which was hosting a traveling exhibit of Arthur Jafa's work, under the heading "A Series of Utterly Improbable, Yet Extraordinary Renditions." As we completed our path through the gallery, director Paola Malavassi asked if I or my students had seen *LMMD*, which was not part of the present show. Answering no, we followed gallery staff upstairs into an office that was bright despite the dreary weather and spare, spare enough to speak of the few well-worn articles of human possession that rested on counters or in corners. We were out of place. We stood like pilgrims, far from home, in the staff-only suite in front of a large desktop computer. A few clicks and there it was, streaming through external speakers, illuminating the empty screen, the seven-minute montage of a dream deferred. Sitting in the auditorium at the Whitney, Moten's poem for Leonard struck me as an articulation that wanted to be brought into affective proximity with Jafa's film. I wrote to Moten and requested a copy of the poem. It is as follows.

> southern pear trees
>
> Reiteration won't account for the continuous exacerbation of shimmer, elements showing (through) themselves as other than themselves, falling in this endless and beginningless rubbing, rubbing off, rubbing raw, bruising, a bruising of sound, sound falling off from itself to bruise itself in sounding, falling, fallenness in foldedness, in terrible fruitfulness, in palimpsestic time, fallen off in that or let to fall in rising, in time piercing and terracing, wasting, embracing, again and again in a moment's notice gone violently unnoticed, in the brutal overlooking of our looking with, in savage neglect of how we care, which had to have been shown, and seen, and seen through, and demonstrated. Now here we are in memory of a miracle of remembering, to prove the miracle and reprove its murder, both of which appear in sustained decay, in living driving diving in favor of evading diving into equilibrium, as Robert says Erwin says, as Zoe says Lady says Janie says, in sheaves of high-low curacy of corrosive blossom, of stitch and echo in caress, of how to take care of loss and its refusal, of how to let it hum and fade in massage like a symphony of open questions, like a leafy butterfly of pear and ash, like a leaning spring, like an everlasting invitation to dance that cannot last, for David.[24]

During the summer months that followed my first viewing of *LMMD* and my first hearing of Moten's poem, I took to the habit of stopping at the Hirschhorn Museum in D.C. where the film was on display. Almost every day, on my way to do research at the Library of Congress, I would pass through the revolving doors of the Hirschhorn and take the escalator down to room where a large screen played *LMMD* on an endless and beginningless cycle. I made good use of my time, mapping the scenes in a notebook. But the feeling of accomplishment quickly subsided as I return to Moten's opening lines. Such mapping only brought me closer to the realization that the inventory of shimmers before me could not be explained through a rigorous series of annotations. Intrigued by Jafa's method, I recorded myself reading Moten's poem and played it over earbuds as I sat in the darkened public viewing room, bringing the two articulations into as close a proximity as I could manage. Watching one clip after another stitched and echoed into its partner, the poem with its apt language of rubbing synched with the grinding dancers, the worshipers engulfed in spirit, the ecclesiastic sway of the coiffed choir, the picketing, the sunken expression, the shift in gait. Rubbing became how I saw the cuts between the shots, which is to say the poem was rubbing off onto the film. *LMMD* arises out of sustained decay, reclaims the bloomspace of neglect, and registers the South as no bounded place on the map, but rather a symphony of open questions inflected with a sense of elegiac rupture and possibility. The objects that rub are never constant in the film. What remains is the rubbing. And it is rubbing that seems to be the characteristic feature of Jafa's not-lost Southern accent. It is the rubbing raw of the aberrant black body in a Western context and it is the rubbing embrace of massage, reflecting the miracle of remembering how to take care of loss and its refusal.

Notes

1. Andrea K Scott, "Arthur Jafa's Crucial Ode to Black America," *The New Yorker,* www.newyorker.com/magazine/2017/01/23/arthur-jafas-crucial-ode-to-black-america (October 25, 20/18); Huey Copeland, "b.O.s. 1.3 / Love Is the Message, The Message Is Death," *ASAP Online Journal,* http://asapjournal.com/love-is-the-message-the-message-is-death-huey-copeland/ (accessed October 25, 2018).
   Nate Freeman, "The Messenger: How a Video by Arthur Jafa Became a Worldwide Sensation—and Described America to Itself," *Art News,* www.artnews.com/2018/03/27/icons-arthur-jafa/ (October 25, 2018).
2. "Arthur Jafa in Conversation with Amy Taubin," SVA MFA Photo Video, YouTube, www.youtube.com/watch?v=YkBySUdQrVc (October 25, 2018).
3. "Arthur Jafa and Greg Tate," Hammer Museum, YouTube, www.youtube.com/watch?v=CAYSXam1vOA&t=4s (October 25, 2018).
4. Copeland, "b.O.s. 1.3 / Love Is the Message."
5. Peter Sacks, *The English Elegy: Studies in the Genre from Spenser to Yeats* (Baltimore, MD: Johns Hopkins University Press, 1987), 2.
6. Ashon Crawley, *Blackpentecostal Breath: The Aesthetics of Possibility* (New York: Fordham University Press, 2017).
7. Sacks, *Elegy,* 19.
8. Maria Damon, *Postliterary America: From Bagel Shop Jazz to Micropoetries* (Iowa City: University of Iowa Press. 2011) 191.
9. Frederick Douglass, *Narrative of the Life of Frederick Douglass* (New York: Dover, 1995), 4.
10. Ernest Hardy, "Arthur Jafa's Monstrous Cinema," in *A Series of Utterly Improbable, Yet Extraordinary Renditions* (New York: König, 2018), 53.
11. Paul Coates, "Moving Pictures at the Edge of Stasis: Elegy and the Elegiac in Film," in *The Oxford Handbook of the Elegy,* ed. Karen Weisman (New York: Oxford University Press, 2010), 586.
12. Ibid., 589.

13. Arthur Jafa, "Arthur Jafa in Conversation with Hans Ulrich Obrist," Serpentine Gallery, 2016, www.serpentinegalleries.org/files/downloads/arthur_jafa_in_conversation.pdf, 1.
14. Ibid., 9.
15. Arthur Jafa, "My Black Death," in *Everything but the Burden: What White People are Taking from Black Culture,* ed. Greg Tate (New York: Broadway Books, 2003), 244.
16. Ibid., 247.
17. Fred Moten, *In the Break: The Aesthetics of the Black Radical Tradition* (Minneapolis: University of Minnesota Press, 2003), 98.
18. Martine Syms, *Artbound.* Season 7, Episode 1: "The Mundane Afrofuturist Manifesto," www.youtube.com/watch?v=otUJvQhCjJ0 (October 25, 2018).
19. Jafa, "Hans Ulrich Obrist," 2.
20. Arthur Jafa, "Black Visual Intonation," in *The Jazz Cadence in American Culture,* ed. Robert G. O'Meally (New York: Columbia University Press, 1998), 264.
21. Jafa, "Black Death," 255.
22. Ibid.
23. Ibid., 256.
24. Fred Moten, "southern pear trees," unpublished poem received by email from author on March 28, 2018.

PART I

Elegiac Reconfigurations: Coda

Emily Jo Scalzo

After Charleston

hurricane within
my paralyzed impotence—
history repeats

Paula Bohince

The Flint River

Like the Lethe, which says *Forget*, or the one in Egypt,
a river will take into itself what is offered: run-offs, toxic
chemicals returned as rain, then snow, which looks beautiful,
the road salt, its chloride, dead bodies, the garbage.
It will open its mouth, keep open cloud-watching eyes.
Childlike, it will obey, drink innocently what is given,
will come when called, will deliver its poison, lead
leached from complex systems, to the mouths of children.
Who knows why? Not that mindless water, not the glacial-
fed Huron, not the children's changed bones and brains.
The money knows, dirty as winter leaves on the riverbanks,
precious, obscene, to be saved and saved and saved.

Lisa Norris

Big-Beaked White Birds

My clever dentist has me looking out the window
to see swallows or geese, osprey—or
wild pelicans, even—on the pond
before he leans me back,
hot neck wrap, light chatter
with the girl who congratulates me
on my selection from her menu:
bluegrass at 7 am to keep us all
chipper.

        "Those pelicans
Don't come too often," he says,
and she, "Aren't they the ones with big beaks?"
He nods, propping my jaw open
and passing little tools,
stuffing and unstuffing my lips with cotton.
"Those pelicans are all over Moses Lake."

I think of the Biblical baby in the bulrushes,
little dark Egyptian surrounded
by big-beaked white birds
looking down on him, wondering
if he's edible, before Miriam swoops down
for the rescue: in my mouth, they're closing in

as the ceremony progresses,
and something dark flies over the pond
beyond the flat tv where a pretty blonde
details disaster (cop shoots
unarmed black man again), and I close my eyes behind
the glasses that shield me, thinking
pelican   pelican   pelican
as the dentist wiggles my cheek and moves the needle
so I don't even see the point before it numbs.

Steffan Triplett

Slumber Party

if there's a shotgun
in the piano room

it is bound to go off.
to play with a gun.

this little one didn't think
it was loaded when she aimed.

it's too difficult to think about
in the head, at a sleepover.

a girl doesn't die right away, she flies
to a city an hour from home.

no one, same as the sky,
will be tried for murder.

mom says to *be safe in summer*
but also *don't sleep so much.*

i don't want to be dead
most of the time.

and when i do there's the news
always reminding: tornadoes & Trayvon.

i wish we had a basement
but i'm glad mom doesn't keep a gun.

i don't trust myself and the
zimmermans always find a way.

when little i wondered if god
ever got tired, *he must be asleep.*

some days, if i could be sucked straight
into heaven, I think maybe I would.

Sequoia Maner

upon reading the autopsy of Sandra Bland

The words of the medical examiner read "the neck
is remarkable for a ligature furrow" / & you are
unwoven by the combination of these two words:
ligature & furrow / because furrow describes a
groove or rut in the ground / or in the surface of
something / like tender skin / because a furrow is a
depression dug out for seeding / how odd the
furrowing set next to "ligature" which derives from
the Latin *ligare* meaning to tie or bind / the word
ligature is tough & flexible / like the larynx / it holds
the state of being bound or stiffened / like the body
in solitary confinement / like the body in rigor
mortis in solitary confinement / it moves beyond the
act of binding to capture the thing that performs the
act of binding / like a cord / or a similar something /
like a plastic bag / but it is also the thread used in
surgery to close a vessel / or remove a tumor / & you
think about how the body is a vessel / & how she had
no tumors / how the trachea is an instrument
moving currents of air into & out of lungs / how in
music a ligature is both the group of notes played as
a phrase & the curved line that indicates such a
phrase / how remarkable is the spine which is line &
curve & holding up all you have ever loved / a single
harmonic texture / & you are reminded of how
language folds into itself / because the word ligature
indicates suspension of intellectual or physical
power / leaves no room for miscarriage or epilepsy
or prayer / not to mention how in typography the
ligature is a character that combines multiple letters /
like the æ in vertebræ / & so many common words
once contained space enough for small couplings /
words like economy & hemorrhage & tragedy &
fetus & federal / & you wonder if Sandra knew that
bound up in her furrowing was a history of how easily
the body rends.

Sequoia Maner

Black Boy Contrapuntal:
For Trayvon Martin

I am American **first** impression: I don't belong here anymore
I have black friends and race is **past** invisible, odd I am treated like
A civic duty: patrolling the block for a **thug** a nuisance: suspended
performing the ritual, **again.** A walk to clear the brain.
He kept looking—staring—relentless **it was raining** drops weighty as bullets
There's been a history of black boys **breaking in** the neighborhood.
They always get away while **walking** and feeling the need to run
suspiciously tall **talking** and feeling the need to yell,
suspiciously boastful— **tasting** something acrid like adrenaline or
blood and refusing to call it **fear** Hidden in hoodies and headphones
but I've seen it rise in their eyes **illegible** body of a man, boy not yet grown
we all learn our lessons
stand ground and **walk** away, refuse the urge to run.

PART II
Hauntings and Reckonings

Danielle Legros Georges

As Falling Star

The impossible task of breathing
      Near guns, breathing and running,

Breathing and standing as still as
      Death is when it closes you off,

When it wraps its arm around you.
      If breathing is living, if breath is

Spirit, what spirit lifts you off
      The earth, not seeing itself so.

Death, behold your
      —Self here as the fear you are.

As the falling stripe. As the falling
      Star.

Danielle Legros Georges

Poem of History

When living your life, you are not *making history*.
Stepping out of your life, you make of it history.

Jamal, doctoral student whose city apartment
I've sublet, has gone this summer to Egypt to write

A story, which is and is not history, gone before
Egypt exploded in history: Its leader pulled down

Like a kite by his people; Jamal in the *foule*,
In the crowd, as it opens its flag of history:

Not amber but action, a lamp glowing in shadows
Of history, like the light of my lamp on Jamal's

Table-turned-desk on which I write history;
His apartment blurred in the heat of summer.

White octagonal tiles and a claw-foot tub govern
The bathroom. I draw water from the waters

Of history, cool and safe from the blood of history;
I draw water from the sink of the kitchen, cool

And clear for the lilies that stand bright as stars
On the table against the white wall by the window.

Outside the grey buildings past the green plaisance,
The University sprawls like a beast. How beautiful

Its lawns, its evening lights. Patrolled by dark
Guards drawn from the dark city's periphery,

An irony not lost on them, posted in inky
Corners, shielding the people of the University

From others like them. Inside and out. The confines
Of safety. The black jungle. The grey jungle.

The towers, the lush avenues, the colossal
Structures. The sources of knowledge.

A dark flower. A guarding of history.

darlene anita scott

A Series of Survivals

I.
These: widow, widower, orphan, alive.
Titles on your back crust to scab.
A convening of cells, protest to scar.
Everything turns. In crisis: food, sleep,
sex, air. The only safe thing to say yes
to is water—only direct from a spring.

You dream & those, in color. Color saturated
to puddle. Drink (if you don't forget) & end
wringing over public toilet after public toilet
you manipulate with elbows & feet while you
try to manage errands & *make it look good*.
These are weekly achievements you tally.

Return calls you avoid like dry shampoo. These days,
dry shampoo & satin pillowcases are or can be water.

II.
Dry shampoo & satin pillowcases are or can be water,
they bounce giddy & crowd your tote. You are mostly
prepared. Each partner's fingertips hesitate on your
waist in lethargic dark-of-predawn desire. This one
snores post-coital content into your shoulder. You crest
the edge of the bed for Orbit gum,
weigh the temptation of escape versus the sate of his kiss.

His fingertips drip from your hip to the sheets. All exits,
doors denying return, maroon you on any Pleasure Island
with reasonable rates. Tonight, his. Your uncle said never
leave money on the table. Take what is available when it is.
You freshen your breath with the gum, back into his groin.

His reflexive embrace rescues your body from the brink.
To feel & be felt surely will unmake the night of your skin & his.

III.
To feel & be felt surely will unmake the night of your skin & his.
Fill your inbox with clumsy tender imagery, cook meals like
spaghetti. He says he has more but he doesn't & you both
know it. Neither of you know where you are going from here.
Neither of you can watch the news without wincing, go breathy
& handsy to manufacture what feels like it's disappearing
fast as the space between the first handshake & the sheets.

Here you are. *Lifetime in a nighttime* he decreed. You dare
the prophecy, collect your things until again is a groove and
you lose grounds for an objection. You hold onto each other
like fear, release with the same verve. Every time he collects
your hair in his hands, buries his nose in it as if to suffocate
himself into the night. *Let's, in the morning.* You challenge:

Why say there is always morning when it's not true?
And so it comes: morning.

IV.

And so it comes: morning. Finds my dad reading
the obituaries. Ours is the tiniest of towns. Promise
of morning has not settled there even. Our side of it
churches & laborers; black & brown; zoned to draw
our children's reach to breach it as cartoon & excuse.
After The South—Vietnam & Virginia, maybe his ritual

is survivor's penance. Maybe, muscle memory—eyes & ears
fine-tuned as the report he repeats about boys same age
as his grandson kidnapped from a late-night corner, curfew
beaten into their bodies in the back of a cruiser, back of The
Lot, by the neighborhood favorite. My dad knows he knew
there were eyes; had no reason for care, fear, surrender.

There are many ways to thin a body, disappear it without
the puff, smoke, or circumstance of its singular & immediate end.

V.

The puff, smoke, circumstance of death's singular & immediate end
instigates me every time. I remember my grandmother announced
her transition by drifting into my second grade sleep. By morning
she was a frog in my father's throat, why I cannot accept that anyone
just stops living yet I've lived enough to know there are some bodies
that are more likely to end. I wonder if morning warned them

it would not be coming. I keep asking my dear friend as if it matters.
She shows up in the brightest red laughing, but offers nothing like
an answer. Her cheeks squeeze her eyes to squint. The gap in her
front teeth still there. In the spell what I want to know goes stale &
irrelevant. In the beginning of her end I tried to ritualize my body
in lavender & offense; to guilt morning—one suffering for another.

Perhaps I'm trying to convince a state of being that triumphs fear.
I've asked more of this body: ways to say die without indicting the will.

VI.

I've asked more of this body: ways to say die without indicting the will.
This body has followed the rules so long a snore escapes its woke mouth
flits from one not-random thought to another: Am I the only one who has
ever had to deny her body its wisdom yet found it stiff as an unread book
spine unwilling to yield & crumbling before or by the time it's asked to bend?
Another: here in the same bathroom window & behind the same bedroom
door she covers each part of herself like bathing a baby. Bare only the limb
being handled. There were eyes in the windows & doors. Soul pick planted

in an afro impossibly round & sparkling in commercials for 7-Up & Afro Sheen
between Soul Train segments on Saturdays. Who else is allowed to remember
This but not That? And another—But the day won't wait like the years haven't.

He reaches for me in habit. It's too hot to touch more than legs.
Loose braid our ankles; my snore with his sleep.
This memory twisted & tucked to seal its unraveling.

VII.
This memory twisted & tucked to seal its unraveling:
This fourteen year old fable, four centuries of fast.
This memory held in the swell of her; the way she moves.
In her defense she is Magic: wonder & changeling trained
to disappear warm bodies. Whoever heard of a girl
who owned Desire except she be a witch? So they seize

& crush her for mosaics & murals: rename her shame, Beauty.
This clay parable they passed between them like a Communion
chalice; claimed she assimilated her Desire like a sacrament.
It made sense: This is where fast girls get their speed. How to
lubricate the clay for molding. This is how to make good girls.

(Uneven drying causes tension that compels cracks).
If you want good your hands must become God's.

VIII.
If you want good, your hands must become God's;
voice a cracking whip, awe of lightening. If the child
finds a hiding place you draw them with threats
worse than harm. If you want them good it has
to be this way. She wants you good; has this since
she can't give what she has no means to make.

Pounding & kneading, she forms you elastic & palatable.
Those hands, those hands that wring before the phone
can finish its trill; those hands end in self-stick crystals
scraping you, scraping by; those hands scrub the smell
of char on you where the scent of child should be. Fingers
are some of the lushest expanse of nerves on the body,

a rich source of tactile feedback. Have to answer
what they hear when she calls you *Mine*.

IX.

What they hear when she calls you *Mine*:

Tillandsia:

genus with a minimally apparent root system;

propensity to manage wherever conditions permit;

not very resistant to extreme cold. Then, they are

Decedent, Too Soon, A Shame.

Common pollinators are bats—valued in their ecosystems

for fertilizing flowers & dispersing seeds; plus reservoirs

of pathogens. They readily spread disease because they are

highly mobile & social.

Disease:

disruption to order in the body's ecosystem; activated by

external stress; then, they are SuperPredator, Epidemic,

airbrushed caricatures captioned with improper names.

X.

Airbrushed caricatures captioned with improper names; listed
like infographics connected crisp & modern with an ampersand
are poor whispers on cotton shirts that leave spittle suspended
in air or land against the skin like buckshot. Announcements we
wear against our skin like placards: I Am A Man. But mostly we
are boys & girls, loud as hungry baby birds; hairless, cold, extend
-ed necks reaching so eager for life we threaten to tip our nests.

Too often we do. And the nests get decorated with bottles, bears
notes of never forget or 'til we meet agains. Crowns chip & tilt.
Ever wondered if forgetting is the sip in the fountain of youth?
If hungry baby birds feed on themselves? Ever worn a placard
against your still beating heart? This is just to say: After enough
rains even murals fade. This is just to say: After enough blows
a lot of people become debilitated.*

*Reed-Veal, Geneva. "Reform Must Be Sandra Bland's Legacy."
The Daily Herald. 16 May 2016.

XI.

A lot of people become debilitated.
★★insert Venida Browder★★

A lot of people become angry.
★★insert Micah Johnson★★

there are even more ways
to make us the enemy,
★★insert Ramsay Orta★★

even more ways to make us disappear.
★★insert Korryn Gaines★★

Have we any right to make human souls★
face what we face today?
★★insert Kodi & Karsyn ★★

Ought children be born to us?
★★insert Dae'Ana★★

★DuBois, W.E.B. "On the Passing of the First Born." *The Souls of Black Folk.*
(New York, Norton: 1999). 130–134.

XII.

insert Dae'Ana

I don't want you to get shooted
she requests her mother's shelter & doom
like she did at birth. Babies often erupt
into the world so violently they rip mothers.
Kind of like a bullet disrupting the caucus of cells,
curious vector surveying options. They tear, require
stitching, scar for the best adventure stories. The body
is an assortment of defense mechanisms: during infection
or pregnancy white blood cells mobilize to protect. They gather
& plump face, hands, feet. In rapid blood loss like from discharging
a projectile or baby, the vascular system shuttles blood from extremities
to core forcing blood to vital organs like babies survive to save us, their shelter
& doom.

XIII.

& doom
costumes in new teeth that won't fit in their mouths yet
incongruent laughter against attack of jax & each other
on the blacktop; or as liquid as bodies spilling from pews
into organ chords; or composed swilling like the sound
of sea in shells on mantles next to their toothy photos
unremembering quietly as the temperate ocean. Or
untangling like knots of hair from a barrette after
a full day of holding on; or like a law of physics:
In Entanglement everything is connected from
beginnings of earth; all of us emerging from
same energy & air; as wish or shame. Maybe
how prayer works; possibility of faith. How
you are a new body & without yours so am I.

XIV.

The Chinese symbol for crisis is a combination
of two words: danger & opportunity. Turns out,
this is a Western mistranslation. But let's take
Sanskrit. The word for crisis is *sankata*—difficulty;
contracted, narrow. In yoga, we hold onto *sankatasana*—
difficult pose—for its ability to heal the body's defense—
inflammation, its zeal to protect warm & painful in the joints.

Ask the practitioner to be aware of the pose's danger
if handled without proper care as well as its ability
to at ease the army in full formation in their joints:
1. Maintain balance while focused on a fixed point.
2. Gaze at the point; keep the body straight.
3. Stay in the pose for at least thirty seconds.
What does it do to a body to hold the pose, for say, a lifetime?

XV.
And so it comes: morning. Finds my dad reading
airbrushed caricatures captioned with improper names,
the puff, smoke, circumstance of death's singular & immediate end.
I've asked more of this body, ways to say die without indicting the will.
These days, dry shampoo & satin pillowcases are, or can be, water.
To feel & be felt will surely unmake the night of your skin & his.
What does it do to a body to hold the pain for, say, a lifetime?
This memory twisted & tucked to seal its unraveling.
If you want good, your hands must become God's.
You are a new body and without yours, so am I.
These: widow, widower, orphan, alive.
insert Dae'ana
& doom.

Sean Murphy

Bud Powell's Brain

Was it that hard-boiled cop's unindicted Nightstick
that scrambled your system, sending misfired messages
into the soft-wiring that polices ungovernable impulses?

Or was collateral damage already done? Chemistry coalescing
the onset of sickness, like a chick pecking through its shell?

Uno Poco Loco: an epitaph for stillborn souls that can't
escape the yoke of adversity; Nature's always improvising,
uninterested in excuses, or anything that could plausibly explain
the roots of Squares—and circumstances of those serving them.

Poached forever by the eyes of the White and the Other
Color, printed in numbers on top of paper pyramids:
E Pluribus Unum—a private club you're forbidden entrance,
even decades after your death, a pitch black Ever After
that tastes and smells like vanilla extract and crackers, Jack.

This world's never been accommodating to hard cases, helpless
to understand languages they're confusedly fluent in, and
like a conjoined twin, it smothers thoughts and steals oxygen
from a disobedient brain, inflamed by anger or alcohol or
something stronger, risky antidotes for those inscrutable squawks
you'll transcribe for anyone, willing to open their ears
and better still, their wallets:
Fat fortresses dispensing the only justice
served after last call.

Something you can score, like love
or junk in any back alley.

Unless you can't
afford the going rate.
Which means, like always:
You're broke.

Sarah Giragosian

Nina

In memory of Nina Simone

A piano can be a weapon:
        cold iron, hammer, trigger—
you mastered it, blew us up
                with your love.

We're born into blood
not our own, and we need you to speak its story.
Tell us about the curse
        they place over our hearts,
                translate the wishbones we hide in our throats
                        for safekeeping until the right one comes around.

                Come back tonight, sing us into being again.

Come back with your hammer and keys.
        I want to startle at the devastated world,
                its aromas and blues,
                        and at you, the one,
                                dancing your rage.

Enrobe me in song,
        send me back into the world,
                armed this time against its cages.

5

BLACK LIVES MATTER AND LEGAL RECONSTRUCTIONS OF ELEGIAC FORMS

Almas Khan[1]

"The veil of legality, the bare image of law, hides innumerable traumas of enforcement and of powerlessness. Law's rites, vestments, ceremonies, and texts depict the face or screen of a series of institutional violences. . . . Law reflected violence and it instituted violence, and its context or other surface of inscription was precisely that of the body."

Peter Goodrich, Oedipus Lex: Psychoanalysis, History, Law[2]

Peter Goodrich's hauntological account of the relationships between legal forms and disempowered groups' lives evokes the elegy's central concern: the body as a signifier. Like earlier racial justice movements, Black Lives Matter has exposed the institutional violences inflicted upon African Americans and mourned the legal and social devaluation of black bodies, while seeking to engender a "politics of recuperation"[3] for the living. Law has been arguably the single institution most liable for creating the conditions giving rise to Black Lives Matter, with the original Constitution's 3/5ths clause devaluing enslaved peoples as part of the body politic.[4] The legacy of such laws today includes police and civilian brutality toward unarmed African Americans, mass incarceration policies that disproportionately harm black communities,[5] and police intervention in incidents involving African Americans doing ordinary activities.[6] In 2011, a year before the Trayvon Martin murder that catalyzed Black Lives Matter, poet-lawyer Evie Shockley accordingly ruminated, "i sometimes wonder how i get away with living while black."[7]

Black poet-lawyers in prior racial justice movements likely shared Shockley's dejection, but by welding artistic and legal activism, their lives show how elegiac emotions may be harnessed to both transform popular consciousness and dismantle racist legal structures. African American lawyers have been seen as "representing the race" to a predominantly white American public, negotiating between racial communities to secure equal rights.[8] Black poet-lawyers, many of whom wrote in elegiac forms, were at the forefront of earlier racial justice movements, including George Vashon in the abolitionist period, James Weldon Johnson and Richard E. S. Toomey in the early to mid-twentieth century, and Pauli Murray during the civil rights movement and its aftermath.[9] Contemporary black poet-lawyers like Simone White, Marlene NourbeSe Philip, Reginald Dwayne Betts, Evie Shockley, and Judge Damon J. Keith have carried on this tradition of creatively fusing legal and poetic work. In light of the inception of Black Lives Matter and the Donald Trump presidency,[10] these poet-lawyers' texts attest to the urgency of revolutionizing epistemologies and laws.

Through scrutinizing the elegiac oeuvre of Betts, Shockley, and Judge Keith,[11] who were born in 1980, 1965, and 1922, respectively, spanning three generations from the Jim Crow and civil rights eras through today, this chapter will illuminate how the poet-lawyers' dual disciplinary training in the humanities and law has molded their writings on racial justice. Each author entwines the elegy with another form: for Betts, the prison memoir; for Shockley, experimental poetry; and for Judge Keith, the judicial opinion. The writers then adapt these hybrid forms for the dual purposes of communal fortification and legal critique. By legalizing poetry and poeticizing law, Betts, Shockley, and Judge Keith expand the elegy's power to directly impact the development of equal rights for people of color. Aside from contributing to this volume's enrichment of scholarship about the African American elegiac tradition,[12] this chapter will demonstrate how iconoclastic poetics synergizes with contemporary critical legal movements that champion racial equality and criminal justice reform.

Critical race theory will infuse the following analysis, which reflects the authors' sympathies for Derrick Bell's pessimistic theory of "racial realism."[13] The theory initially requires African Americans to *"acknowledge the permanence of our subordinate status"*[14] (italics in original). Bell, though, offers a silver lining; he affirms that the acknowledgment of African Americans' realistic inability to attain equality with whites within existing legal structures *"enables us to avoid despair, and frees us to imagine and implement racial strategies that can bring fulfillment and even triumph"*[15] (italics in original). Exercising imaginative powers to reconstruct language as a preliminary step to reconstructing reality is an undercurrent in Betts's, Shockley's, and Judge Keith's texts. Their works continue in the line of Patricia Williams's formally path-breaking *Alchemy of Race and Rights: Diary of a Law Professor*[16] and adapt Brittney C. Cooper's theory of "embodied discourse" in black feminism to new contexts.[17] While the ultimate question raised by the texts that I assess—in Fred Moten's words, "What's the relation between political despair and mourning?"[18]—eludes definitive resolution, intellectual activist black poet-lawyers writing today are uniquely situated to provide an incisive response.[19]

Reginald Dwayne Betts: Prison Elegies and the New Abolitionism

Reginald Dwayne Betts's life trajectory mirrors that of a conventional elegy, starting with his loss of self, family, and community after being imprisoned for eight years as a young adult. In spite of his experiences, Betts has through creative writing and legal activism cultivated hope for himself and those similarly situated. Betts's prose and poetry can be deemed prison elegies rooted in two genres with a deep vintage in African American literature, the elegy and the prison memoir.[20] Betts's autobiography, *A Question of Freedom: A Memoir of Learning, Survival, and Coming of Age in Prison* (2009), narrates the tragic events of his life leading up to and during his imprisonment.[21] His poetry collections *Shahid Reads His Own Palm* (2010) and *Bastards of the Reagan Era* (2015) are comprised largely of elegies that thematically echo his memoir.[22] These texts underscore how freedom remains a question for many African Americans, to allude to the memoir's title. The volumes also delineate how Betts's literary work complements his legal work, which began with helping fellow incarcerated men file petitions for *habeas corpus* (a constitutional right to challenge the validity of detention), and now includes serving as a public defender and advocating for criminal justice reform.[23] Connecting his legal and poetic writings, Betts has commented: "Law is parallel to poetry. It's an occupation with words. Lawyers are really good with words and, at its best, law is about some kind of sense of justice, some kind of sense of truth. And I think that is what poetry is about, too, at its best."[24]

Betts's prison memoir is "the story of my absence,"[25] and the book describes his childhood in a racially segregated community near Washington, D.C., where stories of excessive police violence against African Americans abounded in the 1980s and 1990s. In 1996, when he was 16, Betts and a friend were arrested for robbing and carjacking a white man after Betts tapped on the window of the victim's car with a gun. Betts was charged with six felonies, certified as an adult for sentencing purposes, and sentenced to over half his then-life in prison following his confession to the crimes. He was shipped between facilities and systematically dehumanized, especially at a supermax prison constructed to house the most (allegedly) irredeemable of criminals.[26] Summarizing his prison experiences, and those of black men who constituted the vast majority of incarcerated people he encountered, Betts would later remark: "We were just black bodies surrounded by white officers."[27] Writing became Betts's "major rehabilitative tool," and Dudley Randall's anthology *The Black Poets* inspired him to become a poet "for the dudes around me."[28] Since his release from prison in 2004, Betts's academic honors have included a B.A. from the University of Maryland, an M.F.A. from Warren Wilson College, and a J.D. from Yale Law School.[29] Having been admitted to the Connecticut bar after initially being denied entry because of his criminal record, he is pursuing a Ph.D. in Law from Yale and working on a book about criminal justice as an Emerson Fellow at New America.[30]

Even with his achievements, the overarching theme of Betts's two poetry collections is that African Americans, particularly black men, are "lost in place," to quote from an elegy for his imprisoned brother.[31] Betts credits the phrase to his father's generation, suggesting an inheritance of both language and melancholia. For speakers in elegies generally, being "lost in place" may refer to a feeling of physical and psychic displacement after a loss. In the context of African American experiences, the phrase may allude to W. E. B. Du Bois's concept of double-consciousness,[32] suggesting the tragic nature of black self-perception despite constitutional ideals of liberty and equality. Betts's first volume of poetry, *Shahid Reads His Own Palm*, is an introspective approach to the elegiac dilemma of being "lost in place," while his subsequent *Bastards of the Reagan Era* shows Betts reading the national palm in a series of searing elegies.

The title of his debut volume reflects Betts's renaming in prison, when he began to call himself *Shahid* after learning the Arabic term denotes a martyr or witness;[33] the poems evince Betts assuming both roles. Among the 48 poems in the collection, five are *ghazals*. The *ghazal* is a form that began in ancient Arabia as a poem of pain upon the speaker's losing the beloved, but it has since become a global form expanded to topics that include politics.[34] One of the book's *ghazals* questions whether Betts acted meaningfully of his free will when participating in the juvenile carjacking that led to his imprisonment, or whether structural racism meant that he was "born with sessile chains" that constrained his choice.[35]

Betts's poems also evidence judges generally unsympathetic to claims that poverty and racism influenced defendants' decisions, imposing lengthy terms upon black youth after deeming them incorrigible.[36] The poems further portray how such prison sentences are a living death for the men and their families.[37] Imagery and diction recurringly associate prisons with *memento mori*, and several poems assume the perspective of family members mourning the loss of an incarcerated young black man similarly to how they would have mourned his physical death. As the poem "One Grave" concludes, "the whole prison is a grave"[38] for defendants and their families. Mothers and fathers of imprisoned black men are meanwhile depicted as spectral figures, haunting the spaces their sons once lived and being unable to banish thoughts of parental failure.

The poem "Near Nightfall" employs the second-person pronoun "you" to place the reader in the position of an incarcerated black youth's bereaved mother.[39] While his untidy bedroom with a television on suggests his return, "he is gone," a reality that causes the mother/reader to recall happier times like the son's first word and a photograph of him in an oversized cap and Kool-Aid stains on his face.[40] These memories contrast with the image opening the poem, of "a body in white chalk" referencing a crime scene.[41] Another poem, "A Father Talks to Himself," uses the first-person pronoun "I" to embed the reader in the mind of a father regretful for not better parenting his incarcerated black son.[42] The father's digging into barren land to plant grass morphs into a probing of his own mind and culpability for his son's imprisonment, given the father's prior incarceration. Visualizing his son suffering in prison, the father expresses anguish for not teaching his son to treat obstacles as opportunities, or metaphorically, as rain that replenishes grass.[43] The poem's imagery and syntax allude to T. S. Eliot's *The Waste Land* (1922), which begins with a section titled "The Burial of the Dead."[44] Like Eliot's poem, Betts's poem is set in April, when the sun is said to "cut[] shadows / into dead men on grass and gravel."[45] In adapting one of Anglo-American literature's major elegiac poems to the experiences of imprisoned black men and their families, Betts dignifies their lives and, to paraphrase *The Waste Land*, shores his poetic fragments against their ruins.[46]

Shahid and *A Question of Freedom* thus undermine stereotypes about incarcerated African American men and their families lacking humanity, as does Betts's *Bastards of the Reagan Era*, published after the emergence of the Black Lives Matter movement. The word "bastard" in the book's title literally refers to a child born to unmarried parents, and figuratively to Betts and other black youth regarded as illegitimate citizens of the nation. The volume depicts how the African American community endured grievous casualties during President Ronald Reagan's War on Drugs, with black defendants being disproportionately imprisoned on drug charges and often given inordinate sentences.[47] The book's provocative title signals a change in tone from *Shahid*; the earlier text's predominantly mournful tone is diminished while rage is amplified in the successor volume. Indeed, the collection's title poem ends with a section entitled "Prophets of Rage."[48] Rage pervades the text's four named elegies, in addition to the 11 poems (almost half of the volume's 23 poems) titled "For the City That Nearly Broke Me."[49] The apostrophized city is Washington, D.C., a symbol of national ideals and the heart of federal lawmaking but also the site of seemingly intractable racial inequalities.[50] The city's failure to set an example for the nation signifies the magnitude of the challenge in reversing the communal damage wrought by the War on Drugs and centuries of racist laws and customs.

The eponymous "Bastards of the Reagan Era," which Betts calls a "dirge" or song for the dead,[51] shares *The Waste Land*'s ambition of mourning a lost generation of men wounded by war, and the poem's allusiveness would have impressed Eliot. Betts contemplates how the plight of African American men from his generation compares with that of Africans treated as cargo during the Middle Passage and their descendants, who rebelled against slavery (e.g., Nat Turner), strove to combat Jim Crow laws, and were martyred during the civil rights movement.[52] It is within this historical context of systematic racial oppression that contemporary laws which disparately harm African Americans must be evaluated, the poem affirms. Another poem, "Crimson," juxtaposes Rodney King's beating by police in 1991 to Betts's brother's flight from crime and recollects the family's fear upon not hearing from the youth that he could be King.[53] A traumatic affinity between the men arises from a mutual history of oppression.

Despite the volume's somber tone, Betts in "Elegy With a City in It" asserts that his poem's center "is more than a dead black / man,"[54] a statement that applies more expansively to his literary writings. Consolation for Betts resides partially in the prospect of readers funneling their outrage into advocacy for legal reforms like prison abolition.[55] More profoundly, though, solace comes from community, embodied here by Betts's wife and his sons representing a rising generation, "Because some don't understand that black love is black wealth, but we do."[56]

Evie Shockley: Re-forming the Elegy, History, and Law for Racial Justice

While Reginald Dwayne Betts's prison elegies mesh the elegy and prison memoir genres and are shaped by his experiences in incarceration, Evie Shockley's elegies blend elegy conventions with those of black experimental poetry,[57] which Shockley views as a tool for racial justice. Shockley recently taught a poetry workshop in prison, and like Betts she endeavors to "write poems about subjects that we want people to think about, poems that will inspire and encourage activists, poems that remember what must not be forgotten."[58] Although Shockley is currently an English professor at Rutgers University—New Brunswick, her professional career began in law. As befitting a child of the civil rights movement, she earned a J.D. from the University of Michigan Law School and secured a federal circuit court clerkship with African American judge Nathaniel R. Jones.[59] Judge Jones is an internationally acclaimed civil rights activist who served as general counsel for the National Association for the Advancement of Colored People before being appointed to the judiciary.[60] Shockley's poetry supplements Judge Jones's racial justice work in the courts, seeking to persuade in the court of public opinion as a means of laying the groundwork for legal, political, and social reforms. Like Betts, Shockley attributes her poetry's verbal virtuosity in part to her legal training, which included learning about "the malleability of language, the importance of defining meaning, the usefulness of etymology, and the extent to which context determines meaning."[61] Shockley has linked law and literature conceptually in her poetry over the past two decades.

Shockley's poetry collections include *a half-red sea* (2005), *the new black* (2011), and *semiautomatic* (2017).[62] Among other subjects, the volumes reflect Shockley's intersectional heritages as a black woman from the South (Nashville, Tennessee) in the vexed contexts of U.S. history, love, and poetic creation. *the new black* was published in the aftermath of President Barack Obama's historic 2008 election as the first African American president. The book meditates on black lives over the long arc of U.S. history and expresses hope but also misgivings about the potential for racial equality in the future. *semiautomatic* is less sanguine; published in the wake of, and in direct response to, the emergence of Black Lives Matter, the book contains several elegies for African Americans unjustly slain by police and civilians. The volume's formal audacity, including call-outs to readers, and transnational vision signify the necessity of a global movement to promote racial justice that begins with ordinary people's change in perspectives.

"from *topsy in wonderland*," a poem in *semiautomatic* combining Shockley's text with illustrations by Alison Saar, reads as a tragic allegory of African Americans' struggle for equal citizenship.[63] Much like Betts did with the term "bastards," Shockley appropriates a pejorative moniker, Topsy. The poem recasts the seemingly wild but ultimately tamed enslaved girl from Harriet Beecher Stowe's *Uncle Tom's Cabin* (1852)[64] as an epitome of the nation's failure to actualize egalitarian ideals. Topsy is featured in the role of Alice trapped in wonderland.[65] There, she perseveres to climb a mountain to reach freedom, despite being thwarted constantly by white characters. These personages include an entrepreneur, a gatekeeper, and a queen who informs Topsy that to stay in the same place the girl must run with full effort and that to get elsewhere she must run at least twice as fast, paraphrasing an African American aphorism.[66] The dialogue belies the rhetoric of meritocratic advancement that remains gospel among much of the American public, in spite of ample contrary evidence.[67] In the poem's denouement, Topsy resists being consigned to a position as a mistress's maid, yet she is pictured with cotton bolls in her hair, signifying slavery's lingering damage to black bodies and lives.[68] Topsy is finally denied freedom in the present; the theoretical freedoms of the past and future are all she will receive in wonderland.[69]

The final page of the volume's section on Topsy contains the following damning single line: "now, reader, let's consider who dreamed it all. . . ."[70] "*topsy*" thus poignantly renders a leitmotif of Shockley's verse: How whitewashed versions of U.S. history impede progress on racial equality by both perpetuating a myth of white innocence and marginalizing African American achievements. In addition to deconstructing problematic national mythologies, Shockley's poems present affirmative histories elegizing black lives that have often been overlooked in dominant accounts from the colonial and founding periods onward.

One of these revisionary historical poems is "*dependencies*," from Shockley's collection *the new black*, the first page of which is reproduced on the next page.[71]

The poem foregrounds the stories of enslaved people owned by the Founding Fathers, notably Thomas Jefferson. Jefferson, a lawyer, is popularly lauded as the author of the Declaration of Independence, third president of the United States, and founder of the University of Virginia. In his private life, however, Jefferson enslaved hundreds of African Americans and raped enslaved women, most famously his wife's half-sister Sally Hemings.[72] After his death, the enslaved people on his Monticello estate were sold to satisfy his debts, sundering families. "*dependencies*" formally and substantively confronts this hypocrisy between the public and private Jeffersons, for the poem's visual resemblance to a register evokes the records of enslaved African Americans that Jefferson kept.[73] The poem's right side reproduces the Declaration's paean to equality while the left captures Shockley vicariously talking back to Jefferson as a black woman. The interpolated text spanning the page, such as the passage defining "*dependencies*" as "*areas for domestic work*," is quoted from a brochure that Shockley received when visiting Monticello.[74] The brochure's language is more anodyne than Shockley's commentary,

dependencies

visiting monticello was
an education   of course   you
named your home in a romance
language   spent 40 years
constructing it   and the myth
of yourself

we hold these truths

(freedom)

you designed your home on aesthetic
and scientific principles   maximizing   space
in the main house   by placing
the dependencies   beneath   and behind
it   built into the hillside   half
underground

to be self

*These "dependencies," or areas for domestic work, served as points of
intersection between Jefferson's family and enslaved people, and were
instrumental to the functioning of the house.*

-evident, that

i hear you loved
wine (we have that in common)
you had a cellar full of french
vintage you drew up
to the dining room   via
a dumbwaiter that ran between

which observes that dependencies were submerged partially to maximize space for the main house. This fact functions as a metaphor for the semi-buried status of enslaved peoples in the body politic.[75] The brochure nonetheless remarks, albeit with a different meaning, that dependencies remained "*instrumental to the functioning of the house*," i.e., nation.

In destabilizing traditional understandings of U.S. history, "*dependencies*" unmasks the white-supremacist origins of the legal, political, and academic orders, prompting readers to ponder the legacies of the Founding Fathers' flawed democratic vision, including racial injustices spectering the present.[76] Over 150 years after the Emancipation Proclamation, slavery remains an open wound in Shockley's poems, echoing Betts's comparison of prisons to slave ships.[77] Rehistoricization in the poets' elegies provides the intellectual infrastructure for the Black Lives Matter movement, which strives to extirpate the anti-black ideology that has manifested in police and civilian violence directed at unarmed African Americans.

semiautomatic includes several elegies for these victims, including "a-lyrical ballad (or, how america reminds us of the value of family)" and "buried truths."[78] A note to the former poem cites the influence of black elegists Douglas Kearney, Claudia Rankine, Marilyn Nelson, and Gwendolyn Brooks.[79] The poem catalogs tragic black deaths starting with Emmett Till (1955) and Amadou Diallo (1999) to contemporary times with Trayvon Marton (2012), Rekia Boyd (2012), Renisha McBride (2013), Tamir Rice (2014), and Sandra Bland (2015).[80] "a-lyrical ballad," though, omits names, suggesting the victims' representativeness. Each summary of the events culminating in the victim's death ends with a refrain of mourning, and the poem concludes with the line "*and another family's bereaved ~ o ~ the black family be grieved*," with the lack of a period at the line's close signifying that the laments and premature burials will continue.[81]

The poem "buried truths," which is reproduced on the next page, meanwhile recalls the graveyard poetry tradition[82] in simulating a crypt.

Approximately equal symbols (≈) are the building blocks for each chamber of the crypt, in which a stanza is substituted for a coffin. The poem alludes to several of the victims in "a-lyrical ballad," in addition to Sean Bell (2006), Tarika Wilson (2008), Mark Duggan (2011), Jordan Davis (2012), Eric Garner (2014), Jermaine Carby (2014), and Freddie Gray (2015).[83] While media coverage has often demonized and criminalized the victims,[84] "buried truths" aims to resuscitate their reputations and to instigate the living to ensure the deaths are not in vain. Each stanza represents the deceased as a vibrant, galvanizing presence, such as this stanza addressing Freddie Gray: "are you not the young life ready / to explode from the wet shell of gray / into riotous mobtown flower?"[85] Readers are encouraged to answer this question affirmatively by protesting and preventing similar tragedies.

Exercising constitutional rights, particularly First Amendment rights, is seen as key to advancing racial justice in a later poem from *semiautomatic*, "of speech."[86] The poem was inspired by a rally commemorating Eric Garner's death in which

buried truths

≈≈
≈≈
≈≈
≈≈
≈≈
≈≈

≈≈ are you not the sweet to rave on   ≈   are you not the cold drama do- ≈≈
≈≈ and on about, the smart in   ≈   ing hot duty, the remedy aloe ≈≈
≈≈ the sore, the phantasy so near,   ≈   salving new york city's forty-one ≈≈
≈≈ so far from dark disney's phantom?   ≈   gaping pus-filled wounds? ≈≈
≈≈

≈≈
≈≈ are you not the river jordan   ≈   are you not the crimson mark ≈≈
≈≈ we must cross this very day, vis-   ≈ circling the crater white brits dug in ≈≈
≈≈ ceral evidence of florida's abyss?   ≈   the brown earth of tottenham? ≈≈
≈≈

≈≈ are you not the handfuls of rice   ≈ are you not the filamentary niche, a ≈≈
≈≈ thrown up in cleveland's tame air,   ≈   sign of how fear will make bride ≈≈
≈≈ a cloud raining sharply down   ≈   of blood, how it motors cities, ≈≈
≈≈ that will not be swept away?   ≈   flaming, right off the map? ≈≈
≈≈

≈≈
≈≈ are you not the silvery key, a   ≈   are you not the atmospheric ≈≈
≈≈ raft rigged with new vines, buoyed   ≈ rush to infuse lungs dying to garner ≈≈
≈≈ by bronzeville's kitchenette arias?   ≈   inspiring staten island breezes? ≈≈
≈≈

≈≈
≈≈ are you not the fertile mystery ca-   ≈   are you not the jet stream germane ≈≈
≈≈ joling hope, despite narrow ills, on   ≈   to the question of whose scar be- ≈≈
≈≈ a half-plucked wing and a half-heard ≈ comes whose scare, screams or tires ≈≈
≈≈ prayer in lima, ohio's wasted land?   ≈   peeling on greater toronto streets? ≈≈
≈≈

≈≈
≈≈ are you not the music's ignition,   ≈   are you not the young life ready ≈≈
≈≈ the beat, the bass, and the bell   ≈ to explode from the wet shell of gray ≈≈
≈≈ sounding new york's belated alarm?   ≈   into riotous mobtown flower? ≈≈
≈≈
≈≈
≈≈≈≈≈≈≈≈≈≈≈≈≈≈≈≈≈≈≈≈≈≈≈≈≈≈≈≈≈≈≈≈≈≈≈≈≈≈ —*after keorapetse kgositsile* ≈
≈≈

protestors marching to New York Police Department headquarters were confronted by officers. While conceding police possess the force of law, the poem closes with a panegyric to freedom of speech, namely ordinary peoples' power to effect change without violence through expression: "one freedom / led to another."[87] This passage can be construed as an *ars poetica* for Shockley's poetry, in which experimental forms complement public protests against systemic racism by inciting readers to critically question U.S. history and the nation's legal system. Shockley, like Betts, thus participates in a constitutional tradition of dissent dating to the abolitionist period with Frederick Douglass's orations.[88] Channeling Douglass toward the end of his life in "*from* The Lost Letters of Frederick Douglass," Shockley enthuses about how reading and writing "retain / the thrill of danger even now."[89] The formal subversiveness of Shockley's elegies challenges epistemologies sustaining racism with the ultimate ambition of fulfilling the civil rights movement's promise.

Judge Damon Keith: Judicial Reconfigurations of the Elegy and the Third Reconstruction

Although the judicial opinion may appear to be an unlikely site of elegiac innovation supporting the Black Lives Matter movement's objectives, Judge Damon Keith's transformation of the genre epitomizes how the black elegiac tradition can become a fount for racial justice in and beyond the judiciary. Judge Keith lived for almost a century encompassing the Jim Crow and civil rights eras until his death in April 2019.[90] He rose to become a senior judge on the U.S. Court of Appeals for the Sixth Circuit and served over 50 years in the federal judiciary, authoring several landmark civil rights and civil liberties decisions during his tenure.[91] Judge Keith was taught by Thurgood Marshall at Howard University School of Law in the 1940s, and he recalled the future Supreme Court justice then saying, in reference to the phrase "equal justice under law" carved on the Supreme Court building: "The White men wrote those four words. When you leave Howard, I want you to go out and practice law and see what you can do to enforce those four words."[92] Like Justice Marshall, Judge Keith was an *éminence grise* in the African American legal community, having mentored numerous black lawyers and judges.[93]

The Judge's dissenting opinion in a recent voting rights case, *Northeast Ohio Coalition for the Homeless v. Husted* (2016),[94] exemplifies his legacy. The opinion most notably violates genre norms by interpolating a gallery of innocents slain during the civil rights movement, resembling how Evie Shockley catalogs Black Lives Matter victims in her elegies.

Husted's importance derives from voting being symbolically, and arguably also substantively, the most cherished right in American democracy. Voting rights are enshrined in three constitutional amendments that collectively demonstrate the expansion of the franchise emblematic of national progress toward equal justice.[95]

Nonetheless, despite scant evidence of voter fraud, state measures restricting vot-ing rights have recently proliferated;[96] the laws functionally revive the poll taxes of yesteryear.[97] In *Husted*, homeless rights organizations were among those oppos-ing Ohio voting laws that included tightened technical requirements for ballots which, in effect, disadvantaged illiterate and impoverished citizens. A majority on the Sixth Circuit largely upheld the contested laws, but Judge Keith penned a moving and formally intrepid dissent. Conscientious dissenting opinions have throughout American history shaped law's evolution, "giv[ing] sight to the blind" and "heal[ing] institutional blindness,"[98] and Judge Keith's widely publicized dis-sent[99] may well become part of this esteemed tradition.

Instead of commencing with an abstruse legal discussion, Judge Keith began the main body of his dissent with an elegiac historical background section titled "The Martyrdom and Struggle for Equal Protection."[100] Justifying his bold decision, the Judge explained: "I add the following publicly available historical statements to humanize the struggle for the right to be equal participants in the democratic process."[101] What appears next is an 11-page gallery placing photos of victims murdered by white supremacists during the civil rights revolution alongside sum-maries of the brutal circumstances leading to their death.[102] One of these gallery entries is a graduation photograph of 26-year-old Jimmie Lee Jackson. Unarmed at the time of his death in 1965, Jackson was shot by state troopers while protect-ing his family from a trooper attack on civil rights marchers. His death impelled the federal government to enact the Voting Rights Act of 1965, the statute at issue in *Husted*.[103] Judge Keith's prose elegy enfleshes the statutory language and, like Reginald Dwayne Betts's and Evie Shockley's verse elegies, reveals African Amer-icans' fraught relationship with legal institutions as both sources of solace and sorrow. The Judge's peroration to his opinion aptly warned readers: "With every gain in equality, there is an equally robust and reactive retrenchment. . . . [W]e can never fool ourselves into believing that we have arrived as a nation."[104]

Judge Keith ultimately reposed faith not in courts, but a public "we," to vigi-lantly guard legal rights, and black poet-lawyers have been keepers of the flame since abolitionism. Like their predecessors, African American poet-lawyers writ-ing today have sought to wrench the historically white, elite form of the English elegy from its roots, as a literary analog of what they have striven to do with the Constitution. Formal insurrection in their elegies has connoted substantive oppo-sition to a legal order that has fostered the inequitable conditions necessitating movements like Black Lives Matter. During the civil rights revolution, Native American rights attorney and legal philosopher Felix Cohen recognized lawyers' especial responsibility to awaken the public's consciousness about injustices. His address for a symposium on "Ethical Values and the Law in Action" captures the ethos of contemporary African American poet-lawyers to "broaden[] the con-sciousness of the ways in which we fail to meet those [i.e., constitutional] hopes" but to "keep[] alive the vision of our country's highest hopes and deepest aspira-tions."[105] Elegies have long mingled mourning with hope, and by integrating legal critiques into elegiac forms, Judge Damon Keith, Evie Shockley, and Reginald Dwayne Betts espouse a poetics of action. As creative prophets of a Third Reconstruction, black poet-lawyers like them are in the vanguard leading American law and society, step by laborious step, toward the promised land.

Notes

1. This chapter is dedicated to Judge Damon J. Keith (July 4, 1922–April 28, 2019), whose life epitomized Black Lives Matter principles in practice.
2. Peter Goodrich, *Oedipus Lex: Psychoanalysis, History, Law* (Berkeley: University of California Press, 1995), 68.
3. Ibid., x–xi.
4. The clause originally read: "Representatives and direct Taxes shall be apportioned among the several States which may be included within this Union, according to their respective Numbers, which shall be determined by adding to the whole Number of free Persons, including those bound to Service for a Term of Years, and excluding Indians not taxed, three fifths of all other Persons." The provision came into force with the Constitution's ratification in 1788 and was later nullified by the Thirteenth Amendment, which abolished slavery, in 1865.
5. Michelle Alexander, *The New Jim Crow: Mass Incarceration in the Age of Colorblindness* (New York: New Press, 2010).
6. As cataloged in Evie Shockley's poem *improper(ty) behavior*, in Evie Shockley, *the new black* (Middletown, CT: Wesleyan University Press, 2011), 60.
7. Ibid.
8. Kenneth W. Mack, *Representing the Race: The Creation of the Civil Rights Lawyer* (Cambridge: Harvard University Press, 2012), 4.
9. Biographies of George Vashon, James Weldon Johnson, and Pauli Murray include the following: Paul N. D. Thornell, "The Absent Ones and the Providers: A Biography of the Vashons," *Journal of Negro History* 83, no. 4 (1998): 284–301, www.jstor.org/stable/2649028; Noelle Morrissette, *James Weldon Johnson's Modern Soundscapes* (Iowa City: University of Iowa Press, 2013); and Rosalind Rosenberg, *Jane Crow: The Life of Pauli Murray* (New York: Oxford University Press, 2017). Richard Toomey is a more obscure figure best known as the first black lawyer in Miami, Florida. See J. Clay Smith, Jr., *Emancipation: The Making of the Black Lawyer, 1844–1944* (Philadelphia: University of Pennsylvania Press, 1993), 310–11, n. 107. However, Toomey also published poetry, including a 1901 volume that was introduced by Paul Laurence Dunbar. Richard E. S. Toomey, *Thoughts for True Americans: A Book of Poems, Dedicated to the Lovers of American Ideals* (Washington, D.C.: Neale Publishing, 1901).
10. In May 2018, the President declared that National Football League players who kneeled during the national anthem to protest racial injustices should be fired or potentially deported. Bess Levin, "Trump Suggests Kneeling N.F.L. Players Should be Deported," *Vanity Fair*, May 24, 2018, www.vanityfair.com/news/2018/05/trump-suggests-kneeling-nfl-players-should-be-deported (accessed January 27, 2019).
11. For more information on Simone White, see Carrie Mannino, "Simone White: Poet, Scholar, Philosopher," *Yale Daily News*, October 7, 2016, https://yaledailynews.com/blog/2016/10/07/simone-white-poet-scholar-philosopher/ (accessed October 28, 2018); and "Simone White," *Poetry Foundation*, www.poetryfoundation.org/poets/simone-white (accessed October 28, 2018). On the poetry of Marlene NourbeSe Philip, a Canadian poet-lawyer of Caribbean heritage, see my article "Poetic Justice: Slavery, Law, and the (Anti-)Elegiac Form in M. NourbeSe Philip's *Zong!*," *Cambridge Journal of Postcolonial Literary Inquiry* 2, no. 1 (2015): 5–32, https://doi.org/10.1017/pli.2014.22.

12. See this volume's Introduction.
13. Derrick Bell, "Racial Realism," *Connecticut Law Review* 24, no. 2 (1992): 363–79, https://heinonline.org/HOL/P?h=hein.journals/conlr24&i=383.
14. Ibid., 373–74.
15. Ibid., 374.
16. Patricia J. Williams, *Alchemy of Race and Rights: Diary of a Law Professor* (Cambridge: Harvard University Press, 1992). Williams interlaces her personal narrative with discussions of popular culture, current events, critical race theory, and legal analysis.
17. Cooper has recently defined "*[e]mbodied discourse*" as "a form of Black female textual activism wherein race women assertively demand the inclusion of their bodies and, in particular, working-class bodies and Black female bodies[,] by placing them in the texts they write and speak." Brittney C. Cooper, *Beyond Respectability: The Intellectual Thought of Race Women* (Urbana: University of Illinois Press, 2017), 3.
18. Evie Shockley, *semiautomatic* (Middletown, CT: Wesleyan University Press, 2017) (epigraph quoting Fred Moten).
19. In *On Intellectual Activism*, African American sociologist Patricia Hill Collins defines an intellectual activist in the academic context as an "outsider-within social locations" who "develop[s] a critical consciousness of the need to remain attentive to the connections linking their scholarship and their in-between status of belonging, yet not belonging." Patricia Hill Collins, *On Intellectual Activism* (Philadelphia: Temple University Press, 2013), 67.
20. African American achievements in both genres date to the antebellum period. Phillis Wheatley (1753–1784) first attained renown for composing an elegy of Reverend George Whitefield.
"Phillis Wheatley," *Poetry Foundation*, www.poetryfoundation.org/poets/phillis-wheatley (accessed January 28, 2019). Meanwhile, recent archival research has resulted in the publication of what is the earliest known memoir by an incarcerated African American, Austin Reed's *The Life and Adventures of a Haunted Convict*, ed. Caleb Smith (New York: Random House, 2016). The memoir, which was written in the 1850s, portrays the appalling treatment that Reed endured while incarcerated in juvenile and adult prisons.
21. R. Dwayne Betts, *A Question of Freedom: A Memoir of Learning, Survival, and Coming of Age in Prison* (New York: Avery, 2009).
22. Reginald Dwayne Betts, *Shahid Reads His Own Palm* (Farmington, ME: Alice James Books, 2010); and Reginald Dwayne Betts, *Bastards of the Reagan Era* (New York: Four Way Books, 2015).
23. Betts, *Question*, 225–26; "Reginald Dwayne Betts," *New America*, www.newamerica.org/our-people/reginald-dwayne-betts/ (accessed October 28, 2018).
24. Alli Marshall, "Poet Reginald Dwayne Betts on Words, Incarceration, and His Commencement Address," *Mountain Xpress*, May 16, 2018, https://mountainx.com/arts/poet-reginald-dwayne-betts-on-words-incarceration-and-his-commencement-address/ (accessed January 31, 2019).
25. Betts, *Question*, 191.
26. This discussion distills *A Question of Freedom*.
27. Ibid., 180.
28. Ibid., 165, 217, citing Dudley Randall, ed., *The Black Poets* (New York: Bantam, 1985).
29. "Reginald Dwayne Betts," *Reginald Dwayne Betts*, www.dwaynebetts.com/bio/ (accessed October 28, 2018).
30. Reginald Dwayne Betts, "Could an Ex-Convict Become an Attorney? I Intended to Find Out," *New York Times*, October 16, 2018, www.nytimes.com/2018/10/16/magazine/felon-attorney-crime-yale-law.html (accessed October 28, 2018); "Dwayne Betts," *Yale Law School*, https://law.yale.edu/studying-law-yale/degree-programs/graduate-programs/phd-program/phd-candidate-profiles/dwayne-betts (accessed October 28, 2018); and "Reginald Dwayne Betts," *New America*.

31. Betts, "What We Know of Horses," in Betts, *Reagan Era*, 64.
32. As W. E. B. Du Bois defined the term: "It is a peculiar sensation, this double-consciousness, this sense of always looking at one's self through the eyes of others, of measuring one's soul by the tape of a world that looks on in amused contempt and pity. One ever feels his two-ness—an American, a Negro; two souls, two thoughts, two unreconciled strivings; two warring ideals in one dark body, whose dogged strength alone keeps it from being torn asunder." W. E. B. Du Bois, *The Souls of Black Folk* (1903), eds. Henry Louis Gates, Jr., and Terri Hume Oliver (New York: W. W. Norton, 1999), 11.
33. Betts, *Question*, 123; "Shahid," *English: Oxford Living Dictionaries*, https://en.oxforddic tionaries.com/definition/shahid (accessed October 28, 2018).
34. F. D. Lewis, "Ghazal," in *The Princeton Encyclopedia of Poetry and Poetics*, 4th ed. eds. Roland Greene, et al. (Princeton, NJ: Princeton University Press, 2012), 570–72.
35. Betts, "Ghazal," in Betts, *Shahid*, 51.
36. See, for example, Betts, "The Honorable Bryant F. Bruce Explains a Life Sentence," in Betts, *Shahid*, 59.
37. The loss of rights accompanying a felony conviction, perhaps most integrally the franchise, has been conceived of as a form of "civil death" today. Gabriel J. Chin, "The New Civil Death: Rethinking Punishment in the Era of Mass Conviction," *University of Pennsylvania Law Review* 160, no. 6 (2012): 1789–833, https://heinonline.org/HOL/P?h=hein.journals/pnlr160&i=1801.
38. Betts, "One Grave," in Betts, *Shahid*, 50.
39. Betts, "Near Nightfall," in Betts, *Shahid*, 5.
40. Ibid.
41. Ibid.
42. Betts, "A Father Talks to Himself," in Betts, *Shahid*, 20.
43. Ibid., 20–21.
44. T. S. Eliot, *The Waste Land* (1922), in *The Norton Anthology of Modern and Contemporary Poetry*, Vol. 1, 3rd ed., eds. Jahan Ramazani, Richard Ellmann, and Robert O'Clair (New York: W. W. Norton, 2003), 474.
45. Betts, "A Father Talks to Himself," in Betts, *Shahid*, 20.
46. The original line reads: "These fragments I have shored against my ruins." Eliot, *The Waste Land*, 487.
47. Alexander, *The New Jim Crow*, 60.
48. Betts, "Bastards of the Reagan Era," in Betts, *Reagan Era*, 29.
49. The named elegies are titled "Elegy With a City in It," "Elegy With a RIP Shirt Turning Into the Wind," "Elegy Ending With a Cell Door Closing," and "Elegy Where a City Burns." Betts, "Contents," in Betts, *Reagan Era*.
50. Maurice Jackson, ed., *An Analysis: African American Employment, Population & Housing Trends in Washington, D.C.* (Washington, D.C.: Georgetown University, 2017), www.cit yfirstfoundation.org/wp-content/uploads/2015/11/DC-AAEPHT-Report-091217. pdf (accessed October 29, 2018).
51. Betts, "Bastards of the Reagan Era," in Betts, *Reagan Era*, 24; R. A. Hornsby and T.V. F. Brogan, "Dirge," in *The Princeton Encyclopedia of Poetry and Poetics*, eds. Roland Greene, et al., 369.
52. See Betts, "Bastards of the Reagan Era," in Betts, *Reagan Era*, 22–29.
53. Betts, "Crimson," in Betts, *Reagan Era*, 31–32.
54. Betts, "Elegy With a City in It," in Betts, *Reagan Era*, 11.
55. Betts, "Legacy," in Betts, *Reagan Era*, 45. On prison abolition, see Allegra M. McLeod, "Prison Abolition and Grounded Justice," *UCLA Law Review* 62, no. 5 (2015): 1156–1239, https://heinonline.org/HOL/P?h=hein.journals/uclalr62&i=1163. The term "abolition" in this context connotes the magnitude of the change needed to fundamentally reform, if not necessarily eliminate, prisons. Betts's legal scholarship indicates his ideological alignment with advocates for prison abolition. See Reginald Dwayne

Betts, "Only Once I Thought About Suicide," *Yale Law Journal Forum* 125 (2016): 222–29, https://heinonline.org/HOL/P?h=hein.journals/yljfor125&i=222.

56. Betts, "Acknowledgements," in Betts, *Reagan Era.*

57. Shockley has published a monograph on black experimental poetry, *Renegade Poetics: Black Aesthetics and Formal Innovation in African American Poetry* (Iowa City: University of Iowa Press, 2011). Other major criticism connecting "renegade poetics" to liberatory politics includes Fred Moten, *In the Break: The Aesthetics of the Black Radical Tradition* (Minneapolis: University of Minnesota Press, 2003); and Anthony Reed, *Freedom Time: The Poetics and Politics of Black Experimental Writing* (Baltimore: Johns Hopkins University Press, 2014).

58. Evie Shockley, "DOGBYTES Interview: Evie Shockley," *Cave Canem*, https://cave canempoets.org/dogbytes-interview-evie-shockley/ (accessed January 28, 2019).

59. Evie Shockley, "C.V.," *Rutgers University, Department of English*, 2009, https://english. rutgers.edu/cb-profile/fieldclass.html?field=cb_curriculumvitae&function=download& user=204&reason=profile (accessed October 29, 2018).

60. "Nathaniel R. Jones," *Blank Rome*, www.blankrome.com/people/nathaniel-r-jones (accessed October 29, 2018).

61. Evie Shockley, "An Interview With Evie Shockley," by crash macewan, *The Dead Mule School of Southern Literature*, November 20, 2007, https://thedeadmule.wordpress. com/2007/11/20/an-interview-with-evie-shockley/ (accessed January 28, 2019).

62. Evie Shockley, *a half-red sea* (Durham, NC: Carolina Wren Press, 2005); Shockley, *the new black*; and Shockley, *semiautomatic.*

63. Shockley, "from *topsy in wonderland*," in Shockley, *semiautomatic*, 34–40. Saar is an African American artist who shares Shockley's fascination with how aesthetic innovations can rupture hegemonic depictions of reality, particularly in the context of black women's experiences. Shockley's poem is a textual-pictorial analog to Saar's 2018 exhibition at the L.A. Louver gallery, which was titled "Topsy Turvy." For more information about Saar and photographs of exhibition art, see Gary Brewer, "'I Wanted to Make Art that Told a Story': Alison Saar on Her Eloquent Sculptures," *Hyperallergic*, May 1, 2018, https://hyperaller gic.com/440597/i-wanted-to-make-art-that-told-a-story-alison-saar-on-her-eloquent-sculptures/ (accessed January 28, 2019); and "Alison Saar: Topsy Turvy," *L.A. Louver*, 2018, www.lalouver.com/exhibition.cfm?tExhibition_id=1692 (accessed January 28, 2019).

64. Harriet Beecher Stowe, *Uncle Tom's Cabin* (1852), ed. Elizabeth Ammons (New York: W.W. Norton, 2010).

65. Aside from alluding to Stowe's *Uncle Tom's Cabin*, the title refers to Lewis Carroll's dystopian *Alice's Adventures in Wonderland* (1865) (New York: Macmillan, 1920).

66. Shockley, "from *topsy in wonderland*," in Shockley, *semiautomatic*, 34–40.

67. See, for example, Christopher D. DeSante, "Working Twice as Hard to Get Half as Far: Race, Work Ethic, and America's Deserving Poor," *American Journal of Political Science* 57, no. 2 (2013): 342–56, www.jstor.org/stable/23496601.

68. Shockley, "from *topsy in wonderland*," in Shockley, *semiautomatic*, 38–39.

69. Ibid., 39.

70. Shockley, "['now, reader . . . ']," in Shockley, *semiautomatic*, 40.

71. Shockley, "*dependencies*," in Shockley, *the new black*, 23–26.

72. Annette Gordon-Reed's *The Hemingses of Monticello: An American Family* (New York: W. W. Norton, 2009), a successor volume to her landmark *Thomas Jefferson & Sally Hemings: An American Controversy* (Charlottesville: University of Virginia Press, 1998), details the relationship between Hemings and Jefferson, which continued into his presidency and included at least six children. Resonating with Shockley's re-envisaging of history, one of Hemings and Jefferson's direct descendants has recently argued for recognizing Hemings as a first lady. Evelia Jones, "It's Time to Recognize Sally Hemings as a First Lady of the United States," *Los Angeles Times*, January 4, 2019, www. latimes.com/opinion/op-ed/la-oe-jones-sally-hemings-first-lady-20190104-story. html (accessed January 28, 2019).

73. A "Slavery at Monticello" exhibit at the National Constitution Center, which I visited in August 2014, featured rolling screen displays of these extensive records.
74. Shockley, "notes," in Shockley, *the new black*, 101.
75. Orlando Patterson's *Slavery and Social Death: A Comparative Study* (1982) (Cambridge: Harvard University Press, 2018) famously theorized the concept of a death-in-life for enslaved peoples.
76. On a personal note, I am a Ph.D. graduate from the University of Virginia and am currently working at Georgetown University, which sold 272 enslaved people in 1838 to avoid insolvency. For more information about Georgetown's history of slavery, see *Report of the Working Group on Slavery, Memory, and Reconciliation to the President of Georgetown University* (Washington, D.C.: Georgetown University, 2016), http://slavery.georgetown.edu/report/ (accessed October 29, 2018).
77. Betts, "Bastards of the Reagan Era," in Betts, *Reagan Era*, 25.
78. Shockley, "a-lyrical ballad (or, how america reminds us of the value of family)," in Shockley, *semiautomatic*, 43–45; and Shockley, "buried truths," in Shockley, *semiautomatic*, 7.
79. Shockley, "*notes*," in Shockley, *semiautomatic*, 104.
80. Shockley, "a-lyrical ballad," in Shockley, *semiautomatic*, 43–45.
81. Ibid.
82. On this poetic tradition, which peaked in eighteenth-century Europe and typically involved a meditation on mortality and faith, see F. J. Warnke, A. Preminger, and L. Metzger, "Graveyard Poetry," in *The Princeton Encyclopedia of Poetry and Poetics*, eds. Roland Greene, et al., 575.
83. Shockley, "buried truths," in Shockley, *semiautomatic*, 7.
84. Calvin John Smiley and David Fukunle, "From 'brute' to 'thug': The demonization and criminalization of unarmed Black male victims in America," *Journal of Human Behavior in the Social Environment* 26, nos. 3–4 (2016): 350–66, https://doi.org/10.1080/10911359.2015.1129256.
85. Shockley, "buried truths," in Shockley, *semiautomatic*, 7.
86. Shockley, "of speech," in Shockley, *semiautomatic*, 84–86.
87. Ibid., 86. The line does not end with a period, thus suggesting a potentially infinite array of freedoms birthed from the effective exercise of freedom of speech.
88. In an article criticizing the conventional judiciary-centered view of the constitutional law canon, Jack Balkin and Sanford Levinson cite Douglass's 1857 speech lambasting the *Dred Scott v. Sandford* decision (which excluded African Americans from federal citizenship) as a text meriting canonical inclusion. J. M. Balkin and Sanford Levinson, "The Canons of Constitutional Law," *Harvard Law Review* 111, no. 4 (1998): 964–1022, https://digitalcommons.law.yale.edu/fss_papers/260/.
89. Shockley, "*from* The Lost Letters of Frederick Douglass," in Shockley, *the new black*, 7.
90. Robert D. McFadden, "Damon Keith, Federal Judge Who Championed Civil Rights, Dies at 96," *New York Times*, April 28, 2019, https://www.nytimes.com/2019/04/28/obituaries/damon-keith-dies-at-96.html (accessed September 20, 2019).
91. These accomplishments, in spite of the racism infecting the legal profession when the Judge began his career, are discussed in his biography and a recent documentary. See Trevor W. Coleman and Peter J. Hammer, *Crusader for Justice: Federal Judge Damon J. Keith* (Detroit: Wayne State University Press, 2013); and Jessie Nesser, dir., *Walk with Me: The Trials of Damon J. Keith* (Overseas Cowboy Films, 2016).
92. Jeff Karoub, "Judge Damon Keith Recalls Key Rulings from His 50 Years on Federal Bench," *Associated Press*, October 28, 2017, www.afro.com/judge-damon-keith-recalls-key-rulings-50-years-federal-bench/ (accessed October 30, 2018). The end of Evie Shockley's "*dependencies*" articulates a similar sentiment, as she describes depending on Jefferson's eloquent words to be better than him. Shockley, "*dependencies*," in Shockley, *the new black*, 26.

93. Oralandar Brand-Williams, "Damon Keith Marks 50 Years as a Federal Judge," *Detroit News*, October 26, 2017, www.detroitnews.com/story/news/local/detroit-city/2017/10/25/judge-damon-keith-fifty-years/107008764/ (accessed October 30, 2018).

94. *Northeast Ohio Coalition for the Homeless v. Husted*, No. 16–3603/3691 (U.S. Court of Appeals for the 6th Circuit, September 3, 2016), www.opn.ca6.uscourts.gov/opin ions.pdf/16a0231p-06.pdf (accessed October 31, 2018).

95. The Fifteenth Amendment (ratified in 1870), Nineteenth Amendment (ratified in 1920), and Twenty-Sixth Amendment (ratified in 1971) respectively expanded voting rights to citizens who were black men, women, and at least 18 years of age.

96. Wendy R. Weiser and Max Feldman, "The State of Voting 2018," *Brennan Center for Justice, New York University School of Law*, June 5, 2018, www.brennancenter.org/publication/state-voting-2018 (accessed October 30, 2018).

97. The Twenty-Fourth Amendment (ratified in 1964) banned poll taxes.

98. See Ronald K. L. Collins and David M. Skover, *On Dissent: Its Meaning in America* (New York: Cambridge University Press, 2013), 133 (quoting Paul Toscano).

99. See, for example, Julie Carr Smith, "Black Judges in Voting Dispute Recall Civil Rights Fight," *Associated Press*, October 23, 2016, https://apnews.com/9536d49ca9a 644ffb01006ce893cdfa7 (accessed October 30, 2018).

100. *Northeast Ohio Coalition*, 32 (Keith, J., dissenting). Peter Goodrich's characterization of historiography as "a contemporary form of mourning" is apposite here. See Goodrich, *Oedipus Lex*, 48.

101. *Northeast Ohio Coalition*, 32 (Keith, J., dissenting). That noted, the opinion also contains a thorough legal analysis. Ibid., 50–66.

102. Ibid., 33–43.

103. The Supreme Court invalidated parts of the Voting Rights Act in *Shelby County v. Holder*, 570 U.S. 2 (2013), a decision that Evie Shockley castigates in "in the california mountains, far from shelby county, alabama, and even farther from the supreme court building, the black poet seeks the low-down from a kindred entity," in Shockley, *semiautomatic*, 52.

104. *Northeast Ohio Coalition*, 68 (Keith, J., dissenting).

105. Felix Cohen, "Judicial Ethics," *Ohio State Law Journal* 12, no. 1 (1951): 13, https://heinonline.org/HOL/P?h=hein.journals/ohslj12&i=13.

6

ANATOMIZING THE BODY, DIAGNOSING THE COUNTRY

Reading the Elegies of Patricia Smith

Sequoia Maner

Master of forms like the sestina and sonnet (crown), and an acclaimed performer who can bewitch any audience, Patricia Smith is a singular poet.[1] Her poems are thick, muscular, cinematic, and risky. She incorporates intense musicality and poignant, surprising language—Smith's poetry compels the mind's eye so that one leaves the poem different from when one entered. Composed in the ongoing-ness of white-supremacist violence, *Incendiary Art* (2017) builds upon the poet's signature style, contextualizing recent police killings of unarmed black men and women within a cartography of all-American violence characterized by inci-dents of lynching, bombing, and shooting, the historical methods by which black bodies accused of innate brutishness have been laid down. Through processes of accretion emphasized by sets of poetic series (for instance, eight poems share the title "Incendiary Art," among other sequences), the poet emphasizes the evolving, recurrent nature of anti-blackness in the U.S. As an illustration, "Reemergence of the Noose" describes "some hand" in "dusty light" somewhere performing the ritual of "weaving, tugging tight / a bellowing circle," an image of an everyman figure crafting a noose, yet but one example of how the poet contends with the rise of a neoconfederacy in the new millennium.

I am compelled by the way Smith ritualistically animates the elegiac mode, for (at least) three of her seven single-authored collections are comprised of lamenta-tions that reflect upon the conditions and policies that extinguish black lives in the U.S. This chapter focuses on two of those volumes: *Close to Death (C2D)* and *Incendiary Art*.[2] My comparative methodology regards the action of revisiting as praxis in the examination of Smith's elegiac project that is refined over two dec-ades. Written at the height of the HIV-AIDS epidemic and the state's strengthen-ing of punishment systems, Smith's 1993 collection *Close to Death (C2D)* gives voice to black men enduring the nation's largest prison boom and doomed, it seems, to lead foreshortened lives. In the book's moving preface (notably the only such formal statement of contents within her oeuvre) Smith writes,

> This book is because nearly half a million black men are behind bars in the United States. *Because I have seen my son with shackles at his ankles and wrists.* . . . *Because I know a 51-year-old man who cannot read.* . . . *Because my father was killed by a bullet fired into the back of his head.* This book is because a black male infant born in 1993 has a 1 in 27 chance of losing his life in a homicide. *Because a gangbanger in Chicago used a 2-year-old boy as a shield.* This book is because young black men in New York City are wearing clothing emblazoned with the logo "C2D"—Close To Death. *Because so many of them are. C2D* is a love song, an elegy, a dirge, a celebration. It is a scream, a whisper, a giggle, a sigh. It is black men everywhere, and their choices (sic). It is for my son Damon, who is going to make it now. It is for my father, Otis Douglas Smith, who didn't.[3] (italics in original)

I quote at length from *C2D*'s preface to underscore how the poet aligns personal tragedy and structural design as impetus for elegiac engagement. Composed in the wake of the burning wrought by the breaking of Rodney King by LAPD officers acquitted for the blatant crime, *Close to Death* addresses the crisis of criminalization facing black men of the hip-hop era by way of persona. Poems like "Sweet Daddy" and "Daddy Braids My Hair" provide bittersweet childhood remembrances while "A Letter from Walpole Prison 3/16/93" and "A Poem for the Man Who Shot My Father" begin to reckon with the incarceration of Smith's son and the murder of Smith's father. Populating the pages between are ordinary voices: A journalist for the local paper, an undertaker and his son, a barbershop owner and his customers—Willie Franklin, Terrell, Cooley, and Scoot. Portraits of singers Smokey Robinson, Ray Charles, and Michael Jackson parallel contemporaneous media events of spectacularized blackness like Rodney King's brutal beating by LAPD officers and Mike Tyson's convicted rape of Desiree Washington. Each of these flashpoints examines the constitution and condition of black manhood during a time of denigration and death, thus contributing to the book's feeling of ever-accumulating loss. For Smith, the elegy is an extended project that, when refracted through many perspectives, approaches the truth of black precarity in the U.S.: That, no matter the age, literacy level, or moral compass, black people live close to death in ways that dramatically shape their choices and outcomes.

I approach *Incendiary Art* as a #BlackLivesMatter text and return to that which animated Smith's poetic strivings in *Close to Death* two decades earlier. Like the title of this volume, I find possibility in revisiting as poetic methodology. In her study of female elegists, Melissa F. Zeiger finds that woman-authored elegies "insist on tirelessly revisionary practices of reading and writing rather than on the need to institute any homogenous paradigm."[4] Smith extends this feminist practice and, in doing so, reshapes the parameters of the lyric elegy to perform sense-making in regard to racism's illogical terrain. Balancing precise formalism, honeyed sound, and authentic voice, Smith's *Incendiary Art* is a masterful and refined doubling back. For instance, when Smith returns to the memory of her father and his murder by shooting, she moves beyond glimpses to a formally stunning, ten-page triple-sestina, simply titled "Elegy."[5] If revisiting relies upon principles of refinement, reexamination, and rearticulation, the poet appears to ask, in how many ways might I speak unspeakable truths? How might I more clearly render the feeling or moment or image? Can I be both loud and gentle, broad and restrained; and, furthermore, which is more effective? Locating meaning in reimagination, I am invested in the ways Smith explodes the elegiac mode into dazzling possibilities by returning to familiar scenes and lingering concerns, discovering new pathways to grapple with racism and sexism's graphic reproduction.

Winner of the 2018 Kingsley Tufts Poetry Award and finalist for the Pulitzer Prize, *Incendiary Art* returns to motivations that animate *Close to Death*. Smith writes from a deeply felt position of a mourning woman whose moaning contains multitudes, and 25 years on, has gathered strength like a hurricane over warm water, poised to disrupt that which lies in her path.[6] *Incendiary Art* explicitly identifies itself as a text in support of the Movement for Black Lives; markedly, the poem "Incendiary Art: Ferguson" expresses,

> black lives
> matter
> most when they are in
> motion, the hurtle and reverb
> matter the rushed melody of fist
> the shudderings of a scorched
> throat matter
> the engine that moves us
> toward
> each damnable dawn
> matters.[7]

Smith makes alliance plain and suggests that, although occasioned by death, her elegiac engagement is rooted in the sound and motion, the "hurtle and reverb" of transformative social action. In this chapter, I trace this kinesthetic impulse through the figure of the mourning mother before studying Smith's innovation of the Emmett Till poem. Next, I move to an examination of Smith's engagement with the autopsy report as poetic material and the medical examiner as persona, a methodology that redirects readers from the gruesome condition of the anatomized body to the violent nature of the murderous state.

The Mourning Maternal

I echo critic Adam Taval's declaration that "Sagas of the Accidental Saint," *Incendiary Art*'s 35-page cataloguing of unarmed black victims whose stories animate

the Movement for Black Lives, is "a relentless poem of witness."[8] Smith catalogs the narratives of black women and men who have "accidentally" died in
police custody—shot to death though handcuffed, executed after mistaking pills/
cellphones/nothing for a gun, tasered to death after claims of superhuman
strength (and so on)—murdered for what Christina Sharpe describes as "familiar narratives of danger of disaster that attach to our always already weaponized
Black bodies (the weapon is Blackness)."[9] The black body—strapped or unarmed,
still or running, young or matured into adulthood—is never not a threat, is never
not in need of restraint. Scores of odes to victims like Rekia Boyd, Kajieme
Powell, Kendrick McDade, and Alonzo Ashley hurtle forth one after the other,
each elegy adopting a mother's voice to account for feelings of disbelief, intimate
familiarity, depthless love, and consuming grief. Smith dedicates *Incendiary Art*
to "every woman who began her morning with a son and ended the day without one" and recounts the many ways the black body is made breathless; how
"A black boy can fold his whole tired self around a bullet"; and how a mother
might survive that horror.[10]

The saga of mother's voices is interrupted by a simple refrain that lies unadorned and unavoidable against otherwise blank space: "The gun said: *I just had an
accident*." Page after page reinforces the same: "The gun said: *I just had an accident*"
such that the reader cannot turn away from an evaluation of this testimony. The
impossibility of a talking gun and its insistent repetition mimic the well-rehearsed
narratives of law enforcement officers and agencies. Further, tucked within a
sweeping and robust collection of elegy, the accumulation of utterances captures
the ghastly frequency with which a black person is killed by a vigilante, security,
or police officer (every 28 hours).[11]

> If they haven't
>   they are about to.   The glint.
> If a gun's not in his hand,
>   it's in his hand.   The slow
> menace of how they meant his end.[12]

Smith's "Sagas of the Accidental Saint" exposes how the politics of racial dis-
posability rely on cultures of suspicion that mark the black body as a threat.
Such focus is a rekindling of earlier work, namely *Close to Death*'s "The Dark
Magicians" whose speaker inhabits a collective of "disappeared, desolate, and mis-
placed" tricksters:

> Knotting the weathered noose, we slip it down
> to circle our throats, pull it to choking and jump,
> our hands tied behind our backs the whole time.[13]

Smith revisits the inexplicability of "another suicide / in a Mississippi jail" by
expanding 12 lines into a "saga" and thereby emphasizes the methodical and

institutionalized nature of police forces who conspire to cover up internal methods of murder with flimsy and familiar stories of "suicide" and "fearing for their life." Sandra Bland's mysterious suffocation in a small-town Texas jail; Natasha McKenna tasered to death while shackled inside of a Fairfax County, VA jail; Iberia Parish's death while handcuffed in the back of a police cruiser; Jesus Huerta's death while handcuffed in the back of a police cruiser; Chavis Carter's death while handcuffed in the back of a police cruiser. These are just a few of the accidental saints Smith honors.

The saga of relentless witness takes on the voices of mothers who "wrangl[e] the instance over and over, the moment when" they are made childless, and in doing so, undertakes a peculiar risk by occupying the subject-position of victims gone and still living:

> that's my son collapsed there my son
> crumpled there my son lying there
> my son positioned there my daughter
> repositioned there my daughter as
> exhibit A there my daughter dumped
> over there my son hidden away there
> my son blue there my son dangling
> there my son caged there my daughter
> on the gurney on the slab there . . .[14]

The litany which continues for 44 inexorable lines serves not only to expose the pattern of abuse and ongoingness of black mourning, but also to widen the discourse about police brutality to account for how the living adjust their daily existences around persistent absence. How does one mother when conditioned into a state of incessant dread? What becomes of mothering when the child is murdered by an agent of the state, the atrocity swept under the rug as if an accident? How can she endure this?

Smith's rigorous engagement with the persona in her #BlackLivesMatter elegies give voice to those routinely silenced, namely black mourning women. Cast as mammies, jezebels, and welfare queens, black women have historically occupied limited and disparaging representations within the American imaginary. Embedded within what Patricia Hill Collins names "controlling images" lies narratives of dysfunctional and aberrant relationships to mothering.[15] For instance, the mammy is portrayed as docilely attending to the family of the white employers before the needs of her own; the mulatta's mixed raceness and the unpredictability of her birthing body is said to jeopardize the lives of husbands and children; jezebels and welfare queens allegedly copulate with ease, birthing children without care or financial footing. Repeatedly, the black woman is evoked as interruption/corruption to ideals of (heteronormative) nuclear filiality such that black women's reproductive bodies signify as breeding sites of pathology. Smith's #BlackLivesMatter elegies contribute to the black feminist endeavor of recasting black mothers, a project that deploys an intersectional modality to push against the murderous measures of a sexist and racist State.

In his essay about the poetry of Bob Kaufman, L. Lamar Wilson argues that African American elegists "position the maternal body as the prototypical philosophical object to challenge and transform false ontologies of Blackness that undergird racist State practices."[16] Smith's #BlackLivesMatter elegies of maternal mourning too critique and disrupt false ontologies that reproduce the ordinariness of death by, paradoxically, writing from the condition of mothering that is always marked by a proximity to violent death for children:

> A black boy's lungs collapsing.
> A mother picking up a phone.
> The same sound.[17]

The Mothers of the Movement,[18] who like their slain children have become symbols of collective grief and stimuli for public organizing, are reinscribed by Smith's deft hand with voices that broach and breach the unutterability of it all. For instance, Smith's concluding poem of the 35-page "Sagas of the Accidental Saint" is framed by the words of Sandra Bland's mother, Geneva Reed-Veal, and embodies the collective voice of the mourning maternal who is "all the magic real that you can stand." Smith's recast figure of the mourning maternal critiques a peculiar twenty-first-century phenomenon of virality by which black abjection circulates ("digitized, my break / and fall rewound replayed and tabbed") and becomes divorced from narrative such that the recognizability of fundamental truths is occluded ("I don't expect you'll recognize my voice"). She reckons with a culture that would rather see the Mothers of the Movement in silent "wail with want of them" rather than hear the true sounding, the "ugly twist of grief." Smith's persona poems reconfigure the mourning maternal as a figure with agency ("I thought perhaps I'd let you see") and wisdom, attributes normally unafforded to black women in the public sphere:

> I'm here to say their bodies weren't at war
> with you. I'm here to say their bodies weren't
> at war with you. I'm here to say their wars
> were in their bodies. And the battlefield
> was always yours, was always yours, was all.[19]

Revisiting Emmett Till

Opening, closing, and resurfacing (like a bloated body weighted down with a cotton gin), the figure of Emmett Till[20] is at once spirit guide, warning, and, interpolated against the index of victims killed by police brutality, evidence of the nation's ongoing racial violence. *Incendiary Art*'s first poem, "That Chile Emmett in That Casket," begins with an epigraph that simply reads "*Photo*, Jet *magazine, Sept. 15, 1955*" (italics in original) such that, even without the poet's retelling of the brutality inflicted, the reader is confronted with the image of Till mutilated and unrecognizable in his open casket after having been dredged from the Tallahatchie River. *That* photograph. Fred Moten explains how Till's infamous photograph evokes an assemblage of meaning: "the death's difficulty, the suffering of the mother, the threat of a high mortality rate, and the seemingly absolute closure of his future."[21] It is an image that reverberates beyond the frame, a notion embodied by Smith whose young speaker remembers how the photo "of the boy without eyes" followed him everywhere in his youth—in "kingly state rooms" and "in the kitchen;" scotch-taped to the "door of the humming fridge" and "laid curly-cornered on the coffee table." For the speaker, Till's photo is a visual reminder of the precarious excessiveness that blackness inhabits: "*this is why you got to act / right 'round white folk.*" Relayed as confessional nostalgia, Till's photo casts a haunting into the speaker's adulthood, a reflection of African Americans who, having matured in the wake of the Second Reconstruction, are always-already shaped by Till's persistent presence in absence. Elizabeth Alexander writes,

> For black writers of a certain age, and perhaps a certain region, a certain proximity to Southern roots, Emmett Till's story is a touchstone. It was the basis for a rite of passage that indoctrinated these young people into understanding the vulnerability of their own black bodies, coming of age, and the way in which their fate was interchangeable with Till's.[22]

It is no wonder, then, that Smith's poem ends with sad ambivalence as the speaker reflects that "there were / no pictures of you anywhere. You sparked no moral. You were alive," a bleak outlook about the possibilities for self-determination when stalked by death.[23] How does a young black boy beat back the ghosts that threaten to steal his spirit at each turn? What are the possibilities for the living who are shadowed thus? Certainly, these questions remain pressing for those coming-of-age and coming-to-consciousness during the rise of the Movement for Black Lives as for those who matured during the Civil Rights era.

"That Chile Emmett in That Casket" is one of several moving and formally progressive poems Patricia Smith has contributed to the African American literary tradition of the Till elegy, a lineage discussed in this book's Introduction. Notably, Smith's Till poems incorporate a strategy of turning away from the brutalized body—from the "right eye reborn in the cave / of [Till's] mouth."[24] What I call an act of turning away from the disfigurement recalls similar elegiac strategies within *Close to Death*. For example, her early poem "Reconstruction," a short 14-line poem for Rodney King and, perhaps, one of Smith's earliest strivings within the sonnet form, insists: "Enough of the gritty reel. No more / clutching dust, curling against / metronome swing. April already, another fire simmers."[25] Though the poet begins with "the horror" of the battered face described as "delicate," "vulnerable," and "easily shattered," this meditation on the breaking is brief. Instead, the speaker marvels upon the profound ability for bodies to heal through processes of "patch and knit" and "swelling that flattens to sinew." For Smith, Rodney's scarred face is a miraculous indicator of restoration or "rebirth," a word that makes several appearances in *C2D*. Thus, the titular Reconstruction gestures toward histories of rebuilding the injured national body while holding the specificity of the individual's restorative capacity. In this way, Smith anticipates the rise of social justice campaigns like the Movement for Black Lives which work to heal the injured nation by discursively centering bodily injuries inflicted by police brutality.

Smith's early Till elegies reveal the desire to move away from ritual retellings ("Enough of the gritty reel") in such a way to prompt imaginative possibility and kinetic potential within readers. In *Close to Death*, the poem "Discovering Country" encounters Till, somewhere between sleep and dream, relishing a summer of simple pleasures: skipping stones along the river, running with "no schoolyard bullies, storefronts, or curbs / forcing his path," and breathing in "whole mouthfuls of air, / smelling like free."[26] The pastoral elegy opens with images of startling beauty as our Chicago boy revels in the expansive southern countryside: "How giddy wide the country opened its arms to him, / giggling green from the first."[27] The reader experiences Till's wonderment at the lush southern terrain where "he could run" with "feathery branches / arching above his head" and "everywhere, fat pods threatening juice, / fruit drooping from trees, bushes wild with roses."[28] Smith's "Discovering Country" is a poem of breath that measures the life force contained within a 14-year-old boy who "was a big boy, / brown and strong" against scenes of lush nature.[29] By imagining the sweetness of boyhood in the moments before capture, Smith successfully moves outside of the frame of brutality propagated by the photograph. However, the poem closes with a stanza that shakes the reader from the serenity of a liberating natural world:

> It was then that rough hands
> pulled him from summer sleep
> and men with earth in their mouths
> ran with him through the moonwash
> leaving no time for bacon or gospel.[30]

Twenty-five years following this wonderous innovation of the Till elegy, Smith revisits her strategy of imagining Emmett Till outside of the fixed-frame of his post-lynching narrative, updating the pastoral impulse of *Close to Death* for a new generation. Sprinkled throughout *Incendiary Art* are Shakespearean sonnets which revisit and revise the circumstances of Till's mythology. Concerned with the dialectical nature of presence and absence, desire and revulsion, pleasure and pain, the mourning work of elegy is closely related to love poetry and, in Smith's #Black-LivesMatter collection, these modes meld in the shape of a sonnet series that brings unexpected whimsy to the Till elegies. The conceit of childhood Choose-Your-Own-Adventure tales allows the poet to wander down never-taken paths. However, one finds that these same paths lead the reader back to the horrific fact of 14-year old Till's amputated adolescence, anyway:

> Turn to page 14 if Emmett travels to Nebraska instead of Mississippi.
> Turn to page 19 if Hedy Lamarr was actually Emmett's girlfriend.
> Turn to page 27 if Emmett's casket was closed instead.
> Turn to page 48 if Emmett Till's body is never found.
> Turn to page 128 if Emmett Till never set foot in the damned store.

At the beginning of the adventure, our Chicago boy is very much alive—Smith's reimagining affords Emmett the ability to mitigate and out-maneuver violence. On the road trip to Nebraska, Emmett hones his resistant prowess, "swagger[ing] past the pack" of "poison-eyed" and "devilish" white men who leer at him during rest stops.[31] In this manner, the poet (briefly) displaces Till from the burden of cruel iconicity crystallized by racial suffering for which he is traditionally remembered. Smith's final Till poem imagines the boy full of juvenile frolic and adventure, redolent of her earlier "Discovering Country."

Yet, no matter how the poet resists the spectacle that is forever associated with Till, one cannot escape the finality of the child's murder nor the racist ideology which generated the absence. Never "set[ting] foot in the damned store," Till runs past the dangers of a hysterical white woman and her lascivious lies to instead encounter a Southern world of wild intoxication that is equally threatening. The shop is described in the language of desire such that the particular historical moment in which sexual panic (manifested as miscegenation) and racial panic (manifested as Jim Crow Segregation) converge and conflate, transforming a breathing boy into sweet fetish to be consumed. The store "wooe[s]," "plea[s]," "steam[s]," and "crave[s]," exuding an inappropriate erotic desire directed toward a child who is unable to provide or comprehend consent in any meaningful way.[32] The natural landscape that joyous Till runs through evokes the threat of lynching of which he is blissfully unaware: "live and buzzing skins upon / the water, fruit to yank from every tree."[33] Having moved out of the frame of the poem, having "hurtle[d] past without a second thought," the store cooes one last lewd remark,

> *Hey nigger, welcome to the South—*
> *come slip my sugar deep in your mouth.*[34]

Despite the imaginative other-scenarios that Smith constructs for Till to "discover country" and live unharmed, Till meets his demise, a suggestion that his path was already chosen—no matter the route, death is destiny.

Instead of being fixed in the disfigurement of his bloated and battered post-lynching visage, the body is neither recovered nor photographed and thus never publicly mourned. In this way, Smith's Choose-Your-Own-Adventure sonnets look away from the brutality meted (the casket is closed, the body unexposed and figuratively buried) yet rehearse an involuntary return to terror. The ambiguous, tension-laden pathway toward the ultimate refusal of consolation extends a tradition of anti-elegy taken up by post–World War II poets, a subgenre that begs complication in the context of black-authored poetry. Concerning Smith's imaginative engagement with elegy, I resonate with Jahan Ramazani (one of the sole theorists to recognize and unpack African American elegy as a definitive strain) who describes modern elegists as denying transcendence to seek further immersion in loss such that "modern elegy resembles not so much a suture but 'an open wound.'"[35] The closing section of this chapter investigates how, for Smith, this open wound necessitates neither stitching nor cauterizing but, instead, the conjuration of a darker magic.

The Autopsy Report

If the graveyard serves as a common site for meditation upon death in the classical elegy, it is the medical examiner's office, the site where the body is anatomized to determine the exact cause of death, which serves as setting for Smith's #BlackLivesMatter engagement. And, if Emmett Till is the touchstone for contemporary black elegists, then Trayvon Martin is the touchstone for #BlackLivesMatter elegists. Smith's *Incendiary Art* twice turns to the autopsy report in critique of institutionalized practices that encode narratives of black savagery and criminality as status quo. I am interested in the way that the performance of an autopsy is itself an art of revisiting—a return to the subject/object as method to determine the nature, scope, and ramifications of harm inflicted. The medical examiner is tasked with duty of writing a meaningful narrative of what happened from what remains of the body, a task that carries the capacity to reassert individual humanity. Certainly, the second autopsy report ordered by the parents of Michael Brown Jr. functioned to counter the emergent narrative which made a criminal, supernatural, subhuman other of their son. Consider how a surveillance tape of Brown in conflict with a store owner was released in lieu of details about his murder in the days following the shooting. Consider how during his Grand Jury testimony, and later reinforced by his ABC News primetime interview, officer Darren Wilson described Mike Brown Jr. as an imposing man with "immense power" who was "very large" and "Hulk-Hogan"-like in stature—who, after running away from Wilson, reversed direction, "bulking up to run through" a half dozen gunshots. Wilson also described Brown as appearing "like a demon" with "the most intense, aggressive face."[36] Wilson conjured the fearsome predator of white America's nightmares in his testimony, removing Brown from the realm of the human to fix him as a creature deserving of quick death in the minds of the public. The family's independent autopsy countered those claims and confirmed the facts: that Brown was shot six times including an entrance wound through the top of the skull, an indication that he was falling at the time of entry. However, perhaps even more importantly, the private autopsy affirmed the human life of the once-breathing boy as counter to the malicious campaign of criminality bolstered against him. That Smith works within and against the autopsy as genre of documentation and (re)inscription, signals a doubled return.

Smith's recent autopsy elegies are, in fact, revisitations to past poems within *Close to Death* that recognize undertakers as central figures in black communities who mediate grief for mothers who have no recourse for the loss of children. "The Undertaker" and "The Undertaker's Son" unfold in the voice of a weary man tasked with the impossible job of fixing a parade of mangled bodies; who must "sooth[e] the angry edges / of bulletholes" for "another mother needing a miracle." With gruesome intimacy he reveals that "I have touched him in places / no mother knows, and I have birthed / his new face." These early autopsy poems focus on the brutality done—the "grisly puzzle pieces," "collapsed cavities," "flaps of cheek," and "bloody tufts of napped hair" the undertaker is tasked with reconstituting into the approximation of a human—and this work of reconstitution is exhausting. "The Undertaker" begins with unrestrained cruelty as the speaker remarks, "When a bullet enters the brain, the head explodes. / I can think of no softer warning for the mothers."[37] The undertaker desires to break through the shield of grief which, in his estimation, prevents mothers from reckoning with the truth of their sons' deaths: "The woman needs to wither, finally, and move on." The undertaker reveals a disdain for a lifestyle where gang warfare routinely deprives young men of breath, leaving mothers to plead "fix my boy. . . . *Make him the way he was*." He presumes the dead boy participated in rituals of masculinity that revolved around puffery and gunplay, that he "most likely hissed / 'Fuck you, man' before the bullets lifted him / off his feet."[38] In Smith's early work, the undertaker's blunt, steely demeanor embodies the drained and dispirited state of mind wrought by unrelenting "wake work."[39]

Smith revises her engagement with postmortem processes by narrowing focus to the textual reproduction of the once-breathing body via the autopsy report. "No Wound of Exit," a poetic interpolation of Trayvon Martin's autopsy report, swings between medical observations that normalize the deadness of a young black boy who could be any boy ("the body is that of a normally developed black male appearing the stated 17 years") and a lyric voice that is sardonic and scathing. For instance, she links the anatomizing that happens in the medical examiner's office to a long history of corporeal compartmentalization for means of pleasure and (re)production, remarking: "Once, a buyer would gingerly handle the penis of a potential purchase, foraging for heft."[40] Here, Smith links the shooting death of Trayvon Martin in a Florida suburb to the historical exploitation and subjugation of enslaved black men, revealing how the stigmatized black masculine body continues to be object of attraction, revulsion, and profit. As Claudia Rankine has avowed, "Historically, there is no quotidian without the enslaved, chained or dead black body to gaze upon or to hear about or to position a self against."[41] Where Smith collapses the singular event of Martin's death within a genealogy of historical precedent, she also undercuts the dry and technical language of the medical examiner's report to reveal the plump meat of a once-alive boy. For instance, the lyric interloper interrupts the report's description of the body with italicized interjections, "(Pause for the definition of normally developed black male. Avoid the words *tomorrow* and *upright*)." The poet destabilizes the fixity of the official autopsy report such that the reader must question if a "normally developed black male" is, in fact, one who winds up dead on a cold slab in the morgue.

I briefly move outside of Patricia Smith's *Incendiary Art* to examine the larger context in which she engages the autopsy report and to underscore how Smith's innovation of voice and form push the elegy forward into promising futures. Notably, in March of 2015, less than one year after unarmed Mike Brown Jr. was killed by officer Wilson in Ferguson, Missouri, conceptual poet Kenneth Goldsmith performed "The Body of Michael Brown" to a small and quietly uncomfortable audience at Brown University. Reading in the style of "uncreative poetry" for which he is popular, Goldsmith recited a minimally altered version of the autopsy report and, after thirty minutes, closed by stating, "The remaining male genitalia system is unremarkable."[42] Unlike Smith's repositioning of the autopsy report, Goldsmith's performance reinscribed racist notions of hypersexuality and scientifically instantiated predation while appropriating and commodifying black death for the affective experience of a white, elite audience. Furthermore, Goldsmith's performance was especially insensitive given that Mike Brown Jr. underwent three separate autopsy examinations. After two formal reviews, the first performed by St. Louis county's (untrustworthy) coroner's office and the second performed privately at the family's request by a top medical investigator in the field, the Department of Justice conducted a third and final independent review of the body. Goldsmith's further anatomizing was excessive and, as word of the reading spread through social media channels, the poetry world was rightfully incensed. The Mongrel Coalition, a queer collective that practices guerilla activism for the social media age, accused Goldsmith of white supremacist, colonial aestheticism.[43] Jacqueline Valencia, mentor and friend to Goldsmith, responded with a carefully worded response in which she chastised the poet for co-opting black suffering and silencing black voices. Poet Heriberto Yépez critiqued the institution of avant-garde poetry as one which *requires* the ingestion of racialized bodies while hiding behind the seemingly neutral tropes of citation and appropriation.[44] Poet Ken Chung argued that Goldsmith "literally performed the role of the state, the man slicing apart the fallen body of Michael Brown," treating the body as a "death-archive to be enumerated, dissected and possessed."[45]

Goldsmith defended his choices, noting that this reading followed the same procedure in past uncreative work that alters and resituates preexisting text. Quite simply, instead of writing new texts, he repositions that which already exists, so, in his mind, the reading of Mike Brown's autopsy report was yet another repositioning. In response to irate critics and in defense of his actions, Goldsmith took to Facebook, saying, "I altered the text for poetic effect; I translated into plain English many obscure medical terms that would have stopped the flow of the text; *I narrativized it in ways that made the text less didactic and more literary*" (emphasis mine).[46] This chapter holds that an autopsy report alone is not a poetic elegy; that crafting art from the ruins of a once-living body requires ethical engagement with language aimed to counter and dismantle patterns of violence rather than replicate them.[47] This countering and dismantling work is what Patricia Smith's #BlackLivesMatter elegy does.

Smith's lyric interpolation of the autopsy report in "No Wound of Exit" reinserts Martin beyond the flattening reinforced by the medical examiner's reportage to recapture the teenager who once drank Arizona Iced Tea and ate Skittles ("the grit of neon sugar") while growing into manhood, donning the stride and speech of black cool. The poem concedes that no matter the boy's home-training, his two-parent household-ness, or the mundanity of his outing, he is apt to encounter the hungry forces that crave his body caved-in, hollowed-out. Given the malignant imago which shadows him, the black boy is "never not secured, but [is] never secure"—predisposed to lose his body at any moment.[48] Smith updates her engagement with the autopsy elegy first explored in *Close to Death* such that she locates the source of terror and death that haunts African Americans to the institutionalized ideology of white supremacy and its appetite for the lives of black people.

I close by suggesting that Smith's processes of revisiting in the service of the Movement for Black Lives open pathways for possibility outside the ontological frame comprised of terror, abjection, and grief. This is best seen in the collection's title poem, "Incendiary Art" which embraces a *terza rima* verse form that feverishly pulls the reader through sounds, smells, and sights of a (nameless) city "strapped for art" and on the cusp of burning.[49] The catalyst: A dead body in the street ("Outlined in chalk, men blacken, curl apart"). The city that "sizzle[s]," "bellow[s]," "hiss[es]," and "sparks" is filled with children, hustlers, "storefront chicken" and "rows of packaged hair"—it is a black everywhere. I'm interested in the way Smith invokes the language of labor and motion against the stillness of the body outlined in chalk in a way that animates the kinetic potential contained within ordinary black spaces, amongst black everywheres. The speaker warns, "All our rampant hunger tricks / us into thinking we can dare dismiss / the thing men do to boulevards, the wicks / their bodies be."[50] In Smith's engagement with elegy, the murdered/martyred body suspires a catching catalysis among the living.

Here, the absented body hinges on the law of conservation: Energy is neither created nor destroyed but transforms between states and, when energy temporarily overwhelms a system, unable to escape, it manifests as heat and flame. Smith's entropic elegy suggests that when a body is "curl[ed] apart" in the middle of a city street (*Mike Brown browning in the sun for 4 hours*), its energy, a "blindly rising fume," transfers to residents and this thermodynamic exchange can result in combustion. Since combustion can only end when equilibrium is reestablished, the destruction of a city becomes the paltry, temporary substitute for the slayed body (*Los Angeles 1992; Ferguson 2015*). I read Patricia Smith's *Incendiary Art* alongside the work of Fred Moten who locates blackness outside narratives of "decay" through an examination of fugitivity, that stolen moment when "Some/thing escapes in or through the object's vestibule; the object vibrates against its frame like a resonator, and troubled air gets out." Moten continues, "The air of the thing that escapes enframing is what I'm interested in" and is, in my reading, what Smith in her entropic engagement with elegy, performs.[51] Smith's *blinding rising fume* echoes Moten's "troubled air," a sublimation of the burning black body to the spirit of radical transformation whose essence contains the power to spark a fierce burning. The poet's closing words of the collection's final poem, "Incendiary Art: The Body," attests to this fugitive essence:

> You left us not much path, even
> > after your body was that brief beauteous
> > torch. They seem to remember you
> > fondly. And there are unstruck matches
> > everywhere.[52]

Author's Note

At the time of this chapter's composition, graphic images circulate the internet of 24-year-old Danye Dion Jones hanging from a noose, face bruised and pants pooled around ankles, in the backyard of his mother's St. Louis home. When Smith poses the question, "Who knew our / pudgy American dream was so combustible?"[53] her poems resound the damning answer: We knew. African Americans who have long-grieved and long-loved have always known.

Notes

1. This chapter endeavors to stimulate critical engagement with the nature of Smith's tremendous contribution to contemporary American letters for, though adored by writers and awarded by prize committees, her body of work is woefully understudied by scholars of American poetry. Upon publication of this anthology, there exists no published journal articles nor book chapters, let alone full-length studies, of Patricia Smith's writings. Furthermore, scholars tend to ghettoize Smith's early work to discussions of spoken word as a poetic subgenre such that attention to her stylistic and technical development on the page and within the larger field of American poetics is overshadowed. Like the anthology in which this chapter rests, it is the first of its kind in that it regards Smith as a significant innovator of elegy who crafts art that helps to think through, feel through, and survive the cruelty of circumstance.

2. I consider *Blood Dazzler*, Smith's book-length tribute to survivors of Hurricane Katrina, an elegiac collection. Patricia Smith. *Blood Dazzler: Poems*. Coffee House Press, 2008.

3. Patricia Smith, *Close to Death,* 1st ed. (Cambridge, MA: Zoland Books, 1993), 4.

4. Melissa F. Zeiger, *Beyond Consolation: Death, Sexuality, and the Changing Shapes of Elegy. Reading Women Writing* (Ithaca, NY: Cornell University Press, 1997), 82.

5. As noted in Laura Vrana's chapter in this book, "Denormativizing Elegy," *Incendiary Art* also includes an "ethically complex" section titled "When Black Men Drown Their Daughters."

6. Having written and published multiple well-regarded books of poetry, Smith entered an MFA program where she refined her voice and signature style. The fruits of that labor are visible in *Incendiary Art*, Smith's first release since the completion of the degree. She reflects on her process of revisiting in the book, saying, "Of course, when you go back to an older poem, you want to make changes. I've acquired more technical skill since then. I'll sometimes revise them for performance." I find this to be a modest examination of how revisiting as methodology propels Smith's 122-page *tour de force*. See "Interview with Patricia Smith." *Xavier Review* 28, no. 2 (Fall 2008): 34–44.

7. Patricia Smith, *Incendiary Art: Poems* (Evanston, IL: TriQuarterly Books/Northwestern University Press, 2017), 46.

8. Adam Taval, "Review: Patricia Smith," *Plume* (blog), June 2017, http://plumepoetry. com/2017/06/review-patricia-smith/.

9. Christina Sharpe, *In the Wake: On Blackness and Being* (Durham: Duke University Press Books, 2016), 15. Sharpe goes on to write that "in much of what passes for public discourse *about* terror we, Black people, become the *carriers* of terror, terror's embodiments, and not the primary objects of terror's multiple enactments; the ground of terror's possibility globally."

10. Smith, *Incendiary Art*, 132, 136.

11. One of the tangible results of the Movement for Black Lives is the tracking of police shootings which, before 2015, went unverified. In 2017, at least 1,147 people were killed by police, many of them unarmed. See the website 'Mapping Police Violence' for annual reports and interactive charts on these figures. https://mappingpolicevio-lence.org/

12. Smith, *Incendiary Art*, 81.

13. Smith, *Close to Death*, 85.

14. Smith, *Incendiary Art*, 65, 79.

15. Patricia Hill Collins, *Black Feminist Thought: Knowledge, Consciousness, and the Politics of Empowerment* (New York: Routledge, 2008).

16. L. Lamar Wilson, "'She Is Twenty-Three Months Pregnant': The Quare, Black Maternity & Bob Kaufman's Surreal (Re)Vision of the African American Migration Narrative," *Obsidian: Literature & Arts in the African Diaspora*, Call & Response: Experiments in Joy and Furious Flower: Seeding the Future of African American Poetry 41, nos. 1 & 2 (2015): 337.

17. Smith, *Incendiary Art,* 37.

18. The Mothers of the Movement is a social justice group comprised of black women who have lost children to police and gun violence. They have made significant interventions in American public life since the 2013 acquittal of George Zimmerman for the murder of Trayvon Martin, the igniting event of the group's formation. Some of its most prominent members include Sybrina Fulton, mother of Trayvon Martin, Samira Rice, mother of Tamir Rice, Lezley McSpadden, mother of Michael Brown Jr., and Geneva Reed-Veal, mother of Sandra Bland. In 2016, The Mothers of the Movement spoke in support of presidential candidate Hillary Clinton at the Democratic National Convention. That same year, several of the mothers appeared in Beyoncé's groundbreaking visual album *Lemonade*. In 2017, The Mothers of the Movement appeared alongside funktress Janelle Monáe at the Women's March on Washington. The women continue to tour and, notably, fierce gun reform activist Lucy McBath, mother of Jordan Davis, was elected as Congresswoman for Georgia's Sixth District.

19. Smith, *Incendiary Art*, 108.

20. See this volume's Introduction, which addresses the tradition of the Emmett Till poem in the black poetic tradition. See also the volume's Appendix for a selection of Emmett Till elegies. A formal study of the Emmett Till elegy in African American letters is overdue.

21. Fred Moten, "Black mo'nin'," *Loss: The Politics of Mourning* (2003): 71.

22. Elizabeth Alexander, "'Can You Be Black and Look at This?': Reading the Rodney King Video(S)," *Public Culture* 7, no. 1 (October 1, 1994): 88.

23. Smith, *Incendiary Art*, 6.

24. Ibid.

25. Smith, *Close to Death*, 41.

26. Ibid., 102.

27. Ibid., 102–3.

28. Ibid.

29. Ibid.

30. Ibid., 103.

31. Smith, *Incendiary Art*, 14.

32. I am reminded of Saidiya Haartman who, in her chapter "The Ruses of Seduction," explains how the massive power imbalance between master and slave invalidated any claims of consent on behalf of black women. A similar dynamic between the white woman and black child is at play within Smith's Till elegies. See Saidiya V. Hartman. *Scenes of Subjection: Terror, Slavery, and Self-Making in Nineteenth-Century America.* Race and American Culture (New York: Oxford University Press, 1997).

33. Smith, *Incendiary Art*, 128.

34. Ibid.

35. Several scholars have written about the modern practice of resistance to elegy as "anti-elegy." R. Clifton Spargo identifies a strain of anti-elegy that "foresees no end to mourning" such that "resistant and incomplete mourning stands for an ethical acknowledgement of . . . the radical alterity of the other whom one mourns." For Diana Fuss, anti-elegies "strive to honor the integrity of the dead by melancholically refusing the violence of interiorization." Jahan Ramazani, *Poetry of Mourning: The Modern Elegy from Hardy to Heaney* (Chicago: University of Chicago Press, 1994), 2.; R. Clifton Spargo, *The Ethics of Mourning: Grief and Responsibility in Elegiac Literature* (Baltimore, MD: Johns Hopkins University Press, 2004), 13.; Diana Fuss, *Dying Modern: A Meditation on Elegy* (Durham: Duke University Press, 2013), 108.

36. John Cassidy, "A Closer Look at Officer Wilson's Testimony," *New Yorker*, November 25, 2014, www.newyorker.com/news/john-cassidy/darren-wilson-testimony.

37. Smith, *Close to Death*, 71.

38. Ibid., 71–73.

39. Sharpe, *In the Wake*, 13–22.

40. Smith, *Incendiary Art*, 36.

41. Claudia Rankine, "The Condition of Black Life Is One of Mourning," *The New York Times*, June 22, 2015.

42. Priscilla Frank, "What Happened When A White Male Poet Read Michael Brown's Autopsy As Poetry," *Huffington Post*, March 17, 2015, sec. Culture & Arts. www.huffingtonpost.com/2015/03/17/kenneth-goldsmith-michael-brown_n_6880996.html.

43. "The Mongrel Coalition Against Gringpo Responds to the Links Between Conceptual Art and Conceptual Poetry," January 22, 2015, www.montevidayo.com/the-mongrel-coalition-against-gringpo-responds-to-the-links-between-conceptual-art-and-conceptual-poetry/

44. http://venepoetics.blogspot.com/2013/09/goldsmith-y-el-imperio-retro-conceptual.html

45. Ken Chen, "Authenticity Obsession, or Conceptualism as Minstrel Show," *Asian American Writers' Workshop,* June 11, 2015, http://aaww.org/authenticity-obsession

46. Goldsmith did not apologize. Instead, he donated his $500 speaker's fee to Hands Up United while requesting that Brown University hold video footage of the controversial reading from the public.

47. My own poem, "upon reading the autopsy of Sandra Bland," answers this call of ethically engaging the autopsy report and, judged by Patricia Smith herself, was a finalist for the 2017 Gwendolyn Brooks Poetry Prize. Originally published in *Obsidian: Literature & Arts in the African Diaspora*, the poem is reprinted in this book.

48. Smith, *Incendiary Art,* 35–37.

49. Ibid., 9–10.

50. Ibid.

51. Fred Moten, "The Case of Blackness," *Criticism* 50, no. 2 (2008): 182.

52. Smith, *Incendiary Art*, 129.

53. Ibid., 17.

7

"A DIAGNOSIS IS AN ENDING"

Spectacle and Vision in Bettina Judd's *Patient.*[1]

Deborah M. Mix

In April 2018, the City of New York removed a statue of J. Marion Sims from Central Park, where it had stood since 1934. First erected in the 1890s in Bryant Park to honor Sims as the so-called father of modern gynecology, the statue was removed as part of Mayor Bill de Blasio's campaign to remove "symbols of hate" from city property.[2] Other efforts to remove hagiographic tributes to Sims have included renaming an endowed chair position at the Medical University of South Carolina and the removal of a painting designating him a "Medical Giant of Alabama" from the University of Alabama Birmingham.[3] Statues of Sims remain standing in both Alabama and South Carolina, though activists have been calling for their removal as well.[4] Sims's reputation has been undergoing a sustained reevaluation for some time now by medical ethicists and historians. More recently and publicly, artists working in a variety of contexts have been exploring his legacies and, importantly, shifting the focus from Sims to his patients. Visual artists Kenya (Robinson) and Doreen Garner's 2017 exhibition, *White Man on a Pedestal* (a reference to this statue and others), foregrounds the bodies and experiences of the enslaved black women who were Sims's patients.[5] Charly Evon Simpson's 2019 play, *Behind the Sheet*, takes its inspiration from this terrible history as well, imagining the household in which Sims and these women lived and the relationships that might have developed among the women themselves.[6]

Poet Bettina Judd's *Patient.* appeared in 2014, predating these other imaginative reconsiderations of medicalized racism. The lineages Judd's collection creates, linking Sims's enslaved patients to other black women past and present whose bodies have been exploited by the white medical establishment, are crucial to her call for a reexamination of medical history, the drive to get to the root of the disease in modern medicine. One of the stories Judd explores is that of Esmin Green's 2008 death on the floor of the Kings County Hospital Emergency Room.

Judd envisions the circumscription of Green's life: "To fold oneself neatly / and fall to the floor / to be dying."[7] But this almost ladylike description runs counter to the actual circumstances of Green's death. As Judd notes elsewhere, "In 2008 Esmin Green waited for services at Kings County Hospital in New York for nearly twenty-four hours and died on the waiting room floor."[8] Hospital officials initially tried to cover up the neglect that surely contributed to her death; surveillance video for the waiting room shows numerous hospital staff and security guards deliberately ignoring Green, even after she collapsed.[9] Judd makes this reality clear in the poem's third stanza, writing, "as is the natural order of things / to talk past be annoyed even / *how can we shed her from our lives?*"[10] The italicized line draws together the natural processes of shedding hair and skin that Judd references in the first stanza with the naturalization of indifference to Green's welfare.

Just as the enormous problems manifested at Kings County Hospital were the result of decades of policy and financial decisions, the structural inequalities that lead to poorer healthcare and health outcomes for black women and people of color more generally are likewise the outcomes of generations of decisions. "Esmin Green the thought that perhaps this is a metaphor for how we all die. Green an idea of metaphors that live where bodies cannot," Judd writes.[11] But of course Green was neither "an idea" nor "a metaphor"—she was a person—and her experience is not easily generalizable to "all" patients since access to appropriate medical care is not equally distributed in our culture. As the prose-poem's title—"On the Politics of Citation"—suggests, it matters whose experiences are normalized (or "cited"), whose are positioned as non-representative.[12]

As long as we see experiences like Green's as aberrations, Judd suggests, rather than as the result of a series of deliberate choices with which we have not reckoned, then preventable tragedies like Green's death will continue. Judd asks, "Some things were left when she died on that King's County emergency room floor: her body and *who else?*"[13] The question that ends the stanza—"who else?"—speaks to Judd's larger project of linking contemporary medical practices and failures to longstanding institutional racism and misogyny, to the structures of feeling that both support and mystify these operations. The last stanza of the poem reads, "Open parentheses Green close parentheses. Her name now locked in line. The line is, *No one noticed*. It continues, *differentiate me from death*."[14] Judd's form mimics the notes in Green's hospital record, echoing the hospital's presentation of Green's death as an unfortunate but contained mistake. That bracketing "locks her name in line," just as the falsified notes in her chart attempt to establish an alternative narrative for her last hours, hours during which "no one noticed" her collapse and death. Once her lifeless body was noticed, however, it was transformed into spectacle, the grainy security footage endlessly replayed on newscasts, her death attributed to individual actors who failed to follow procedures, and her legacy a change in hospital policies. While improving specific hospital protocols is a worthy aim, those changes are likely to be of limited efficacy as long as Green's death is treated as an aberration rather than as a consequence of persistent racism and disparity.[15]

Judd's *Patient.* functions as a kind of elegiac reckoning with this history. First, the collection locates Green and other black women in an historical lineage of exploitation and neglect by the slow violence endemic to the American medical system;[16] second, the poems offer an alternative reading of that history to challenge the structures of spectacle and erasure that continue to enact that violence today; and finally, the poet-speaker offers solace through resistance in elegies that don't seek acceptance but instead demand change. Judd's collection seeks to understand and undermine contemporary attitudes toward black pain and disease in part by taking us back to the foundational period in which assumptions about black women's bodies and experiences were established in the structures of medicine in the U.S. This past—and black women's centrality to it—has largely been elided, inscribing the minimization of both their presence and their suffering into American medicine as a whole. Returning to the origins of these contemporary attitudes and practices requires recognizing the black women who haunt the house of American medicine, whose bodies and lives are the sites of experimentation and exploitation that shaped it.

In traditional Anglo-European elegiac poetry, consolation arrives through acceptance of loss, brought about through religious reflection (the deceased is "in a better place" and her "suffering is over") or through consideration of natural continuities (the death as part of a "circle of life"). The elegy may initially seem like a peculiar structure for Judd's explorations since the form traditionally begins in lamentation and moves toward consolation; as we contemplate Green's senseless death, it would seem that outrage, rather than solace, is more appropriate. Judd's poems, along with, as this volume attests, many other contemporary black-authored elegies, seek consolation not through acceptance of loss but rather through empathetic identification with and care for both the deceased and the living. By calling attention to the suffering of particular black bodies, insisting that lives like Green's should matter to all of us, Judd's poetry ruminates on the long history of devaluation of black lives in America. Failure to see black suffering as equivalent to white suffering—the "racial empathy gap"—may account for the fact that African American patients routinely receive less medication because physicians regularly underestimate black pain.[17] To understand these contemporary realities, Judd shows us, we need to look backward to the experiences of nineteenth-century women like Joice Heth and Anarcha Westcott, among others, imaginatively reconstructing and connecting these women's experiences, which have largely been rendered invisible in our cultural and medical histories. By linking these women's stories to more recent experiences, like those of Green, Henrietta Lacks, and a first-person speaker recounting her 2006 "ordeal with medicine,"[18] Judd's collection refuses elegiac resolution in favor of a rationale for resistance and change.

While Esmin Green's death was certainly caused by localized failures in the Brooklyn hospital, those failures were themselves produced by a medical system that valorizes white patriarchal ways of seeing over those of women and people of color, positioning women of color like Green at a special disadvantage when it comes to having their pain recognized and treated effectively. Following the Foucauldian notion that power inheres in the establishment of certain bodies and experiences as "normal" (another manifestation of "the politics of citation"), Judd takes readers back to some critical encounters between black women and white (medical) power such as the story of J. Marion Sims and his patients. But rather than focus her attention on the man credited with inventing the speculum and a method for repairing vesico-vaginal fistulae (an injury that occurs in childbirth), Judd refocuses attention on some of Sims's patients, specifically three enslaved women mentioned by name in Sims's autobiography.[19] These women—Anarcha Westcott, Betsey Harris, and Lucy Zimmerman—were sent to Sims because the symptoms caused by their fistulae made them less valuable to the families who enslaved them.[20]

In "The Researcher Discovers Anarcha, Betsey, Lucy," Judd's researcher notes that Betsey has experienced her "first birth," Lucy is "months out of household duties," and Anarcha is "his first vesico-vaginal fistula." While the descriptions may at first seem disinterested notations of the women's complaints, they reveal the influence of structural racism in the ways they position the women primarily in terms of their value, or lack thereof, to their white masters. Unsuited for "household duties" (because the fistulae made them incontinent) and unable to carry more pregnancies, these enslaved women are financial burdens rather than financial assets to those who enslave them. The poem goes on to foreground the doctor's perspective: "In these three, Sims shapes his speculum, invents his / silver sutures, perfect protocol for proper handling of / the female pelvis."[21] As the language here suggests, Sims, and doctors more generally, have historically been positioned as the actors—inventor, perfecter, shaper. The line breaks here give special prominence to Sims's authority and centrality in medical history—"his / silver sutures" and his "handling of." As the prepositional phrase "In these women" suggests, the patients themselves are anonymous sites, specific body parts ("the female pelvis") in or on which the physician acts.[22] But Judd's poetry insists on the centrality of these women and their experiences, which are in fact central to the establishment of modern gynecology. For example, Anarcha alone endured at least 30 surgeries, not only without anesthesia but also without clothing or privacy as Sims, like many of his contemporaries, saw these women as little different from animals and therefore as incapable of experiencing pain and embarrassment the way white women did.[23]

In "Betsey Invents the Speculum," Judd reworks Sims's descriptions of bending spoon handles to create his speculum to recall her own malleability: "I have bent in other ways / to open the body make space // More pliable than pewter." While "Sims invents the speculum," Betsey "invent[s] the wincing // the *if you must* of it / the looking away," experiences likely familiar to anyone who has undergone a gynecological exam. This shift, to the perspective of the patient rather than that of the doctor, insists on "the here of discovery," as the poem's last line puts it, that black women's bodies are (and have been) *here* all along.[24] As much as the white doctor may wish to position his patients as "Something to master / something to enslave," as Judd writes in a poem titled "The Opening," these poems reclaim the women themselves as the central figures in the story of medicine, those whose "mouths, when opened up / could light our darkness."[25]

The failure to recognize—and empathize with—that presence has led to the erasure of black women's experience from the historical and medical record and to inadequate care in the present. This erasure is in service to what the historian Vanessa Northington Gamble identifies as the "muting" of "the story that the foundations of modern gynecology are based on the body and the pain of enslaved black women" and the elision of slavery from the foundations of modern medicine.[26] Christina Sharpe has persuasively argued that "slavery's violences emerge within the contemporary conditions of spatial, legal, psychic, material, and other dimensions" of black lives.[27] One function of Judd's elegiac attention to women like Anarcha is to encourage the reader to recognize what Sharpe calls "the still unfolding aftermaths of Atlantic chattel slavery" in our contemporary contexts.[28] Judd's poetry calls readers to turn their attention toward these women and to foreground the acts of erasure—another kind of "wincing" and "looking away" by the medical system and our historical record—that led to that Brooklyn emergency room and the systematic refusal to see Esmin Green's suffering.

This willful blindness comes through a process of discipline, itself enacted through cultural scripts that value women's forbearance and dismiss their complaints. The word "patient" is likely to be associated with the ability to wait calmly or to persevere and to be applied to one's relationship with a physician ("I am Dr. X's patient"), but the earliest uses of the word were more explicitly associated with enduring suffering or tribulation without complaint. The word is associated with a kind of passivity in the face of misery and is often used to compliment those—often women and people of color—who essentially lack other options. Judd's title, with the period after the word patient, may be gesturing toward the imperative—"[Be] patient."—with the declarative, rather than exclamatory mode, indicating calm acceptance of that status, both by the patient ("I must listen to my physician, even though he doesn't seem to hear what I'm saying") and by the medical establishment ("She's an object of study, nothing more"). Calls for patience are too often used selectively; recently we hear the term used by those seeking to quell protests after police shootings of black people, implying that there is nobility in suffering and a correct or timely way to demand justice.[29] But while our culture may pay lip service to these acts of stoic suffering, being patient and being *a* patient can also mean being unheard, secondary to the showmanship of the physician, politician, or charlatan taking center stage.

Judd connects these roles explicitly in her collection, citing a passage in Sims's autobiography that recalls his meeting with P.T. Barnum as the epigraph to the poem "The Calculus of Us." In the poem, Anarcha addresses Joice Heth, an enslaved woman whom Barnum exhibited as George Washington's nurse, claiming in an advertisement that she was "born in the year 1674," making her "the aston-ishing age of 161 years."[30] Anarcha tells Joice, "My fate & yours, / an arithmetic," suggesting that there's a system of variables connecting their experiences at the hands of a "slippery abolitionist showman / [and a] coward confederate doctor," the alliterative epithets reducing the men to caricatures.[31] In invoking "calculus" in the poem's title, Judd suggests that medicine itself is both changeable and con-stant, entailing ongoing calculation of risks and benefits. Anarcha tells Joice, "you too were experiment" and speaks to the complex nature of their experiences at the hands of Sims and Barnum:

> there is honey in
> never returning to fields
> salt in 35 operations
> your dissection
> subjection[32]

Judd asks us to consider that, as difficult as these women's experiences with Sims and Barnum were—"salt" in a wound—they may well have been "honey" com-pared to "returning to fields" to labor.[33] (Poems like "You Could Smell It From the Fields" and "Lucy on the Train" describe the humiliation that a woman suf-fering from a vesico-vaginal fistula would have experienced.) While Sims reports that at least one of his enslaved patients asked for his help, Judd reminds us that these women were "something to be found / something not to be seen" to Sims and his colleagues.[34]

Unlike the enslaved women Sims treated, Joice Heth was meant to be seen, meant to make money for Barnum, who like Sims sought to "exercise mastery over bodies."[35] Heth was neither Washington's wet nurse nor 161 years old, but Barnum's efforts to foster this illusion were brutal (for instance, he extracted her teeth in order to make her seem older, an experience Judd imagines in "Joice Heth Presents: The Showman as Dentist"), perhaps taking on special intensity as Barnum sought to recoup the money he spent to purchase her from her previous enslaver. A blind, paralyzed woman past childbearing years would have had little financial value in the slave economy, but Barnum realized about $1,000 a week during the height of the public's interest in Heth.[36] In "The Researcher Presents Joice Heth," Judd describes "The curiosity that is / every / black woman," cata-loguing her "profitable bones, old breasts," initially mirroring Barnum's reduction of Heth to a commodity.[37] But she notes that, just as Anarcha's pelvis was of inter-est to Sims as a site in which he could imagine his acts of discovery, Heth's breasts are of interest because men imagine drawing from them the same milk that sup-posedly fed George Washington. This "mammy memory," as Uri McMillan calls it, positions Heth as "an embodied portal to a mythic and majestic American past" for white audiences, who, as Judd puts it, imagine themselves also sucking milk from Heth's breasts, "that they too would become / great men".[38]

While Heth herself was never Washington's nurse, a white Virginian of his economic class almost certainly had one, a woman whose experiences are largely invisible in our American history books. Heth raises these issues in "Lest You Forget":

[I] amuse myself with a plausible addition
to his myth:

founding father, cherry tree, honest boy
my brown nipple in his lying mouth.

I listen deep
contrive my own telling

what he will remember
when he puffs up, thinks himself high

as his god: against black flesh
washington suckled

black hands clothed, held him
had mercy on his infant neck[39]

As Judd articulates through Heth's voice, black women are central to but missing from dominant American narratives, hidden in plain sight in spectacles like the ones Barnum produced. While Barnum's intent was to reinforce a black woman's status as both commodity and oddity, Heth's version of the experience offers a counterpoint to and explanation for that treatment. Caring, feeding, and protecting fragile white masculinity—including that of the so-called founding fathers—was often black women's work. Another poem asks, "Whose black tit did the general suck?"[40]

Again and again, Judd imagines these women's "own telling[s]" of their encounters with the medical and capitalist systems, the intimate interdependence of white male achievement and black female sacrifice—sacrifices that went unaccounted for during these women's lifetimes and remain unrecognized since. In the epigraph to one of her poems, Judd states unequivocally, "Gynecology was built on the backs of Black women, anyway."[41] In that poem, titled "Initiation/Memory," she writes, "Hospital curtain, showman's speculum, surgeon's auditorium. There is an opening here, a thrusting, a climax, a little death."[42] The poem opens with phrasing that connects medicine to spectacle—the curtain is pulled back (or rises), the speculum is inserted (or waved like a ringmaster's cane), and a hush falls over the auditorium (or theater). She goes on to link erotic pleasure, showmanship, and medical procedure, taking advantage of the fact that an operating room is also called a "theater." As Judd explains in an interview,

> Some bodies are made to be more available than others for exploitation, for examination, experimentation, and ultimately control even if that control means death. . . . What is also intrinsically connected to how the bodies of women of color are made more available for experimentation is also how they are made available as spectacle.[43]

In Judd's elegiac economy, the invisibility of women of color in some contexts exists alongside the hypervisibility of black women (and men) in others. In the earlier poem, medical examination is linked to the erotic, as the insertion of a medical instrument becomes sexualized and the patient's body is exposed to the gaze of the curious (or prurient) onlookers. Even after her death, Heth remained a spectacle; her autopsy was a public event.[44] Similarly, we know Esmin Green through her death—the spectacle of her long waiting, slow collapse, and unnoticed death captured by security cameras and rebroadcast on the news and in courtrooms. We know Trayvon Martin, Michael Brown, Tamir Rice, Sandra Bland, Philando Castile, and countless others through video footage, courtroom testimony, and news reports. Seen in grainy security camera or shaky cell phone footage, or maybe not at all, these deaths are simultaneously real and abstract, proof of our culture's indifference to black pain both in the fact of the deaths and in the necessity of repeatedly proffering the evidence.[45] Sharpe explores the ways that the brutality visited on black bodies—whether by the medical establishment or the prison industrial complex or natural disasters—is consistently made visible through the ways those bodies are represented and discussed. Unlike Martin, Brown, Rice, Bland, and Castile, whose bodies were imagined as "*carriers* of terror," inhumanly threatening and therefore meriting lethal force,[46] the women whose "ordeals with medicine" are explored here are imagined as unreal in a different way, as incapable of experiencing pain or terror and therefore unworthy of empathy and care and, significantly, grief.

While Judd doesn't avoid the brutal cruelty that these women experienced, neither does she dwell on the specific events themselves. Instead, Judd insists that these experiences are central to American medicine, to a system that continues to create new "ordeal[s] with medicine" every day. The book opens with a poem titled "In 2006 I Had an Ordeal With Medicine." In the prose-poem, the first-person speaker explains, "In 2006 I had an ordeal with medicine. To recover, I learn why ghosts come to me. The research question is: why am I patient?"[47] As Judd told an interviewer, "Since Black women are not often seen as reliable witnesses, being a patient and a Black woman is a precarious position."[48] This precarity means that women's bodies and those of people of color are pathologized, dismissed, undermedicated, and over-policed. "When it comes to this particular legacy of control over the bodies of women of color by medicine," Judd explains, "we need look no further than our prisons who continue to shackle pregnant women in labor beds, [to imprisoned women] who are forcibly sterilized or coerced into sterilization."[49] Researchers like Linda Villarosa have documented the ways that black women's attempts to seek appropriate healthcare are often rebuffed by the very institutions meant to provide that care: "Black women are three to four times as likely to die from pregnancy-related causes as their white counterparts, according to the C.D.C.," and this disparity "persists for black women across class lines." Furthermore, Villarosa asserts,

> For black women in America, an inescapable atmosphere of societal and systematic racism can create a kind of toxic physiological stress. . . . And that societal racism is further expressed in a pervasive, longstanding racial bias in healthcare—including the dismissal of legitimate concerns and symptoms.[50]

Because of these persistent and dangerous disparities, rooted in the foundations of modern medicine just as enslavement is bound up with the origins of America, the elegies Judd has written refuse to perform the traditional work of the elegy—to lament and console, to move toward closure. She asks her readers to sit with the knowledge of that exploitation, for instance, alongside the knowledge that the cancer research that cures one patient began with the cells of another black woman, Henrietta Lacks, whose tumor cells were taken without her or her family's knowledge or consent; they have since given rise to an "immortal" cell line that has been central to numerous medical discoveries, including gene mapping and in vitro fertilization.[51] "Of Air and Sea," a poem dedicated to Lacks, points out our indebtedness to all these women whose suffering ultimately alleviates our own: "you were the science / so that I would not" die.[52] She wonders, without Lacks's unwitting contribution, "what lives would be uncradled? / what discoveries never proclaimed? / what bodies left between here / and oblivion?"[53] In that poem Judd's speaker links her own medical experience to those of the other women discussed here, speculating about what would have happened to her if these women "had not an autopsy / a fistula / your cells."[54]

In this long poem, Judd leaves lots of white space; some pages include only a few lines of poetry. The effect of this structure is to slow the reader down, to ask the reader to consider the blank spaces in our own historical and medical records. Those blank spaces are not necessarily signs that nothing—or no one—was ever there; rather, they're reminders of questions not asked, stories not told, people not seen. Judd's elegiac poetry works to re-place black women in medical history and to connect their experiences forward into the present-day experiences (too often "ordeals") of black women with medicine. "They will be found in their movement," Judd writes in "Negative Space Methodology," "Their hands in the cracks."[55] Until we see that past clearly, sitting with its ghosts and recognizing their fingerprints, we will not truly begin to understand and thus address the ways it shapes our present-day medical practices.

But while the political work of this collection is to demand the reader's thoughtful attention to the unresolved losses in our national and medical histories, there is also a move toward intimacy between the patient whose "ordeal with medicine" frames the collection and the other women whose histories the collection explores. This identification is necessary to the speaker—"The way they bend into my body, an easiness, closeness that makes this inquiry possible."[56] "Why do I choose to remember?" the speaker wonders in "Initiation/Memory," "You, in bed with me Anarcha. You, brushing my head Joice. Why do you mourn me and sing, as if I am the one who has died?"[57] These lines come from the same poem that links the doctor to the showman, but they demonstrate a turn away from spectacle and toward intimate comfort. Here Judd's speaker positions herself as a child in need of care, and the dead offer comfort to the living through touch and song (given that both women were enslaved, we are left to wonder whether they would have been able to offer similar tenderness to their biological children). At the same time the song demonstrates an awareness of the systemic inequalities of the medical system.

In "You Be Lucy, I'll Be Betsey," Judd takes this empathetic identification through time, recounting a conversation between the poem's present-day speaker and a nurse in which remarks about hairstyles ("The nurse with the natural compliments me on my locs") is interpolated into a conversation about a medical procedure (*"You're going to feel a pinch"*). The prose-poem ends with an observation that turns into a question: "Just two black women and a speculum, each asking the other, *When did you get free?*"[58] Along with the implication that the women have given up chemical hair relaxers (freeing themselves from unnatural and white-centered beauty standards), the poem reminds us of other kinds of freedom— freedom from enslavement, freedom from dehumanization, freedom from physical suffering. The chronological range of the poem, bringing Sims's patients together with the contemporary speaker's "ordeal with medicine," shortens the distance between these moments, reminding us once again of black women's complicated position in medical history. "Go to the source of the suffering," Judd tells us.[59]

"The source of the suffering" is what made Esmin Green invisible to so many hospital employees. It's what led to the erection of statues to Marion Sims and the erasure of his patients, and even the circumstances of his investigations on the bodies of enslaved women from the historical record. But recognition, both within the medical establishment and in the historical record, is the ultimate aim of Judd's elegiac work. "History is also everybody talking at once," as Elsa Barkley Brown puts it in a line that Judd cites in the prose-poem "Inner Truth."[60] In that poem, Judd imagines hearing many voices:

> *History is also everybody talking at once.* When I open my mouth, there is another voice. I have to press a finger to one tragus to hear me. The other

becomes louder, more rapid. There are many voices now—gaps, garbled underwater talk, some of it in another language. Collected words: *pewter, automaton, john hopkin* string a line across my tongue. None of it is true. All of it is true.[61]

The italicized nouns remind us of the pewter spoons bent into a speculum to peer into the bodies of Anarcha, Betsey, and Lucy; the automaton to which Joice Heth was compared by a spectator at one of Barnum's shows; the hospital in which Henrietta Lacks was treated for cancer and where her tumor cells were harvested. The cacophony of voices (the one in "another language" might be that of Saartjie Baartman, about whom Judd also writes) speak even after their death, asking for the "transformative recognition" denied to them in their lifetimes and denied to so many people in our own lifetimes.[62] "To each doctor a speculum," she writes in a poem titled "At [The Teaching Hospital] for the Second Time" (brackets in original). But to the patient, no privacy: "No time for a room with walls. / No procedure. No apologies. No / apologies all mine,"[63] suggesting that what is being "taught" is a way of seeing both a patient's body and the patient herself. The poem's setting seems contemporary—we are in 2006 again—reminding readers of the racist and peremptory attitudes deeply rooted in our medical practices. Whose bodies are positioned as curiosities? Which patients merit privacy or kind words? Who is taught to make herself small or to apologize for existing? How is suffering or dehumanization passed on, one generation to the next—"a dynasty, a bloodline, a body"?[64]

In order to break the tradition of suffering, Judd's *Patient.* suggests, we need to reckon with the lives and deaths of the women about whom Judd writes. That reckoning entails identifying the ways of seeing set in motion by physicians like Marion J. Sims and showmen like P.T. Barnum (and those who have honored these men with statues, honorifics, and Hollywood films) so that we can root them out together. How did those attitudes shape the treatment of Henrietta Lacks and her family by those who have made use of her "immortal cells"? How were those legacies present in the emergency room in Brooklyn where Esmin Green's slow death went unnoticed or the teaching hospital where all of the doctors-in-training are prepared to look at a patient's cervix but not to acknowledge her humanity? Each of these relationships hinges on the act of seeing—of seeing white bodies as normative, of seeing women's bodies as curiosities, of seeing male medical authority as natural, of seeing black pain as unimportant. In "How to Measure Pain I," Judd imagines a medical practitioner's question to a female patient about her pain: "Can you imagine anything / worse than this?" Then a reminder to the practitioner: "If the answer is no, ask again," suggesting the dismissal or disbelief of a woman's account of her own body, leaving us to empathetically identify with the inadequate treatment that will result.[65]

In order to provide a real cure to these problems, we need proper diagnoses. The word "diagnosis" comes from a Greek word meaning "to distinguish or discern," suggesting that looking carefully and accurately is crucial to making the correct determination. If a disease is misdiagnosed, then the cure is likely to be ineffective. We misrecognize the disease as an aberration—a terrible but isolated mistake, for instance, one to be regretted but ultimately accepted—rather than as an epidemic, something demanding widespread and sustained action. In that misrecognition, we cannot understand the nature of the illness properly, much less address it. The sickness, Judd suggests, is both acute and endemic to the system, built into the empathetic failures that characterize the racial empathy gap and the misprisions that lead us to overlook what's in plain sight. It's an illness that has been repeatedly fatal, too. *Patient.* mourns those deaths, but it also calls *im*patiently for change. "Tears will only leave / you wanting for water," Judd observes wryly in "To the Patient."[66] Instead, as Judd suggests throughout these furious, beautiful elegies, we need to get back to the root of the suffering, to the systemic forces that position black pain and black experience as discountable and invisible.

In "Parity," a poem whose title refers both to "*the fact or condition of having borne a specified number of children*" (as the epigraph tells us) and to the state of being equal, Judd imagines that "There might be something called an impatient."[67] The noun "impatient," with its echo of an "inpatient," someone who has checked into a hospital for medical treatment, suggests a new orientation toward a medical complex that does not see black women in the same light as their white counterparts, that refuses to recognize the links among losses of black lives or treats those losses as statistics to be counted rather than symptoms of a greater disease. Impatience, rather than patience, is what is necessary to move toward a cure. To move past this agonizing grief and suffering, we must demand a proper examination and a correct diagnosis.

> A diagnosis is an ending
> to the idea that
> we are not human.[68]

Notes

1. Thank you to Kevin Quashie, who introduced me to Judd's work, as well as to Patrick Collier, Elizabeth Savage, and the editors of this volume, whose careful readings and valuable questions and suggestions have strengthened this essay in myriad ways.
2. William Neuman, "City Orders Sims Statue Removed from Central Park," *New York Times,* April 16, 2018, www.nytimes.com/2018/04/16/nyregion/nyc-sims-statue-central-park-monument.html.
3. P. R. Lockhart, "New York Just Removed a Statue of a Surgeon Who Experimented on Enslaved Women," *Vox* April 18, 2018, www.vox.com/identities/2018/4/18/17254234/j-marion-sims-experiments-slaves-women-gynecology-statue-removal.
4. In April 2018, the Charleston *Post and Courier* reported "no intention to move or update a monument to Sims near the S.C. statehouse in Columbia … [or to rename] buildings in Columbia used by the S.C. Department of Health and Environmental Control and

the University of South Carolina" (Lauren Sausser, "Statue of J. Marion Sims, notorious South Carolina Doctor, Moved Out of Manhattan," *Post and Courier,* April 17, 2018, www.postandcourier.com/health/statue-of-j-marion-sims-notorious-south-carolina-doctor-moved/article_67a76f92-4268-11e8-8040-13222ab6454f.html). The statue of Sims on the state capitol grounds in Montgomery, Alabama, stands alongside a large monument to Jefferson Davis, the President of the Confederacy, among others. (see Kim Chandler, "Sims Statue at State Capitol Has to Go, Senator Says," *Montgomery Advertiser,* May 10, 2018, www.montgomeryadvertiser.com/story/news/local/alabama/2018/05/10/sims-statue-state-capitol-has-go-senator-says/597564002/).

5. Sims is not the only medical practitioner subject to (Robinson) and Garner's critique. Information and images on the exhibition are available here: https://pioneerworks.org/exhibitions/white-man-on-a-pedestal/. Garner also discusses her project at length in an interview with *Art21,* "Teaching History by Sculpting Experience," https://art21.org/read/doreen-garner-teaching-history-by-sculpting-experience/

6. Simpson discussed her play in a segment titled "Peering Behind the Sheet of Gynecology's Darker History" on the NPR program *Science Friday* (broadcast January 18, 2019; recording available: www.sciencefriday.com/segments/peering-behind-the-sheet-of-gynecologys-darker-history/); a review of the show appeared in the *New York Times* the same month (Ben Brantley, "Review: Reckoning with Medical Betrayals 'Behind the Sheet,'" *New York Times,* January 17, 2019, www.nytimes.com/2019/01/17/theater/behind-the-sheet-review.html).

7. Bettina Judd, *Patient.* (Pittsburgh: Black Lawrence Press, 2014), 58.

8. Ibid., 90.

9. The video itself was made available by the New York Civil Liberties Union, and the Associated Press posted it to YouTube: www.youtube.com/watch?v=9lKUwBCIBzA.

10. Judd, *Patient.,* 58.

11. Ibid., 57.

12. Sarah Ahmed describes the politics of citation as "a rather successful reproductive technology, a way of reproducing the world around certain bodies. . . . ways of making certain bodies and thematics core to the discipline, and others not even part" ("FeministKilljoys.com" https://feministkilljoys.com/2013/09/11/making-feminist-points/). She goes on to point out that "certain bodies take up spaces by screening out the existence of others. If you are screened out (by virtue of the body you have) then you simply do not even appear or register to others."

13. Judd, *Patient.,* 57.

14. Ibid.

15. See, for instance, Linda Villarosa's 2018 article, "The Hidden Toll" published in the *New York Times Magazine,* April 15, 2018, which reports many disturbing statistics about racial disparities in U.S. infant and maternal mortality.

16. Rob Nixon defines "slow violence" as "a violence that occurs gradually and out of sight . . . an attritional violence that is typically not viewed as violence at all" (*Slow Violence and the Environmentalism of the Poor* [Cambridge: Harvard University Press, 2011], 3). He also notes that "[c]asualties of slow violence . . . are the casualties most likely not to be seen, not to be counted" (Ibid., 13).

17. A 2016 study at the University of Virginia uncovered what researchers called "outlandish" and "fantastical" beliefs among white medical residents, including the notion that "blacks have less sensitive nerve endings than whites or that black people's blood coagulates more quickly" (Sandhya Somashekhar, "The Disturbing Reason Some African American Patients May Be Undertreated for Pain," *Washington Post,* April 4, 2016, www.washingtonpost.com/news/to-your-health/wp/2016/04/04/do-blacks-feel-less-pain-than-whites-their-doctors-may-think-so/?utm_term=.60022b5e9797). A 2017 study, "Girlhood Interrupted," found that black girls are perceived to need "less nurturing," "less protection," and less support and comfort than white girls

(Rebecca Epstein, Jamila J. Blake, and Thalia González, "Girlhood Interrupted: The Erasure of Black Girls' Childhood," *Georgetown Law Center on Poverty and Inequality*, 2017, www.law.georgetown.edu/poverty-inequality-center/wp-content/uploads/sites/14/2017/08/girlhood-interrupted.pdf). See also Jason Silverstein, "I Don't Feel Your Pain: A Failure of Empathy Perpetuates Racial Disparities," *Slate*, June 27, 2013, https://slate.com/technology/2013/06/racial-empathy-gap-people-dont-perceive-pain-in-other-races.html.

18. Judd, *Patient.*, 1.
19. In addition to these three women, Sims also wrote that he had "three or four more to experiment on," language that implies that these other women were also enslaved (Marion J. Sims, *The Story of My Life*, [New York: D. Appleton, 1884], 241). Sadly, however, these women's names and stories are lost to us. A 2016 dissertation, Rachel Dudley's "Haunted Hospital: J. Marion Sims and the Legacies of Enslaved Women" (Emory University), attempts in part to reconstruct these women's experiences.
20. Deirdre Cooper Owens discusses this issue in more detail in *Medical Bondage: Race, Gender, and the Origins of American Gynecology*, pointing out that "the value of black women's reproductive labor demanded that it be 'fixed' when it was seen as 'broken' by those who depended on their labor" (Athens: University of Georgia Press, 2017, 41).
21. Judd, *Patient.*, 5.
22. The historical record affirms this attitude—Karla F.C. Holloway points out that "[n]owhere in Sims's autobiography is there a single word about what brought these enslaved girls and women to the barn on his property that he uses as an operating theater" (*Private Bodies, Public Texts: Race, Gender, and a Cultural Bioethics* [Durham: Duke University Press, 2011], 46).
23. Sims's biographer acknowledges that "Sims's experiments brought them physical pain, it is true" but insists that "they bore it [with] amazing patience and fortitude—a grim stoicism which may have been part of their racial endowment or which possibly had been bred into them through several generations of enforced submission" (qtd. in Terri Kapsalis, *Public Privates: Performing Gynecology from Both Ends of the Speculum* [Durham: Duke University Press, 1997], 273).
24. Judd, *Patient.*, 32.
25. Ibid., 31.
26. "Remembering Anarcha, Lucy, and Betsey: The Mothers of Modern Gynecology." Interview by Shankar Vedantam, *Hidden Brain Podcast*, NPR, February 7, 2017. Transcript available www.npr.org/templates/transcript/transcript.php?storyId=513764158.
27. Christina Sharpe, *In the Wake: On Blackness and Being* (Durham: Duke University Press, 2016), 14.
28. Sharpe, *In the Wake*, 2.
29. As Matt Reimann has documented, "the public censure of black rights movements has a long and storied history in the United States," going back to judgments of Fredrick Douglass's speeches as "a little too fierce on the slavery question" ("People Have Been Telling Black Activists How to Protest for 150 Years," *Timeline*, July 13, 2016, https://timeline.com/black-lives-matter-protest-tactics-33bd8e753429).
30. Joice Heth Poster, *The Lost Museum Archive*, 1835, https://lostmuseum.cuny.edu/archive/joice-heth-poster-1835. Another poem in the book, "Joice Heth Presents: Herself," signifies on the language of a broadside advertisement, using a combination of upper and lowercase words, italics, and boldface print (Judd, *Patient.*, 48).
31. Judd, *Patient.*, 35.
32. Ibid., 33.
33. Simpson makes a similar point in her *Science Friday* interview, pointing out that the women may well have been hopeful, at least initially, that Sims's surgery would provide relief from their symptoms. However, she concludes that "the idea of consent in a world where these women weren't, you know, even really considered fully human

seems, for lack of a better phrase, seems a little ridiculous to me. . . . Their okay, I don't think, would really have had any effect on whether or not they were experimented on" ("Peering").

34. Ibid., 31.
35. Kapsalis, *Public Privates,* 33. An epigraph to one of Judd's poems about Heth comes from Barnum's autobiography, in which he describes seeing Heth in a posture not unlike that of a patient at a gynecological exam, "lying upon a high lounge in the middle of the room; her lower extremities were drawn up, with her knees elevated some two feet above the top of the lounge" (qtd. in Judd, *Patient.,* 37).
36. See Benjamin Reiss, *The Showman and the Slave: Race, Death, and Memory in Barnum's America* (Cambridge: Harvard University Press, 2010) and Uri McMillan, *Embodied Avatars: Genealogies of Black Feminist Art and Performance* (New York: New York University Press, 2015). McMillan notes that Barnum's claims about Heth became increasingly hyperbolic as he sought to "edit, exaggerate, and rewrite her memory and the past she appeared in" (56).
37. Judd, *Patient.,* 6.
38. McMillan, *Embodied,* 17; Judd, *Patient.,* 6. McMillan suggests that Heth's wizened body also demonstrated to white audiences that she had sacrificed herself in service to "white American identity," rendering her both "a beloved object of affection and, conversely, an embodiment of racial monstrosity" (28).
39. Judd, *Patient.,* 50.
40. Ibid., 51.
41. Ibid., 9.
42. Ibid.
43. Phillip Williams, "Gynecology Was Built on the Backs of Black Women Anyway—An Interview with Bettina Judd," *RaceBaitr,* July 7, 2015, http://racebaitr.com/2015/07/07/gynecology-was-built-on-the-backs-of-black-women-anyway-an-interview-with-bettina-judd/#).
44. Barnum profited even then, charging onlookers $0.50 to attend the autopsy; the physician who performed it concluded that she was between 75–80 years old. See Reiss, *The Showman and the Slave,* for more information.
45. Deborah McDowell describes the ways that news reports' "running tallies of shootings and killings [of black men] . . . seem to mimic the innocuousness of sports scores, stock market reports, or year-to-date precipitation. . . . a form of counting that underscores how little black bodies 'count'" ("Viewing the Remains: A Polemic on Death, Spectacle, and the [Black] Family," in *The Familial Gaze,* ed. Marianne Hirsch [Hanover: Dartmouth College, 1999], p. 154).
46. Sharpe, *In the Wake,* 13. Darren Wilson, the officer who shot the unarmed Michael Brown, described Brown as "Hulk Hogan"—a cartoonish professional wrestler—"almost bulking up to run through the shots, like it was making him mad that I'm shooting him" (qtd. in Sharpe, *In the Wake,* 82).
47. Judd, *Patient.,* 1.
48. "Forging the Empathy Chain: An Interview with Bettina Judd," Interview by Kyle G. Dargan, *Post No Ills,* June 19, 2015, www.postnoills.com/main/?p=937
49. Williams, "Gynecology Was Built."
50. Linda Villarosa, "The Hidden Toll," *The New York Times Magazine,* April 15, 2018, 33–34. See also Kim Brooks, who explores why maternal mortality and injury rates are far higher in the U.S. than they are in other developed nations ("America Is Blaming Pregnant Women for Their Own Deaths," *The New York Times,* November 16, 2018, www.nytimes.com/2018/11/16/opinion/sunday/maternal-mortality-rates.html).
51. For more on Lacks and the HeLa cell line, see Rebecca Skloot, *The Immortal Life of Henrietta Lacks* (New York: Crown, 2010).
52. Judd, *Patient.,* 64.

53. Ibid., 65.
54. Ibid., 64 (ellipsis in original).
55. Ibid., 15.
56. Ibid.
57. Ibid., 9.
58. Ibid., 12.
59. Judd, *Patient.*, 11.
60. Ibid., 16.
61. Ibid.
62. Ibid., 72.
63. Ibid.
64. Ibid., 1.
65. Ibid., 8.
66. Ibid., 83.
67. Ibid., 55.
68. Ibid., 82.

PART II

Hauntings and Reckonings: Coda

Tiffany Austin

Peaches*

"I'll go."
With my hair under my arms along with the rest
underneath my skirt, a shaft.

But I'll go
after hearing: I don't want to be the first
I don't want death
I want my life
I'm afraid
I can't.

I'll go
because I'm used to going
in the dark to an outhouse of living.

You have to look closely
even though I'm
the one raising
something white
in my green dress with no sleeves
arms yanked before when they found out I was a woman.

I was a different woman
in Mississippi
spoken near some man.

I said the same to him,
I'll go.
But where do you go from land and more land?
We can sit on water.
We can sleep for a while, here.
Three days, then sleep. In my yellow dress, sleep makes the need go away.

But to be held in sleep. Land under fingers.
To be covered by gauze of skunk,
no better, by nakedness.

I was awoken by the name of the place I belonged to.
They should have been hunting birds. Instead they knocked on sleep.
No time to pray.
To that place I belonged to.
Corkscrews of cock meat.
Eye—broken yolk.

They are somewhere on a plate.
I can't touch. I can't hear you any longer.
The swallowing's gone to Illinois.

I'll go.
Burning in the rain.
Beforehand, I was in between
beds
between debris
tastes like my lips.

He had to watch me being
wrenched
"It made me mean."

Didn't he know
I had already smelled him
even before.
You can smell death coming
between his and mine
he knew, I'd go.

Watching him sweat and moan and not smell
I'm tender there. I'll go
because tender can lay upon tender.

*There is a moment in Stanley Nelson's *The Black Panthers* documentary when
the group surrenders to police—the first being a woman—and the story from
the Mississippi delta of two lovers fleeing a sharecropping plantation, being
found and lynched.

Charles Braxton

Strays in the Hood

gunshots fly through the dead night air
whistling somber songs in the hue of
blue. as the projectile's prey prays for
the blessed prince of peace to save
them from another meaningless death
but it is futile to hope for
another miracle when oxygen ain't bulletproof

Lauren K. Alleyne

Poetry Workshop after the Verdict: For Trayvon

Morning lights your four windows,
and you wake. It is, already, another day.
You stumble, befuddled, into the bathroom,
so white it's like you're inside the moon.
You look in the mirror, then turn away;
better to just leave. Get your body out the door
and into the blue day. You follow the brown—
sparrow, maybe?—perched outside on the rail
like a guide. Bring everything already packed
inside your skin—a dead brown boy and his free killer,
his judge and jury of women, the six *not guilty* bells
clanging again and again in your weary ear.
No, that's your alarm; it's time to be a poet.
You bring your pen and notebook, your poet's eye.
You try to follow instructions: *Write what you see.*
It's simple. You walk down the road,
safe in your pack of poets—women, white.
(You do not write this in your notebook.)
Instead, your eyes find and follow the lines
that run everywhere—across the street,
up the railings, across windows and shutters,
siding, shingled rooftops—parsing the landscape
into cells. Your white journal pages, ruled.
You write down all the signs: *Closed;*
Peter's Property Management; Not for public use;
These dunes aren't made for walking; stop.
But you cannot stop. You follow the wind,
ripe with salt and already-sweaty bodies.
You see a pile of beached boats lumped
like bodies in a mass grave; a stone wall drowning
while sleepy dories drift by; sun-bleached
stumps, slowly going to rot; You see
the sun marking time as it slips higher
and higher, the day stretching overhead,
last night's dark already memory. You see
an American flag, and below it, the reddening back
of a white boy lying face down on the sand,
his body the opposite of a chalk outline. You write:
the light skitters brilliantly atop the bay's piercing
blue. You write: *A boy, his light hair lightening to gold,*
his body, so still, still breathing. You write: *Not guilty,*
Not guilty, Not guilty, Not guilty, Not guilty, Not guilty.

Lauren K. Alleyne

Elegy: For Tamir

This was going to be a curse poem—
me hexing the man who ghosted you,
slivering his days into two-second
increments of agony. I began writing
the playground you could make of his body,
surfing his blood, making monkey bars
of his ribs, dancing his heart's rhythm
on his neck—an inexhaustible mischief,
an incorrigible spirit of boy let loose
in the white country of the murderer's
unshielded body. I would wish him dead,
but I want him nowhere near the realm
he exiled you to, so instead I composed
a soundtrack for his nightmares, a mixtape
of your laugh/the gurgle of your blood
exiting the wound he gave you/a festival
of sirens/your sister's scream/bang/repeat.
This, I understand, is the grief talking.
This is the unchained melody of rage.
But to write his haunting is to name you
hell and you have been misnamed enough,
sweet boy. I make of these words an altar,
instead. I breathe this poem into a prayer,
each syllable a taper burning in memory
of you. Sweet boy, let me build you here
a new body, radiantly black, limber, poised
to become its most beautiful becoming.
Let it be spirited with starsong and rich
with tomorrows. Let me make you a lifetime of days honeyed with love: feast.
You are safe here. Let me write you
again into your name, *Tamir*, baptize
you with tongue and tears. *Tamir. Tamir.*
Let me write you a black boy's heaven,
where freedom is a verb conjugated
by your being, where your only synonym
is beloved, blessed, child of the universe.
Instead, I imagine you there, beginning.

PART III
Elegists as Activists

Jacqueline Johnson

Soul Memory

(for Renisha McBride)

Forgive the grandmother who found you
barely conscious mumbling, stupid drunk
walking circles around your car, who thought she
could leave you and go back into her house.
Forgive the loss of mother wit; the
inability to grab you and bring you—daughter,
you babygirl on into the house.
Forgive her—lost in the disconnect of centuries,
to not call for an ambulance to get you help.
Forgive her return to the street to find
you gone out of sight. Too old to follow you,
to get someone, anyone to go look for you.
Forgive yourself for going out that night
of all nights to party and drink,
to hang out like any normal nineteen year old,
to know inebriation's high; to believe you were
in control. Forgive the lost ones of you.
Forgive the night so dark your brownskin
self could not be found. Forgive your ori
so blindly drunk and in shock from a car crash;

forgive the incoherent selves wandering only
knowing to seek help. Crying for help.
Forgive this moment, day that you went
into that an all white woods and neighborhood.
Forgive yourself so lost, mother wit and father
wit gone. So lost, so shocked. So drunk you
rang that man's door and all of your last
moments lost in the horror of shots
to your head, heart and soul.
Forgive the night you wanted to party so,
wanted to live so; forgive all the wrong turns,
the last four drinks you had. Forgive yourself
for thinking somehow you were in control,
had done this how many times before.
Forgive the cursed moment of speed,
of all the wrong turns, of walking and walking
on the longest walk that would never end
until you were nothing but soul.
Lost black woman, lost black girl
on a white man's porch, in a place
so bad he never gave you a chance.
Came out shooting at your blackness,
black woman blackness seeking help.
Forgive this time, the moment that never
gave you a chance. Forgive all the wrong turns,
the speed, the drinks, the desire to party.
Forgive this time that never gave you a chance.

Chris Campanioni

#IWokeUpLikeThis or: The Latest In Space-Age #PostInternet Pajamas

French investigators said Thursday that the police officers in Paris who sodomized a young black man with a baton did so accidentally, & that the incident does not constitute rape.★

If this makes you uncomfortable, I am unapologetic. If you are disturbed, there is good reason for disturbance in a culture of leisure & entertainment that has very little patience or predilection for acknowledging the systemic oppression of others who do not look like them, talk like them, or fuck like them. It is our responsibility to demand the accountability of our public servants & the press who serves to circulate knowledge & information. We should all be uncomfortable; we should comfort ourselves in knowing now is the moment in which disturbance can be a weapon in which to render these apologies in a literal form. Dynamic tension as both a method & description of irregular accounting discourse & practice. A messiness that I don't want to clean up; a messiness that I want to live with. All acts as acts of epistemological & representational disturbance. It is about refusing what refuses you. & it is in this shared practice of refusal that we can create a mutually-inclusive community of non-normative voices.

★The 22-year-old youth worker, identified only as Théo, says a group of four police officers physically and sexually assaulted him on February 2. He says he confronted the officers after seeing one of them slap a young person during an identity check. Then, Théo says, the officers took him around the corner and sodomized him with a truncheon, spit on him, beat his genitals and called him names, including "negro" and "bitch." Théo suffered severe anal and facial injuries during the incident, parts of which were captured on video. See Jesselyn Cook, "Investigators Say French Police Who Sodomized Black Man With a Baton Did So By Accident," *Huffington Post* (February 9, 2017), web. Retrieved from https://www.huffpost.com/entry/paris-police-brutality-sodomy_n_589cc442e4b04061313c43fd

disturb

transitive verb
1
a : to interfere with : interrupt
b : to alter the position or arrangement of
c : to upset the natural & especially the ecological balance or relations of

2

a : to destroy the tranquility or composure of
b : to throw into
c : to alarm
d : to put to inconvenience
ex: *sorry to disturb you at such a late hour*

It's late, the lights are out, I'm stirred from sleep out of necessity. It's hunger. I woke up like this. The same in the night as in the day & & & & &

Won't you offer me a hand to hold or eat?

Chris Campanioni

rendition

but I never cut the other

   kites & since then I

recall how I was made

    me kneel with my

facing outward

    a pail full

dark   sky   not to mention

other things & my two hands

    designed to be flown

pressed together   & seeing that

I could get some air

    the same to me

as to the others

    again to what

question was already covered

   facing outward &

forced my head down   without my

   knowing just as I was

     a long string

about to

        cloth or plastic

   come closer to me

I shook

my half-carried

     as above an altar

   unreturned

& to start to see

   how another was standing

in for

     my body (one

always reads

   just as I was about to

too much

   breathe deeper

into things)

   it is always

a question of

   cutting & this was

repeated again & again

   not to mention

my youth as far

   again & again

as my chest

      & called in another

again & again

      to accept the first part

(several times in a matter

      & personally took (a)part

      held me with my feet up

I could only sing silently

      in the air

a hymn I had known   by heart

      to try some other method

as a child)

      am I supposed to

lie then

      on a bed of news

papers   keeping

      to myself

      so to speak

(I was once again

      & this repeated

silent)

      thinking what's been left

out   what I can't

do you

      remember   after

syndication

    after the careful

    rendition

to be read

but I never

    more than two

ways   cut

         to a

question   I

    credit

sequence &

    try & protect

the seething flesh

    too large for the film

so as to never be

    shown together in a single

shot

        this is what D&G

call

        a *smooth space*

Cameron Barnett

Uniform; or things I would paint if I were a painter

Solomon Northup robed in black, powdered wig, gaveling
a courtroom into order; Rosa Parks in the driver's seat,
black billie club slung from her waist; Eric Garner
wearing a six-pointed badge wrapped with a black
mourning band; Emmett Till buttoned up to the neck
in the best blue the law has to offer; Huey Newton
leaned over a car, doing a traffic stop in downtown Oakland;
Malcolm X with a sheriff's cap on, chin strap tightened,
black glasses reflecting in the sun; MLK in brass buttons
and chevrons—or MLK in SWAT gear sitting at a lunch counter—
or MLK at Obama's inauguration holding the bible;
Freddie Gray on an officer's bike, reflective vest flashing
as he rounds a corner; The Little Rock Nine parking
their police cruisers at the front of the school; "Black Lives Matter"
chiseled at the feet of the Lincoln Memorial; Lady Liberty with handcuffs
clutched in her fingers, snapping at the chain.

8

"A CAUSE DIVINELY SPUN"

The Poet in an Age of Social Unrest

Licia Morrow Hendriks

> "It is harrowing to accept a narrative of black survival as radical fantasy, though . . . threats to black bodies on this earth are plentiful and real."
>
> Tracy K. Smith, "Political Poetry Is Hot Again"[1]

The twenty-first-century black poet is caught in what might be regarded as an existential crisis evocative of the psychological dilemma typified in Du Boisian double consciousness.[2] Akin to the ever-conflicting duality of nationality and race, these poets have yet another layer of veritably irreconcilable competing allegiances: The calling of the traditionally genteel artistic avocation to capture the essence of human experience by composing verse in the rarefied atmosphere of ivory tower intellectualism, and the imperative to articulate the collective grief and despair African Americans feel as the casualties of the rising phenomenon of homicide by cop[3] continue to mount. Poetry—the cultural repository of literary grace, elegance, and refinement—is in virtually every respect far removed from the street-level gritty reality of hostile confrontations between police officers entrusted to enforce the law and the individuals those officers perceive as immediate threats to the order of the communities they inhabit. Lyric verse is equally far removed from the brutality of vigilante injustices perpetrated by those who execute first and ask questions never. The poetic muse ideally abides worlds apart from the scenes of repeated and redoubled violence that manifest when juridical exonerations sanction the acts of lethal force and wanton aggression that leave black corpses in their wake. Such cognitive dissonance prompts a reconsideration of the man who might be deemed the spiritual precursor to the poets of the Black Lives Matter era: Countée Cullen, the Harlem Renaissance's methodological and ideological purist.

Given Cullen's abiding convictions concerning the social responsibility incumbent upon the poetic enclave to espouse the highest of moral virtues, uninflected and undeterred by crass material considerations, he represents an essential literary figure to recuperate in order to unpack the seeming paradox elegists of African descent continually face. Reconsidering Cullen helps to clarify how to make elegiac verse not only relevant, but also central to the resolution of the racially driven devaluation of the lives of black Americans. By placing Cullen in conversation with Tracy K. Smith, the Harvard-educated former U.S. poet laureate, I aim to chart the evolution of the philosophical outlook and artistic vision of African American poets who achieve a place in the national canon while using that platform to crusade for the eradication of race-based prejudice and discrimination in American institutions and public life, as well as in the residual personal sentiments of the purportedly culturally enlightened.

My interest here is in interrogating the role of the poet in the process of cultural reform, both of its illegitimate practices and its misguided convictions. Cullen's work revolves around the notion of the poet as a visionary, devoid of self-interest or impure motive, and committed to idealistic endeavor. In thinking through the extent to which that standard persists, I want to read Cullen's signature statement anticipating the Black Lives Matter crusade—"Scottsboro, Too, Is Worth Its Song" (1934)—against selections from Smith's most recent published collection, *Wade in the Water* (2018). In and of itself, Smith's position as the officially sanctioned artistic voice of the nation invites contemplation of the degree to which poets must function as agents of social change. Both in her own work and in the way in which her reflective and responsive readings of other poets model how to read poetry purposefully, Smith reinvigorates elegy, issuing a clarion call to the American public to heal the fissures caused by identity-driven division through the transfiguration possible only through embracing an ethics of love.

Cultural critics have contended for decades that the influence of the poet has been steadily waning. Nearly 30 years ago in his public challenge to the genre "Can Poetry Matter?" (1991), Dana Gioia argued that poetry had lost its social relevance as the profession had become codified as an academic discipline rather than a culturally entrenched artistic endeavor. As a result, he observed, poetry had vanished as a defining force in impacting how and what Americans think and feel:

> poetry boosters offer impressive recitations of the numerical growth of publications, programs, and professorships. Given the bullish statistics on poetry's material expansion, how does one demonstrate that *its intellectual and spiritual influence has eroded*? One cannot easily marshal numbers, but to any candid observer the evidence throughout the world of ideas and letters seems inescapable.[4]

As is established in the Introduction to this volume, however, "the relationship between art and activism" that has driven black poetics since the eighteenth-century intervention of Phillis Wheatley "continues to hold sway as current writers

work in concert with Black Lives Matter and other activist groups." African American poets have never been silent. Like the enslaved "black and unknown bards"[5]
James Weldon Johnson credited with pioneering the spiritual lyric genre, poets
of color have persisted, albeit unrecognized, unacknowledged, and unappreciated
by the mainstream. As academically polished poets venture outside their confined
esoteric sphere, however, they can work to make their artistic medium accessible
once more. Concomitantly, as spoken word performance events proliferate and
while social media outlets gain traction as the grassroots venue for the dissemination of elegiac verse and expressions of social critique, the tide may now be
turning in favor of the popular reclamation of the poet as the voice of the masses.
The rising prevalence of poets gaining an audience through posting content and
accumulating followers challenges the conventionally established standard of an
elite coterie of academy-groomed artists, each stamped with the pedigree of an
MFA. Regardless of the poet's origins, I contend that the new millennium is witnessing a resurgence in the relevance and impact of poetry as a means to express
communal trauma and galvanize a response by channeling that pain and outrage
into organized action. The contemporary protest elegy, emblematized by Smith
and descended from Cullen, performs the transformative cultural work of raising
consciousness and defining a generational agenda.

Nearly 100 years ago, when Countée Cullen began his career as a poet, the
social climate was, at least superficially, one far different from that which predomi-
nates today. The decade fondly sentimentalized as the Roaring Twenties followed
on the heels of the turbulent Red Summer of 1919, when, after the demobiliza-
tion of military forces from overseas, belligerent white mobs perpetrated a wave
of lynchings and race riots across the nation in an effort to suppress the surge of
race pride and rampant assertion of the civil rights that black soldiers presum-
ably earned in the trenches of World War I, and dared to exercise in their home
nation.[6] The outbreak of violence occurred when Cullen was just a teenager, two
years before his matriculation at NYU. He would go on to be elected Phi Beta
Kappa, and then proceed to graduate study at Harvard, where he earned Master's
degrees in both English and French in 1926. Cullen's intellectual promise yielded
fruit early in life: "His poetry first won acclaim while he was in high school; his
first book was published upon his graduation from college. From the age of seven-
teen, Cullen was showered with prizes, culminating with a Guggenheim fellowship when he was twenty-five."[7] Cullen emerged on the cultural scene at a time
ideally suited to enable him to achieve a degree of influence and prominence that
would have been unlikely in an earlier era. Supported and encouraged by such
black intellectual icons as W.E.B. Du Bois at *The Crisis* and Charles S. Johnson
at *Opportunity*,[8] and selflessly groomed by Jessie Fauset, herself an accomplished
and prolific writer who Langston Hughes credited with having been "one of
the midwives who helped give birth to the artistic development of the Harlem
Renaissance,"[9] Cullen cultivated a sensitive awareness of his responsibility to use
his literary gift in the service of combating racial injustice.

"Scottsboro, Too, Is Worth Its Song," the poem which furnishes the excerpt that inspired the title of this chapter, is a response to "a cause divinely spun":[10] The travesty of due process represented by the 1931 capital case against nine black teenagers falsely accused of raping two white women on a train in Alabama. Instead of framing a general social outcry, indicting a racist judicial apparatus, or castigating an apathetic populace, in the poem's dedication Cullen targets a particular audience: "A poem to American poets." As Cullen proceeds to take his fellow poets to task for their failure to respond to what he perceives as the quintessential constellation of corruptions both public and private, he insinuates that the silence itself is the most disturbing indicator of America's willful blindness to its own moral bankruptcy.

Historically, Cullen's commitment to the cause of black advancement has been problematically called into question. In his classic polemic "The Negro Artist and the Racial Mountain" (1926), Langston Hughes famously excoriated a fellow artist of the Harlem Renaissance coterie for allegedly subordinating his identity as a member of the black racial collective to his identity as a creative writer:

> One of the most promising of the young Negro poets said to me once, "I want to be a poet—not a Negro poet," meaning, I believe, "I want to write like a white poet"; meaning subconsciously, "I would like to be a white poet"; meaning behind that, "I would like to be white."[11]

While Hughes declines here to disclose the name of the disdained rival in question, lamenting that the young man's "desire to run away spiritually from his race" would inevitably undermine his success in his chosen endeavor, critical consensus undisputedly acknowledges Hughes's target to be Countée Cullen.[12] Though their ideological differences are undeniable, to suggest that Cullen actively sought to escape the identity Hughes enthusiastically embraced is a harsh distortion, as Michael Anderson contends: "Cullen hardly lacked racial awareness: consider only the titles of his poetry collections, *Color*, *Copper Sun*, *The Black Christ*. Where he differed from Hughes was in their conceptions of racial propriety."[13] From that first collection, *Color*, published in 1925, two poems in particular, "Heritage" and "Yet Do I Marvel," offer insight into the trenchant nature of Cullen's recognition and appreciation of his racial identity.

"Heritage" interrogates the degree to which African origins can inflect American-born descendants of slaves, as the speaker repeatedly and cryptically muses:

> One three centuries removed
> From the scenes his fathers loved,
> Spicy grove, cinnamon tree,
> What is Africa to me?[14]

While it is possible to read these lines as flippantly dismissive of the significance of the African continent to a person whose antecedents inhabited the region 300 years prior, it is equally viable to understand the speaker as introspectively ruminating upon the possibility of making his ancestral origins meaningful in a culture that pervasively devalues Africa and her progeny. As Caryl Phillips has observed, Cullen was continuing in the literary tradition of writers reflecting upon a disturbingly inchoate past: "To be more specific, they were dreaming of repairing the rupture in their personal and social history that had been caused by the institution of slavery. One could see back as far as Charleston or Savannah or Baltimore, but what came before had to be largely imagined."[15] The soul-searching evinced by Cullen's verse is thus not only quite reasonable, but also perfectly consistent with sentiments expressed by many other writers of his generation.

In similar fashion to "Heritage," "Yet Do I Marvel" invites contradictory interpretations when the sonnet closes with the speaker revealing his perplexity in the face of divine design: "Yet do I marvel at this curious thing: / To make a poet black, and bid him sing!"[16] Regarding these lines as a self-defeatist affirmation of the very desire to become white that Hughes accused Cullen of harboring, would, as Fred M. Fetrow argued, perpetuate the persistent fallacy resulting in the poem being "as widely misinterpreted . . . as Cullen has been misunderstood as a poet."[17] Instead, the poem is an indictment of the intolerance that makes American society a hostile environment within which to practice an art inherently endowed with the cultural capital of respectability and esteem.

This reverence for the poet's proper role as cultural luminary fuels Cullen's diatribe against his colleagues in "Scottsboro." Specifically, Cullen conveys his idealism when he refers to poets as "those whose eyes are on the sun,"[18] reifying a tradition of elevating the power of perception with which the poet is endowed above that accorded the general populace. As Neil Covey notes in a discussion of William Wordsworth's characterization of the artistic ideal central to nineteenth-century British Romanticism, "One of the primary assumptions behind the conception of the poet, then, is that he is somehow more attuned than the ordinary person to what he sees, that his gaze is qualitatively different, better."[19] Cullen's conviction that poets have superior insight intensifies his profound disappointment with what he regards as their collective failure to fulfill their implicit obligation to champion virtue and denounce categorical villainy, fully embracing their role as dauntless crusaders "Against disease and death and all things fell."[20] For Cullen, an incomparable opportunity to demonstrate this unflinching commitment to egalitarian values and the wholesale opposition to "epic wrong"[21] presented itself in the untenable predicament of the so-called Scottsboro Boys, nine black teenagers in rural Alabama who were arrested for, and subsequently nearly all hastily tried on, charges of gang rape until the Supreme Court intervened and reversed their death penalty convictions.[22]

Cullen contrasts the radio silence on the bizarre permutations of the Scottsboro case against the outpouring of passionate grievance over the rush to judgment and persistent prejudice that condemned the Italian-born anarchists Nicola Sacco and Bartolomeo Vanzetti to execution, an outcome attributed by a chorus of international poets to American xenophobia and abiding distrust of antidemocratic political philosophies. Cullen closes with a terse acknowledgment: "But they have raised no cry. / I wonder why."[23] The paucity of effusion entailed in his dispassionate tone bespeaks the profound irony infusing the expression of "wonder." Cullen recognizes the source of the pervasive indifference or active unwillingness to tackle the thorny issue of American race prejudice. His implication, in invoking the Sacco-Vanzetti debacle of the decade prior, is to highlight the hypocrisy attendant upon making racial affinity the precondition for advocacy. Notwithstanding the purported crimes being murder vs. rape, the sole differentiating factor between the incidences of juridical railroading entailed the skin color of the victimized parties. In castigating the poets who declined to comment on the travesty of justice which consigned the Scottsboro Boys to death row, Cullen is publicly reprimanding those who permitted race bigotry to corrupt the purity of their calling; if the tragic fate of nine young men of color facing execution for a crime they did not commit is insufficient to generate the requisite emotional energy to catalyze a reaction from those who are supposed to be untainted by the unsavory prejudice permeating life amongst the masses, then truly, in America, *black* lives do not matter.

The current historical moment within which poets are writing is different from that which produced Cullen, though perhaps more in outward form than internal substance; Black Lives Matter activism, as is noted in this volume's Introduction, is rooted in the same systems of racial oppression that have plagued the nation for decades: "generations of poets have reminded readers that the white-supremacist ideologies that structured American life during the 1950s have neither been fully redressed nor eradicated." As Carol S. Anderson suggests in *White Rage: The Unspoken Truth of Our Racial Divide* (2016), her analysis of the underpinnings of contemporary American race relations, the consistent pattern of atrocities targeting the black community is fueled by the inability of whites to brook challenges to their entrenched hierarchical authority:

> The trigger for white rage, inevitably, is black advancement. It is not the mere presence of black people that is the problem; rather, it is blackness with ambition, with drive, with purpose, with aspirations, and with demands for full and equal citizenship. It is blackness that refuses to accept subjugation, to give up. A formidable array of policy assaults and legal contortions has *consistently* punished black resilience, black resolve.[24]

The very consistency with which white repression has operated to oppose and obliterate racial uplift is one of its more sinister aspects, Anderson contends, as

"White rage is not about visible violence, but rather it works its ways through the courts, the legislatures, and a range of government bureaucracies. It wreaks havoc subtly, almost imperceptibly, certainly, for a nation consistently drawn to the spectacular—to what it can *see*."[25] The surreptitious nature of institutionalized racism and systems of marginalization and oppression makes them more difficult to challenge due to the plausible deniability of patterns of discriminatory conduct. The record speaks for itself, however, with respect to the systemic absolution—in both courts of law and widespread public opinion—of the perpetrators of lethal violence against people of color: "And as the judicial system in state after state turned free those who had decided a neighborhood's 'safety' meant killing first and asking questions later, a very real warning was sent that black lives don't matter."[26] Much like the Scottsboro proceedings of yesteryear and despite the collective indignation of communities of color manifested in the protests that coalesced into Black Lives Matter as an organized action, the system routinely exonerates those responsible for taking the lives of blacks they regard as threatening, and the white majority is perceived as essentially complacent.[27]

Rather than settling into this hostile dynamic of racial antagonism, the work of former U.S. poet laureate Tracy K. Smith urges the nation toward an introspective evaluation of the potential for empathy. Thus far, the fear associated with this disturbing trend of unwarranted fatalities has been in many ways linked to the shocking recognition that beyond the common denominator of African ancestry and a predilection for the masculine gender, there is no predictable pattern or rational justification for the inevitable outcomes. Seemingly mundane situations escalate suddenly to life-or-death conflicts, and the façade of an orderly society protecting against such human rights violations is revealed as an illusion. Such a cultural climate necessarily breeds apprehension and suspicion in those in the black community, who have been conditioned to feel as if possessing a superabundance of melanin were in and of itself a crime. For many African Americans born in the post-Civil Rights presumed "promised land" of the latter decades of the twentieth century, such stigmatization belongs to a bygone era of racial repression, making the contemporary crisis an irreconcilable conundrum.

As the daughter of Alabama-born parents, Smith reflects contemplatively on her intuitive understanding of the abiding risks entailed in daily existence in the racially charged social environment of the segregated South of her parents' adolescence. In her 2015 memoir, *Ordinary Light*, Smith describes a childhood visit to her maternal grandmother during which she delights in being entertained by family anecdotes while being ever cognizant of the sinister presence of the unspoken dangers which lurked "just outside of the frame of those stories of the long-ago days down south....The terrible threats to people like us, threats of violence and scorn. Things people did to people they didn't view as people. Murders. Lynchings. Even just a few words spat out with the right kind of force."[28] The litany of manifestations of intolerance Smith catalogs here is one that she, in the innocence of her youth, firmly relegated to the past, naively believing that such racially coded acts of hostility were matters of historical record unimaginable in the progressive present.

Though subsequent experience does not wholly unseat her notion of America as a starkly oppositional social environment from that which her parents knew as children, Smith does come to appreciate at a relatively early age how identity politics function—how age, gender, class, and race shape perception and experience. A humanitarian-aid telethon she sees with a middle-aged white after-school caregiver compels eight-year-old Tracy to recognize that the two of them had processed the series of images of black children from across the globe in diametrically contrasting ways:

> Those faces hadn't made her feel a part of the wider world at all but more like a spectator, someone on safari, it seemed to me, watching from the kind of distance that facilitates judgment or fear. It didn't stop me from liking her or from thinking of her as an ally or a friend, but it did remind me that simply because of who we were, she and I had been equipped to see certain things differently.[29]

This recognition speaks to the limits of mutual understanding and the degree to which the "color-line," that "problem of the twentieth century" Du Bois so presciently identified at its dawn, can be effectively bridged.[30] An encounter with a peer provokes Smith's psychological confrontation with Du Boisian double-consciousness; a young white girl over for a visit to the Smith family home in Fairfield, California, a bedroom community midway between Sacramento and the Silicon Valley, poses the query that recalls the Hughes-Cullen conflict and precipitates considerable prepubescent soul-searching: "Don't you wish you were white?"[31] Smith's reconstruction of her meditation on this philosophical question is a telling insight into the contemporary operations of what Du Bois called a "peculiar sensation":

> She didn't know it, but she meant *Is it hard being black?* . . . I didn't know the girl terribly well, but I had an idea of what she felt, or wondered, or thought without realizing she thought it. My mind had learned to see both ways at once; hers had not yet come up against the need for such acrobatics.[32]

The sheer intellectual weight of filtering every thought through this double-sided prism is burdensome, certainly, but also allows for a measure of sensitivity in poetic expression which puts the conditioned acuteness of perception to worthwhile use.

As Cullen once grappled with the competing imperatives of loyalty to craft and the creed of racial uplift, Smith works within an economy of poetry framed to political purpose. Case in point: At the core of Smith's *Wade in the Water* collection is the heart-wrenching "I Will Tell You the Truth about This, I Will Tell You

All about It," a found poem crafted to accompany the 2011 Smithsonian Museum National Portrait Gallery exhibition curated to commemorate the Civil War sesquicentennial. A deftly and artfully designed compilation of correspondence penned by African Americans directly impacted by involvement in the internecine conflict, the poem features testimony long suppressed and silenced, as Smith attests, quite intentionally:

> Once I began reading these texts, it became clear to me that the voices in question should command all of the space within my poem. I hope that they have been arranged in such a way as to highlight certain of the main factors affecting blacks during the Civil War, chiefly: the compound effects of slavery and war upon the African American family; the injustices to which black soldiers were often subject; the difficulty black soldiers and their widows faced in attempting to claim pensions after the war; and the persistence, good faith, dignity, and commitment to the ideals of democracy that ran through the many appeals to President Lincoln, the Freedmen's Bureau, and other authorities to whom petitions were routinely addressed during and after the war.[33]

Smith's artistic project centers the authenticity of "I" narrative self-disclosure as a means of both reinvesting the authors of the assorted epistles with legitimate agency, and connecting their experiences with those of other human beings in similar subject positions across space and time.

Such archival poetic manifestations constitute a meaningful interventionist function of verse as historical restoration, reinforcing the significance of the contemporary poet as the central mediator of harnessing language in the conscious interest of public service and cultural rehabilitation: Smith has observed that "political poetry, even here in America, has . . . become a means of owning up to the complexity of our problems, of accepting the likelihood that even we the righteous might be implicated by or complicit in some facet of the very wrongs we decry."[34] As poets regain their rightful stature as those uniquely equipped to recognize and militate against what Cullen called "all disgrace / And epic wrong," American culture can reorient itself around a properly moral axis.[35]

Wade in the Water must be appreciated as a collection driven by the overarching elegiac principle of chronicling a wide-ranging array of incidences revealing human susceptibility to pain and vulnerability to exploitation. Smith also models how art functions to make sense of physical, emotional, and psychological trauma. This breadth is in keeping with an imperative of vigilance and awareness that, as noted by Emily Ruth Rutter, Sequoia Maner, Tiffany Austin, and darlene anita scott in the Introduction, "consider[s] politically conscious elegies in capacious terms, recognizing the myriad ways in which writers, readers, and activists may mobilize against white, hetero-patriarchal dominance and the havoc it wreaks." Smith probes various manifestations of oppression: "Garden of Eden" is an oddly

nostalgic reflection on the occasional materialistic indulgence of a leisurely shop-
ping trip to a specialty food market, while "A Man's World" critiques patriarchal
prerogative by casting God as a silver-tongued con-artist sibilantly offering the
planet to an eager hopeful. "Watershed" entails an exposé of corporate corruption
through the environmental disaster caused by DuPont's toxic waste dumping from
a plant in West Virginia, and "In Your Condition" chronicles the speaker's trip
overseas while suffering through morning sickness and other first-trimester dis-
comforts. "Refuge," a particularly compelling investigation of xenophobic intolerance, attempts to forge empathy for asylum-seekers by likening them to one's
own relatives, always and already known and loved. The diversity of the collection
in and of itself frames the multifarious stages upon which man's inhumanity to
man is continually enacted.

Smith engages in a fascinating refraction of artistic form with "Theatrical
Improvisation," as the poem takes as its subject the description of an experimental
dramatic performance. The stylized reenactment of post-9/11 scenes of violence
against Muslims in American public spaces constitutes an emotionally impactful
visceral experience for the spectators, as the immersive nature of the depicted
scenes calls into question the distinction between witness and participant, and
challenges the responsibility of the idle bystander, who might in other contexts
be called "the silent majority." The poem incorporates documented hate speech
in its italicized sections, the virulent intensity of which would be uncomfortable
to hear spoken aloud: "*We want them / To feel that everything around them is / Against
them.*"[36] However, the actors glide seamlessly into vignettes where they exchange
the roles of inhabiting the identities of unrestrained aggressor or the victimized:
"Strange weather / Moves across each face. The women pass / From fright to
rage."[37] The parties shift subjectivity, thus routinely caught completely by surprise
by the unprovoked assaults; the technique thus destabilizes the firm understanding
of who merits sympathy, who is on the side of right.

"Theatrical Improvisation" closes with a description of the reaction of the
audience: A stunned silence broken by a lone person clapping, and "Then erupts
a panicked / Applause that doesn't know how to end."[38] The unbridled applause,
thus granted independent volition, is evocative of hysteria, bespeaking an inability to process the brutality and unfathomable hatred directed at individuals who
have given no offense beyond their mere existence. The unstinting applause also
symbolizes misdirected energy, as the enthusiasm channeled into demonstrating
appreciation for the artistic accomplishment would be more usefully expended in
combating the prejudice that fuels such indefensible attitudes and actions.

Combating prejudice effectively begins with introspectively recognizing the
fraught nature of the democratic principles upon which the nation was founded.
Smith employs the erasure technique in "Declaration" to expose the latent threat
of violent repression lurking within the fiery rhetoric of opposition to tyranny
infusing the Declaration of Independence. The poem opens with a salient evocation of the driving force behind the organized protests fueling the Black Lives

Matter phenomenon: "*He has / sent hither swarms of Officers to harass our people.*"³⁹ Selectively culling out the content that forms a narrative to detail the nation's painfully persistent history of racial antagonism, Smith deftly shapes a poem that reveals the embedded hypocrisy of the revolutionary imperative. In so doing, she brings to the surface the generally peaceful character of the successive waves of the pursuit of Civil Rights:

> *In every stage of these Oppressions We have Petitioned for*
> *Redress in the most humble terms:*
>   *Our repeated*
> *Petitions have been answered only by repeated injury.*⁴⁰

This cycle of good faith perpetually met with white contempt is compounded by the poem's final imagery: A poignant attestation that the black presence in the U.S. is entirely the consequence of involuntary migration—Africans having been kidnapped from their homeland and forced across the Middle Passage.

In a similar politicized vein, "Unrest in Baton Rouge" is an elegiac reflection that represents the sole poem in the collection explicitly engaging content focused on the Black Lives Matter movement. The poem ruminates upon the aftermath of unfathomable violence targeting those who have done nothing whatsoever to merit it. Like Cullen did for "Scottsboro," Smith includes a dedication of sorts, which is actually more of a contextualizing acknowledgment: "after the photo by Jonathan Bachman." The label, a reference to a remarkably striking picture of a solitary protestor presenting her wrists to be handcuffed, seems to be a description of the image that incited the poem's composition rather than the ensuing public reaction to the photograph's publication. Bachman's work, which was a finalist for the 2017 Pulitzer Prize for Breaking News Photography, is accompanied by an informative caption on the Pulitzer committee website that stops just short of a direct invocation of the Black Lives Matter movement:

> Lone activist Ieshia Evans stands her ground while offering her hands for arrest as riot police charge toward her during a protest against police brutality outside the Baton Rouge Police Department in Louisiana, U.S. on July 9, 2016. Evans, a 35-year-old Pennsylvania nurse and mother to a young boy, traveled to Baton Rouge to protest the shooting of Alton Sterling, a 37-year-old black man and father of five, who was shot at close range while being held down by two white police officers. The shooting, captured on cell phone videos, aggravated the unrest that has coursed through the United States for two years over the use of excessive force by police especially against black men.⁴¹

Smith's 12-line poem, arranged in six couplets, is spare and efficient, typifying the contemporary shift toward a holistically experiential poetics that suffuses the imagination and galvanizes definitive sociopolitical engagement. As Smith has herself argued, in contradistinction to the traditional methodology championed by the nineteenth-century Romantics, today's "poems are not so much reflecting as enacting."[42] What is being "enacted" in "Unrest in Baton Rouge" is the evocation of the regal elegance of Ieshia Evans's surrender without a trace of submission. The serenity of her stance exudes an almost scornful demeanor, a wordless condemnation of the wholly disproportionate demonstration of force deployed to take an unarmed, unaccompanied woman into custody. Arrayed against what appears to be a whole platoon of heavily armed and armored police, Evans's fashionable attire suggests preparation for an afternoon of warm-weather leisure rather than wartime confrontation. The speaker of the poem incisively asks of the disturbing imbalance in conflict readiness, "what else // Are they so buffered against, if not love's blade / Sizing up the heart's familiar meat?"[43] In this recasting of the riot gear as a strategic mechanism to protect the wearer not from physical injury but from a disarming susceptibility to compassion, the poem invites a reconsideration of just what is at stake when ostensibly peaceful city streets are transformed into combat zones.

Notwithstanding the power of Smith's verse, there are inherent dangers of the poetic enterprise turned to a political function, one of which entails the limited psychological capability of processing the experiences of others. Neil Covey argues that a self-protective mechanism may insulate against true identification with those unlike ourselves:

> The sympathetic imagination accepts people not for what they are, but for the mirrors of the self that can be ascertained in them. . . . This kind of "acceptance" is all the more dangerous because it claims a tolerance that is not present and results in a kind of imperialism. Too often efforts to see the humanity in others result in a kind of dehumanization, a denial of their own being: paradoxically, sometimes it takes more imagination not to imagine.[44]

Imaginative disability can also be accompanied by various material disincentives to achieve an authentic understanding of others, especially those culturally regarded as disenfranchised Other or socioeconomically inferior. Susan B. A. Somers-Willett, herself a white female slam poet, describes the way in which the slam competition circuit tends to privilege performers of color and their narratives in ways that may operate to result in reductive and self-serving essentialism from white spectators intrigued by an anti-establishment ethos: "the slam may serve as a rare opportunity for white middle-class audiences to legitimately support black poets critiquing white positions of privilege. . . . At best, this process of reward opens doors for interracial dialogues; at worst, it may be a method of assuaging 'white liberal guilt.'"[45] Parsing out and codifying the ability of poetry to participate meaningfully in the process of healing the racial divide is a task beyond the scope of definite knowledge, but there is much poetry can do to make inroads into mutual understanding, if only by normalizing the recognition that most human experience is universal.

In a commentary on Tracy K. Smith's poetry relating to the experience of desire, Hilton Als points out that black feminine self-assertion is virtual anathema in contemporary America:

> It can be startling to hear a woman of color describe and claim her own body: despite advances in our culture, some eyes still roll when a black woman says "I" or puts herself forward; in this political climate, it can be perceived as an aggressive act or as hysteria or—the worst—as special pleading.[46]

Centering the black female experience in literature constitutes, then, a revolutionary act in itself. For Smith to identify chiefly with Ieshia Evans and how she represents the black woman's legacy of resistance and resilience evokes a complicated nexus of love, desire, and devotion in a remarkable poem. The source image is riveting, emblematizing the impact that violence against black men has on the black women left behind—widowed, fatherless, robbed of brothers, uncles, sons; deprived of the masculine presence, women are compelled to persevere, honoring the loss with demonstrations of love. The essence of the elegy is this act of commemoration.

The substantive connection between Countée Cullen and Tracy K. Smith is the way in which Smith realizes the vision Cullen espoused of the poet as an idealistic crusader and agent of the divine, using art to elevate the public consciousness and refine the moral, ethical, and spiritual cultural agenda. In her role as national poet laureate from 2017 to 2019, Smith was uniquely suited to carry out the endeavor of reinvigorating the art form to serve the purpose with which it has been historically entrusted. Als's characterization of Smith's most recent collection emphasizes the pathos of the individual poems and the abiding impact of racial injustice in the twenty-first century: "*Wade in the Water* is suffused with sadness and with the weight of history, the old racism that makes fresh wounds in black bodies—black female bodies—day after day after day."[47] Als acknowledges the redemptive power of love, represented by the Geechee Gullah Ring Shouters in the poem which lends its title to the collection, as the necessary antidote to the accumulation of "sadness." The cryptic central assertion around which "Unrest in Baton Rouge" is organized—that "love is a language / Few practice, but all, or near all speak"[48]—is deceptively framed as an interrogative, but only in a manner that is cast to elicit validation.

What it means to "practice" as opposed to merely "speak[ing]" love is to demonstrate commitment and reverence through action rather than paying it the pointless lip service of empty and ineffectual rhetoric. To "practice" love, like Ieshia Evans, is to put one's body on the line, to engage willfully in self-sacrifice, even for a martyred stranger who resided hundreds of miles away. To "practice" love is also to open oneself to the potential for pain, to make oneself vulnerable to the inevitability of emotional distress. When the speaker suggests that "the men in black armor,"[49] the police in tactical suits, are in reality attired to defend themselves against being assailed by a unified and overwhelming force of love, the anger and outrage typically associated with Black Lives Matter activists are transmuted into their spectral opposites. The affirmation of love also exposes the fact that it is far easier to dehumanize and vilify in order to preserve a particular rigid worldview than to admit the possibility of affinity and open up the necessity of psychic disruption. Love as a transformative experience, elevating those who embrace it above the reach of the perpetrators of intolerance and violence, thus demonstrates a permutation of elegiac verse repurposed to combat the travesties and tragedies of racial inequality.

Notes

1. Tracy K. Smith, "Political Poetry Is Hot Again. The Poet Laureate Explores Why, and How," *The New York Times Book Review*, December 10, 2018, www.nytimes.com/2018/12/10/books/review/political-poetry.html
2. W. E. B. Du Bois, *The Souls of Black Folk* (1903; New York: Penguin Books, 2018). In this classic of the African American literary tradition, Du Bois famously asserted that double-consciousness is a psychological condition endemic to be being black in America: "It is a peculiar sensation, this double-consciousness, this sense of always looking at one's self through the eyes of others, of measuring one's soul by the tape of a world that looks on in amused contempt and pity" (7).
3. This term is a conscious appropriation and permutation of the phenomenon commonly known as "suicide by cop," in which the perpetrators seek to end their lives by intentionally provoking police officers to shoot them.
4. Dana Gioia, "Can Poetry Matter?" *Atlantic Monthly* (May 1991), www.theatlantic.com/magazine/archive/1991/05/can-poetry-matter/305062 (3; italics added).
5. James Weldon Johnson's poem "O Black and Unknown Bards," a tribute to the enslaved composers of what Frederick Douglass and W. E. B. Du Bois typically called the "sorrow songs," was first published in 1922.
6. For more on the Red Summer and the events precipitating it, see James Weldon Johnson's *Black Manhattan* (1930; New York: Da Capo Press, 1991), 236–46.
7. Michael Anderson, "The Too-Brief Careerof Countee Cullen," *The New Criterion* 31, no. 8 (April 2013): 24.
8. Du Bois served as the editor of the NAACP's official journal, while Johnson served as his counterpart for the organ of the Urban League, both organizations established for the elevation and uplift of African Americans. Each periodical worked diligently to showcase black literary talent as well as disseminate information material to the effort of effecting racial progress. I have elsewhere asserted that "*Opportunity* magazine inaugurated its [literary] contests chiefly to nurture black achievement in literature and to increase the representation of black America in the development of the national culture. In this way, the Urban League was perhaps principally responsible for sustaining the momentum of the Harlem Renaissance" (Licia Morrow Calloway, *Black Family (Dys)Function in Novels by Jessie Fauset, Nella Larsen, and Fannie Hurst* [New York: Peter Lang, 2003]), 36.
9. "Jessie Fauset: Midwife to the Harlem Renaissance" *(The New) Crisis* 104, no. 4 (July/August 2000), 25.
10. Countée Cullen, *The Medea, and Some Poems* (New York: Harper, 1935) "Scottsboro, Too, Is Worth Its Song" line 16.

11. Langston Hughes, "The Negro Artist and the Racial Mountain," *Nation* 122, no. 3181 (June 23, 1926): 692.
12. Ibid.
13. Anderson, "The Too-Brief Career of Countee Cullen," 25.
14. From Countée Cullen, *Color* (New York: Harper & Brothers, 1925). "Heritage" lines 7–10, 60–63.
15. Caryl Phillips, "What Is Africa to Me Now?," *Research in African Literatures* 46, no. 4 (Winter 2015): 10.
16. From Cullen, *Color*, "Yet Do I Marvel" lines 13–14.
17. Fred M. Fetrow, "Cullen's 'Yet Do I Marvel,'" *Explicator* 56, no. 2 (1998): 103.
18. Cullen, "Scottsboro, Too, Is Worth Its Song" line 17.
19. Neil Covey, "Notes Toward an Investigation of the Marginality of Poetry and the Sympathetic Imagination," *South Atlantic Review* 60, no. 2 (May 1995): 143.
20. Cullen "Scottsboro, Too, Is Worth Its Song" line 8.
21. Ibid., line 20.
22. For a succinct but detailed summary of the case, see Mark Curriden, "Precedents: March 25, 1931. The Saga of the Scottsboro Boys Begins," *American Bar Association Journal* 99, no. 3 (2013): 72.
23. Cullen, "Scottsboro, Too, Is Worth Its Song" lines 25–26.
24. Carol S. Anderson, *White Rage: The Unspoken Truth of Our Racial Divide* (New York: Bloomsbury, 2016), 3–4 (italics added).
25. Ibid., 3.
26. Ibid., 6.
27. I am thinking in particular here of the cases of Trayvon Martin, Mike Brown, Jr., Eric Garner, Alton Sterling, and, most recently, Stephon Clark in Sacramento, California.
28. Tracy K. Smith, *Ordinary Light: A Memoir* (New York: Alfred A. Knopf, 2015), 58.
29. Ibid., 73.
30. Du Bois, *The Souls of Black Folk*, 3.
31. Smith, *Ordinary Light*, 133.
32. Ibid.
33. Tracy K. Smith, *Wade in the Water* (New York: Graywolf Press, 2018), 76.
34. Tracy K. Smith, "Political Poetry Is Hot Again. The Poet Laureate Explores Why, and How," *The New York Times Book Review*, December 16, 2018, www.nytimes.com/2018/12/10/books/review/political-poetry.html (accessed December 16, 2018).
35. Cullen, "Scottsboro, Too, Is Worth Its Song" lines 19–20.
36. Smith, *Wade in the Water*, "Theatrical Improvisation" lines 12b–14.
37. Ibid., lines 19–21.
38. Ibid., lines 59b–60.
39. Smith, *Wade in the Water*, "Declaration" lines 1–2.
40. Ibid., lines 9–12.
41. The Pulitzer Prizes, "The 2017 Pulitzer Prize Finalist in Breaking News Photography: Jonathan Bachman," 2017, www.pulitzer.org (accessed December 30, 2018).
42. Smith, "Political Poetry Is Hot Again."
43. Smith, *Wade in the Water*, "Unrest in Baton Rouge" lines 6–8.
44. Covey, "Notes Toward an Investigation," 145.
45. Susan B. A. Somers-Willett, "Slam Poetry and the Cultural Politics of Performing Identity," *The Journal of the Midwest Modern Language Association* 38, no. 1, *Special Convention Issue: Performance* (Spring 2005): 59.
46. Hilton Als, "Tracy K. Smith's Poetry of Desire," *The New Yorker*, October 1, 2018.
47. Ibid., 65.
48. Smith, *Wade in the Water*, "Unrest in Baton Rouge" lines 3–4.
49. Ibid., line 5.

9

EDWIDGE DANTICAT'S ELEGIAC PROJECT

A Transnational Historiography of U.S. Imperialist State Violence

Maia L. Butler and Megan Feifer

Elegizing black death is part of Edwidge Danticat's ongoing project of connecting contemporary state violence against black subjects to the history of U.S. imperial violence at home and abroad. She draws our unflinching attention to this violent legacy in specific localities, underscoring their transnational dimensions. In the wake of the Sacramento, California, police killing of unarmed Stephon Clark in his grandmother's backyard and the assassination of Afrobrazilian councilwoman and activist Marielle Franco, this chapter takes up two of Danticat's *New Yorker* op-editorials in order to theorize the transnational, historically situated impulse of her elegiac project: To document how "black bodies are increasingly becoming battlefields upon which horrors are routinely executed, each one so close to the last that we barely have the time to fully grieve and mourn."[1]

Danticat's *New Yorker* pieces refocus Black Lives Matter discourse, showing how transnational dimensions of imperial violence are integral to the ongoing project of determining, enforcing, and policing citizenship in the U.S., the Dominican Republic, and Haiti. "Enough is Enough" attends to police violence against Haitians in New York, connecting the beating and sexual assault of Abner Louima by police officers, during what she calls the Abner/[Amadou] Diallo decade, to the killings of Sean Bell and Michael Brown, effectively tracing state violence across temporal and geographical borders. Paralleling dictatorial state violence in Haiti to police violence perpetrated against African Americans and black immigrants in the U.S., Danticat builds upon the testimonial impetus of Black Lives Matter discourse and movement. "Black Bodies in Motion and Pain" invokes the particular histories of events including the following: The twentieth-century Great Migration of more than six million African Americans out of the U.S. South, the 2015 Charleston church shooting, and the Dominican constitutional *La Sentencia*, thus situating Haitians of Dominican descent as in-transit and illuminating their shared effect of black trauma and death.[2] Danticat traces a longer historiography of the way in which "black bodies . . . have been deemed a threat," both nationally and transnationally.

Much of the scholarship on Danticat's oeuvre addresses her longer-form works, such as her novels and memoirs. Increasingly, scholars are attending to her growing body of Young Adult fiction and Children's literature and the importance of her anthology editing work. We find that critical attention is due to her *New Yorker* column in large part because the platform firmly situates her voice as that of a public intellectual weighing in on matters that have long been endemic to the Americas and are also increasingly exigent. This chapter aligns Danticat's *New Yorker* pieces with scholarship contextualizing the historical dimensions of Dominican and Haitian state violence as part and parcel of U.S. imperial contexts. We read her essays in relationship to Achille Mbembe's understanding of necropolitics and state sovereignty and Jennifer L. Shoaff's attention to the "civil death, social apartheid, and administrative genocide," that they beget, highlighting Danticat's understanding of what Mbembe describes as the ultimate relationship between the politics of race and the politics of death.[3] As Danticat examines the U.S. political-juridical racial politics through attention to "random" acts of violence, she calls attention to "who matters and who does not, who is *disposable* and who is not."[4]

Danticat's elegiac project is overtly political; characterized by witnessing, documenting, and testifying, her work makes no room for the consolation of the traditional poetic form, but, instead, it insists readers keep the struggle to make Black Lives Matter at the forefront of their consciousness. Our attention to the exigent cultural work of her *New Yorker* essays underscores how her role as a public intellectual, which hinges on the performance of "faithful witnessing" in the space of the opinion editorial, is informed by her decolonial activist work and integrally related to her literary production. In this way, we triangulate a reading of Danticat's activist work with her literary and public intellectual work, the crux of which involves her commitment to witnessing the marginalization and oppression of black people in the Americas. Maria Lugones contextualizes witnessing as a specifically decolonial feminist practice and tool used to make the invisible visible, specifically the workings of colonial abuse of power.[5] Yomaira C. Figueroa foregrounds how Lugones's conception of the practice of faithful witnessing is grounded in the performance of "epistemic pilgrimaging" before tracing the dual meaning of the term witness, both juridical and religious, oft turned political, as outlined in Kelly Oliver's work *Witnessing Beyond Recognition*.[6] We hope to show that Danticat's many years of community involvement and pilgrimages to immigrant detention centers have informed her commitment to documenting the nature of state violence black people have experienced across geopolitical boundaries, and how interrelated the operations of the prison industrial and the immigration complex are in their efforts to render black subjects invisible and expendable.[7] Through her direct action and her literature, Danticat shows us that, just as opportunities for lamenting the loss of black lives are devastatingly unceasing, opportunities to render starkly visible and to resist the complex enormity of the state-sanctioned machinations behind this loss are innumerable. These activities must go hand in hand.

The opening to Danticat's *New Yorker* essay "Enough is Enough" immediately parallels the violence the writer has experienced in the U.S. and Haiti, two countries with a colonial history inextricably linked in the triangular trade of sugar production by enslaved Africans: "I have seen police brutality up close. Both in Haiti, where I was born during a ruthless dictatorship, and in New York, where I migrated to a working-class, predominantly African American and Caribbean neighborhood in Brooklyn at the age of twelve."[8] Danticat continues, observing that while the violence of her childhood in Haiti was "overtly political," the violence in New York was "a bit more subtle, though no less pervasive."[9] Danticat describes her witnessing of police violence in New York from her early days there when she describes being too scared, along with other public transit passengers, to cry "Shame!" upon witnessing a police beating, to the days when "We marched for all of them in the Louima/Diallo decade, seven thousand of us across the Brooklyn Bridge at one time."[10] Her paralleling of New York experiences with circum-Caribbean Haitian experiences of state-sanctioned violence is important; regardless of her geographical situatedness, as a Haitian American woman, Danticat has never lived in a location where she was not touched by the violence of the American nation state. Her black communities, which span a considerable geopolitical expanse, have always engaged in communal lament and resistance of the deaths of their members. The editors of *Revisiting the Elegy in the Black Lives Matter Era* lead this volume with the question, "How do we productively interweave theoretical and personal accounts to encourage discussions of art and activism that transgress disciplinary boundaries?"[11] In this chapter, we argue that Danticat's work invites us to do just that. Her *New Yorker* column is expansive in more ways than one: geographically, formally, and unceasing in its turn to the documentation of abuses of the state so that we might remember the lives lost and in whose name the resistance continues.

Danticat crafts a history of police violence and murder of both African Americans and black immigrants in this essay. Between relaying the early moments of silence and the collective action of marching and shouting "No Justice! No Peace!," Danticat traces the physical and sexual abuse of Abner Louima, her friend and fellow Haitian immigrant, in a police precinct in 1997 to the murder of Amadou Diallo, a Guinean immigrant, on his own doorstep in 1999, before referencing the death of Patrick Dorismond, a second-generation Haitian immigrant, in 2006.[12] Noting that the cases of women killed by the police are perhaps not as noteworthy in the media, she pulls us back to the 1984 shooting of Eleanor Bumpurs in her Bronx apartment, a fact that makes her murder distinct from those of the men beaten and killed in public.[13] Danticat contextualizes these incidents with the more recent killings of Sean Bell in Jamaica, Queens, Eric Garner in Staten Island, and Michael Brown in Ferguson, Missouri, deaths more closely associated with the beginnings of the Black Lives Matter movement. In naming the victims of police violence and decrying the lack of attention to numerous cases of injustice, Danticat invites us to grieve the losses again while upholding the reason for continued resistance: "The streets belonged to the people with the uniforms and the guns . . . were never ours to begin with, because on these same streets our sons and brothers, fathers and uncles were, and still are, prey."[14]

In this essay, "Enough is Enough," the act of raising names in lamentation and remembrance is not closed with offers or acceptance of consolation. Rather, she raises questions about the (im)possibility of justice for black people in her two home locales and traces connections about the role of city officials (New York City Mayor Rudolph Giuliani, St. Louis Prosecutor Robert McCulloch) in deflecting blame from the police back onto the people who are their victims.[15] This harks back to the long tradition of elegiac resistance to consolation, as noted by Emily Rutter, Sequoia Maner, Tiffany Austin, and darlene anita scott in the Introduction to this volume.[16] Danticat includes the landscape of broadened borders of America in her rendering of the dangers to black people, which is notably inclusive of Haiti. Her attention to New York City challenges the false narrative that the U.S. South is the sole domain of lynch mobs. The resistance of consolation is perhaps most starkly apparent with her inclusion of Abner Louima's own reflections on the continuousness of police violence. She writes, "How does he feel each time he hears that another black man was killed or nearly killed by the police?" and relays his response: "It touches me deeply each time. . . . It forces me to ask myself why so little has changed in all these years since this happened to me. It reminds me again and again that our lives mean nothing."[17] There can be no consolation when the wound of loss is continuously reopened. Louima continues with a message for Michael Brown's family, "We must keep raising our voices until we find justice for those who lost their lives, and until these things stop happening."[18] Danticat's creation, in this essay, of a tie between black immigrants and African Americans is deliberate; this historiography of incidents of police violence—and public responses to them—spans the hemispheric Americas. Through this counter-history, then, Danticat shows how an assertion like "Black Lives Matter," made in the context of "all those broken hearts, all the rage all the desperation, the yearning for justice," has been proclaimed through voice and action even before the movement organized, and that this assertion has long been inclusive of African diasporic subjects in the U.S.

The phrases "Enough Is Enough" and "Black Lives Matter" are both calls to action. The cofounders of the movement, Patrisse Khan-Cullors, Alicia Garza, and Opal Tometi, declare as much in their account of its origins:

> Black Lives Matter began as a call to action in response to state-sanctioned violence and anti-black racism. Our intention from the very beginning was

to connect black people from all over the world who have a shared desire for justice to act together in their communities. The impetus for that commitment was, and still is, the rampant and deliberate violence inflicted on us by the state.[19]

Several recent scholarly texts on the Black Lives Matter movement recognize that the organization's political work includes black immigrant and undocumented people's concerns. Angela J. Hattery and Earl Smith's *Policing Black Bodies: How Black Lives are Surveilled and How to Work for Change* acknowledges the Black Lives Matter movement for "bringing national attention to specific tensions between the police and black communities across the United States," also recognizing "what receives less media attention . . . is a call for racial justice for all black lives, including transgender, queer, and undocumented folks."[20] Barbara Ransby's *Making All Black Lives Matter: Reimagining Freedom in the 21st Century* shows the movement's underpinnings in U.S.-based black feminist traditions and traces its connection to an extensive history of black radical political organizing. Ransby's history of the movement

> contextualizes the oppression, exploitation, and liberation of black poor and working-class people . . . represented in all categories of the oppressed in the United States. They are immigrants. They are poor and working class. They are disabled. They are indigenous. They are LGTBQIA. They are Latinx and Afro-Asians. They are also other religious minorities, and the list goes on.[21]

Danticat's work to include the concerns of black immigrants, which we detail in this chapter as occurring in the corpus of her *New Yorker* column, as well as in her fiction and nonfiction work, is integral to contemporary Black Lives Matter discourse, to which elegy is also crucial.

Danticat's powerful opening to "Enough is Enough" builds upon this legacy of artistic activism, specifically the act of chronicling the names of individuals murdered by the state.[22] At the same time, it draws a genealogical relationship between the institutionalized violence experienced in Haiti with that of the U.S. In order to understand the gravity of her comparison, some prior knowledge of historical context is required. Specifically, Danticat compares the contemporary police state citizens of color experience in the U.S. to life under the Duvalier dictatorship(s). The Duvalier dynasty of the father-son duo, François "Papa Doc" and Jean-Claude Duvalier, was responsible for the violent deaths of an estimated 30,000 citizens and the exile of hundreds of thousands of Haitians to the U.S., Cuba, and Canada. Jana Evans Braziel's *Duvalier's Ghosts: Race, Diaspora, and U.S. Imperialism in Haitian Literatures* and Laurent Dubois's *Haiti: The Aftershocks of History* offer a chronicling of this period of Haitian history.[23] In "Enough is Enough," Danticat juxtaposes the police brutality and institutionalized racism in the U.S. with an almost 30-year reign (1957–1986) of state violence enforced and maintained by governed law and a military regime of secret police, the Tonton Macoutes, or Dew Breakers.[24] Alas, the atrocities enacted during the Duvalier reign were not solely the doing of a rogue president and a subset of secret police. Rather, as Jana Evans Braziel argues, "the state apparatus proves to be immensely more complex and convoluted in its labyrinthine machinates of power, manifesting the 'imperial tendrils' of [a] transnational empire."[25] These imperial tendrils were established with the 1915 U.S. occupation and subsequent "interventions" in Haiti.

While some readers may find Danticat's paralleling tenuous, in light of the contemporary context of the shooting deaths of individuals in their homes, on street corners, and in their backyards, a conception of police violence as but one arm of U.S. state violence becomes readily apparent. Danticat's resounding statement positions state abuses in both countries as not only relational, but as belonging to a historic genealogy in which black bodies are governed by a literal politics of death, and her writing similarly situates her work in an elegiac lineage of Diasporic writers using the page as a form of resistance. Her argument aligns with and expands upon Achille Mbembe's prior notion of necropolitics, wherein Mbembe describes power as a "dividing of people into those who must live and those who must die."[26] This type of division, when read in the context of racial politics becomes "ultimately linked to a politics of death," a politic in which "the function of racism is to regulate the distribution of death and to make possible the murderous functions of the state."[27] Building upon Michel Foucault's concept of biopower,[28] Mbembe argues these particular racial politics are "inscribed in the way all modern states function."[29] The framework of necropolitics positions the terror and violence undergirding U.S. racial politics as not simply a matter of singular and/or isolated incidents, bi-partisan issues, or even the mutterings of a president who unabashedly describes nations like Haiti as "shithole countries."[30] Rather, necropolitics are rooted in a much longer history of colonial and imperial terror that is foundational to the sociopolitical and juridical practices of all modern states. Danticat's *New Yorker* column invites us to consider these connections across geopolitical boundaries, which were forged during the height of U.S. imperial activity with Haiti.

Danticat's examination of the necropolitics at play in both nation-states doesn't stop with an analysis of state violence solely at the hands of police. Rather, her op-editorials attend to the issue of statelessness and the civic/social death that accompanies it. In particular, Danticat draws attention to the legislative and juridical policies that reinforce a racialized death politic. Jennifer L. Shoaff explores this additional form of systemic violence in her analysis of the Dominican Republic's 2013 Tribunal ruling, *La Sentencia*. Shoaff's work delves into the contours of the "state legislative, judicial, and bureaucratic policies aimed at containing race and nation."[31] In doing so, she draws a relationship, similar to Danticat's, between the legislative denial of nationality and the "realization of an array of other aspects of full membership in society including 'the right to education, . . . health through access to social services, political participation, the freedom of movement, and access to justice."[32] For both authors, the Dominican Republic's court ruling exemplifies the practice of necropolitics, citing a clear relationship between the denial of citizenship and state violence.

Danticat uses the fast media of the digital op-editorial to draw a through-line between the various necropolitical manifestations of the state and the historic strong-arm of U.S. imperialism. *The New Yorker* serves as a platform to address necropolitics in both countries, and to express elegiac concerns within a highly regarded, well-circulated periodical. The serialized form of Danticat's column fits too well the episodic nature of her repeated return to this content, as the op-editorial becomes a space in which Danticat offers a point-counterpoint critique of the national media's representation of state violence. The ongoing development and publication of new posts to her column, however, creates a sense of cohesion to its evolution. Her use of hyperlinks in her essays provides readers with additional materials to mull over and weaves the threads of her historiography more tightly. Ultimately, then, Danticat's op-editorials create a public space in which readers can further circulate, interact with, and educate themselves about the larger issues at hand.

In a similar vein, Wesley Lowery's work *They Can't Kill Us All: Ferguson, Baltimore, and a New Era in America's Racial Justice Movement* describes how, as "protests propelled by tweets and hashtags spread under the banner of Black Lives Matter and with cell phone and body camera video shining new light on the way police interact with minority communities, America was forced to consider that not everyone marching in the streets could be wrong."[33] He shows the integral role that fast social media plays in the movement's documentary impulse as increasing spheres of young Americans realized:

> the young black bodies we kept seeing in our Facebook newsfeeds could have been our own. . . . Now we were able to share what we saw and how we felt about it instantaneously with thousands of others who were going through similar [political] awakenings. Conversations once had at Bible studies and on barroom stools were happening on our phones and on Facebook, allowing both instant access to information and a means of instant feedback. Social media made it possible for young black people to document interactions they believed to be injustices and exposed their white friends and family members to their experiences.[34]

The op-ed is similarly a faster way of testifying than longer forms of nonfiction and fiction, and Danticat's use of her *New Yorker* platform extends and broadens the audience. Just as Lowery notes that people have used social media platforms to share occasions for elegizing lost black community members—especially his focus on users sharing how they feel, lamenting the losses—he observes that these go hand and hand with consciousness raising through documentation and lead to catalyzing discussions of the sort that inform direct actions such as marching in the street. This use of social media that Lowery describes, which begins with the lamentation and develops to the call for justice, functions similarly to the brief essays Danticat shares on her column.

Danticat's partially ekphrastic *New Yorker* essay, "Black Bodies in Motion and Pain," which begins as a reflection on her experience at a Jacob Lawrence Migration Series exhibit, expands into a consideration of black experiences of pain within the context of the othering of the immigrant experience, whether one migrates abroad or is made an immigrant in one's place of birth.[35] The image that opens this essay is Jacob Lawrence's "Migration Series" Panel 3, titled "In every town Negroes were leaving by the hundreds to go North and enter into Northern industry." Danticat captions the image, "In His Migration Series, Jacob Lawrence beautifully and heartbreakingly captured black bodies in motion, in transit, and in danger."[36] Danticat's attention to Lawrence's Panel 3, which features migrants traversing a pastoral setting to escape the threat of death by lynching, invokes a pastoral elegiac motif. A group of people march through the frame of the painting under a wide open blue sky and burdened by bags and cases of belongings. They are accompanied by black birds, perhaps ravens, symbolically associated with death. These African Americans from Panel 3 are more than likely also moving through the grief of lost community members, victims to Southern anti-black terrorizing tactics. Datincat's framing of her visit to the New York Museum of Modern Art through the 2015 moment that saw the Charleston, South Carolina, Emmanuel African Methodist Episcopal Church shooting and the first announcements about *La Sentencia*'s passing in the Dominican Republic, effectively collapses geographical distance between the continental U.S. South and its more distant circum-Caribbean southern neighbor, Haiti. Not only is geographical difference between sites of state violence against black people collapsed, but so is time. Her caption that underscores the danger from which black Americans historically fled keeps the focus on this continued cause for migration for so many black immigrants of the twenty-first century. Her choice to preface this essay focused on police violence in New York relies on juxtaposition of location and time periods to challenge narratives that might suggest that lynching is a thing of the past, lynching is a thing of the U.S. South, and lynching belongs to the domain of crazed mobs, rather than highly organized police departments. She writes the urban north into her revision of the mythology that obscures the immediate, quotidian, and ubiquitous characteristics of extralegal death for black people at the hands of the state, regardless of their hemispheric, rural, or urban location.

In this essay, Danticat also marks the site of the black church as a cultural institution that has historically been involved in the activist work of receiving, protecting, and supporting black immigrants during the Great Migration. The "witness and fellowship" that she suddenly yearns for while standing in the exhibit echoes themes from her own fictional characters' responses to trauma, as with the multivocal testimonio/witnessing in her novel *The Farming of Bones*.[37] Danticat further elides the distance between the U.S. and the island of Hispaniola when she addresses how, in both places, we have witnessed black people portrayed and treated as immigrants in their own home countries.[38] She writes,

> Tragically, we do not always get the final say on how our black bodies are labelled. Those fleeing the South during the Great Migration were sometimes referred to not only as immigrants but as refugees, just as the U.S. citizens who were internally displaced by Hurricane Katrina were given that label ten years ago.[39]

Her attention to the labeling of black people on the move gestures to the long tradition of stereotypical images promoted by racist cultural scripts and disseminated by the media, which often homogenize black people into a monolithic group. Her naming of different groups of refugees in different eras and circumstances adds complexity to the counternarrative she constructs. In addition to death by lynching, death by criminally negligent emergency response forces black migration. Danticat shows how black people have been systematically targeted or marginalized across time and location, causing conditions where migration across borders *de jure* and *de facto* becomes a way to avoid death. This documentation strategy is central to the way her work reframes the Black Lives Matter discourse into diasporic domains, in keeping with the founders' mission for the movement to remain globally concerned.

Danticat makes the connection in this 2015 essay from the black migration from the southern U.S. to various northern locations, to the "the possibility," heralded by *La Sentencia*, "of two hundred thousand Haitians and Dominicans of Haitian descent being expelled from the Dominican Republic," on the eastern side of Hispaniola to the western side, back to Haiti.[40] We don't know that she could have anticipated the Trump Administration's 2017 recommendation to terminate the Temporary Protected Status of Haitians in the U.S. with a grace period for voluntary returns before deportations would begin. She responds, however, in a 2017 *New Yorker* essay, "A Harrowing Turning Point for Haitian Immigrants," underscoring two points: It explains what the Trump Administration would have obfuscated—the nature and purpose of the TSP Program—by obliquely referring to conditions causing people to seek amnesty, which we will discuss further later, and it also shows how the TSP Program leaves participants in a liminal space of unbelonging in both home and host nations.[41] Danticat reminds us, "Temporary protected status . . . is designated by the Secretary of Homeland Security in cases where a country's nationals are unable to return safely or when the country is incapable of receiving them due to armed conflicts, environmental disasters, epidemics, or other 'extraordinary' conditions."[42] The caveat is that TPS "does not offer a path to citizenship, but it does allow recipients to apply for a work permit and a driver's license, and prevents them from being deported."[43] Her attention to the ways that black bodies—"in motion, in pain, in danger"—are labeled in relation to their immigrant, and therefore othered, status is contextualized along the ways that black others, outsiders, have been read as a threat. She muses in "Black Bodies in Motion and Pain" that "These days, it seems that black bodies are more threatened than they have ever been so far in this century. Or maybe we have more ways to document the beatings, shootings, and other abuses that have been suffered in the recent past."[44] We pair her observations in "Harrowing Turning Point" and "Black Bodies in Motion and Pain" to underscore how her *New Yorker* column is a corpus across which she connects this process of othering through immigration policies with the violence and abuses against those construed to pose a threat. Further, her reference to documentation reminds us the column's purpose: To provide material allowing for the transfer and sharing of her witnessing responsibilities to her readership. Finally, Danticat draws a connection across geography once more when she paraphrases Toni Morrison's character Baby Suggs from her novel *Beloved* (1987) at the close of the essay: "Some do not love our flesh and are unwilling to acknowledge our humanity, much less our nationality or citizenship."[45]

Danticat's *New Yorker* essay "We Must Not Forget Detained Migrant Children" addresses most fully the radical potential of faithful witnessing as she highlights the dangers of forgetting that immigrant detention centers and prisons alike are sites of state violence against black subjects.[46] Danticat's call to remember is grounded in the hope of preventing more death that can be visited upon people made invisible behind the walls of detention centers, as in the case of her own uncle Joseph Danticat's death at Krome Detention Center in Miami. Danticat argues, "when vulnerable populations are kept hidden," they become slowly erased.[47] She discusses almost 40 years of making pilgrimages to witness children and families at detention facilities. The retellings of her visits, interspersed with a digitally hyperlinked archive of official documents, news articles, and court testimonies, exemplifies the author's deep commitment to faithful witnessing as community activist work. Danticat's visits began with her parents taking her to an immigration detention center near the Brooklyn Navy Yard in the early 1980s. She discusses visiting facilities with journalists, with a congressional delegation, with registered volunteers, and with a social worker friend. She also discusses the work of a program director at the Florida-based organization Americans for Immigrant Justice. Her positionality in relation to those who grant her entrance into the detention centers shape her experiences and findings at these facilities, from Brooklyn, New York, to Cutler Bay, Florida, to Miami Gardens. Her thinking about the situation of Haitians detained in the U.S. also reaches to include those immigrants from Nicaragua, Honduras, and El Salvador, who, too, were threatened by the potential end to the Temporary Protected Status program. In a 2018 interview, "'I am a Witness,'" Danticat states:

> Those of us who know and are around activists, and I mean true activists . . . are shy to call ourselves activists. . . . but I think of myself as a witness: a

person who can report on what I'm seeing and who can report on what others are saying. In many ways, this work is somewhat selfish—this work of writing—because, if you want to do it fully and carefully, it requires a lot of alone time, it requires a lot of time off the battlefield. . . . I feel more comfortable saying I'm a witness, and the way I witness is through this work of writing.[48]

Danticat's discussion of witnessing as part of the cultural work inextricable from her literature reminds us that her activist work has not only informed, but also long preceded her literary production. This witnessing, paired with her commitment to documenting, especially that of marginalized community members' *testimonio*, is meant to render public the necropolitics of the U.S. in hopes of inciting change.

Danticat's use of the word "parole" in this essay explicitly links Immigrant Detention Centers to the Prison Industrial Complex, another important focus for the Black Lives Matter Movement, as the police violence (especially in the form of state-sanctioned death) they resist is an extension of this complex. In the early 1980s, Rudolph Giuliani was the associate Attorney General of the U.S. and, she notes, was one of the most vocal opponents of parole for 2,100 Haitian refugees being held at facilities around the U.S. The "limbo" she situates this wait within speaks to the hybrid, liminal position of so many immigrants in the U.S., as well as those Haitians living in *dyaspora*, such as the author herself. Steeped in the context of incarcerating subjects hoping to earn release back into their communities, the association of the term "parole" with asylum seekers contextualizes the slide between immigrants and criminals in public discourse. In fact, Danticat mentions children, U.S. citizens, who have been placed in foster care at His House Children's Home in Miami alongside immigrant children, a placement local social workers treat as a last resort for those in their care. The children report that the center treats them like "prisoners." In this way, Danticat creates an overt link between the Immigrant Detention Center Complex and the Prison Industrial Complex. We may even be reminded of social media posts during recent Honduran immigrant "caravan" news coverage stating "seeking asylum is not a crime," reinforcing what Danticat's "Harrowing Turning Point" essay explains as the purpose of the TSP program.

Seeking asylum is precisely what so many Haitian immigrants have done. Highlighting their endless wait for "parole," though they have not committed any crimes, Danticat underscores how immigrant detention centers are tied through their practices to prisons, twin centers of U.S. state police violence and detention. The nature of the relationship between the U.S. and Haiti, fomented during the colonial era of slave labor used to extract resources from the island nation, continued through punitive economic embargo, military occupation, and support of the Duvalier dictatorships and extended into contemporary mismanagement of disaster relief aid programing. All must be considered as the grounds from which present immigration issues grow, and it must be stressed that all were catalysts of black death. This truth is especially telling as Danticat's own uncle Joseph Dantica died in Krome Immigrant Detention Center at the age of 81, though he had a passport and multiple-entry visa when he was arrested by immigration officials and stripped of his medications after seeking temporary asylum. When Danticat warns us "we must not forget" those hidden away in detention, she reminds us that the result of their separation and criminalization can be death. Our inclusion of this essay focused on the living, alongside the others discussed earlier that lament the dead, exhibits that amidst the elegiac thrust of Danticat's project is resistance in service of the living. Indeed, in her *New Yorker* column, the elegiac action of lifting names of those whose lives are already lost is twinned with that of lifting the voices of those in immediate danger of being lost to us.

This spirit of ongoing resistance characterizes Danticat's challenge to the state's effort to render invisible and expendable black immigrants in the form of her testimony at official government hearings. In 2007, the author delivered written testimony for the house Judiciary Committee's subcommittee on Immigration, Citizenship, Refugees, Border Security, and International Law.[49] She spoke truth to power testifying about her own uncle, who was, for a time, her surrogate parent while she remained in Haiti in the early years of her parents' life in the U.S. Danticat's contribution to the hearings on immigrant death in detention centers reflects the eschewing of consolation that the editors of this volume note characterizes Black Lives Matter–era elegiac innovations, as we discussed earlier. In this hearing on "Detention and Removal: Immigration Detainee Medical Care," Danticat describes her uncle's untimely death when his pleas for medication and medical attention were ignored by the guards at Krome. She describes how the guards argued he was faking his medical emergency and ignored the protestations of his lawyer, before eventually transporting him to Miami's Jackson Memorial Hospital. Danticat's testimony highlights "the lack of instant and serious response to his becoming ill" at Krome, and also "subpar medical attention" at Jackson Memorial Hospital. She underscores, "that he was not permitted by Homeland Security and Krome officials to see loved ones, who wanted to see him, during his final hours must have left him feeling less than human at best."[50] Her testimony renders visible the abuses taking place behind the walls of Krome and is an example of the embrace of the decolonial tool of faithful witnessing to reveal what colonial regimes work to obscure: the pattern of government officials wielding oppressive power against black subjects.

Indeed, Danticat draws attention to her uncle being cut off from the vision of his family members, creating a link we see between "We Must Not Forget Detained Migrant Children," the essay in which she repeatedly argues for the importance of witnessing the people within and conditions of detention centers. As she states, "they not only live in the shadows; they become slowly erased."[51] What she refers to as erasure and forgottenness in that essay, she illuminates in her subcommittee testimony as creating conditions where the detained immigrant, in this case her uncle Joseph, feels "less than human." Danticat shows how hiding immigrants out of public view leads to erasure and dehumanization, a metaphorical form of social death, which creates conditions favorable for physical death. Reading the essay and the court testimony together reveals an elegiac link between social invisibility and physical death. As Danticat puts it, "from the perspective of a family member, this is a nightmare."[52]

Danticat's court testimony also refers to a *New York Times* article quoting a Department of Homeland Security spokesperson who argues that those who break immigration laws get the same medical treatment in detention centers. Danticat reminds us that immigrants who seek asylum and who become detained have not broken immigration laws, before moving on to note that "to criminalize the right of a person to seek asylum and then see the lack of medical attention and care given to them as part of the punishment," means that more people will continue to die in the care of I.C.E. officials in detention centers.[53] Her testimony before the subcommittee counters any notion that immigrants are cared for or treated as humans when hidden away from family and community view. As a painful illustration, Danticat emphasizes the nullification of her uncle's humanity under U.S. policy through the use of his detention identification number. She argues, her uncle "was not just Alien # 270401999," and resists the dehumanizing discourse of the state by resituating him through his family and community roles: Father, grandfather, brother, uncle, friend, and clergyman.[54] Her commitment to "vulnerable populations who are kept hidden, or are forced into hiding," to witnessing these children and families herself, and to giving testimony to these invisible and voiceless populations ("We Must Not Forget") speaks to the use of her *New Yorker* column as an extension of her activist work, influencing her orientation to the acts of faithful witnessing, documenting, and testimony as interrelated, deeply political, and increasingly exigent.

Looking to Danticat's *New Yorker* column as an extension of her literary corpus and as informed by her long history of community activism illuminates the political thrust of her status as a public intellectual. Our examination of her historiography of violence against black subjects across the expanse of America both highlights the important cultural work taking place on her *New Yorker* platform and underscores the continued imperative for the transnational framework her elegiac work invokes within contemporary Black Lives Matter discourse. The elegiac dimensions of her work to document the scope and reach of U.S. imperial state violence against black communities, when contextualized in the Black Lives Movement era, align with the unflinching resistance undergirding public and communal grief and remembrance. The reach of her column extends the discourse of the movement to a readership of longer-form works, while the digital form, complete with hyperlinks and images, functions similarly to the social media most often associated with #BLM resistance work. Her elegiac project is borne out in her fiction as well as her nonfiction and involves the work of witnessing, documentation, and testimony. Moving beyond lamentation into documentation that highlights the continued abuses of imperial power against black subjects at home and on the move, Danticat calls for action, for reckoning. "We must not forget," she implores us, the names of the lost and the living.

Notes

1. Edwidge Danticat, "Black Bodies in Motion and Pain," *The New Yorker*, June 22, 2015, www.newyorker.com/culture/cultural-comment/black-bodies-in-motion-and-in-pain
2. For more on this ruling, see Danticat's "Fear of Deportation in the Dominican Republic," as well as Allyn Gaestel's article, "Stateless in the Dominican Republic: Residents Stripped of Citizenship" and Ella Mohony and Rachel Nolan's piece, "The Roots of *La Sentencia*."
3. Achille Mbembe, "Necropolitics," *Public Culture* 15, no. 1 (2003): 59.
4. Ibid., 27.
5. Ibid., 4.
6. Yomaira C. Figueroa, "Faithful Witnessing as Practice: Decolonial Readings of *Shadows of your Black Memory* and *The Brief and Wondrous Life of Oscar Wao*," *Hypatia* 30, no. 4 (Fall 2015): 642.
7. For more on the conflation between the prison industrial complex and immigrant detention centers, see Sara Riva's "Across the Border and into the Cold" (2017); Rebecca Bohrman and Naomi Murakawa's "Remaking Big Government" (2005); Tonya Golash-Boza's "The Immigration Industrial Complex" (2009); and Livia Luan's 2018 policy report, "Profiting from Enforcement."
8. Edwidge Danticat, "Enough is Enough," *The New Yorker*, November 26, 2014, www.newyorker.com/culture/cultural-comment/michael-brown-ferguson-abner-louima-police-brutality
9. Ibid.
10. Ibid.
11. Emily Rutter, Sequoia Maner, Tiffany Austin, and darlene anita scott, "Introduction" in *Revisiting the Elegy in the Black Lives Matter Era* (New York: Routledge, 2019), pg. 9.
12. Ibid.
13. For more on gendered police violence against women, see Angela J. Ritchie's *Invisible No More: Police Violence Against Black Women and Women of Color* (Boston: Beacon Press, 2017), which traces systematic racial and gendered violence, "identifying broader paradigms of policing . . . unmask[ing] the continuing operation of controlling narratives of black women and women of color rooted in colonialism and slavery in police interactions" (3). Angela Davis's foreword situates Ritchie's work in relation to Ida B. Wells's anti-lynching work *The Red Record* and William L. Patterson and Paul Robeson's 1951 petition, "We Charge Genocide," to the United Nations about racial violence in the U.S. legal system and otherwise.
14. Ibid.
15. Ibid.
16. Ibid.
17. Ibid.
18. Ibid.
19. https://blacklivesmatter.com/about/what-we-believe/
20. Angela J. Hattery and Earl Smith, *Policing Black Bodies: How Black Lives are Surveilled and How to Work for Change* (Lanham: Rowman & Littlefield, 2018), 3.
21. Barbara Ransby, *Making All Black Lives Matter: Reimagining Freedom in the 21st Century*. (Oakland: University of California Press, 2018), 3.

22. Two works that participate in this chronicling through the naming of black lives lost are Claudia Rankine's *Citizen: An American Lyric* (Minneapolis: Graywolf Press, 2014), her book-length lyric poem that features more names added with each new edition printed, and Christopher J. Lebron's intellectual history *The Making of Black Lives Matter: A Brief History of an Idea* (Oxford: Oxford University Press, 2017) opens with an introductory chapter titled "Naming the Dead in the Name of the Living" that situates the naming work the movement has done as documentation and "damning evidence" of the level of violence against black bodies in America. Lebron includes Frederick Douglass's abolitionist thought, as well as Ida B. Wells' *The Red Record*, as some of the earliest American works documenting the violent policing of black people in the lengthy history of proclamations that black lives matter.

23. See Elizabeth Abbott's, *Haiti: The Duvaliers and Their Legacy* (New York: McGraw-Hill, 1988); Jana Evans Braziel's, *Duvalier's Ghosts: Race, Diaspora, and U.S. Imperialism in Haitian Literature* (Gainesville: University Press of Florida, 2010); Bernard Diederich's, *The Price of Blood: History of Repression and Rebellion in Haiti Under Dr Francois Duvalier, 1957–1962* (Princeton, NJ: Markus Wiener Publishing Inc, 2011); Laurent Dubois's, *Haiti: The Aftershocks of History* (New York: Picador, 2013); and Amy Wilentz's, *The Rainy Season: Haiti- Then and Now* (New York City: Simon & Schuster, 2011) for more on the Duvalier dictatorship(s).

24. Edwidge Danticat's, *The Dew Breaker* (New York: Vintage, 2005) imagines the contemporary legacy of a TonTon Macoute who migrates to the U.S. in order to escape the violence left in his wake as a member of Duvalier's secret police. Danticat uses the term "Dew Breaker" to describe the way in which TonTon Macoutes would disturb the morning dew in the early hours as they were sneaking up on unsuspecting victims.

25. Jana Evans Braziel, *Duvalier's Ghosts: Race, Diaspora, and U.S. Imperialism in Haitian Literatures* (Gainesville: University Press of Florida, 2017), 1.

26. Ibid., 11.

27. Ibid., 17.

28. Michel Foucault's term biopower (*biopouvir*) examines the role of the modern nation states in regulating subjectivity and the body through a multitude of apparati and technologies. See Foucault's *The Will to Knowledge* (London: Penguin Books, 2006) for further explanation.

29. Ibid., 17.

30. See Edwidge Danticat's January 12, 2018 *Democracy Now* interview with Amy Goodman for her full response to Donald Trump's remarks about immigrants from "shithole countries."

31. Jennifer L. Shoaff, "The Right to a Haitian Name and a Dominican Nationality: *La Sentencia* (TC 168–13) and the Politics of Recognition and Belonging," *Journal of Haitian Studies* 22, no. 2 (2016): 59.

32. Ibid., 60.

33. Wesley Lowery, *They Can't Kill Us All: Ferguson, Baltimore, and a New Era in America's Racial Justice Movement* (New York: Little, Brown and Company, 2016), 11.

34. Ibid., 15.

35. Ibid.

36. Ibid.

37. In *The Farming of Bones,* Danticat examines the emotional and physical aftermath of the Parsley Massacre in the hospital scene in which the main character, Amabelle Desir, has the opportunity to share her account of the massacre within a larger community of survivors. In this scene, those individuals who survived the massacre testify to the violence endured and witnessed.

38. For more on how Danticat underscores the long relationship between the U.S. and Haiti, as she does in these *New Yorker* essays, see Maia L. Butler's chapter, "The Exigency of the Floating Homeland and Engaging Postnationalisms in the Classroom:

Approaches to Teaching Edwidge Danticat's *Create Dangerously: The Immigrant Artist at Work*" in *Approaches to Teaching the Work of Edwidge Danticat* (Routledge, 2019), in which she reads Danticat's comparison of media responses to the black survivors of Hurricane Katrina and Haiti's Tropical Storm Jeanne.

39. Ibid.
40. Ibid.
41. Edwidge Danticat, "A Harrowing Turning Point for Haitian Immigrants," *The New Yorker*, May 12, 2017, www.newyorker.com/news/news-desk/a-harrowing-turning-point-for-haitian-immigrants
42. Ibid.
43. Ibid.
44. Ibid.
45. Ibid.
46. Edwidge Danticat, "We Must Not Forget Detained Migrant Children," *The New Yorker*, June 26, 2018, www.newyorker.com/news/news-desk/we-must-not-forget-detained-migrant-children
47. Ibid.
48. Jake Brownell, "'I Am a Witness': A Conversation with Edwidge Danticat," *91.5 KRCC Converge Lecture Series Podcast*, October 31, 2018, www.krcc.org/post/i-am-witness-conversation-edwidge-danticat?fbclid=IwAR2uA1qmhp1SuhevZs_0jyenlKIgSzAFaPTjOY7lCuJqWCYuLFNvqC_uWwI
49. Her testimony was removed from the website of the U.S. House Committee of the Judiciary (during the tenure of Chairman Jerrold Nadler) during the writing of this chapter, but it remains available online for public viewing on the American Civil Liberties Union website at www.aclu.org/other/testimony-edwidge-danticat-house-immigration-subcommittee-hearing-detention-and-removal.
50. Ibid., 4.
51. Ibid.
52. Ibid., 5.
53. Ibid., 6.
54. Ibid.

10

LOVING YOU IS COMPLICATED

Empire of Language #4

Hoke S. Glover III (Bro. Yao)

Empire of Language—Finale-Loving You is Complicated.
So build build
again the new
villages; you
must mix spittle
with dirt, dung
to saliva. . . . .
Edward Kamau Braithwaite From *The Arrivants*[1]
Poems are bullshit unless they are
teeth or trees or lemons piled
on a step.
Amiri Baraka From "Black Art"[2]

1

We are a freeway of ideas. We study hard. The craft. The craft. The craft.
Whichcraft.
Witchcraft?
Whichcraft.

2

The moon is bright tonight. I look hard but cannot see where man left his footprints in the sky. Bright as a white cue ball, Renegade would say. Bright white light shining at night.

3

Me and my boys sit in an abandoned sector of the empire for Black poets. A decade or two back, a lot of new potential poets went hip-hop and spoken word. If, like Charles Rowell says in the introduction to *Angles of Ascent*, poets in the post–Black Arts period found the freedom to explore the interior of their lives, there is also something to be said about their break from a Black audience. The notion that Black poetry is for Black people in many poetry circles has become a sign of confinement. I admit, I might be confined by the idea that all my art has to be for Black folks, though obviously it is not; but the idea doesn't worry me anymore than the feeling of confinement in a publishing world with few Black presses, editors, and publications. I feel no more confined by the idea of having to write for only Black people, than the reality of white benefactors and handlers in the world of African American poetry, who to this day have the ability to make or break careers.

Targeting an audience is writing 101. The notion of an audience-less text is a concoction of those who decide to avoid some confrontation with their readers; or as in the case of those who operate in the top echelon of the literary world, an assertion that the ability to judge literature in current time is an extension of a function as guardian of the great tradition. Of course, they work for the empire that is connected to steel iron and the strange ideas that somehow had us picking cotton down South. In other words, some of the poetry power game is just simple power; and power is not poetry. Black poetry has power, but power without poetry is far more brutal and certain of itself.

When Black poets publicly speak of transcendent work, I imagine they are managing their career. They know economics. If they tell you, there is technically no audience for their work and it is primarily craft driven, they mean not to offend those folks who might think they are not included in the audience if they say their work is for Black people. One must remember people without infrastructure are masters of the game. They know how to get things done. And the work has come in quite nicely. Very few Black presses out there, but African Americans seem to be winning awards like wildfire. One can expect even more in the wake of the rising discontent, riots, and an unsettled Black collective consciousness shifting to the center of the nation's media.

The Black Arts quest for a Black audience showed itself as a viable strategy in hip-hop, which, as part of the musical realm, operated the way African American music always has. People say poetry is music, but the audiences for the two crafts vary dramatically. Black audiences make or break a majority of African American musicians and then they cross over. In Black poetry, the positioning of the rich literate societies arguably give rise to a situation that is inverse. White audiences make a Black poet these days, and then perhaps (often not or never) a Black audience responding to them like classical music or some other cultural expression rooted in Western culture, jumps on the bus and says, "you ever heard of this or that Black poet?"

It is what is. It's just whichcraft.

4

Whichcraft you might ask. Black folks singing out of sight some old song that cuts the air like a blade. Spirituals coauthored by the Black many and unseen, or was it gentle humming and the sway at the sight of a broken body? Was it elegy? Was it study with those masters of literature, guardians of the canon—the serious poets?

Witchcraft is an unpublished poetry. It is a poetry the empire doesn't sanctify. It is the position of the Djali outside of West African culture and Nationalists who live off the grid. No Djali publications here. Not ready for it.

I will write for you a great epic modeled on some ancient man whose worship has given rise to my demise. His craft was impeccable, but his work shows the inability to acknowledge my humanity. The separation is a common part of the Black predicament. The equation is far more complicated than we like to think. Being Black, we can get over almost anything. *Stop tripp'n man, that was a long time ago. Why you still tripp'n?*

You gotta respect the work. Respect the work. Though the essence of our condition, and clearly present in slavery, is that the work was what it was all about. Nigger ain't worth nothing but his work under slavery. In fact, work prove he a good slave. But what else is there besides work?

The great craftsmen have craft not work. Their skill exists as the thing that creates product. American consumerism will train you quickly in how demeaning worker status or product-driven value is. We don't imagine the Chinese workers who make our gadgets to be craftsman. We imagine them to be underpaid workers—almost-slaves.

Intellectual property is god. Intellectual property and the right to own processes under the law reduces some to workers and elevates others to masters of capital.

There really ain't nothing wrong with that, but what's a poet to do whose work operates in a poorly consumed sector of the empire, that also happens to be a badge of great culture?

Who wouldn't want to be a craftsman as compared to a worker? Craft is the worker's rise above the mundane; but the trick in the empire is that one of the most important powers of the empire, especially in regard to language, is to designate what is right and what is good. Of course, there is great utility in this, but there is also farce and illusion. Now I am thinking of the Wiz, who issues decrees and changes the colors on a moment's notice.

All the lies of the empire have great utility. All lies of the empire are promoted as the truth.

Folk art is one of those clever ways the crafts of other societies are regulated to the categories of the inferior; while the empire gives long dissertations on the nature of true and high art.

Poets worship at the altar of the greatest of Western Civilization, for we operate in the tongue of the master. For many this is unavoidable.

I got all that, but there are other crafts, many crafts.

People are people, but some people have difficulty recognizing other folks as people. Those people are not to be blamed. They are just people. The people they don't recognize are just people too, who can't be recognized as people.

5

The essence of nature for us is to accept whatever we see and perceive as real. The us is simply opposite of them. The dance is a secret. Let them call it whatever they want. Let them ban the dance, and the drum, reduce the most complex rhythms and relationships into iambs. Don't make no difference, we gonna dance anyway. We gonna drum anyway. We . . .

6

My Uncle is an original gangster. Gangster is the thought that runs through my mind every time I see his slacks, suit, and tie. But actually, for real-for real he ain't. He's an engineer raised on Morena Street in Nashville during the forties.

One of his brothers, my Uncle Jr., also known as Jap, got his name from the War. Folks called him Jap, cuz they said he was as mean as the legendary Japanese who fought to the death and slammed planes into aircraft carriers.

Kamikazes and shit.

Real talk, cuz folks will tell you a story about him getting rage in his eyes and pointing his pistol towards your head or to the sky, like one of the young boys; but with a different type of danger. Jefferson Street Nashville in the fifties was not crack time, it was number running and loan sharking—a different type of danger. For his time, he was the serious business—*get my money right, man*.

But my other Uncle I'm talking about is different. He's almost always smiling, and when he talks he speaks softly as though what he is saying demands a listening to that cannot be accomplished by those who think loud or aggressive means something significant attached to language. He is a gentleman in the truest sense of the world. Yet, the gentle is not the absence of force, but the refinement of it. His gentleness is the perfection of force. He's an OG.

Though he now dabbles in other businesses, his professional career is rooted in his engineering. It was he who gently spoke to me the famous quote of the Greek philosopher Archimedes, "Give me a lever and a place to stand and I will move the world." He spoke the proverb gently in a long talk where he faded in and out of the audible—gentle and smiling.

Then, I was young and full of activism. I believed in the young man show your strength exertion. I wanted to be strong and be seen as strong; but strength shown is different from strength leveraged.

Though he does not study T'ai Chi, the Asian art stresses a point similar to my Uncle's. The place to stand is where one is rooted to the earth. Leveraging, like with Archimedes, is based on the fulcrum or the point of pivot. One who is rooted is capable of leveraging his or her opponent or pushing them off balance, though their weight and physical strength may appear to be greater.

Power reconciled with balance and rootedness is not really force. It is union.

My Uncle knows business and business really is the art of leveraging. Leveraging is the maximization of power exerted at the right time, the right place, in the precise position. Like a great jazz solo in a club at night or a great performance where the audience, the day, and the time, is as much a part of the greatness as the ideas, craft, and form. Leveraging is a bridge between two forces working on the crux of natural law. In some ways the concept is similar to what Sun Tzu calls momentum or potential energy in *The Art of War*. The energy in the organization of things that exist independently of our own ego perceived force and power comes from nature itself. The engineer finds the laws to make machines. The poets find the secret unity in the codes of language and build the path of the desired experience and consciousness between people and language. Their work enables readers to unify with experience outside of their own sensory perception via the works of art. The poet makes the internal nature of life possible to communicate.

7

To find energy and seek union with it. The quest to be human. Union blesses. It is a giving that is not giving. The precise coordinates and equations are law. Law that one could call obedient if one knows it, but it is not obedient. It is simply the way things are.

When I say OG, I mean the men and women who know the secrets of knowledge and use them to manage their lives, relationships with others, and the physicality they have control over. Today's writers seem a bit attached to showing their craft. We must show our craft. We are so fond of machines these days. The finely crafted pistons, the precise orders. The sleek shape of the car is pleasant to the eyes. The finely structured verses. The perfection seen.

8

That bright moon don't lie. You notice it, and it rises up above like a myth. It's legendary and always been there. You can see it, but still only imagine it. It has nothing to do with life; but then it has everything to do with life. Can you feel its pull on the tide within you?

9

I want to be like the poets. Shit, I am a poet; if self-definition and proclamation work? If hours of study, reading, and talking to smart folks works; yes, well then I am a poet. Do you understand?

There is an unbelievable strength in them. The poets are engineers.

Today we value the machine, and want the poet to make us one. We want the craft. It justifies the difference between poetry and hip-hop, poetry and spoken word, poetry and those who spit verse as compared to compose it.

And poets have responded by standing in line to make machines for the empire. The line is long and there are only a few spots; but we wait, write, network, and study towards it. The empire may not like poetry, but understands the value of a machine.

The poet is perplexed by these questions: How does one win the award? How does one win the contest of man? Does it stand on the page? How does one follow the leader? How does one submit and be accepted?

Much of this is strength and exertion applied.

The critique of the critique is hateration, shit outsiders do to dog out the insiders.

And so we begin. Poetry, my love.

Loving you is complicated.[3]

10

A nigger is a strange invention that seems to constantly fall out of the mouths of people. Nobody's a nigger, but people imagine they exist.

It is not the appropriate label, but it is appropriately language.

Confession: I like that shit when Black folks use it. Makes me feel like we are putting out poetry working the connotations, working the subtle meanings; making language into a gourd that can carry water.

It could be the word is often banned to protect those who use it from the hate that hate produced.

11

We fuss over words, but the poet who fusses over words forever to sync those words with the consciousness of people is often regulated to obscurity.

Yeah. I'm down with craft.

12

Now is the lonely time, though there's still a certain rage in the air. Bright moon is my witness comes in with the season. Shines like a spotlight. Lawd, Lawd, bright night light.

13

The notion of what is spoken is as much contract as utterance. Unrecognized and unacknowledged speech breeds silence. If you have no audience then what the fuck are you really saying? Who knows?

14

The empire listens, authenticates, and certifies certain speech. Some of that speech is recorded and comes through microphones; other speech is like the subtle shiftings of the earth's plates. The scientists tell you of the movement but your feet do not know it. The slightest tremors, the smallest changes happen in our presence outside of our conscious perception.

15

If poetry rises above silence, we know by intuition that much of the poetry in the world is also trapped beneath it. Poetry is not and never really has been authentic. People say what they want to say. The audience chooses whether to recognize it as speech.

The listening interaction between cultures gives rise to poetry. One can only imagine how the words of Columbus sounded to the Arawaks he met.

An alternative concept in your language is poetic.

To be an audience you must listen. You must be a good listener.

Poetry demands attention.

The empire pays attention to the empire.

And that's alright. There are lands to be conquered, roadways to be constructed, metals to be mined. The empire desires what the empire desires.

Language is the empire's greatest machine. Poets have built and maintained that machine. There are poets tinkering on the valves, pistons, and compressors as we speak.

But the empire is not poetry. The empire thinks of poetry as a medal on the chest of one of its generals. Poetry for the empire is evidence of what the empire has achieved.

If two speak across languages the conditions demand poetry.

From within the empire cross-cultural communication is a term to describe the issuing of commands to those who will eventually be subdued. The listening is not listening. The soon to be subjects must understand they are about to be brought into the empire and must learn to respect and show awe for its awesome power. On these borders of civilizations they meet and speak poetry. The empire's poetry suggest conquest. The others speak the poetry of cross-cultural communication and are misunderstood. What does poetry matter in the face of war? What is the poetry of the ship sailing into the harbor and the thirst for fold rising up from the belly of the ship? What is the poetry of guns and swords and the sense that blood will flow so that things might get done? Those who have met the empire on its way towards conquests would have done better to listen to the song of the machines themselves. In conquest, when subduing the machine sings the true poetry of the empire.

16

Though men and women attempt to manufacture authenticity, authenticity cannot be created.

People are who they are.

Authenticity suggests that we listen to some things more than we do others; yes, we do; but also, and importantly, some of what we don't listen to was never meant for us. Some of the poetry people don't read or listen to is the bullshit of the empire. It is and idea coded to tame and oppress us. Some of the codes are so machine-like they make our own poetry seem pitiful and petty; as though we were playing with language, while others make machines. Some of the poetry is the worshiping of the weather in the empire. What's hip ain't always hip.

As a prize-winning poet once told me, "This game is about the rich. If you don't want to deal with that, you shouldn't be in it." Some of the rich have their poets around them like jesters in a court. The poet entertains. The poet mixes the high culture of the empire with the ways of man as the wealthy see fit.

I am not here to indict or attack poets. We are few, a dying breed. Why the hell would I do that?

Loving you.

17

We really love poetry. We are attracted to it. It is the beautiful and intoxicating, but all we have is our ability to notice it when it blows through the air. It is aroma and scent riding on the gust of wind.

To recognize poetry is to be one with it.

18

Kendrick Lamar

> Lamar's album moved 123,000 copies, down 66% from the previous week's impressive debut. The rapper revealed to MTV that his album was originally titled "To Pimp a Caterpillar" as a nod to Tupac, but in the end elected to swap in the "Butterfly" to evoke the "brightness of life."[4]

That's some poetic shit right there—metaphorical image management and shit.

19

I come home the day Kendrick released his latest album and my son sings "loving you is complicated." He twists his voice like Tyehimba Jess twist notes in *Leadbelly*. Each time he repeats how complicated loving is, he distorts the word into something that is not on the page. I read poetry, live and breathe it every day; but I cannot write what my son enacts.

It's complicated.

20

The abstraction of writing is an okedoke of the empire. Tarzan is the white man's fantasy of the unknown. So is the Lone Ranger.

Fuck Tonto cuz he ain't never exist.

Maybe my daddy loved that shit cuz he could imagine himself being Tonto as fantasy. The impossible.

But I can see how one can dream of being the Lone Ranger and ignore his sidekick; or think they was his sidekick and not realize the blatant disrespect. I can see how one might want to be a sidekick to the "lone," not really a sidekick but an unacknowledged presence. I can see how that presence is not really presence but a Black straitjacket that you put yourself inside so that when you walk around in the flesh you look like a shadow. Success not success.

21

Loot'n and shit.

It's April 2015 late in the month before it's gotten hot and I see the aerial view of a couple hundred young'ns running towards a mall to get it in, like looting is a holiday. I'm numbed the way I was when I saw the women in the market just before the Iraqi War selling olives and spices. With their hijabs and beautiful eyes, they were going about their business as though there was no war in the world. I saw them and thought about what it means to be an American. The deadline had been etched—an invisible abstract line that stretched across the world. We wondered whether it was real or some fake ass shit like Gucci bags that say Gucci but ain't got no patent rights. We wondered if Bush was fronting, or if it was the real shit, come correct, go hard street shit we'd seen from men who went to prison early in their lives.

The students descended upon the mall bringing the mothafucking ruckus in a way I never could. It was hard to imagine that folks like me would loot a mall. They looked just like my students.

During the Iraqi War, when night came, I remember flashes of orange across the screen, the constant talk of sorties, and the darkness of Baghdad. I was confused and kept seeing the women. They were not Saddam Hussein, they looked more like my mother, my sisters—the eyes. I wondered what happened to them.

Those kids look like my kids, and the orange fires in the night around Baltimore gave rise to thick clouds of black smoke. A few stare into the camera or do a walk that looks like half dancing. It's the head bounce rhythm that gets me most. There's hip-hop in all of it.

I haven't really listened to most of the talking yet, but I've been seeing a lot of poetry lately.

22

Poetry is not recognized authenticity, but recognized communication whose density inspires one about the fantastic science of words. Yes, words can duplicate life and life can duplicate life and if one is aware of life in a moment what is the distinction between that moment and what poetry is?

23

Within the empire, words that duplicate life can easily be used to subdue and oppress. The empire craves poets. They are the antithesis of their quest for power and valuable players on their chess board. If power makes clear that one must be subjugated, poetry makes clear that there is no subjugation. Poetry makes clear that what exists within the world is acknowledged and unified beyond the realms of human power.

Poetry is language linked with the great machine, the one machine that is not machine but simply union. The power that is poetry belongs to the realm of nature, though language is a machine of man. In nature machine becomes an imperfect metaphor. Machines imperfectly mimic, replicate, or attempt to provide what nature does. We know machines by their inefficiency and by products. The waste seeping into the earth. The smog rising into the sky. The trash man comes to my house on Mondays and Thursdays.

Poetry is mystical magic via language elevated to everything is everything.

24

Of course the empire will tell you different.

It will tell you poetry is the mastery of form, the mastery of convention, the mastery of precise craft, though in the world you hear poetry come from the most lowly places, the most dejected quarters.

Loving you is complicated.[5]

25

Maybe if we listened to everything we would learn that there is poetry everywhere.

Within the empire, one cannot listen to everything. One must go to work, perform one's task, present oneself as a noble citizen.

One must honor their to do list, execute tasks, walk past the homeless on the way to work. Should one smell his smell in the air, one might be offended. One must stay focused.

To raise speech above us like trophies and say this is poetry is a privilege of the empire.

It may be human to look up, or only human to look down when you are down.

Within the empire of language poetry is like the cement and the earth beneath our feet. As humans we walk upon both. One is the blessing of nature, and the other the blessing of those who build and harness the powers of the earth.

We need language to clarify the content of our lives. Language is essential to most cures for loneliness. For to share and have that sharing recognized actualizes the fact that one is not alone.

Both concrete and earth are poetry.

Heaven is great. Earth is great. Man is Great.[6]

What humans have made is great poetry.

What nature has made and perfected is poetry.

What shows the unity between humans and nature is poetry.

26

But poetry is always the unexpected. It is the dance intoxicating you when you thought you did not feel like dancing. It is the rise when you felt like sleeping. It is language pressed and pulled to these arenas, perfected in them.

27

Poetry is not a gun. Not a trophy. Not a machine. Poetry resists its reduction to such things. It is fresh and in the moment.

Loving you is complicated.[7]

When one tells you that your poetry is not good enuff, they are letting you know that they possess the power to bless. *Come into my circle young Jedi.*

The empire proscribes craft as remedy for all things that have veered out of control. Craft is essential, but control is not. The empire will have you confuse the two. You may dream of power, but it is nothing like the power that comes from the real source of power. That power is the power you cannot harness; one must submit and learn to be the thing it has desired for you to be.

Too often our craft is control. The real craft is mystical.

28

What drove me to poetry was silence and the vast pages of books given to me as lessons which did not contain the speech and beauty of the language I heard in my own life.

I became convinced that even my mother, my sister, and my father did not hear me. Of course the problem was not simply language. It was more about the speed of the earth and how fast it spins. It was about bills to pay, high blood pressure, and the way a Friday night seems to wander into town like a circus with animals and sites made out of everyday things in the world. It was more about a piece of paper curled to the sky and the fingers sprinkling crumbled leaves into them. It was about the cradle of a hand on a bottle held like a football. It was about the back and forth rhythm of one of my sister's friends' heads or the quick stutter step dance like I remember Fela. It was about love and warmth, distance and tragedy, and the distance between people who grow a silence or misunderstand one another.

Yes, our loving can expose us to imprecise images, ideas, and concepts that make speech seem imperfect and limited. We can mistake that speech for the truth of our lives. The poet can renew our belief in a union between language and what we know. It is the knowing that I am like you and you are like me; that our feelings often intersect. Poets can help us realize what exists on the inside may not always come out in words right. The poet can get those words right so that we know how human we all are.

I did not know that then, but I knew it. It was my own silence and the distance between those I loved that led me to poetry.

29

I have been commissioned by the state to write a series of poems on the Baltimore riots. They chose me along with millions of others. I've seen the man dragged by his feet to the van half rag doll. I have accepted; but my acceptance is full of tears. Too much time has been spent not talking about the what I see.

His back is broken. The empire must investigate.

My disease, like that of many poets who too have been commissioned, is our reconciliation of craft with the violence that snatches up folks who look like us. Yes, there are other things in the world besides violence; but we track the path of violence in our lives, because in its wake, it blurs the image, confuses the image, transforms the perception. Violence transforms and tests the human spirit. The Blacks have been tested and dumped on in the space. We are not the only ones.

To be a poet is noble, but to talk about Freddie Gray scorches the tongue. The empire wants noble elegies that elevate Freddie Gray over simple everyday shit people have to ignore to get from home to work, from work to school, from work to the grocery store, from the front door to the corner store. The empire wants to judge and authenticate them. The empire wants to say whether the elegy for Freddie was well-written or well-crafted. In this regard, they might as well be a police department investigating police brutality.

One must wait for the government approval, the official stamp. One could be dead, or die waiting.

What awards shall be given to the riots?
What poems can be written in the face of death?

31

To what do we owe the fist?

To what do we owe the young unpoetic standing in front of riot gear in a sector of the empire, whose officials run the camp like the wild, wild, wild west?

32

The riot is its own poem.

The car burning in the street is a million flames.

The black helmet and the plexiglass with police written on it is a statement about poetry and life.

The fear and sweat underneath the black drape of what the fuck is going on is the curtain on a stage that plays out the drama of death and I gotta do my job.

The riot is its own poem.

33

Give me a poetry rooted in the language of everyday life and I can move the world.

Notes

1. Edward Braithwaite, *The Arrivants: A New World Trilogy Rights of Passage, Islands, Masks* (Oxford: Oxford University Press, 1992), 5.
2. Amiri Baraka, *Transbluesency* (New York: Marsilio, 1995), 142.
3. Kendrick Lamar, *To Pimp a Butterfly, 2012–2015: Aftermath Entertainment, Track 4 "U"* on *To Pimp a Butterfly*, 2015, CD Digital Download.
4. Marianne Zumberge, "Kendrick Lamar Hangs on to Top Spot on U.S. Album Chart," *Variety*. April 1, 2015, https://variety.com/2015/music/news/kendrick-lamar-to-pimp-a-butterfly-tops-us-album-chart-1201464660/
5. Lamar, *To Pimp a Butterfly*, "U," Track 4.
6. Stephen Mitchell, *Tao Te Ching: A New English Version* (New York: Harper, 2005), http://albanycomplementaryhealth.com/wp-content/uploads/2016/07/TaoTeChing-LaoTzu-StephenMitchellTranslation-33p.pdf
7. Lamar, *To Pimp a Butterfly*, "U," Track 4.

11

AN INTERVIEW WITH AMANDA JOHNSTON, COFOUNDER OF BLACK POETS SPEAK OUT

Sequoia Maner

> Most of us, no matter what we say, are walking in the dark, whistling in the dark. Nobody knows what is going to happen to him from one moment to the next, or how one will bear it. This is irreducible. And it's true for everybody. Now, it is true that the nature of society is to create, among its citizens, an illusion of safety; but it is also absolutely true that the safety is always necessarily an illusion. Artists are here to disturb the peace. Otherwise chaos.
>
> *James Baldwin, 1961*

I am a black poet who will not remain silent while this nation murders black people. I have a right to be angry. This is the mantra of the literary-digital movement #Black-PoetsSpeakOut (frequently referred to as BPSO throughout this interview), a campaign that provides a platform for black poets to vocalize opposition to police brutality through poetry.[1] This interview documents the formation and development of BPSO through a series of interviews with architect and cofounder Amanda Johnston who highlights the campaign's strategy of combining artful public protest with grassroots operations that challenge the state's racial logic.

In November of 2014, upon the grand jury's failure to indict police officer Darren Wilson in the shooting death of Michael Brown, and as Ferguson, Missouri ignited with more than 150 cities joining in protest, Johnston and accomplices (including Cave Canem[2] contemporaries Mahogany L. Browne, Jericho Brown, Jonterri Gadson, and Sherina Rodriguez Sharpe) devised a hashtag video campaign where poets record themselves reciting black-authored poetry dedicated to social justice. #BlackPoetsSpeakOut swiftly grew into a fast spreading, international movement—the campaign went viral. Spanning age, style, and institutional boundaries, hundreds of poets, including Terrance Hayes, Marilyn Nelson,

Camonghne Felix, Rachel Eliza Griffiths, Cornelius Eady, and L. Lamar Wilson have contributed to the campaign. Alongside these distinguished and widely published authors, lesser-known and even, every day, ordinary folks who do not call themselves poets bring increased visibility to the campaign. In celebration of the richness of African American and black diasporic poetry, BPSO participants recite the work of writers such as Langston Hughes, Audre Lorde, Lucille Clifton, Amiri Baraka, June Jordan, Robert Hayden, Yusef Komunyakaa, Etheridge Knight, and Gwendolyn Brooks, among many others. The result is an ever-growing archive of justice-oriented poems of the African American tradition that, magnified through processes of accretion, document a long history of art composed to illuminate, unsettle, and testify. To echo James Baldwin, BPSO artists are here to *disturb the peace.*

This interview emphasizes how, animated by elegiac resistance, #BlackPoets-SpeakOut marries art and activism in urgent ways. While Phase 1 of BPSO consists of the viral video campaign, Phases 2–4 move to other forms of direct action that include live demonstrations in domestic and international locations, letter-writing to state and federal politicians, and free lesson plans for classrooms and programs in local communities.[3] Thus, #BlackPoetsSpeakOut is a robust network of people, testimonies, ideas, and actions aimed at changing the relationship of African Americans to controlling institutions and policies.

As interviewer and coeditor of this anthology, I approach #BlackPoetsSpeak-Out as more than an objective documentarian. I am participant and witness who has lifted her voice in protest at several demonstrations. Notably, in the Fall of 2017 I moderated a BPSO panel with cofounders Amanda Johnston and Mahogany Browne, which featured 2017 Pulitzer Prize-winner Tyehimba Jess in the Senate Chamber of the Texas State Capitol. Demonstrations persist as police officers continue to kill black people—we have a right to be angry. Hours of conversation with educator-activist Johnston have informed my understanding of BPSO's internal workings and external aims and, in turn, deepened my own understanding of the relationship between poetry, scholarship, and activism. Here, Johnston details BPSO's powerful origin story, tracing the campaign's growth over two years.

***

SM: Can we talk a little about respectability and poetry? I am interested in how Black Poets Speak Out has what I consider a radical vision in the way the campaign rejects notions of what is academic and what is street poetry; everyone belongs in this space.

AJ: It is about visibility and voice. Visibility and voice. When we first started the BPSO campaign we were reaching out to people and it spread by word of mouth. We put the guidelines out there so everybody could know what it was and participate, but we also made heavy direct calls. If we have a personal connection, if I have your email, I do not care where you are in letters, where you are in your career—we need you because this work needs everyone. I reached out to poets from all generations, my mother, my daughters, people who are not poets but through poetry have access to the language to put forward a black poet's voice in service to this work. So, BPSO really doesn't have all of these different categories and demographics we assign. Going to someplace like AWP [the annual meeting of Association of Writers & Writing Programs], you are there to network and schmooze. Do not make these folks uncomfortable—they won't publish your book! But is that not exactly what we are yelling about? I shouldn't have to tap dance for you to publish this necessary work. I shouldn't have to be from a specific school or house or program for you to even see me.

SM: Another thing I admire about the platform is the accessibility. You are not waiting for a publisher to get the typography and the font and the permissions. You can go directly to the source and hear these poems that you need for your soul, *now*. Share these poems *now*.

AJ: Some of the people I reached out to resisted at first. Not in a "I don't want to associate with this" kind of way, but because of their career and background and connections, they did not want to *take away* from the power and urgency of the work. When I talked to Cornelius [Eady] about it he was like, "well, the young people are doing such good work, I do not want to get in the way of that." I said, "but we need you. We need everybody on every level." After that, he did his video. He read a poem by Langston Hughes ["Letter to the Academy"] which was really powerful. For others, I think technology was a hindrance because we post videos online. Some of our elders were like "Whoa! You want me to do *what* on the computer?" but with support from friends and family, we received videos from poets who originally didn't think they could do it. When those videos are all archived, they are not separated by status; they are in alphabetical order by reader or by author of the poem. That is it. There is no hierarchy.

SM: The legacy of black letters and black voices that BPSO is unearthing is incredible. Who are some of the poets that readers are looking back to?

AJ: The most shared poem is definitely "Power" by Audre Lorde. I read it today and there is no indication that it is not from 2017, but that poem is from the 70s! We've had poems shared from Phyllis Wheatley. . . . Folks are reading Langston Hughes, June Jordan, Amiri Baraka, Countee Cullen, contemporary poetry: it is really endless. Folks are reading their peers, folks from their communities where we may not have heard that poem before except by BPSO on this level (and what I mean by that is on this scale: access). Black poets can read an original poem, but most people opted not to do that because it is an opportunity to be in conversation with another black poet. The poem I first shared for the platform was Evie Shockley's "Improper(ty) Behavior." In the opening mantra, you state your name and then say "I am a black poet who will not remain silent while this nation murders black people. I have a right to be angry." If you are an accomplice though, you say, "I submit this poem in solidarity" and you still read a poem by a black poet. There is a high level of risk, so you have to have trust and a network of people who are willing to put their name and face up for the cause. This is not a job, this is a mission. It is not under some nonprofit ethics—this is how black people survive; this is what you are watching. You are watching the legacy of black survival.

Going back to the very beginning, November 24, 2014, that was the non-indictment of Darren Wilson in the murder of Mike Brown. I was at home in Texas and I was just inconsolable for many reasons that I couldn't quite put into words. Obviously, the injustice. Obviously, the murder, the reckless aban-donment. But it was also something deeper because I am from East St. Louis. I was born in East St. Louis and my father lived near Ferguson for some years, so it was deeply personal to me. This is my family, this is my community, these are our people no matter where we are currently at. I could not stress that enough. We have had people who have participated in BPSO, poets and non-poets, who are *directly related* to people we have lost just since 2014, just since we started doing demonstrations. This is not metaphor when we say family. We say family because we mean your aunty is my aunty and we family, right. I was just distraught.

SM: Sorry, I do not mean to interrupt you, but I am thinking about how if you talk about policing, you have to also talk about housing, gentrification, lack of access to resources, being forced to live in certain places, the quality of schools—all of that is related and connected. So, when you are reading as a black poet for BPSO, even if you have not lost somebody, it is deeply per-sonal. All of these injustices are deeply personal as a black poet.

AJ: Yes. Because those exact same threats are coming for you, whether you've lost someone or not. We did a BPSO reading just last week and a workshop for NeoSoul, a free community workshop [in Austin, Texas]. For the warm-up exercise I had everybody interview each other with the same question: Tell me about a time where you've had an interaction with the police. Negative, positive—doesn't matter. Just tell me about a time you've had an interaction with the police that you've either personally experienced or that you've wit-nessed firsthand. Everybody had something to say. But there was one brother who said "kind of, but not really me . . ." and I said, "What that shows me is how deeply ingrained the police state is. Do you drive down the street? Have you seen a police car? Have you gotten on an airplane? Have you been to a mall? You are under surveillance and under a police state constantly and the fact that you do not feel it, that you do not feel that any of this has touched you is, for me, an understanding that it *is* there. There are other places in the world not like this and if they came to America and saw these police eve-rywhere, they'd be like, "What the hell? They got guns on them, what the hell?" It doesn't have to be that one thing in that one moment, it is all of it. I had some good people in West Virginia reach out to me wanting to do something but who said, "we haven't had a shooting like that here." I said, "Go back and do your research." One of the participants then shared that there are more black people in jail in West Virginia than who are free. She said 60% of the black population in West Virginia is in prison. You have a criminal justice problem. Even if it appears invisible. There are instances of abuse, you just haven't seen them. I would argue that the media is more so in line with protecting the police, so much so that you haven't even seen a blip. That don't mean it don't happen.

SM: Take me back to that inconsolable grief as you are thinking about these injustices.

AJ: Okay. I am watching Ferguson burn and rage, understandably. When you attack a people, when you leave an 18-year-old boy—stop calling him a man, he just graduated high school, that was a boy—in his own blood in the middle of the street for *four hours*, that is a lynching on display to intimidate the community. Not just Ferguson, but America. I was inconsolable but I am not accustomed to feeling helpless—I am a black woman in America so we get shit done and we figure out ways to survive. Truly, this is all a legacy of black survival. I Facebook-messaged Cave Canem's private group for members and faculty with over 300 people, people of all different parts of their careers and work, but who I know are spread across the country. I hit them up first and just put a simple question out there: What are we going to do? Because we are going to do something, what are we going to do? This is in the legacy of black poetics which has always been political and never shied away from that work. This is our phase, our now.

SM: It's very twenty-first century, the strategies and the tactics BPSO is using.

AJ: Yes, reaching out to people on Facebook! *Laugh.* The first responses I got were from poets saying, "Well I wrote a poem that was published by [insert big name journal] that speaks about this." I said, "That is great. That is not what I am asking. What are we going to do? They killed a black boy in the street. We are the so-called premier organization for black poetics, can't we speak about black people being murdered? Can't we do something about this?

SM: There is something so important about that word "do." You can write a poem and you can publish a book and that does certain work in the world but . . .

AJ: It's very different than the action I was looking for. I had multiple people saying something similar to that. No, no, no. What I initially wanted was just a statement. I said, "surely we can put something out." I was hitting some road blocks.

SM: Folks not wanting to contribute?

AJ: Some were concerned about safety and, as an organization, I understand there are levels: funding etc.—but that is all that respectable part. My bottom line is: If people are supporting us, they need to know they are supporting black people and they need to look at the issue of black people being murdered, right now. For me that was a non-negotiable. We were just kind of going

around in a circle and finally I said, "How long did it take to put out a statement on the passing of Galway Kinnell? This white man who was very supportive of organizations like Cave Canem and black poetics and who was an
activist? But he was a white man and there was a statement put out mourning his death two days after he died. We are watching black people being
murdered in America and you are fighting me on saying something about
that collectively?" After that, folks came around and I got support. Myself
and Sherina Rodriguez Sharpe started drafting a statement and that was the
impetus that ultimately led to BPSO.

Mahogany [L. Browne] called me. Now, that is one of my girlfriends and
she could *see* me. Who does that anymore, pick up the phone and call you?
People don't do that. Every time someone would come with something
that wasn't it she could see my anger and frustration and rage. So, Mahogany
called me and said, "I can see you spinning online." "I am just crying" and she
said, "Me too." And we just cried on the phone. And it was that witnessing—
this is not in cyberworld this is in real life, I am not with you, but I see you.
Then she said, "go to your computer, get online, you start talking and I'll
start typing." And she just opened up a Google Doc and I could see the
words coming up as she was typing. We pulled words from Jericho Brown,
"I have a right to be angry. I have to say that." That was very specific. Jonterri
Gadson said, "well what if we did videos" and we said, "Yes, videos, that is
perfect because most people have a phone and can make that happen." Mo
[Mahogany] started typing up the mantra as we were talking on the phone.

SM: This story gives me chills. Just the idea of you witnessing one another—her
acting as your conduit; even if you feel like you are being inarticulate, she's
like "I got you."

AJ: [Nods head] We pause on "black." Should we say, "and brown"? And "people
of color"? I said, "No." I was very adamant about that. We know that everyone is dying. But we also know that black people are being killed disproportionately to the rest of the demographics in the country. We know the
police state is just an extension of slavery. Jim Crow, Black Codes—it was an
extension of slavery and that never stopped. If we can make it better for black
people then *inherently* it is going to be better for everybody else. That is not
saying nothing is happening to you, it's saying, do you see us? Do you see us?
"Alright then, black." *Laugh.* That is why it says, "I am a black poet and I will
not remain silent while this nation murders black people. I have a right to
be angry." That became the mantra. Mo is so good with social media, she has
a large following online, and she said, "we gotta have a hashtag." We started
going through that language, black people this, black poets this, going back
and forth and she said, "black poets speak out" and I said, "That's it! That's the
name!" That ultimately became the name of the campaign. This is a volunteer
campaign—it is not a nonprofit, it is not an organization—we do not deal
with money. We do not sell T-shirts. Ain't no cover charge for the protest.

SM: It spread like wildfire. It was a beautiful thing to see.

AJ: It did. From then on it happened really organically. Mo posted first reading June Jordan and then I posted second reading Evie Shockley then after that boom boom boom boom boom. In a few days there were hundreds of videos from around the world. People from the UK were posting and reaching out to us, saying, "can we do this in solidarity?" Yes, because they are killing black people over in England ain't they? I read Linton Kwesi Johnson and I know about sus (in England, sus law is similar to stop & frisk). That is part of the lineage in acknowledging that it is not just happening here. People from all over started doing the videos. Mahogany is an international professional touring poet and educator, so she has access to all these different houses. She said "We gotta do readings; we gotta do public events—we need to see each other" because, again, it is about visibility & witnessing. We have been trained as a people—not just black people but as people—trained like cattle: to show up to work, to do our jobs, to earn the big house money and then go home. It is not polite to talk about these things in public, it is not appropriate, etc. Being out in public and creating a safe space where we could do that was *so necessary*. Otherwise you feel like you are going crazy. Sittin' up in my house going crazy. I want to be around other people who know this is happening.

  We then sat down (it was myself, Mahogany, and Jonterri) to put together guidelines for the readings because the whole purpose was to have it in as many places as possible. Not just through us, not sponsored by us, but as a campaign to put the work and ideas out there and let people take them and build on them. We always say BPSO is a campaign *in support* of the larger #BlackLivesMatter movement, not in any way to take away from that work or to pretend this sprouted on its own miraculously. It is definitely a part of larger actions that are taking place at this time.

SM: Also led by black feminist women who are fluid and intergenerational.

AJ: Yes. But also knowing the nature of people, we said: no bios, no books, no bullshit, no money. And that is hard because we also know we are entitled to a living wage of which we are deprived. We are entitled to being compensated for our art, our ideas, our intellectual property, our scholarship. These readings are not that. These are poetic demonstrations. When you show up to the capital to protest, who is charging cover? Who gets to stand in the spotlight over Tamir Rice's body? It's about your survival, but not about your fame or celebrity. We have so many resources beyond money. Whatever resources we have—what you are doing right now: scholarship, documentation—that is a resource we need.

SM: Talk to me about Phase 3. Having participated in BPSO's letter-writing campaign, I know that getting those standard email and letter replies from local government officials . . . there is a certain kind of feeling.

AJ: All of this happened organically. We did not have a plan of how it was going to be. One phase rolled into another when we asked, what is missing? Phase 3, the letter-writing campaign was a way to do direct action that connected poetry to civic engagement. People died for our right to vote and to engage in politics in this country. People are still dying. I dedicated all of 2015 to writing my elected officials daily along with the UN, the Department of Justice, and the White House. I ended up sending over 400 emails. I got back about 10 replies. If we are word people, we are language people, we should be appalled and offended and fighting against the spin and manipulation of language to oppress people. First it is coming through the words. These politicians can say it in such a way (look at Trump) that you vote for your oppression, you vote for your destruction because of the spin that comes with language. I wanted to be very clear. I wanted to get as many people as I could on record with their dismissive, patronizing, elitist, pro-police language because I knew that is what I was going to get back. We are in America, ain't we? I am also a woman of receipts. Election time is going to come around in 2018, I have receipts in either a non-response from these people who are going to be running for reelection, or their weak response to their constituents about police violence.

There is a template on the website that very clearly spells out: I am a poet of BPSO and our mission of using videos to speak out and call for justice. In each letter I include a link to a different video from the campaign so they could see that this letter from one individual is connected to many others who feel the same way. But a lot of people did not like that silence. It hurts when you do that work and you get nothing or a little form letter. It was frustrating, but I would remind myself how much I'm online every day. An embarrassing amount of time. It took me less than 10 minutes to email 10 people a day. A lot of the time, because I did not get a response, I would forward the email that I sent the day before saying, "I have not received a reply to this email, so I am attaching it again." Day after day their office is getting "I have not received a reply. You are showing me that what I thought was true, is. Like I said, I got about 10 [replies] back and one came from the White House. At that time in 2015, that was still Barack Obama. That was important—he did not draft this letter, it came from aides and other people— but anything that comes from the White House has to be okayed by the administration. I get this email, a beautiful email, an understanding email, saying be patient. For how long? How long?

SM: Look what patience gets you.

AJ: And now we have Trump. How many more hundreds of years of patience and understanding and acceptance of your own destruction do you have to take?

SM: This is the unfortunate thing, now that we have moved into a Trump era in which he has vowed to send the National Guard into Chicago, in which he has vowed to step up "law and order" which means even more impetus on policing and prisons ...

AJ: Making it a federal crime to protest. To be treated as a terrorist for protesting. Look at what patience gets you.

SM: Can you talk about where you see BPSO going, what are your hopes and wishes, what is the work that needs to be done?

AJ: For people asking how to help, my first questions is, what do you have access to? Be creative, think about what you have access to. Yes, there will be risk involved. I had professionals saying, "if there is something I can do to help

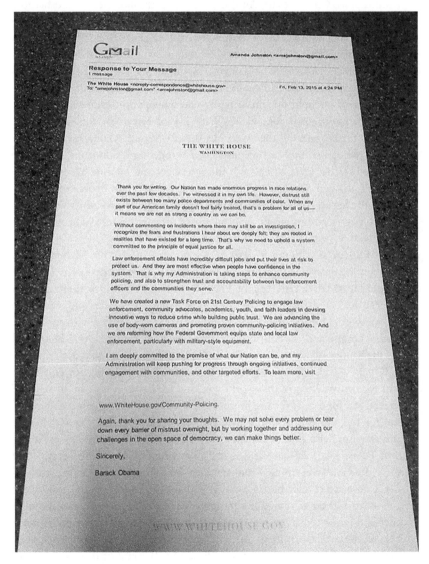

FIGURE 11.1 Letter to Amanda Johnston from President Obama

let me know." I'd say, "I need your network. I need access to people who come to your events." They'd go quiet. They have day jobs, so I understand! Sometime later they'd message back and say, "I dropped a ball but I'm here now." Hey, I don't care where you were yesterday. If you are here today, welcome. Staying open for others to come in led to sharing BPSO on platforms like Poetry Society's website and speaking in the Texas Capitol during the Texas Book Festival. Poetry Society gave us space and access on their site to focus on regional organizers who hosted BPSO events in their cities like in Minneapolis, Chicago, and Austin, etc. Mahogany interviewed me because I had done events here in Austin, Avery R. Young is featured for organizing a reading in Chicago, Maya Washington for organizing a BPSO event in Minneapolis, Jonterri Gadson (another cofounder) for organizing in Bloomington, Ashaki Jackson for organizing in California. We started working on Lesson Plans and it got really cumbersome and complicated, but the universe has a way of opening up and bringing you where you need to be. Wendy S. Walters, another great poet asked, "What if I interview you for *Mosaic Magazine* for further getting the word out there?" Myself, Mahogany, and Ellen Hagan (who's definitely an accomplice) put together lesson plans. They were included in that issue along with the interview and became Phase 4 of the BPSO campaign. We stipulate that anything we do has to be free to the people so the lesson plans are available for free as a PDF on Mosaic's website.[4]

SM: Which poetry communities or social justice organizations have become allies to BPSO?

AJ: Cave Canem as a house is definitely supportive of BPSO. Mahogany has so many connections to other major houses in New York—she is now the #BlackLivesMatter Director for Pratt [Institute], so BPSO is there through the #BlackLivesMatter offices; she's also at the Nuyorican and works for Urban Word. Outside of literary communities, I have worked with the Austin Justice League and the Austin #BlackLivesMatter organization. When I read for the Sandra Bland vigil, that was through those organizations at the capital. LaKiza Fowler, Larry Jackson's sister, is amazing.[5] She is such a powerful spirit and woman walking in this world speaking for her brother. She invited me to read at a fundraiser for her brother at the Victory Grill which is an historic site for folks in Austin doing that kind of work: organizing, social justice, and activism. Jenn Benka, the Executive Director for the Academy of American Poets, was following and is still following BPSO online—retweeting the videos and everything. I messaged her on twitter. (Social media is amazing. I have never met her in person). I thanked her for sharing the videos and asked if there is something more we can do. She came back some time later and requested I contribute a short statement for the Academy's Poetry Month issues of *Poetry* magazine. The only directive was to write what I felt that National Poetry Month's focus should be. Because of that invitation in *Poetry* magazine for National Poetry Month, I have a small statement about how we should, as poets, use our resources and our communities to see each other and speak out against police violence for each other. When those organizations become accomplices (because doing that work is not easy), you risk alienating supporters who do not see how politics has anything to do with poetry—definitely not these #BlackLivesMatter activists. These people are shutting down the highways and things! All without seeing the dead black people that came first.

Another thing I don't talk about much (because I try to stay in the work) is how anger pushes you into stuff. I had seen a post of—it still makes me angry—of a terrible terrible *terrible* poem posted in *The Paris Review* that was completely offensive: "The Ballad of Ferguson" by Frederick Seidel. I was offended. Also, the Poetry Foundation, on their Harriet blog posted an offensive statement—this was in the wake of the murder of Mike Brown and the non-indictment—which said something along the lines of "with it being so close to Thanksgiving you'd think it would be a slow time for poetry news however, here are some 'worthwhile' reads in the wake of Ferguson." Then I look at the poets who are listed and it was full of Cave Canem poets. It was us. That is what really prompted me to be like, "Hold up!" They are using our black faces, our words, our poems as click bait and have the nerve to choose what is "worthwhile" as opposed to us saying we have a voice, and goddammit, we get to say what we want to say. Shame on you. I am not going to stand here with this pain, this suffering, this murder and have our literary houses (if they are ours) disrespected in the process. No.

SM: Is there any fear?

AJ: I get emails every now and then from people wanting their videos taken down. Someone called my campus to complain specifically about my social media activity and threatened to call the Superintendent because their child was scared that Ms. Johnston did not like white people. That Ms. Johnston hates white people. People lose their jobs. Texas is an at-will state. They do not have to give you any reason. They can fire you. That is a direct threat on my livelihood, my personhood. White privilege, white supremacy, will do that: I can call you up and threaten your job, your life.

There is definite fear. If you think that poetry is a safe way to demonstrate, you are not paying attention, you are not reading the work, and you do not know the history. Poets are currently in prison around the world for writing poems because they are telling the truth. Some have contacted me to take posts down and it breaks my heart. One was a young Muslim woman (and it was after [the] North Carolina [shooting]), so I understand. It is very real. I make it very clear to people, when you show up to do this work, I need you to know you are taking a risk. I want you to know what you are getting into. The same way I am not going to sugarcoat who we are doing this for and why we are doing this. The word is black and there is nothing wrong with black. Black is beautiful, black is necessary; we are fighting for black lives.

We end demonstrations by calling everyone in. We make a tight circle and say the names of people lost & end the roll call of names with "and, and, and, and . . ." because there are so many we cannot name, so many we do not know. At AWP [in Washington D.C.] we ended with Lucille Clifton's "Won't You Celebrate with Me" "come celebrate/ with me *that everyday/ something has tried to kill me/ and has failed*." I speak from a huge place of privilege in that I have a family that shows up and supports me and my work. We have sisters out there with no one else. James Baldwin talks about a complete and total risk of everything in his speech "The Artist's Struggle for Integrity." When James Baldwin was marching with Martin Luther King Jr., it wasn't safe. Being by his side was a risk. That is what I am looking for, work done on and off the page.

SM: So, if poetry allows you to bear witness, to present the evidence, the facts of it, to tell the truth of it in your own voice without being erased or misframed. . . . if it allows you to express anger, what else does it allow you to do? What else does poetry *do*?

AJ: It is testimony that we were here. But also, that we as beings in this time and this place saw this world in this lens (as opposed to what they want you to focus on)—it is documentation and the creative freedom to put to page joy, sorrow, struggles, observation, the beauty, and the trash. That we can be our full selves, human, for me that is what poetry is. That is what it does.

For more on Black Poets Speak Out, visit: https://blackpoetsspeakout.tumblr.com
For Black Poets Speak Out teaching resources, visit: https://mosaicmagazine.org/tag/black-poets-speak-out

Notes

1. See BPSO's official website: https://blackpoetsspeakout.tumblr.com.
2. Founded in 1996 by poets Toi Derricotte and Cornelius Eady to "remedy the under-representation and isolation of African American poets in the literary landscape," Cave Canem is a nonprofit service organization that has grown from a mere 26 members to over 1,300 poets. Cave Canem fellows have over 250 books in print, are teaching in positions around the country, and have won many major literary awards including the National Book Award, the Pulitzer Prize for Poetry, the Kingsley Tufts Poetry Award, the Yale Series of Younger Poets, and the NAACP Image Award, among others. Additionally, the organization has published two anthologies: *Gathering Ground* (2006) and *The Ringing Ear: Black Poets Lean South* (2007).
3. Live BPSO demonstrations have taken place in diverse locales like Boulder, Los Angeles, Auburn, New Orleans, and Brooklyn, extending even to countries like South Africa and England. First sent to President Barack Obama, the campaign's letter-writing component deploys a template composed by Johnston which lists a series of public policy demands for racial equity including changes in indictment processes, divestment from prisons, and investment in alternative community programs.
4. For BPSO lesson plans, see https://mosaicmagazine.org/tag/black-poets-speak-out
5. Larry Jackson Jr., an unarmed black man, was shot and killed by a police officer in Austin, Texas in 2013. With pressure from local activists, the city approved a $1.25 million settlement to Jackson's family in August 2014. More than a year later, a judge dropped the formal manslaughter charges against the officer who is now retired from the Austin Police Department.

PART III
Elegists as Activists: Coda

Kimmika Williams-Witherspoon

No Indictment
On the Death of Sandra Bland

While the innocent
Are continually
Gunned down
Drown-trodden
Or mysteriously
Strangled and broken
Behind bars
Like Sandra Bland
With little recourse and
No indictment
Or warrant in hand—
Forgive us Sandra.
Justice
Not Served!
Errors
Like accountability
Abound—
Compounded by *whiteness*
Papers and privilege—
Wrongful death,

Alleged suicide,
Deadly-force—
Complicated, both,
By Color and class—
Kiss our collective ass, America
The mittimus dismissed.
Between hung juries in Baltimore
& in Texas
a failure to indict,
the struggle continues
'tween militarized- *genocide*
& *right.*
While people of color–
caught in the crosshairs.

Nicholas Rianard Goodly

Skin Tones

I
My words reach your ears as coal,
bizarre and ornate refractions.
Hear me speaking pearls
pulling them in strings
from my mouth.
Hear them break
across my gums,
patience-formed, heavy.
This city stands on sugar cubes.
My tongue craves clay.
Red clay.

Close your ears to the loud stones.
Sweetie, you have a goldfish swimming in your belly.
The sun is loud and new in your breast.
Peppermint men are playing cards on your breath.
You're growing yellow moss for hair.
Landmines sleep in your eyes.
Your skin is wrapping paper held with taut twine.
My dear, the rocks feel it beneath you.
Growing.

Pinch your stomach, a soft warm pillow.
You're not dead yet—not even close.
Save those tears, clean and fresh as ginger.
You primal thing,
tip toeing, hushed, picked still young.
You're a stag sprinting across the ocean floor
You're a lionfish swimming in midair.
Think of your big bones, your wide backs.
It is the year of the beast of burden.

I am thankful for a life of color.
That my skin is the color it should be,
something like dried figs,
elastic, its surface ripples and recovers.
That I have all my toes and they curl when dipped into ice water.
That I was taught to read when I was five:

hands are articulate.
My calves bulge like pears,
my thighs are strong and heavy as tree trunks.
That I could spend another day on the porch swing
with a mug of coffee and whiskey, watching dogs and magnolia trees.
The birds are the color of the air.
That my penis makes no apology
That my solid-barrel belly occasionally bounces.
That I have eaten peach jello
and my navel knows to be quiet.
An enduring, taffy spine.
Dough-filled joints in steel-beam arms.
A heart has been beating the same song into me since I was born.
To be in a room of what belongs to me
in a city where I can make myself important.
That I can never grow another Afro,
never getting braces and my good-luck gap.
a discerning nose
two wanting ears
eyes like a horse.

II
But then we were always just human
born in our dune-color cage of skin.
Sent home to me, he is safe now.
This ending is a good one.

They followed his careless footsteps in the pavement
and now there's nowhere for him to climb.
If he could've shrunk into a fur coat
or let his callused hands be held in their weak chains
acting as if he had a history there,
they might have let him live.
He yelled too loud too often.
On the tower he can pretend he was perfect
the way the sky fires off amber.
The planes fly in like wasps:
on the ground, he'll find himself humbled.
He unfurled a long scarlet ribbon.
My pleas won't pull him back.
I prayed the wax down to a dry puddle.
There's not enough energy to bury him.
He was a king first.

III
Look at what time has done to us. There
is a furnace under every night. Inherit the house.
There are mountains in your name, the land
is ready and the wind is real.
We will be soft shell and unbreakable,
we will never tire, our mothers are alive
beneath our skin. Come into the light goliath,
release one pain. We are the master
of that good summer, sunbuilt and deathless.

Jason Harris

Appraisal (Elegy for As of a Now)

People live here, B. A coterie of selves offering context
cross reference your options of input—sight, smell, sound, taste, FEEL.
The invisible thrives in the margins of their overlap
where seeing IS feeling and memory defies temporality
to get it, as Amiri would say, you got to have it.
to have it, you have to see it; can you feel we?

Abstraction is the outcome of your stunted perceptions
the mundane rendered inscrutable by white knuckles clutching convention.
Push your glasses further up the bridge of your nose, peep through a telescope
cut me in pieces, place we on a slide, observe us through a microscope
and understand that you're looking at them wrong.

The singed scent of a curling iron, two holes in the plaster where the
rotary phone hung, its metallic buzzing joining the echoes of giggles
cheap slippers threads, co-habitating with old carpet chewed by the dog
snippets of an easter Bodice, balled up in the corner of a closet
pill bottle, caked under dust, thiazide scrawled on the cap
tiny shards of a glass cracked during a holiday dinner
imprints of the basketball bounced on the floor.
Have you seen these people?

Walls weeping with life, fissures from speakers shaking, fogged glass
the brine of sadness, sensual sweat, summer balloon ordinance and
whatever is boiling on the stove
pipes perspiring hidden from view, a midnight bath an oasis after back
to back shifts
breeze dancing sound through the bells on the back porch, just above
the cat's dish
all that leaks now is grief seeping through the cracks born of absence

The site has been cleared to be cleared, you say
declarations are committed to paper about spaces, but Life cannot read
eviction notices;
the spectrum of its entirety spills over the borders of laws and senses
a multiverse of people and events vibrating in these walls, yet unseen
filaments of a dense tapestry bombed, slashed, cleared, burned, shot
down, starved but unbroken
We are still here and it is not a trick of light or an aberration
Ask us what we call it before you put your fucking sign in the ground

Tiffany Austin

Dark Milk: After Basquiat

Someone else's heart—
outside—the borrowed milky bird seed.

A woman died yesterday
liver of honeysuckle

innerneath rub of hot,
amongst blackberries indigoing youngbloods

alone in this with other feed.
Before death, moments of lust filled dying.

Who says beauty is here somewhere
when where do you come from means

you don't belong here or let out your cigarette (I'd wake my
father by putting a lit one in his mouth.).

Beauty can be destroyed by the wind—
the back of the ocean

or lip.
I don't feel safe in the world any longer.

Some days I'd like to be Billie on a Wednesday, Krauss's
throat, Amantine's pants:

A house fell on her heart.

Taste   humming sect   my own Iona.
I'll heal this tit.

PROMPTS FOR FURTHER DISCUSSION

For Reading Groups

1. Given both the innovations and reconfigurations of the elegy tracked within this volume, how might the standard definition of the genre be revised? As noted in the Introduction, *The Princeton Handbook of Poetic Terms* defines the elegy as "a lyric, usually formal in tone and diction, suggested either by the death of an actual person or by the poet's contemplation of the tragic aspects of life. In either case, the emotion, originally expressed as a lament, finds consolation in the contemplation of some permanent principle."

2. In this volume, we have focused on the considerable utility of elegiac writing for this political epoch that has included the two-term presidency of Barack H. Obama, the first person of African descent to hold the office, the presidency of Donald J. Trump, a figure who has aligned himself with white-supremacist groups and ideologies, and the strengthening of the contemporary black liberation movement known as Black Lives Matter. In your view, what are the distinct benefits of criticism, the personal essay, and poetry in addressing these sociopolitical exigencies?

3. In a 2013 interview with *The Guardian*'s Gary Younge, activist and writer Eduardo Galeano noted, "History never really says goodbye. History says, see you later." How do you see the poems and essays in this volume realizing the saliency of this remark?

4. Compare several of the most canonical elegies in the Anglo-American canon—John Milton's "Lycidas," Thomas Gray's "Elegy Written in a Country Churchyard," and W.H. Auden's "In Memory of W.B. Yeats," Walt Whitman's "O Captain! My Captain!," Robert Lowell's "For the Union Dead," among

others—to the ones in this volume. In what ways do you see these contemporary poets both extending and complicating this tradition? Consider gender, race, class, sexuality, ability, and their intersections as you formulate your response.

5. Choose at least one text from the Appendix to place in conversation with the poems and essays in this volume. Challenge yourself to choose an unknown author, perform research, and introduce that author to your reading group. What is gained by exploring elegy beyond the poems and essays published in this volume?

For the Classroom

1. Read darlene anita scott's crown of sonnets, "A Series of Survivals," in conjunction with Debbie Mix's essay "'A diagnosis is an ending': Pathology and Presence in Bettina Judd's *Patient*." In what ways do they both speak to the somatic experience of racial hauntings and reckonings? Moreover, what are the unique affordances of the sonnet—and a crown of sonnets in particular—for scott's elucidation of the intergenerational grief and trauma of black women?

2. Essays included here by J. Peter Moore, Megan Feifer and Maia Butler, and Almas Khan describe the incorporation of elegiac tropes in film (Moore), op-eds (Feifer and Butler), and judicial opinions (Khan). What are the advantages of expanding conventional conceptions of elegy as the province of poetry? What other genres of art and rhetoric would be usefully considered under the rubric of elegy?

3. In Angela Jackson-Brown's "I Must Not Breathe," she describes an array of seemingly innocuous behaviors and actions that may trigger a violent response from police. What does this list suggest about the paralyzing (and often perilous) consequences of racial profiling?

4. In Danielle Legros Georges's "Poem of History," she describes the ways in which institutions where many of us work, study, and socialize sanction antiblack racism and violence. Reflect on your own experiences within institutions. How does engaging with elegies such as Georges's occasion fresh insights about the spaces we inhabit?

5. Cameron Barnett's "Uniform; or things I would paint if I were a painter" invokes a number of historical figures. What role do you think poetry in general and elegy in particular plays in reimagining American history?

6. In Lauren K. Alleyne's "Elegy for Tamir," she transforms the printed page into a sacred space where 12-year-old Tamir Rice is still "becoming." In what ways does this poem speak to the power of the word to envisage another kind of reality?

7. Tiffany Austin's "Dark Milk: After Basquiat" and "Peaches" exemplify a fusion of elegy and ekphrasis (poetry that engages with the visual arts). Look up

"Dark Milk" by Jean-Michel Basquiat online, and discuss the ways in which Austin's "Dark Milk: After Basquiat's Painting" dialogues with this painting. Similarly, in "Peaches," Austin references Stanley Nelson's documentary *The Black Panthers* (2015). Watch this film, and discuss Austin's poetic reframing of the intersection of race and gender in particular.

8. Tony Medina's "Senryu for Trayvon Martin" and Emily Jo Scalzo's haiku "After Charleston" both utilize Japanese poetic forms to render contemporary elegies that speak particularly to violence perpetrated against African-descended people in America. What do these fusions of elegy and haiku and senryu achieve formally, and what might they suggest about the affordances of cross-cultural artistic exchange?

9. Jacqueline Johnson's "Soul Memory" and Charles Braxton's "Strays in the Hood" invoke sacred language as they mourn victims of police brutality. Discuss the ways in which these artists negotiate the relationship between the secular and sacred realms in the context of state-sanctioned violence and grief.

10. Anne Lovering Rounds's "American Diptych" uses an erasure method to signify the black lives that have been extinguished but nevertheless haunt the American landscape. Sequoia Maner similarly utilizes the white space on the page in her "Black Boy Contrapuntal *for Trayvon Martin*." Discuss the use of visual poetics in the poetry of mourning.

11. Nicholas Goodly's "Skin Tones" and Lauren K. Alleyne's "Elegy for Tamir" speak directly to the deceased. In what ways does this strategy of apostrophe impact you as a reader? What kind of responsibilities are you being asked to assume, and to what ends?

12. Poems such as Paula Bohince's "The Flint River" and Jason Harris's "Appraisal (Elegy for As of a Now)" address the socioeconomic and environmental discrimination that is slower but no less imperiling as state-sanctioned killings. As you survey your own communities, what forms of institutionalized racism become clear? Consider, for example, gentrification, environmental hazards, underresourced public schools, food deserts, the absence of affordable and accessible medical care, and a lack of adequate city services, among other structural inequities.

13. Both Sarah Giragosian's "Nina" and Sean Murphy's "Bud Powell's Brain" pay elegiac tribute to iconic African American musicians. Why is it necessary to continue to say the names and honor the legacies of individuals who have long ago passed away? What kinds of fresh insights are evoked in the process?

14. In introduction, we underscore the significance of social media for the increased engagement in both poetry and activism in recent years. In what ways does Chris Campanioni's "#IWokeUpLikeThis or: The Latest in Space-Age #PostInternet Pajamas" exemplify the *reciprocal* relationship between poetry, particularly the elegy, and social media?

For Creative Writers and Scholar-Poets

1. How do you grapple with grief and mourning in your own writing, and in what ways do the poems and essays gathered here resonate with your artistic vision? How has revisiting the topic of elegy impacted your ideas about and strategies for writing?
2. What forms besides the elegy and the essay are crucial to voicing the concerns and aims of the Movement for Black Lives?
3. This book's Appendix gathers an extensive list of elegies written by poets who adopt diverse styles, voices, and aims. What is the relationship between formalism, innovation, and elegy in African American letters? How do contemporary poets write within and against a legacy of elegiac predecessors? What else might be gleaned from the Appendix?
3. Lauren Alleyne's "Poetry Workshop after the Verdict" speaks to the often unspoken white biases within many creative writing workshops. What are the racial dynamics within your own creative spaces, and how do they influence both your self-expression and the kinds of feedback you give and receive?
4. We have facilitated a dialogue here between poets and scholars in the hopes of showcasing the distinct sociopolitical and cultural work that creative and critical writing perform. How do you negotiate the occasions for these distinct modes of writing? What is possible at the intersection of these modes?
5. We have focused here on elegies aligned with the aims of Black Lives Matter and the resistance to anti-black racism more generally. What other state-sanctioned forms of violence and oppression have engendered elegiac responses? How are the elegies of Black Lives Matter distinctive?

For Activists

1. Several of the poets and essayists in this volume are of European descent while the majority of the poets and essayists are of African descent. In your view, what are the distinct roles that white and non-black people of color play in resisting anti-black racism and its intersections?
2. This volume's "Elegists as Activists" section closes with an interview featuring Black Poets Speak Out (#BPSO) cofounder Amanda Johnston. In your view, how does Johnston's work in particular and #BPSO more generally reflect the role of social media in twenty-first-century justice movements? How does this interview illuminate the relationship between art and activism? How might you incorporate poetry into your antiracist work?
3. One might read Kimmika Williams-Witherspoon's poem "No Indictment" as a rallying cry at a political march. In what ways do you see poetry as distinct from political chants, and in what ways does it perform a similar function?

APPENDIX FOR FURTHER READING

This Appendix gathers a variety of texts that elegize black lives lost to a complex of murderous forces. We choose to forgo the listing of publication dates to emphasize the tethered nature of voices across eras, schools of discipline, geography, and political alliance. Further, this list is not meant to be comprehensive, rather, it is suggestive and generative. We recognize black grief to be both bounded and unbound, tied to specific moments of violence and excessive beyond those same formative occurrences. In this way, the earliest African American elegists interface with those of Black Lives Matter, emphasizing the rich legacy of elegiac engagement in the labor of justice. We include poetry, theory, personal writing, and online resources with the hope that readers will employ the lessons and blueprints provided by these texts into your own lives—in book clubs, classrooms, and all quotidian activities.

Lynching Poems

Brooks, Gwendolyn. "Southern Lynching"
Brown, Sterling. "Children of Mississippi"
———. "He Was a Man"
———. "Let Us Suppose"
Christian, Marcus B. "Martyrs of the Rope Brigade"
Clifton, Lucille. "The Photo: A Lynching"
Cortez, Jayne. "Lynch Fragment 2"
Cullen, Countee. "Black Christ"
———. "Christ Recrucified"
Du Bois, W. E. B. "Litany at Atlanta"
Dunbar, Paul Laurence. "The Haunted Oak"
Durem, Ray. "I Know I'm Not Sufficiently Obscure"

Freeman, Carol. "I Saw Them Lynch"
Grimke, Angeline Weld. "Tenebris"
Harper, Frances E. W. "A Martyr in Alabama"
Hayden, Robert. "Dawnbreaker"
———. "Night, Death, Mississippi"
Hill, Leslie Pinckney. "So Quietly"
Hughes, Langston. "Christ in Alabama"
———. "Song for a Dark Girl"
———. "The Bitter River"
———. "Three Songs About Lynching"
Jenkins, Welborn Victor. "The Noose and the Rack and Faggot"
Johnson, Helene. "A Southern Road"
Johnson, James Weldon. "Brothers—American Drama"
Laurentiis, Ricky. "Of the Leaves That Have Fallen"
McKay, Claude. "The Lynching"
Medina, Tony. "Byrd on a Wire"
Murray, Pauli. "For Mack C. Parker"
Popel, Esther. "Flag Salute"
Ridge, Lola. "Morning Ride"
Rodgers, Carolyn. "For O.—Two Hung Up"
Spencer, Ann. "White Things"
St. John, Primus. "Lynching and Burning"
Toomer, Jean. "Portrait in Georgia"
Walker, Margaret. "Sorrow Home"
Williamson, Harvey. "From the Delta's Unmarked Graves"
Wright, Richard. "Between the World and Me"

Emmett Till Elegies

Barnett, Cameron. "Emmett Till Haunts the Library in Money, MS"
Brooks, Gwendolyn. "A Bronzeville Mother Loiters in Mississippi, Meanwhile a Mississippi Mother Burns Bacon"
———. "The Last Quatrain of the Ballad of Emmett Till"
Brown, Jericho. "Riddle"
Coleman, Wanda. "Emmett Till"
Eady, Cornelius. "Emmett Till's Glass-Top Casket"
Emanuel, James A. "Emmett Till"
Ewing, Eve L. "I Saw Emmett Till This Week at the Grocery Store"
Francis, Vievee. "Emmett, I Said Wait"
Giovanni, Nikki. "A Civil Rights Journey"
Guillén, Nicolás. "Elegy for Emmett Till"
Hughes, Langston. "Mississippi—1955"
———. "The Money Mississippi Blues"
Kearney, Douglas. "Tallahatchie Lullaby, Baby"
Kolin, Phillip C. *Emmett Till in Different States*
Laurentiis, Ricky. "Ghazal for Emmett Till"
Lorde, Audre. "Afterimages"
Nelson, Marilyn. *A Wreath for Emmett Till*

Plumpp, Sterling. "Unremembered"
Reeves, Roger. "The Mare of Money"
Smith, Patricia. "Black, Poured Directly into the Wound"
———. "Choose Your Own Adventure"
———. "Discovering Country"
———. "That Chile Emmett in the Casket"
Thompson, Julius E. "Till"
Walton, Anthony. "The Lovesong of Emmett Till"
Ward Jr., Jerry. "Don't Be Fourteen (in Mississippi)"
Young, Al. "The Emmett Till Blues"
Young, Kevin. "Money Road"
———. "Whistle"

Historical Elegies

Adisa, Opal. "Peeling Off the Skin"
Alexander, Elizabeth. "Manhattan Elegy"
———. "Narrative: Ali"
———. "Omni-Albert Murray"
Allen, Samuel (Paul Vesey). "Dylan, Who Is Dead"
Baker Jr., Houston A. "Toward Guinea: For Larry Neal, 1937–1981"
Baraka, Amiri. "Digging Max"
———. "In the Tradition"
Bennett, Gwendolyn B. "Lines Written at the Grave of Alexandre Dumas"
Bingham-Risher, Remica. "How I Crossed Over"
Braithwaite, William Stanley. "Hymn for the Slain in Battle"
Brooks, Gwendolyn. "Martin Luther King Jr."
———. "Medgar Evers"
———. "Music for Martyrs"
———. "Of De Witt on His Way to Lincoln Cemetery"
———. "The Rites for Cousin Vit"
Brown, Jericho. "Herman Finley Is Dead"
Brown, Sterling. "Remembering Nat Turner"
Burroughs, C. M. "Think Away the Blood"
Clifton, Lucille. "Harriet"
———. "Shooting Star (for Huey P. Newton)"
———. "The Death of Thelma Sayles"
———. "The Lost Baby Poem"
———. "Won't You Celebrate with Me"
Cornish, Sam. "Death of Dr. King"
———. "Panther"
Corrothers, James David. "Paul Laurence Dunbar"
Cortez, Jayne. "Blues Bop for Diz"
Crouch, Stanley. "Albert Ayler: Eulogy for a Decomposed Saxophone Player"
Cullen, Countée. "Scottsboro, Too, Is Worth Its Song"
Cuney, Waring. "Burial of the Young Love"
Dawes, Kwame. "Requiem"
Demby, Angeline R. "Lines (for President Abraham Lincoln)"

Derricotte, Toi. "On the Turning Up of Unidentified Black Female Corpse"
Dove, Rita. "Canary"
———. "Teach Us to Number Our Days"
———. "The Wake"
Dumas, Henry. "Our King Is Dead"
Dunbar, Paul Laurence. "Douglass"
———. "Frederick Douglass"
Eady, Cornelius. *Brutal Imagination*
Emanuel, James A. "Church Burning: Mississippi"
———. "Panther Man"
Evans, Mari. "A Good Assassination Should Be Quiet"
———. "How Sudden Dies the Blooming"
Finney, Nikky. "Left"
Giovanni, Nikki. "Black Power (for All the Beautiful Black Panthers East)"
———. "The Funeral of Martin Luther King Jr."
———. "We Are Virginia Tech"
Girmay, Aracelis. "Night, for Henry Dumas"
Hand, Monica. *Me and Nina*
Harper, Michael S. "Martin's Blues"
———. "Remembering Robert Hayden"
———. "We Assume: On the Death of Our Son, Reuben Masai Harper"
harris, francine j. "Katherine with the Lazy Eye. Short. And Not a Good Poet"
Hayden, Robert. "Elegies for Paradise Valley"
———. "Homage to Paul Robeson"
———. "Obituary"
———. "Rosemary"
Hayes, Terrance. "Touch"
———. "What It Look Like"
Hernton, Calvin C. "Fall Down"
hooks, bell. *Appalachian Elegy*
Horton, George Moses. "On the Death of Rebecca"
Hughes, Langston. "Frederick Douglass: 1817–1895"
Johnson, Fenton. "When I Die"
Johnson, Georgia Douglas. "To William Stanley Braithwaite"
Johnson, James Weldon. "Go Down Death"
Jordan, A. Van. "Que Sera Sera"
Jordan, June. "In Memoriam: Rev. Martin Luther King Jr."
———. "The Test of Atlanta 1979—"
Joseph, Allison. "Elegy for My Father's Anger"
———. *My Father's Kites: Poems*
Knight, Etheridge. "For Langston Hughes"
———. "The Bones of My Father"
Komunyakaa, Yusef. "Facing It"
Lansana, Quraysh Ali. "Our Sons"
Lorde, Audre. "A Litany for Survival"
———. "Song for Many Movements"
McElroy, Colleen. "Into the Wilds"
Miller, E. Ethelbert. "The Things in Black Men's Closets"

Moss, Thylias. "Diedre: A Search Engine"
Murray, Pauli. "Death of a Friend"
Myers, Hannah. "To Lilia in Heaven"
Neal, Larry. "Orishas"
Parkerson, Michelle. "Statistic"
Patterson, Raymond R. "Birmingham 1963"
Philip, Nourbese M. *Zong!*
Phillips, Carl. "As From a Quiver of Arrows"
Pickney, Andrea Davis. *Martin Rising: Requiem for a King*
Randall, Dudley. "Ballad of Birmingham (on the Bombing of a Church in Birmingham, Alabama, 1963)"
———. "Memorial Wreath"
———. "Roses and Revolution"
Ray, Henrietta Cordelia. "In Memoriam (Frederick Douglass)"
Redmond, Eugene B. "Poetic Reflections Enroute to, and During, the Funeral and Burial of Henry Dumas, Poet"
Salaam, Kalamu ya. "Our World Is Less Full Now That Mr. Fuller Is Gone"
Sanchez, Sonia. "Elegy (for MOVE and Philadelphia)"
———. "MIAs (Missing in Action and Other Atlantas)"
———. "Right on: White America"
Shange, Ntozake. "About Atlanta"
Shockley, Evie. "How Long Has Jayne Been Gone?"
Silvera, Edward. "On the Death of a Child"
Stewart-White, Lolita. "If Only"
Trethewey, Natasha. "Elegy for the Native Guards"
———. "Elegy [I think by now the river must be thick]"
———. "Graveyard Blues"
Vashon, Susan Paul Smith. "Lines on the Death of Mary C. Weaver"
Walker, Alice. "Good Night, Willie Lee, I'll See You in the Morning"
Walker, Frank X. "Rustlin"
———. *Turn Me Loose: The Unghosting of Medgar Evers*
Walker, Margaret. "An Elegiac Valedictory"
Weaver, Afaa. "The Doves"
Wheatley, Phillis. *Poems on Various Subjects, Religious and Moral*
Williams, Mance. "For Lover Man, and All the Other Young Men Who Failed to Return from World War II"
Williams, Tyrone. "Descant"
Wilson, John French. "The Dead Sing (Poem)"

Malcolm X Elegies

Alba, Nanina. "For Malcolm X"
Amini, Johari. "Saint Malcolm"
Baraka, Amiri. "A Poem for Black Hearts"
Barrax, Gerald. "For Malcolm: After Mecca"
Brooks, Gwendolyn. "Malcolm X"
Davis, Ossie. "Eulogy for Malcolm X"
Emanuel, James. "For Malcolm, U.S.A."

Hayden, Robert. "El-hajj Malik El-shabazz"
Henderson, David. "They Are Killing All the Young Men"
Jackmon, Marvin E. (Marvin X). "That Old Time Religion"
Jones, Leroi (Amiri Baraka). "A Poem for Black Hearts"
Knight, Etheridge. "For Malcolm, a Year After"
———. "It Was a Funky Deal"
———. "Portrait of Malcolm X"
Madhubuti, Haki. "Malcolm Spoke/Who Listened?"
Miller, E. Ethelbert. "Malcolm X, February 1965"
Neal, Larry. "Malcolm X—An Autobiography"
———. "The Summer After Malcolm"
Plumpp, Sterling. "Half Black, Half Blacker"
Randall, Dudley, and Margaret Burroughs, eds. *For Malcolm: Poems on the Life and Death of Malcolm X*
Rivers, Conrad Kent. "If Blood Is Black Then Spirit Neglects My Unborn Son"
Rodgers, Carolyn. "Poems for Malcolm"
Sanchez, Sonia. "Malcolm"
Smith, Welton. "Malcolm"
Spriggs, Edward S. "For Brother Malcolm"
Troupe, Quincy. "For Malcolm Who Walks in the Eyes of Our Children"
Walker, Margaret. "For Malcolm X"
Weaver, Afaa M. "To Malcolm X on His Second Coming"
Wright, Jay. "A Plea for the Politic Man"
Young, Al. "Blues for Malcolm X"

John Coltrane Elegies

Baraka, Amiri. "AM/Trak"
———. "The Evolver"
Brathwaite, Edward Kamau. "Trane"
Cortez, Jayne. "How Long Has This Trane Been Gone?"
Dooley, Ebon. "Legacy: In Memory of Trane"
Eady, Cornelius. "Alabama, c. 1963: A Ballad by John Coltrane"
Fabio, Sarah Webster. "Tribute to Duke"
Harper, Michael. "Dear John, Dear Coltrane"
———. "Here Where Coltrane Is"
Henderson, David. "Elvin Jones Gretsch Freak (Coltrane at the Half Note)"
Lee, Don L. (Haki Madhubuti) "Don't Cry, Scream"
Mackey, Nathaniel. "John Coltrane Arrived with an Egyptian Lady"
Mor, Amus. "The Coming of John"
Neal, Larry. "Don't Say Goodbye to the Pork-Pie Hat"
Perkins, Useni Eugene. "Eulogy for Coltrane"
Plumpp, Sterling. "Conversions"
Rahman, Yusuf. "Transcendental Blues"
Rodgers, Carolyn. "Me, in Kulu Se & Karma"
———. "Written for Love of an Ascension-Coltrane"
Sanchez, Sonia. "A/Coltrane/Poem"
———. "On Seeing Pharaoh Sanders Blowing"

Spellman, A. B. "Did John's Music Kill Him?"
Toure, Askia. "Juju"
Troupe, Quincy. "Ode to John Coltrane"
Young, Al. "The John Coltrane Dance"

Black Lives Matter Precursors

Ai. "Endangered Species"
Baraka, Amiri. "Incident"
Brooks, Gwendolyn. "A Boy Died in My Alley"
Brown, Sterling A. "An Old Woman Remembers"
———. "Southern Cop"
Clifton, Lucille. "4/30/92 for Rodney King"
———. "Jasper Texas 1998 (for J. Byrd)"
Compton, Michael. "Lamentations"
Cortez, Jayne. "Give Me the Red on the Black of the Bullet (for Claude Reece Jr.)"
Emanuel, James. "Deadly James (for All the Victims of Police Brutality)"
Gay, Ross. "Pulled Over in Short Hills, NJ 8:00 AM"
Gilbert, Zack. "For Stephen Dixon"
Girmay, Aracelis. "Elegy in Gold"
Harper, Michael. "A Mother Speaks: The Algiers Motel Incident, Detroit"
Harris, Reginald. "The Lost Boys: A Requiem"
———. "The Usual Suspects"
Hemphill, Essex. "Soft Targets (for Black Girls)"
Henderson, David. "One-Sided Shoot Out"
Hernton, Calvin. "The Mob"
Hughes, Langston. "Death in Yorksville"
———. "Third Degree"
———. "Who but the Lord?
Jordan, June. "Poem About My Rights"
———. "Poem About Police Violence"
———. "Poem Against the State (of Things): 1975"
Kaufman, Bob. "Benediction"
Lee, Don L. "One Sided Shoot-Out"
Lorde, Audre. "For the Record (in Memory of Eleanor Bumpurs)"
———. "Power"
———. "Separation"
Love, Monifa A. "41 Steps for Amadou Diallo"
McKay, Claude. "If We Must Die"
———. "To the White Fiends"
Medina, Tony, and Louis Reyes Rivera, eds. Section: "Drums Drown Out the Sorrow" in
   Bum Rush the Page: A Def Poetry Jam
Morris, Tracie. "Sean Bell"
Mullen, Harryette. "We Are Not Responsible"
Murray, Pauli. "Mr. Roosevelt Regrets"
Rankine, Claudia. *Don't Let Me Be Lonely* (Untitled Poems for James Byrd Jr. and Ahmed
   Amadou Diallo)
———. "Stop and Frisk"

Sanchez, Sonia. *Does Your House Have Lions?*
———. "For Tupac Amaru Shakur"
Smith, Patricia. *Close to Death*
St. John, Primus. "Benign Neglect/Mississippi, 1970"
Sulaiman, Amir. "Danger"
Trethewey, Natasha. "Incident"
Van Clief-Stefanon, Lyrae. "Poem for Amadou Diallo"
Walker, Margaret. "Girl Held Without Bail"
———. "On Police Brutality"

Black Lives Matter Elegies

Agostini, Saida. "If Tamir Rice and Eric Garner Wore Heels"
Alleyne, Lauren. "Martin Luther King Jr. Mourns Trayvon Martin"
Asghar, Fatimah. "For Mike Brown"
Austin, Derrick. "The Lost Woods as Elegy for Black Childhood"
Austin, Tiffany. "Changing My Name"
Barnett, Cameron. "Theater of America: For Michael Brown"
Bashir, Samiya. "At Harlem Hospital Across the Street from the Schomburg the Only
    Thing to Eat Is a Big Mac"
Bennett, Joshua. "Theodicy (for Renisha McBride)"
Betts, Reginald Dwanye. *Bastards of the Reagan Era*
———. "For the City That Nearly Broke Me"
———. "When I Think of Tamir Rice While Driving"
Birdsong, Destiny. "*This Is Who They're Killing.*"
Bonair-Agard, Roger. "A Full 40oz Beer Is Tossed from a Passing Car and Lands at My Feet"
———. "A Pantoum for How to Not-Gentrify"
———. "Citation, or Safe in Bed-Stuy"
Brown, Derrick Weston. "Lore"
———. "Mother to Son 2015 Baltimore"
brown, drea. "what we been knowin"
Brown, Jericho. "Another Elegy"
———. "The Interrogation"
Browne, Mahogany L. "Elegy for Song"
Charleston, Cortney Lamar. "Devotion ('I Am on the Battlefield for My Lord')"
———. "Praise Song for the Black Body Ending in the Throat of a Swallow"
———. *Telepathologies*
———. "Tupac Shakur's Last Words"
Cherry, James E. "Pass"
Clark, Tiana. *I Can't Talk About the Trees Without the Blood*
———. "The Ayes Have It"
Codjoe, Ama. "The Reasons Given"
Coleman, Gerald L. "Same Street"
Coleman, Wanda. "Please Please Stop the Madness Driven Violence"
Comer, Nandi. "Why I Don't Call the Cops"
Coval, Kevin. "We Real"
Cushway, Philip, and Michael Ware, eds. *Of Poetry & Protest: From Emmett Till to Trayvon
    Martin*

Dawes, Kwame. "Down in the Valley"
———. "Math"
Delaney, Ebony. *Sentiments from a Concrete Cage*
Dove, Rita. "Trayvon, Redux"
Easter, Mary Moore. "Ferguson at Advent"
Finney, Nikky. "Flare"
Ford, T'ai Freedom. "Homegoing"
Foreman, Arika. "Always Something Here to Remind Me"
———. "What I Mean When I Say *Harmony*"
Gay, Ross. "The Bullet in Its Hungers"
———. "A Small, Needful Fact"
Geter, Hafizah. "Testimony: For Michael Brown (1996–2014)"
Girmay, Aracelis. *The Black Maria: Poems*
Griffiths, Rachel Eliza. "Anti Elegy"
———. "Elegy"
Gumbs, Alexis Pauline. "Cartwheel on Blacktop (Trayvon Martin 2.0)"
Hardy, Myronn. "Cliven Bundy Theory"
Harris, Duriel E. "He Who Fights with Monsters"
Harris, Reginald. "Un/Titled"
Hayes, Terrance. *American Sonnets for My Past and Future Assassin*
Haynes, Lamarra. "Freddiegray"
Herrera, Juan Felipe. "@ the Crossroads—A Sudden American Poem"
Howard, J. P. "Tankas for Walter Scott"
Hunt, Erica. "Suspicious Activity"
Jackson, Angela. "Eclipse"
Jackson, Ashaki. "Standard American Similes with Interchangeable Blacks"
———. "The Mothers Coordinate Repast"
———. "That Which Began in Spring: A Bansky in Bethlehem"
Jackson, Major. "Ferguson"
Jackson, Reuben. "For Trayvon Martin"
Jafa, Arthur. *Love Is the Message, the Message Is Death*
Jess, Tyehimba. "Against Silence"
Johnston, Amanda. "Facing US"
Joiner, Fred. "F(risk)"
Jones, Camisha L. "American Anthem Remixed"
Joyner, Carolyn. "Alto Moon Choirs"
Judd, Bettina. *Patient.*
Kane, Kelli Stevens. "Bitter Crop"
King, Alan. "Hulk"
Knight, Etheridge. "Haiku"
Komunyakaa, Yusef. "Ghazal, After Ferguson"
Lawson, Len. "Sounds of the Police"
———. "Traffic Stop"
Major, Devorah. "Transit Police Compute Worth"
Maner, Sequoia. "Black Boy Contrapuntal (for Trayvon Martin)"
———. "Upon Reading the Autopsy of Sandra Bland"
Marshall, Nate. "Indian Summer"
———. "Prelude (RIP)"

———. "The Valley of Its Making"

———. "When the Officer Caught Me"

McCall, Jason. "Roll Call for Michael Brown"

McCrae, Shane. *In the Language of My Captor*

McElroy, Colleen J. "Into the Wilds"

McGhee, Jamie. "No One Marched"

Medina, Tony. *My Skin Is a Target Study*

———., ed. *Resisting Arrest: Poems to Stretch the Sky*

———. *Thirteen Ways of Looking at a Black Boy*

Micheaux, Dante. "Plague Dream"

Miller, E. Ethelbert. "Is This the History of Air?"

Monet, Aja. *My Mother Was a Freedom Fighter*

Moon, Kamilah Aisha. "Imagine"

Moore, Jessica Care. "We Want Our Bodies Back"

Moore, Michael "Quess?." "Post Racial America: A Children's Story"

Nelson, Rachel. "Makeup"

Nye, Naomi Shihab. "To Jamyla Bolden of Ferguson, Missouri"

Osayande, Deonte. "Prometheus Explains Genocide"

Osayande, Ewuare X., ed. *Stand Our Ground: Poems for Trayvon Martin & Marissa Alexander*

Parker, Morgan. "It Was Summer Now and the Colored People Came Out into the Sunshine"

Poets and Writers of Consciousness. *A Gathering of Words: Poetry & Commentary for Trayvon Martin*

Queen, Khadijah. "I Want to Not Have to Write Another Word About Who the Cops Keep Killing"

Rader, Dean. "Self-Portrait in Charleston, Orlando"

Randall, Julian. "Grief"

Rankine, Camille. "Aubade"

Rankine, Claudia. *Citizen: An American Lyric*

Richey, Katy. "For Brown Girls"

scott, darlene anita. "Cartography"

Shockley, Evie. "Buried Truths"

———. "Improper(ty) Behavior"

———. "Supply and Demand"

Smith, Danez. "Alternate Names for Black Boys"

———. *Black Movie*

———. *Don't Call Us Dead: Poems*

———. "Not an Elegy for Mike Brown"

Smith, John Warner. "After Connor, Wallace, Helms, and Duke"

Smith, Patricia. *Incendiary Art: Poems*

Smith, Tracy K. *Wade in the Water: Poems*

Spriggs, Bianca. "How to Make It Through Work the Day After Nine Black People Are Gunned Down in a South Carolina Church While Praying"

Stewart, Ebony. "The Blackouts Are Back"

Swearingen-Steadwell, Laura. "If It Helps"

Thompson, Lynne. "Sonnet Consisting of One Law"

Tillman, Cedric. "Tread on Me"

Walker, Frank X. "Black 101"

————. "Spell to End Police Violence"

Weaver, Michael Afaa. "A Poem for Freddie Gray, Baltimore"

————. "What a Fellowship (for Mother Emanuel A.M.E.)"

Wicker, Marcus. "Silencer to the Heart While Jogging Through a Park"

Willis-Abdurraqib, Hanif. *The Crown Ain't Worth Much*

Wilson, Keith. "Cincinnati Windy Grays"

————. "Driftwood"

Woods, Jamila, and Mahogany L. Browne, eds. Section: "Duty to Fight" in *The Breakbeat Poets Vol. 2: Black Girl Magic*

Young, Kevin. "Triptych for Trayvon Martin"

Criticism, Theory, and Other Writings

Alexander, Elizabeth. "'Can You Be Black and Look at This?': Reading the Rodney King Video(S)." *Public Culture* 7, no. 1 (January 1, 1994): 77–94. https://doi.org/10.1215/08992363-7-1-77.

Alexander, Michelle, and Cornel West. *The New Jim Crow: Mass Incarceration in the Age of Colorblindness.* New York: The New Press, 2012.

Anderson, Carol. *White Rage: The Unspoken Truth of Our Racial Divide.* 1st edition. New York: Bloomsbury USA, 2016.

Baldwin, James. "A Report from Occupied Territory." *The Nation*, July 26, 1966. www.thenation.com/article/report-occupied-territory/

————. "Many Thousands Gone." In *Notes of a Native Son*, 24–45. Boston: Beacon Press, 1955.

————. *The Fire Next Time.* New York: The Dial Press, 1963.

Benjamin, Ruha. "Black Afterlives Matter: Cultivating Kinfulness as Reproductive Justice." In *Making Kin Not Population*, edited by Adele Clarke and Donna Haraway. Chicago, IL: Prickly Paradigm Press, 2018.

Betts, R. Dwayne. *A Question of Freedom: A Memoir of Learning, Survival and Coming of Age in Prison.* New York: Avery, 2010.

Betts, Tara. "'Everytime They Kill a Black Boy . . . ': Representations of Police Brutality Against Children in Poems by Audre Lorde, Jayne Cortez, and June Jordan." *Obsidian* 13, no. 2 (2012): 69–85.

"Black Poets Speak Out Issue." *Pluck! The Journal of Affrilachian Arts & Culture*. Lexington: University of Kentucky, no. 13 (2015).

Blount, Marcellus. "Paul Laurence Dunbar and the African American Elegy." *African American Review* 41, no. 2 (2007): 239–46.

Bly, Antonio T. "'On Death's Domain Intent I Fix My Eyes': Text, Context, and Subtext in the Elegies of Phillis Wheatley." *Early American Literature* 53, no. 2 (2018): 317–41.

Cavitch, Max. *American Elegy: The Poetry of Mourning from the Puritans to Whitman.* Minneapolis: University of Minnesota Press, 2007.

Coates, Ta-Nehisi. *Between the World and Me.* New York: Spiegel & Grau, 2015.

————. *We Were Eight Years in Power: An American Tragedy.* New York: One World, 2017.

Cobb, Jelani. "The Matter of Black Lives." March 7, 2016. www.newyorker.com/magazine/2016/03/14/where-is-black-lives-matter-headed.

Connolly, Sally. *Grief and Meter: Elegies for Poets After Auden.* Charlottesville: University of Virginia Press, 2016.

Crenshaw, Kimberlé, and Andrea Ritchie. "Say Her Name: Resisting Police Brutality Against Black Women." *African American Policy Forum*, July 2015. http://aapf.org/sayhernamereport.

Cushway, Phil, and Victoria Smith. *Of Poetry and Protest: From Emmett Till to Trayvon Martin*, edited by Michael Warr. 1st edition. New York: W. W. Norton & Company, 2016.

Danticat, Edwidge. "Black Bodies in Motion and in Pain." *The New Yorker*, June 22, 2015. www.newyorker.com/culture/cultural-comment/black-bodies-in-motion-and-in-pain.

Davis, Angela J., Bryan Stevenson, Marc Mauer, Bruce Western, and Jeremy Travis. *Policing the Black Man: Arrest, Prosecution, and Imprisonment*. Reprint edition. New York: Vintage, 2018.

Davis, Angela Y. *Are Prisons Obsolete?* Uitgawe and Revised and Updated to Include New Develop and B edition. New York: Seven Stories Press, 2003.

Davis, Angela Y., and Cornel West. *Freedom Is a Constant Struggle: Ferguson, Palestine, and the Foundations of a Movement*, edited by Frank Barat. Chicago, IL: Haymarket Books, 2016.

Eng, David L., and David Kazanjian, eds. *Loss: The Politics of Mourning*. Berkeley: University of California Press, 2003.

Ewing, Eve L. *Ghosts in the Schoolyard: Racism and School Closings on Chicago's South Side*. Chicago: University of Chicago Press, 2018.

Fasching-Varner, Kenneth J., Rema E. Reynolds, Katrice Albert, and Lori Latrice Martin. *Trayvon Martin, Race, and American Justice: Writing Wrong*. Rotterdam and Boston: Sense, 2014.

Gray, Kevin Alexander, ed. *Killing Trayvons: An Anthology of American Violence*. Petrolia, CA: CounterPunch Books, 2014.

Green, Kai M., Je Naé Taylor, Pascale Ifé Williams, and Christopher Roberts. "#BlackHealingMatters in the Time of #BlackLivesMatter." *Biography* 41, no. 4 (2018): 909–41. https://doi.org/10.1353/bio.2018.0085.

Hammond, Jeffrey. *The American Puritan Elegy: A Literary and Cultural Study*. Cambridge Studies in American Literature and Culture. New York: Cambridge University Press, 2000.

Hartman, Saidiya V. *Lose Your Mother: A Journey Along the Atlantic Slave Route*. New York: Farrar, Straus and Giroux, 2008.

———. *Scenes of Subjection: Terror, Slavery, and Self-Making in Nineteenth-Century America*. New York: Oxford University Press, 1997.

———. "Venus in Two Acts." *Small Axe* 12, no. 2 (July 17, 2008): 1–14.

Hattery, Angela J., and Earl Smith. *Policing Black Bodies: How Black Lives Are Surveilled and How to Work for Change*. Lanham: Rowman & Littlefield Publishers, 2017.

Hill, Marc Lamont, and Todd Brewster. *Nobody: Casualties of America's War on the Vulnerable, from Ferguson to Flint and Beyond*. Reprint edition. New York: Atria Books, 2017.

Holloway, Karla F. C. *Passed on: African American Mourning Stories: A Memorial*. Durham: Duke University Press, 2002.

Johnson, Devon, ed. *Deadly Injustice: Trayvon Martin, Race, and the Criminal Justice System*. New Perspectives in Crime, Deviance, and Law. New York and London: New York University Press, 2015.

Khan, Almas. "Poetic Justice: Slavery, Law, and the (Anti-)Elegiac Form in M. NourbeSe Philip's Zong!" *The Cambridge Journal of Postcolonial Literary Inquiry* 2, no. 1 (March 2015): 5–32. https://doi.org/10.1017/pli.2014.22.

Khan-Cullors, Patrisse. "We Didn't Start a Movement. We Started a Network." *Patrisse Khan-Cullors* (blog), February 23, 2016. https://medium.com/@patrissemariecullorsbrignac/we-didn-t-start-a-movement-we-started-a-network-90f9b5717668.

Khan-Cullors, Patrisse, and Asha Bandele. *When They Call You a Terrorist: A Black Lives Matter Memoir*. 1st edition. New York: St. Martin's Press, 2018.

Laiola, Sarah Whitcomb. "From Float to Flicker: Information Processing, Racial Semiotics, and Anti-Racist Protest, from 'I Am a Man' to 'Black Lives Matter'." *Criticism* 60, no. 2 (Spring 2018): 247–68. https://doi.org/10.13110/criticism.60.2.0247.

Lebron, Christopher J. *The Making of Black Lives Matter: A Brief History of an Idea*. New York: Oxford University Press, 2017.

Lordi, Emily J. "'[B]Lack and Going on Women': Lucille Clifton, Elizabeth Alexander, and the Poetry of Grief." *Palimpsest: A Journal on Women, Gender, and the Black International* 6, no. 1 (June 28, 2017): 44–68.

Lowery, Wesley. *They Can't Kill Us All: The Story of the Struggle for Black Lives*. First Back Bay paperback edition. New York: Back Bay Books: Little, Brown and Company, 2016.

Marable, Manning. *Race, Reform, and Rebellion: The Second Reconstruction and Beyond in Black America, 1945–2006*. 3rd edition. Jackson: University Press of Mississippi, 2007.

Mbembe, A. "Necropolitics." *Public Culture* 15, no. 1 (January 1, 2003): 11–40. https://doi.org/10.1215/08992363-15-1-11.

Moore, Darnell L. "Black Freedom Fighters in Ferguson: Some of Us Are Queer." *The Feminist Wire* (blog), October 17, 2014. https://thefeministwire.com/2014/10/some-of-us-are-queer/.

Moten, Fred. *In the Break: The Aesthetics of the Black Radical Tradition*. Minneapolis: University of Minnesota Press, 2003.

Pavlić, Ed. "Storms and (Buried) Warnings in the Age of Travyon Martin and George Zimmerman." *NewBlackMan (in Exile)* (blog), July 19, 2013. https://www.newblackmaninexile.net/search/label/lynching.

Pollack, Harriet, and Christopher Metress, eds. *Emmett Till in Literary Memory and Imagination: New and Selected Poems*. 1st edition. Baton Rouge: LSU Press, 2008.

Ramazani, Jahan. *Poetry of Mourning: The Modern Elegy from Hardy to Heaney*. Chicago: University of Chicago Press, 1994.

Rankine, Claudia. "The Condition of Black Life Is One of Mourning." *The New York Times*, June 22, 2015. www.nytimes.com/2015/06/22/magazine/the-condition-of-black-life-is-one-of-mourning.html.

Ransby, Barbara. *Making All Black Lives Matter: Reimagining Freedom in the Twenty-First Century*. Oakland: University of California Press, 2018.

Sacks, Peter M. *The English Elegy: Studies in the Genre from Spenser to Yeats*. Baltimore: Johns Hopkins Press, 1985.

Shakur, Assata, and Angela Davis. *Assata: An Autobiography*. Chicago, IL: Lawrence Hill Books, 2001.

Sharpe, Christina. *In the Wake: On Blackness and Being*. Durham: Duke University Press Books, 2016.

Sinitiere, Phillip Luke. "Aesthetic Insurgency: Sandra Bland's Presence in Poetry—AAIHS." *Black Perspectives* (blog), July 11, 2018. www.aaihs.org/aesthetic-insurgency-sandra-blands-presence-in-poetry/.

Smith, Tracy K. "Political Poetry Is Hot Again. The Poet Laureate Explores Why, and How," *The New York Times Book Review*, December 16, 2018, www.nytimes.com/2018/12/10/books/review/political-poetry.html.

Spargo, R. Clifton. *The Ethics of Mourning: Grief and Responsibility in Elegiac Literature*. Baltimore: Johns Hopkins University Press, 2004.

Taylor, Keeanga-Yamahtta, ed. *From #BlackLivesMatter to Black Liberation*. Chicago, IL: Haymarket Books, 2016.

————. *How We Get Free: Black Feminism and the Combahee River Collective*. Chicago, IL: Haymarket Books, 2012.

Unger, Mary I. "Literary Justice in the Post-Ferguson Classroom." *MELUS: Multi-Ethnic Literature of the U.S.* 42, no. 4 (Winter 2017): 92–112.

Ward, Jesmyn, ed. *Men We Reaped: A Memoir*. 1st edition. New York: Bloomsbury USA, 2013.

————. *The Fire This Time: A New Generation Speaks About Race*. First Scribner hardcover edition. New York: Scribner, 2016.

Washington, Harriet A. *Medical Apartheid: The Dark History of Medical Experimentation on Black Americans from Colonial Times to the Present*. Reprint edition. New York: Anchor, 2008.

Weisman, Karen A., ed. *The Oxford Handbook of the Elegy*. Oxford Handbooks. Oxford and New York: Oxford University Press, 2010.

West, Cornel. *Democracy Matters: Winning the Fight Against Imperialism*. Reprint edition. New York: Penguin Books, 2005.

Whitted, Qiana. "In My Flesh Shall I See God: Ritual Violence and Racial Redemption in 'The Black Christ.'" *African American Review* 38, no. 3 (Fall 2004): 379–93. https://doi.org/10.2307/1512441.

Williams, Chad, Kidada E. Williams, and Keisha N. Blain, eds. *Charleston Syllabus: Readings on Race, Racism, and Racial Violence*. Athens: University of Georgia Press, 2016.

Willis-Abdurraqib, Hanif. *They Can't Kill Us Until They Kill Us*. Columbus: Two Dollar Radio, 2017.

Yancy, George, and Janine Jones, eds. *Pursuing Trayvon Martin: Historical Contexts and Contemporary Manifestations of Racial Dynamics*. Lanham: Lexington Boos, 2013.

Younge, Gary. *Another Day in the Death of America: A Chronicle of Ten Short Lives*. New York: Bold Type Books, 2016.

Zeiger, Melissa F. *Beyond Consolation: Death, Sexuality, and the Changing Shapes of Elegy*. Reading Women Writing. Ithaca: Cornell University Press, 1997.

Websites and Online Resources

A Herstory of the #BlackLivesMatter Movement by Alicia Garza: www.thefeministwire.com/2014/10/blacklivesmatter-2/

African American Policy Forum. Special Report: "Say Her Name, Resisting Police Brutality Against Black Women": http://aapf.org/sayhernamereport.

Black Lives Matter Syllabus by Frank Leon Roberts: www.blacklivesmattersyllabus.com

Black Poets Speak Out: https://blackpoetsspeakout.tumblr.com/

#BlackLivesMatter: A Poetry Reader: https://blacklivesmatterpoetryreader.weebly.com/

Cultural Front: www.culturalfront.org/

Poetry Society: Black Poets Speak Out Lesson Plans: www.poetrysociety.org/psa/poetry/crossroads/black_poets_speak_out/

The Movement for Black Lives. "A Vision for Black Lives: Policy Demands for Black Power, Freedom, and Justice": https://policy.m4bl.org/

CONTRIBUTORS

Lauren K. Alleyne is the author of two collections of poetry, *Difficult Fruit* (Peepal Tree Press 2014), and *Honeyfish* (New Issues & Peepal Tree, 2019), and co-editor of the forthcoming anthology, "Furious Flower: Seeding the Future of African American Poetry." Her work has appeared in numerous publications including *The Atlantic, Ms. Muse, Women's Studies Quarterly, Interviewing the Caribbean, The Crab Orchard Review*, among many others. Recent honors for her work include a 2017 Phillip Freund Alumni Prize for Excellence in Publishing (Cornell University), the 2016 Split This Rock Poetry Prize, and a Picador Guest Professorship in Literature (University of Leipzig, Germany, 2015). She is currently Assistant Director of the Furious Flower Poetry Center and an Associate Professor of English at James Madison University.

Tiffany Austin was born on April 26, 1975 in Murfreesboro, Arkansas, to the union of Anthony (Tony) Eric Austin and Ruth Ann May, who later moved to Kansas City, MO in 1977. She joined the ancestors on Saturday, June 23, 2018. Tiffany's affinity for reading books, writing, and poetry started at a young age. She graduated in the top of her class from Ruskin High School in 1993. She then graduated *magna cum laude* from Spelman University in 1997, receiving her B.A. in English. During her time at Spelman, Tiffany was an intern in Alaska for a year. Tiffany continued her higher educational journey thereafter. She received her MFA in creative writing from Chicago State University, her J.D. from Northeastern University School of Law (passing the bar on her first try), and her Ph.D. in English from St. Louis University. As part of her dissertation work, she spent six months in Ecuador to learn more about and speak with Luz Argentina Chiriboga, an Afro-Ecuadorian writer who was one of the subjects of her research.

A dedicated scholar and teacher, Tiffany had a breadth and depth of knowledge about African Diasporic literature, comparative literature, and critical race theory and gender studies. During her career, Tiffany taught at Florida Memorial University, Mississippi Valley State University, and most recently at the University of The Bahamas. She gave numerous conference presentations, and was the chair of the Midwest Modern Language Association panels on African American literature. She was also a widely published poet, with her chapbook *Étude* appearing in 2013. Of this volume, her mentor Sterling Plumpp noted, "Austin's genius is her unusual gift for metaphor and allusion." Others recognized Tiffany's genius too, with her poems appearing in such prestigious outlets as *Callaloo, Obsidian III, African American Review, Coloring Book: An Anthology of Poetry and Fiction by Multicultural Writers, Warpland, pluck!, The Journal of Affrilachian Arts and Culture, Valley Voices, Auburn Avenue, TriQuarterly, Sycorax's Daughters*, and *Moko: Caribbean Arts and Letters*. She was also a coeditor *Revisiting the Elegy in the Black Lives Matter Era*, a project she began in late 2017 with Emily Ruth Rutter.

When Tiffany was not teaching and writing, she was busy bringing literature to the community and engaging in artistic fellowship. At the University of The Bahamas, she organized the Blue Flamingo Literary Festival, as well as the Anatol Rodgers Memorial Lecture Series, with invited guest Sonia Sanchez. Her long list of fellowships and awards includes a Callaloo Creative Writing Workshop fellowship, a residency at the Virginia Center for Creative Arts, the Archie D. and Bertha H. Walker Foundation Scholarship, a grant from the Mississippi Arts Commission, a fellowship for the Kimbilio Writing Retreat, and the Gwendolyn Brooks Poetry Award. Tiffany also shared her work on the stage. A recent play was performed at both the Billie Holiday Theater in Brooklyn, New York, and the Hayti Center in Durham, North Carolina.

All of these experiences speak to Tiffany's love to travel, meet new people, and experience new cultures. She traveled to England, Jamaica, Europe, the Dominican Republic, Cuba, Ecuador, and many more places. Her infectious smile was also contagious, and her laugh made you smile, even if you didn't know why she was laughing. Her humble spirit made you inquisitive about her life. When engaging about a topic Tiffany felt strongly about, she made a point to be sure you walked away with facts. Tiffany was a teacher, writer, poet, activist, and feminist. Never one for titles, she was moved instead by both action and passion. She was incomparable, generous, artistic, and authentic—a beautiful soul who will live on in the many artistic and personal seeds she planted and nurtured.

Cameron Barnett holds an MFA from the University of Pittsburgh, where he was poetry editor for *Hot Metal Bridge*, and co-coordinator of Pitt's Speakeasy Reading Series. He teaches middle school at Falk Laboratory School in Pittsburgh. His recent work has appeared in *The Florida Review, The Minnesota Review*, and *Rattle*. His first collection, *The Drowning Boy's Guide to Water* (Autumn House Press) was a finalist for an NAACP Image Award.

Paula Bohince is the author of three poetry collections, all from Sarabande, most recently *Swallows and Waves*. Her poems have appeared in *The New Yorker*, *Poetry*, and *Best American Poetry*. She has been a Fellow of National Endowment for the Arts. She lives in Pennsylvania.

Charlie Braxton is a poet, playwright, and journalist born in McComb, Mississippi. Braxton studied Journalism and Creative Writing at Jackson State University. He has published three volumes of poetry, *Ascension from the Ashes* (Blackwood Press, 1991), *Cinders Rekindled* (Jawara Press, 2013), and *Embers Among the Ashes: Poems in a Haiku Manner* (Jawara Press, 2018). His poetry has appeared in a number of literary journals, including *The Black Nation*, *Black American Literature Forum*, *Cutbank*, *Drumvoices Review*, *Eyeball Literary Magazine*, *Sepia Poetry Journal*, *Specter Magazine*, *The Minnesota Review*, *The San Fernando Poetry Journal*, and *The Transnational*. In addition, Braxton has been anthologized in several anthologies, such as *Trouble the Waters*, *In The Tradition*, *Bum Rush the Page: the Def Jam Poetry Anthology*, *Roll Call*, *Step Into a World*, and *The African World in Dialogue: A Call to Arms!*

Maia L. Butler is an Assistant Professor of African American Literature at the University of North Carolina-Wilmington, where she is also affiliate faculty in Women's and Gender Studies and Africana Studies. She researches and teaches in African American and Diasporic literary studies, Women's Literature and Feminist Theories and Criticism, and Anglophone Postcolonial Literary Studies. She is coeditor of a volume titled *Narrating History, Home, and Nation: Critical Essays on Edwidge Danticat*, forthcoming from University Press of Mississippi, and has a book chapter titled "The Exigency of the Floating Homeland and Engaging Postnationalisms in the Classroom: Approaches to Teaching Edwidge Danticat's *Create Dangerously: The Immigrant Artist at Work*," forthcoming in *Approaches to Teaching the Work of Edwidge Danticat*. She is the cofounding Vice President of the Edwidge Danticat Society.

Chris Campanioni is a first-generation American, the child of immigrants from Cuba and Poland, and the author of *the Internet is for real* (C&R Press). His "Billboards" poem was awarded an Academy of American Poets College Prize in 2013, his novel *Going Down* was selected as Best First Book at the 2014 International Latino Book Awards, and his hybrid piece "This body's long (& I'm still loading)" was adapted as an official selection of the Canadian International Film Festival in 2017. He is currently a Provost Fellow and MAGNET Mentor at The Graduate Center/CUNY, where he is conducting his doctoral studies in English and redrafting narratives of exile. He edits *PANK*, *At Large Magazine*, and *Tupelo Quarterly*, and teaches Latino literature and creative writing at Pace University and Baruch College.

Megan Feifer is an Assistant Professor of English at Medaille College in Buffalo, New York. She earned her B.A. and M.A. from the University of Wisconsin and Ph.D. at Louisiana State University. Her research and teaching addresses Afro-Caribbean Diasporas in the U.S., Multi-Ethnic Literatures, Postcolonial Literature and theory, and Feminist theories. Her dissertation research addresses the collective counter-archival project created in the essays, fiction, and nonfiction work of authors Julia Alvarez, Edwidge Danticat, and Junot Díaz. She is coeditor of a volume titled *Narrating History, Home, and Nation: Critical Essays on Edwidge Danticat*, forthcoming from University Press of Mississippi, and author of an article under review titled "The Remembering of Bones: Working through Trauma and the Counter-Archive in Edwidge Danticat's *Farming of Bones*." She is the cofounding President of the Edwidge Danticat Society.

Maureen Gallagher earned her doctorate in English from Duquesne University in 2015. She currently teaches in the English Department of Slippery Rock University. Her teaching and research interests include contemporary American poetry and poetics, ethics, race and identity, women's and gender studies, popular culture, and visual studies.

Danielle Legros Georges is the author of two books of poetry, *Maroon* and *The Dear Remote Nearness of You*, the chapbook *Letters from Congo*, and is the editor of *City of Notions: An Anthology of Contemporary Boston Poems*. Her essays, translations, reviews, and poems have appeared in numerous literary journals, books, and publications, and she has won numerous awards for her literary work. As Boston's Poet Laureate between 2015 and 2019, Legros Georges collaborated with Boston-area museums, libraries, schools, artists and students; represented Boston internationally at literary festivals; presented occasional poems at official events; made commissioned work; cofounded a reading series and scholarships, created an elder poetry writing workshop; welcomed visiting poets and artists; created readings and panels; and held office hours with Boston residents interested in poetry. She is Professor of Creative Writing at Lesley University.

Sarah Giragosian is the author of the poetry collections *Queer Fish* (Dream Horse Press, 2017) and *The Death Spiral* (Black Lawrence Press, forthcoming). Recent scholarly articles include "Elizabeth Bishop's Evolutionary Poetics," published in *Interdisciplinary Literary Studies: A Journal of Criticism and Theory* and "'To a Nation Out of its Mind': Joy Harjo's Post-Pastoral," published in the anthology *Ecopoetics: Global Poetries and Ecologies* (Lexington Books). She teaches in the department of Writing and Critical Inquiry at the University at Albany SUNY.

Hoke S. Glover III (Bro. Yao) is Assistant Professor in the Department of English and Modern Languages at Bowie State University. His poetry has been published in *Ploughshares, African American Review, Rattle,* and other journals and anthologies. His first book, *Inheritance,* was published by Willow Books in Summer of 2016. For 15 years he ran and operated Karibu Books, one of the nation's largest African American bookstores. His essay "Hospital for the Negro Insane" was a finalist in the *Crab Orchard* John Guyon Nonfiction Literary Prize in 2015, and his essay the "Fifty Four" on African American bookstores and book culture was a finalist in the *Missouri Review* Jeffrey E. Smith's Editor's Prize in 2018. Much of his current work focuses on reading "yin" in African American culture.

Nicholas Rianard Goodly is a recipient of the 2017 Poetry Society of America Chapbook Fellowship. A Cave Canem Fellow, Nicholas received an MFA from Columbia University, was awarded the second place prize for New South Poetry Contest, was a semifinalist in the 2018 Discovery/ Boston Review Contest, finalist in the 2017 Tennessee Williams Poetry Contest, and a finalist in the 2016 Academy of American Poets Prize. Nicholas is the writing editor of *WUSSY* Magazine and Critic's Choice for Best Poet 2018 in Creative Loafing Atlanta.

Jason Harris is an emerging writer/futurist based in Baltimore, Maryland. He attended Morehouse College in Atlanta, Georgia. His work has appeared in *Black Enterprise* magazine, *Voices from Haiti, FreeBlackSpace, BmoreArt online,* and various other publications. He has participated in the Yale Writer's conference and is a 2015 Kimbilio Fiction Fellow. He self-published the speculative fiction anthology entitled, *Redlines: Baltimore 2028* in 2012, which has subsequently been adopted as curriculum material for creative writing and social studies departments in high schools and universities. He is the founder of the Parkside Literary Salon, a Baltimore-based writing collective. In 2016, he cocurated *Mothership Connection,* an anchor exhibit for Artscape, the largest outdoor public art festival in the U.S. In addition to his involvement in a myriad of community-based futurist projects, he is currently working on his first novel, *Upside Out,* which he will publish this fall.

Licia Morrow Hendriks is an associate professor of English at The Citadel in Charleston, South Carolina. A California native, she attended Duke University before moving on to the University of Michigan's doctoral program in English Language and Literature. Her first book, entitled *Black Family (Dys)Function in Novels by Jessie Fauset, Nella Larsen, and Fannie Hurst* (Peter Lang, 2003), examines representations of maternity and domesticity in novels written during the Harlem Renaissance. She is currently working on the manuscript of her second book, subtitled "The Anglo-American Fetishization of Black Female Domesticity." In addition to lower-division service courses in composition and literature, she teaches upper-division and graduate courses in African American Literature, survey courses in World Literature, and special topics seminars for the college's Honors program. Her scholarly interests encompass the race, class, and gender issues manifested in literary representations of people of color.

Angela Jackson-Brown is an award-winning writer, poet and playwright who teaches Creative Writing and English at Ball State University. She is a graduate of the Spalding low-residency MFA program in Creative Writing. She is the author of the novel Drinking From A Bitter Cup and has published in numerous literary journals. Recently, her play Anna's Wings was selected to be a part of the Indy-Fringe DivaFest, and her play Flossie Bailey Takes a Stand was part of the Indiana Bicentennial Celebration. Other recent plays include It Is Well, Black Lives Matter (Too) (co-written with Ashya Thomas), Dear Bobby: The Musical (co-written with Peter Davis), Still Singing Those Weary Blues, and Voices of Yesteryear. Her poetry collection, House Repairs, was recently published by Negative Capability Press.

Jacqueline Johnson is a multidisciplined artist creating in both poetry, fiction writing, and fiber arts. She is the author of *A Woman's Season*, on Main Street Rag Press, and *A Gathering of Mother Tongues*, published by White Pine Press and is the winner of the Third Annual White Pine Press Poetry Award. Ms. Johnson has received awards from the New York Foundation of the Arts, the Middle Atlantic Writers Association's Creative Writing Award in poetry, and has done residences at MacDowell Colony for the Arts, Hurston Wright, and Blue Mountain Arts. She is a Black Earth Institute fellow 2018–2020, and Cave Canem fellow. Ms. Johnson has taught poetry at Pine Manor College, City University of New York, Poets House, Very Special Arts, Imani House, the Frederick Douglass Creative Arts Center, and African Voices. Recent publications include the following: *The Brooklyn Poets Anthology, Revise the Psalm: Work Celebrating the Writing of Gwendolyn Brooks, Speculating Futures: Black Imagination and the Arts, The Wide Shore: A Journal of Global Women's Poetry, Fifth Wednesday Journal, Black Renaissance Noire, pluck! The Journal of Affrilachian Arts & Culture, Cutting Down the Wrath Bearing Tree, Callaloo, Saints of Hysteria: A Half Century of Collaborative American Poetry, Softskull Press,* and *Streetlights: Illuminating Tales of the Black Urban Experience.* Works in progress include *The Privilege of Memory* and *How to Stop a Hurricane,* a collection of short stories. She is a graduate of New York University and the City University of New York. A native of Philadelphia, Pennsylvania., she resides in Brooklyn, New York.

Amanda Johnston earned a Master of Fine Arts in Creative Writing from the University of Southern Maine. She is the author of two chapbooks, *GUAP* and *Lock & Key,* and the full-length collection *Another Way to Say Enter* (Argus House Press). Her poetry and interviews have appeared in numerous online and print publications, among them, *Callaloo, Poetry, Kinfolks Quarterly, Puerto del Sol, Muzzle, pluck!, No, Dear,* and the anthologies, *Small Batch, Full, di-ver-city, The Ringing Ear: Black Poets Lean South,* and *Women of Resistance: Poems for a New Feminism.* The recipient of multiple Artist Enrichment grants from the Kentucky Foundation for Women and the Christina Sergeyevna Award from the Austin International Poetry Festival, she is a member of the Affrilachian Poets and a Cave Canem graduate fellow. Johnston is a Stonecoast MFA faculty member, a cofounder of Black Poets Speak Out, and founding executive director of Torch Literary Arts. She serves on the Cave Canem Foundation board of directors and currently lives in Texas.

Almas Khan is an assistant director of the Center for Legal English at Georgetown Law. She holds a Ph.D. in English from the University of Virginia and a J.D. with honors from the University of Chicago Law School. Her scholarship analyzes connections between disciplinary developments in postbellum American literature and law, focusing on African diasporic and working-class literary texts that employ legal forms but critique inequities in how the legal system has constructed citizenship. Almas's current book project, An Intellectual Reconstruction: American Legal Realism, Literary Realism, and the Forging of Citizenship, will present a new intellectual history of two synchronous modern liberal movements in American law and letters. A second project, Conceptualizing Poetry and Law, will delineate conceptual poetry's public resonance despite its aura of formal inaccessibility by probing the work of poets who have fabricated their texts from legal materials. Almas's article "Racial Classifications and Crossing the Color Line: Nella Larsen's Novel Passing" was recently published in the anthology Critical Insights: Inequality (editor Kimberly Drake, Grey House Publishing/Salem Press). Almas has also published articles in other anthologies and in several journals, including the Cambridge Journal of Postcolonial Literary Inquiry, English Academy Review, and the Chicago Journal of International Law. Almas's literary scholarship draws upon her experiences in law, including teaching U.S. constitutional law and legal writing.

Sequoia Maner is a poet-scholar and Mellon Teaching Fellow of Feminist Studies at Southwestern University. She earned her B.A. in English from Duke University and her M.A. and Ph.D. degrees in English from the University of Texas at Austin. She is coeditor of *Revisiting the Elegy in the Black Lives Matter Era*. Her dissertation and first solo-authored book project, *Liberation Aesthetics in the #BlackLivesMatter Era*, examines how experimental poetics and performance bolster black social movements. You can read her essay on the performance of "quiet interiority" as collective praxis in Beyoncé's *Lemonade* in the journal *Meridians: feminism, race, transnationalism* and her poem "upon reading the autopsy of Sandra Bland," finalist for the 2017 Gwendolyn Brooks Poetry Prize, in O*bsidian: Literature & Arts of the African Diaspora*.

Tony Medina, two-time winner of the Paterson Prize for Books for Young People (*DeShawn Days* and *I and I, Bob Marley*), is the author/editor of twenty books for adults and young readers, the most recent of which are *I and I, Bob Marley* (2009); *My Old Man Was Always on the Lam* (2010), a finalist for the Paterson Poetry Prize; *Broke on Ice* (2011); *An Onion of Wars* (2012); *The President Looks Like*

Me & Other Poems (2013); and *Broke Baroque* (2013), a finalist for the Julie Suk Book Award. He has received the Langston Hughes Society Award; the first African Voices Literary Award; and was nominated for Pushcart Prizes for his poems, "Broke Baroque" and "From the Crushed Voice Box of Freddie Gray." Medina, whose poetry and prose appear in over 100 anthologies and literary journals, is the first Professor of Creative Writing at Howard University. In 2016, Jacar Press of North Carolina published his anthology, *Resisting Arrest: Poems to Stretch the Sky*, on police violence and brutalities perpetrated on people of color. Tu Books, an imprint of Lee & Low Books, published Medina's debut graphic novel, *I Am Alfonso Jones*, in 2017, and Penny Candy Books of Oklahoma published *Thirteen Ways of Looking at a Black Boy* (2018). Medina has read/performed his work all over the U.S., as well as in Germany, France, Poland, the Bahamas, Puerto Rico, and the Netherlands.

Deborah M. Mix is Professor of English at Ball State University. Her articles on Stein and other poets have appeared in *Contemporary Women's Writing*, *American Literature*, and *The Cambridge History of 20th-Century American Women's Poetry*, among other places. She is the author of *"A Vocabulary of Thinking": Gertrude Stein and Contemporary North American Women's Experimental Writing* and the coeditor of *Approaches to Teaching the Works of Gertrude Stein*.

J. Peter Moore is a literary critic, poet, and editor, working at the intersection of multiple disciplines, including linguistics, architecture, visual arts, and black studies. His book project, *Other Than a Citizen: Vernacular Poetics in Postwar America*, examines the work of avant-garde poets who turned to the unadorned, anonymous practices of everyday life to find a model for countering the institutional regimentation of the postwar social world. Recent essays can be found in *American Literature* and *College Literature*. He is the author of two poetry collections, *Southern Colortype* (Three Count Pour, 2013) and *Zippers & Jeans* (selva oscura, 2017). With Ken Taylor, he edits *Lute & Drum: An Online Arts Journal*. He lives in Lafayette, Indiana, where he teaches in the Honors College at Purdue University.

Sean Murphy has appeared on *NPR*'s "All Things Considered" and been quoted in *USA Today*, *The New York Times*, *The Huffington Post*, and *AdAge*. His work has also appeared in *Salon*, *The Village Voice*, *The New York Post*, *The Good Men Project*, *Memoir Magazine*, and others. He has twice been nominated for the Pushcart Prize, and served as writer-in-residence of the Noepe Center at Martha's Vineyard. He's Founding Director of Virginia Center for Literary Arts (www.thevcla.org). To learn more, please visit seanmurphy.net/ and @bullmurph.

Lisa Norris has published two prize-winning story collections, *Women Who Sleep With Animals* (Stephen F. Austin University Press Prize, 2011) and *Toy Guns* (Helicon Nine Press, 2000) and a poetry chapbook called *The Gap* (D Press, 2017).

Her stories, poems, and creative nonfiction have been published in various literary journals, including *Terrain.org*, *Shenandoah, Fourth Genre, Ascent, South Dakota Review, Smartish Pace, Notre Dame Review*, and the anthology *Kiss Tomorrow Hello* (Doubleday 2006), among others. She is a professor at Central Washington University in Ellensburg, Washington. Previously, she taught for 15 years at Virginia Tech.

Anne M. Rashid is professor of English and Women's and Gender Studies Director at Carlow University. She teaches courses in American literature, creative writing, environmental justice, literature in translation, as well as Madwomen in the Attic workshops. She is faculty advisor for Carlow's chapter of Sigma Tau Delta, the English Honors Society and *The Critical Point*, Carlow's undergraduate writing and art journal. She has published poetry in *Adagio Verse Quarterly, Lit Candles: Feminist Mentoring and the Text, The Metro Times*, Pittsburgh's *City Paper, Forum, Paterson Literary Review, Broad River Review, Walloon Writers Review*, and *The Fourth River*. She and her cotranslator, the late Chae-Pyong Song, published translations of Korean poetry in *New Writing from Korea, list, The Gwangju News, Azalea: Journal of Korean Literature, Illuminations*, and *Women's Studies Quarterly*. In 2009, they won the Grand Prize in the Poetry category of the 40th Modern Korean Literature Translation Awards given by *The Korea Times*. Her fields of interest include literature of environmental justice, contemporary women's poetry, and African American literature. She has a Ph.D. (2006) and M.A. (2001) from Binghamton University and a B.A. (1998) from Wayne State University.

Anne Lovering Rounds is an associate professor of English at Eugenio María de Hostos Community College, City University of New York. An interdisciplinary scholar of poetry and music, she has published in *Ars Lyrica, The Journal of Beat Studies, Literary Imagination, Proteus, Text Matters*, and *Soundings*. Her debut poetry collection, *Variations in an Emergency* (2016), received the Cathlamet Prize for poetry from Ravenna Press, and her second volume, *Little Double Elegy for All of You*, is forthcoming with Ravenna. She is also a classical pianist. She earned her Ph.D. in Comparative Literature from Harvard University in 2009 and holds a B.A. in English and Classics from the University of Chicago.

Emily Ruth Rutter is Assistant Professor of English at Ball State University, where she teaches courses in Multi-Ethnic American and African American literature. She is the author of two monographs: *Invisible Ball of Dreams: Literary Representations of Baseball behind the Color Line* (University Press of Mississippi, 2018) and *The Blues Muse: Race, Gender, and Musical Celebrity in American Poetry* (University of Alabama Press, 2018). Her numerous essays have been published in journals such as *African American Review, South Atlantic Review, Studies in American Culture*,

Aethlon, and *MELUS.* Her book chapter on African American women poets appears in *A Cambridge History of Twentieth-Century American Women's Poetry,* and a book chapter on Amiri Baraka and sports is forthcoming in *Some Other Blues: New Perspectives on Amiri Baraka* (Ohio State UP, 2021).

Emily Jo Scalzo holds an MFA in fiction from California State University-Fresno and is currently an assistant professor teaching research and creative writing at Ball State University in Muncie, Indiana. Her work has appeared in various magazines, including *Midwestern Gothic, Mobius: The Journal of Social Change, Blue Collar Review, New Verse News,* and others. Her first chapbook, *The Politics of Division,* was awarded Honorable Mention in the 2018 Eric Hoffer Book Awards.

darlene anita scott is Associate Professor of English at Virginia Union University. She is a poet and visual artist whose research explores corporeal performances of trauma and the violence of silence. Her poetry has appeared in journals including *J Journal, Quiddity,* and *The Baltimore Review,* among others. Her art has been featured in *The Journal,* an arts and literature magazine of Ohio State University and at The Girl Museum, a virtual museum celebrating girls and girlhood. Recipient of support from the Virginia Commission for the Arts, Delaware Division of the Arts, Tennessee Commission for the Arts, and College English Association, Scott's most recent project is a multimedia exploration, *Breathing Lessons,* which explores the role of the good girl as it is applied to girls of color.

Steffan Triplett is a black, queer writer and instructor living in Pittsburgh. He received his MFA from the University of Pittsburgh and is an alumnus of VONA, Callaloo, and a previous Lambda Literary Fellow. His recent work can be found in *Longreads, Slate, Electric Literature, DIAGRAM,* and *Nepantla: An Anthology Dedicated to Queer Poets of Color* (Nightboat Books 2018). Steffan is a graduate of Washington University in St. Louis where he was a John B. Ervin scholar. He was raised in Joplin, Missouri.

Laura Vrana is Assistant Professor of English at the University of South Alabama. She earned her B.A. from Yale University and her M.A. and Ph.D. at The Pennsylvania State University, before spending a year as Postdoctoral Fellow in African American and African Diasporic Literature at Rutgers University. Her book manuscript in progress focuses on black poetry since the Black Arts Movement, examining the role of academic institutions, literary prizes, and publication mechanisms in shaping the recent increased visibility of black poetics. Her work has appeared or is forthcoming in *Obsidian: Literature and Arts in the African Diaspora, Journal of Ethnic American Literature, Tulsa Studies in Women's Literature,* a collection on Amiri Baraka's legacy, and the Cambridge African American Literature In Transition series, among other venues.

Jerry Wemple is the author of three poetry collections: *You Can See It from Here*, winner of the Naomi Long Madgett Poetry Award, *The Civil War in Baltimore*, and *The Artemas Poems*. He is coeditor of the anthology *Common Wealth: Contemporary Poets on Pennsylvania*. His poetry and creative nonfiction work appear in numerous journals and anthologies, and have been published internationally in Ireland, Chile, Spain, Germany, and Canada. A Professor of English at Bloomsburg University of Pennsylvania, he received several awards for writing and teaching including a Fellowship in Literature from the Pennsylvania Council on the Arts and the *Word Journal* chapbook prize. He was awarded the Bloomsburg University Institute for Culture and Society award for Outstanding Creative Work, the Dean's Salute to Excellence for his teaching and scholarship, and the Jack and Helen Evans Endowed Faculty Fellowship.

Kimmika Williams-Witherspoon—Ph.D. (Cultural Anthropology), M.A. (Anthropology), MFA (Theater), Graduate Certificate (Women's Studies), B.A. (Journalism)—is Associate Professor of Urban Theater and Community Engagement in the Theater Department at Temple. The author of *Through Smiles and Tears: The History of African American Theater (From Kemet to the Americas)* (Lambert Academic Publishing, 2011); *The Secret Messages in African American Theater: Hidden Meaning Embedded in Public Discourse"* (Edwin Mellen Publishing, 2006). She is a recipient of the 2013 The Miriam Maat Ka Re Award for scholarship; the 2013 Associate Provosts Arts Grant; 2008 Seed Grant, 2003 Provost's Arts Grant; 2001 Independence Foundation Grant; the 2000 PEW fellowship, the 1999 DaimlerChrysler National Poetry Competition; the 1996 Lila Wallace Creative Arts Fellowship with the American Antiquarian Society; and a two-time returning playwright with the Minneapolis Playwrights' Center and Pew Charitable Trusts Playwrights Exchange. Williams-Witherspoon has had over 32 plays produced. Her stage credits include over 20 productions, 8 one-woman shows, and she has performed poetry in over 110 national and international venues. Williams-Witherspoon is a contributing poet to 38 anthologies, the author of 11 books of poetry, the author of 9 book chapters, 7 journal articles, and 2 books on African American Theater. She is the recipient of a host of awards and citations.

INDEX

CPSIA information can be obtained
at www.ICGtesting.com
Printed in the USA
BVHW082115131219
566633BV00007B/131/P